THE WORLD OF THE CHILD

Edited,

with an introduction,

by

Toby Talbot

Clinical

and

Cultural Studies

from

Birth to

Adolescence

Jason Aronson, New York

"The Two Concepts of Childhood" is reprinted from *Centuries of Childhood*, by Philippe Ariès, translated by Robert Baldick, by permission of Alfred A. Knopf Inc. Copyright © 1962 by Jonathan Cape Ltd.

"On Memory and Childhood Amnesia," from *Metamorphosis* by Ernest G. Schachtel, Copyright © 1959 by Basic Books, Inc., Publishers. Reprinted by permission of Basic Books and The William Alanson White Psychiatric Foundation, Inc.

"The Magic Wand" is a new translation by Toby Talbot of "La Varita de Virtudes" by José Ortega y Gasset, *El Espectador*, Tomo III, pp. 185–93, published by Ediciones de la Revista de Occidente S.A., Madrid.

"Man's Part as Child," from *The World of Man* by Georg Groddeck, reprinted by permission of Vision Press, Ltd.

"The Trauma of Birth," published as "Infantile Anxiety" in *The Trauma of Birth* by Otto Rank, Basic Books, Inc., Publishers. Reprinted by permission of Basic Books and Routledge & Kegan Paul, Ltd.

"Infancy: The Role of Anxiety in the Beginning Differentiation of Experience," reprinted from *The Interpersonal Theory of Psychiatry* by Harry Stack Sullivan, M.D., by permission of W. W. Norton & Company, Inc. Copyright 1953 by The William Alanson White Psychiatric Foundation, Inc.

"Early Stages of the Oedipus Conflict," from *Contributions to Psychoanalysis* by Melanie Klein, reprinted by permission of The Hogarth Press, Ltd.

"The Origins of Love and Hate," Chapter III from *The Origins of Love and Hate* by Ian Suttie, reprinted by permission of Julian Press, Inc.

"Psychic Conflicts in a Child," from Volume 17, *The Development of Personality*, of *The Collected Works of C. G. Jung*, translated from the German by R. F. C. Hull, Bollingen Series XX.17, Pantheon Books. Copyright 1954 by Bollingen Foundation.

"Babbling," from *Infant Speech* by M. M. Lewis. Reprinted by permission of Routledge & Kegan Paul, Ltd.

For Nina, Emily and Sarah

Contents

Introduction

Alfred North Whitehead has said that all men are more alike than they are dissimilar. Every man experiences at least one childhood; usually he experiences another vicariously through rearing his own children. Yet few men remember with any clarity what it feels like to be a child.

Childhood, with its lightning changes of mood, its gratifications and deprivations, its fantasies and yearnings, its helplessness and power, is a purgatory to be traversed and a paradise lost, as well as a key to the adult's psychic life. Childhood is a unique stage in man's growth, not merely an anteroom to maturity.

Through the centuries, the real and imposed length of childhood has varied with our changing notions of one generation's obligations to the next and its demands upon its children. We live in an era that is hypersensitive to the physical and emotional needs of its offspring. The child is no longer regarded merely as a cunning *bambino* or *poupin* to be dandled and indulged until he miraculously emerges, full-grown, into maturity. He is not a miniature adult, nor is he an unnatural force whose spirit must be broken and reformed according to a rigid ideal of human nature. The child has become an entity in his own right, the object of investigation by many disciplines—cultural anthropology, sociology, psychology, psychoanalysis, pediatrics, and pedagogy.

One of the foremost investigators of childhood was Sigmund Freud. His work on the psychic life of the infant remains one of the influences dominating our view of childhood and our practice of parenthood. Although his emphasis on infantile sexuality and the Oedipus complex has provoked much protest, Freud's pronouncements have affected everyone involved with children today, from parent to child analyst.

Modern educators, however, respect the emotional life of the child and try to tap the benevolent forces within him.

Freedom in education has developed steadily through the centuries. In accordance with former views about children, educators valued obedience over individual liberty and applied compulsion rather than encouraging spontaneity. Plato advised parents "to avoid compulsion and let your children's lessons take the form of play." Rousseau insisted that the education of the young child rest largely on his natural development. Pestalozzi held that the home should be the model for education and called for similarly concrete experiences in the school. Friedrich Froebel pointed to the fundamental importance of play in the child's development. Montessori stressed the importance of muscular skills and spontaneous expression in the formation of a child's mental life. John Dewey and other psychologists affirmed that the interplay of a child's native instincts and his social activity are his primary means of learning. Modern psychologists believe that, rather than clip the wings of children to make them tolerable to adult society and its standards of virtue, educators should use the child's physical development as the instrument of his intellectual and moral training; as Dewey would put it, pupils must learn by doing.

Today's concepts of childhood and education, then, stress and encourage the uniqueness of each child. But a question must be faced which is generally more puzzling now than in eras which readily accepted a repressive view of child-rearing: how is the individual to find his own fulfillment, an organic manhood, while simultaneously becoming a social being? Can we preserve social continuity, staff our institutions, man our factories and enrich our arts and learning while encouraging a high degree of individuality? The conflict between obedience and liberty is the affliction of childhood for which real life generally offers three solutions: submission, revolt or cooperation. Childhood represents one's first attempt to balance the demands of the inner and outer worlds and, in seeking equilibrium, to sacrifice wholly to neither.

If there is a theme to unite the views in this book, it is this quest for integrating the individuality of the child with the external world. How can parents and educators avoid an erratic course between freedom and prohibitions, laissez faire and authoritarian morality, while steering the child toward activity that calls forth all his experimental energies? How can we discourage mental and physical docility in children, the condition reflex response heretofore typical of the "good" child and the "A" student? How does one respond to the increasing alienation of American youth, who largely reject (as younger generations of a few years ago seemed indifferently to accept) the highly touted values of American life?

Finally, within the present crowded framework of our society, whose media assault one's senses with more stimuli than can be reasonably absorbed, whose rhetoricians and politicians seem to the young to often speak at cross-purposes of civil rights and peace, is it sensible to seek a more authentic, individual youth?

While such questions in themselves fill volumes, this collection has assembled some reflections of broad and subtle minds upon them. I have chosen contributions from both specialists and gifted amateurs, since some of the liveliest, most empathetic writing about the universal experience of childhood has come from people not professionally involved with child study. Obviously this collection is a sampler from the large literature on childhood, but within it is a fair range of agreement and disagreement. Due to their wide familiarity and availability, however, certain names are conspicuously absent, though without their work the making of this collection would have been impossible.*

Beginning with a consideration of the adult's power to recollect his own childhood, selections discuss the infant's abrupt arrival in the world, his tentative explorations and growing sense of self and sexuality. The private world of children's play, art and language is explored, especially where it meets adult demands and conventions with stratagem and conventions of its own. What happens to children in other cultures, and the child's reactions to certain universal realities of adult life—among them death, war and bigotry—are considered. A final section places childhood in perspective of the most momentous question it raises for adults: how one generation can best prepare the next to contribute to a society whose future lies with the educated individual.

* See Bibliography for the works of Sigmund Freud, Erik Erikson, Margaret Mead, John Dollard, and Arnold Gesell, among others.

I

The Nature of Childhood

The Two Concepts of Childhood

PHILIPPE ARIÈS

(1959)

The length of human childhood has varied from culture to culture through history according to adults' definitions and expectations of a child. Medieval societies little understood the educational process and vaguely designated the "ages of man" as childhood, puerility, adolescence, youth, senility and old age. While medieval children were considered unformed souls, for practical purposes they were also treated as adults at a very much earlier age than modern children. In our view, the child contains a potentially adult personality that must be developed and trained over a prolonged period. Family life centers around the child, and his education is a major concern of our society. In this essay from his book *Centuries of Childhood*, Philippe Ariès, the French demographic historian, traces the evolution of the concept of childhood in its relation to the family.

In medieval society the idea of childhood did not exist; this is not to suggest that children were neglected, forsaken or despised. The idea of childhood is not to be confused with affection for children: it corresponds to an awareness of the particular nature of childhood, that particular nature which distinguishes the child from the adult, even the young adult. In medieval society this awareness was lacking. That is why, as soon as the child could live without the constant solicitude of his mother, his nanny or his cradle-rocker, he belonged to adult society. That adult society now strikes us as rather puerile: no doubt this is largely a matter of its mental age, but it is also due to its physical age, because it was partly made up of children and youths. Language did not give the word "child" the restricted meaning we give it today: people said "child" much as we say "lad" in everyday speech.* The

* For etymological treatment of the word "child" cf. Georg Groddeck's *Man's Part as Child*. (Editor)

absence of definition extended to every sort of social activity: games, crafts, arms. There is not a single collective picture of the times in which children are not to be found, nesting singly or in pairs in the *trousse* hung round women's necks,[1] or urinating in a corner, or playing their part in a traditional festival, or as apprentices in a workshop, or as pages serving a knight, etc.

The infant who was too fragile as yet to take part in the life of adults simply "did not count": this is the expression used by Molière, who bears witness to the survival in the seventeenth century of a very old attitude of mind. Argan in *Le malade imaginaire* has two daughters, one of marriageable age and little Louison who is just beginning to talk and walk. It is generally known that he is threatening to put his elder daughter in a convent to stop her philandering. His brother asks him: "How is it, Brother, that rich as you are and having only one daughter, *for I don't count the little one,* you can talk of putting her in a convent?"[2] The little one did not count because she could disappear.

The quotation from Molière shows the continuance of the archaic attitude to childhood. But this survival, for all that it was stubborn, was precarious. From the fourteenth century on, there had been a tendency to express in art, iconography and religion (in the cult of the dead) the personality which children were seen to possess, and the poetic, familiar significance attributed to their special nature. We have followed the evolution of the *putto* and the child portrait. And we have seen that in the sixteenth and seventeenth centuries the child or infant—at least in the upper classes of society—was given a special costume which marked him out from the adults. This specialization of the dress of children and especially of little boys, in a society in which clothes and outward appearances had considerable importance, bears witness to the change which had taken place in the general attitude toward children: they counted much more than Argan's brother imagined. In fact, *Le malade imaginaire,* which seems as hard on little children as do certain remarks by La Fontaine, contains a whole conversation between Argan and little Louison: "Look

[1] Père Michault, *Doctrinal du temps présent,* edited by T. Walton, 1931, p. 119.
[2] *Le Malade Imaginaire,* Act III, Scene III, cf. Montaigne, *Essais,* II, 8.

at me, will you!" "What is it, papa?" "Here!" "What?"
"Haven't you anything to tell me?" "If you wish, I can tell
you, to amuse you, the story of the Ass's Skin, or else the
fable of the Fox and the Crow which I was taught not so long
ago." A new concept of childhood had appeared, in which the
child, on account of his sweetness, simplicity and drollery, became a source of amusement and relaxation for the adult.

To begin with, the attitude was held by women, women
whose task it was to look after children—mothers and nannies.
In the sixteenth-century edition of *Le Grand Propriétaire de
toutes choses* we are told about the nanny: "She rejoices when
the child is happy, and feels sorry for the child when he is ill;
she picks him up when he falls, she binds him when he tosses
about, and she washes and cleans him when he is dirty."[3] She
brings the child up and teaches him to talk: "She pronounces
the words as if she had a stammer, to teach him to talk better
and more rapidly . . . she carries him in her hands, then on
her shoulder, then on her lap, to play with him when he
cries; she chews the child's meat for him when he has no
teeth so that he can swallow profitably and without danger;
she plays with the child to make him sleep and she binds his
limbs to keep them straight so that he has no stiffness in his
body, and she bathes and anoints him to nourish his flesh . . ."
Thomas More dwells on the subject of the schoolboy being
sent to school by his mother: "When the little boy will not
rise in time for her, but lies still abed and slugg, and when he
is up, weepeth because he hath lien so long, fearing to be
beaten at school for his late coming thither, she telleth him
then that it is but early days, and he shall come time enough,
and biddeth him: 'Go, good son, I warrant thee, I have
sent to thy master myself, take thy bread and butter with
thee, thou shalt not be beaten at all.' " Thus she sends him off
sufficiently reassured not to burst into tears at the idea of
leaving her at home, but she does not get to the bottom of
the trouble and the late arrival will be well and truly beaten
when he gets to school.[4]

Children's little antics must always have seemed touching to
mothers, nannies and cradle-rockers, but their reactions
formed part of the huge domain of unexpressed feelings.
Henceforth people would no longer hesitate to recognize the
pleasure they got from watching children's antics and "cod-

[3] *Le Grand Propriétaire de toutes choses,* 1556.
[4] Quoted by Jarman, *Landmarks in the History of Education,* London,
1951.

dling" them. We find Mme. de Sévigné admitting, not without a certain affectation, how much time she spends playing with her granddaughter: "I am reading the story of Christopher Columbus's discovery of the Indies, which is entertaining me greatly; but your daughter entertains me even more. I do so love her . . . she strokes your portrait and caresses it in such an amusing way that I have to kiss her straight away."[5] "I have been playing with your daughter for an hour now; she is delightful." And, as if she were afraid of some infection, she adds, with a levity which surprises us, for the death of a child is something serious for us and nothing to joke about: "I do not want her to die." For, as we have seen from Molière, this first appreciation of childhood went with a certain indifference, or rather with the indifference that was traditional.

The "coddling" attitude toward children is even better known to us by the critical reactions it provoked at the end of the sixteenth century and particularly in the seventeenth century. Peevish persons found insufferable the attention paid to children. Montaigne bristles: "I cannot abide that passion for caressing new-born children, which have neither mental activities nor recognizable bodily shape by which to make themselves lovable, and I have never willingly suffered them to be fed in my presence." He cannot accept the idea of loving children "for our amusement, like monkeys," or taking pleasure in their "frolickings, games and infantile nonsense."[6]

Another example of this state of mind, a century later, is to be seen in Coulanges, Mme. de Sévigné's cousin.[7] He was obviously exasperated by the way his friends and relatives fussed over their children, for he composed a song dedicated to "fathers of families," urging them not to spoil their offspring or allow them to eat with adults.

It is important to note that this feeling of exasperation was as novel as "coddling," and even more foreign than "coddling" to the indifferent attitude of people in the Middle Ages. It was precisely to the presence of children that Montaigne and Coulanges, like Mme. de Sévigné, were hypersensitive; it should be pointed out that Montaigne and Coulanges were more modern than Mme. de Sévigné in so far as they considered it necessary to keep children apart from adults. They held that it was no longer desirable that children should mingle

[5] Mme. de Sévigné, *Lettres*, April 1st, 1672, cf. Letter of August 19, 1671.
[6] Montaigne, *Essais*, II, 8.
[7] Coulanges, *Chansons Choisie*, 1694.

with adults, especially at table; no doubt because if they did they were "spoiled" and became ill-mannered.

The seventeenth-century moralists and pedagogues shared the dislike felt by Montaigne and Coulanges for "coddling." Thus the austere Fleury, in his treatise on studies, speaks very much like Montaigne: "When little children are caught in a trap, when they say something foolish, drawing a correct inference from an irrelevant principle which has been given to them, people burst out laughing, rejoice at having tricked them, or kiss and caress them as if they had worked out the correct answer. It is as if the poor children had been made only to amuse the adults, like little dogs or little monkeys."[8]

The author of *Galatée*, the manual of etiquette commonly used in the best colleges, those of the Jesuits, speaks like Coulanges: "Those persons are greatly at fault who never talk of anything but their wives, their little children and their nannies. 'My little son made me laugh so much! Just listen to this . . .' "[9]

M. d'Argonne, in his treatise on education, *L'Éducation de Monsieur de Moncade* (1690), likewise complains that people take an interest in very small children only for the sake of their "caresses" and "antics"; too many parents "value their children only in so far as they derive pleasure and entertainment from them."

It is important to remember that at the end of the seventeenth century this "coddling" was not practiced only by people of quality, who, in fact, were beginning to disdain it. Its presence in the lower classes was noted and denounced. J.-B. de La Salle in his *Conduite des écoles chrétiennes* (1720) states that the children of the poor are particularly ill-mannered because "they do just as they please, their parents paying no attention to them, even treating them in an idolatrous manner: what the children want, they want too."

In the moralists and pedagogues of the seventeenth century, we see that fondness for childhood and its special nature no longer found expression in amusement and "coddling," but in psychological interest and moral solicitude. The child was no longer regarded as amusing or agreeable: "Every man must be conscious of that insipidity of childhood which disgusts the sane mind; that coarseness of youth which finds pleasure in scarcely anything but material objects and which

[8] Fleury, *Traite du choix et de la méthode des études*, 1686.
[9] Della Casa, *Galatée*, French translation, 1607, pp. 162–68.

is only a very crude sketch of the man of thought." Thus
Balthazar Gratien in *El Discreto,* a treatise on education published in 1646 which was still being translated into French in
1723.[10] "Only time can cure a person of childhood and youth,
which are truly ages of imperfection in every respect." To be
understood, these opinions need to be put back in their temporal context and compared with the other texts of the period.
They have been interpreted by some historians as showing
ignorance of childhood, but in fact they mark the beginning
of a serious and realistic concept of childhood. For they do
not suggest that people should accept the levity of childhood:
that was the old mistake. In order to correct the behavior of
children, people must first of all understand it, and the texts
of the late sixteenth century and the seventeenth century are
full of comments on child psychology.[11] The authors show a
great solicitude for children, who are seen as witnesses to
baptismal innocence, comparable to the angels, and close to
Christ who loved them. But this interest calls for the development in them of a faculty of reasoning which is still fragile, a
determined attempt to turn them into thinking men and good
Christians. The tone is sometimes grim, the emphasis being
laid on strictness as opposed to the laxity and facility of contemporary manners; but this is not always the case. There is
even humor in Jacqueline Pascal, and undisguised tenderness. In the texts published toward the end of the century, an
attempt is made to reconcile sweetness and reason. Thus the
Abbé Goussault, a counselor at the High Court, writes in
Le Portrait d'une honnête femme: "Familiarizing oneself
with one's children, getting them to talk about all manner of
things, treating them as sensible people and winning them over
with sweetness, is an infallible secret for doing what one wants
with them. They are young plants which need tending and
watering frequently: a few words of advice offered at the right
moment, a few marks of friendship and affection given now
and then, touch them and bind them. A few caresses, a few
little presents, a few words of cordiality and trust make an impression on their minds, and they are few in number that
resist these sweet and easy methods of making them persons
of honor and probity."[12]

[10] B. Gratien, *El Discreto,* Huesca, 1646, French Translation of 1723
by Père de Courbeville, S.J.

[11] As can be seen in the 1586 ratio of the Jesuits and in Jacqueline
Pascal's regulations for little girls brought up at Port Royal.

[12] Goussault, *Le Portrait d'une honnête femme,* 1693.

The first concept of childhood—characterized by "coddling" —had made its appearance in the family circle, in the company of little children. The second, on the contrary, sprang from a source outside the family: churchmen or gentlemen of the robe, few in number before the sixteenth century, and a far greater number of moralists in the seventeenth century, eager to ensure disciplined, rational manners. They too had become alive to the formerly neglected phenomenon of childhood, but they were unwilling to regard children as charming toys, for they saw them as fragile creatures of God who needed to be both safeguarded and reformed. This concept in its turn passed into family life.

In the eighteenth century, we find those two elements in the family, together with a new element: concern about hygiene and physical health. Care of the body was not ignored by seventeenth-century moralists and pedagogues. People nursed the sick devotedly (at the same time taking every precaution to unmask malingerers), but any interest shown in healthy bodies had a moral purpose behind it: a delicate body encouraged luxury, sloth, concupiscence—all the vices in fact!

General de Martange's correspondence with his wife gives us some idea of a family's private life and preoccupations about a century after Mme. de Sévigné.[13] Martange was born in 1722 and married in 1754. He shows great interest in everything concerning his children's life, from "coddling" to education; he watches closely over their health and even their hygiene. Everything to do with children and family life has become a matter worthy of attention. Not only the child's future but his presence and his very existence are of concern: the child has taken a central place in the family.

[13] *Correspondance inédite du général de Martange, 1756–1782*, edited by Bréard, 1893.

On Memory and Childhood Amnesia

ERNEST G. SCHACHTEL

(1947)

In the following essay, Ernest Schachtel explains that
conflicts in man, aggravated by his life in society, prevent
him from remembering his early childhood. Childhood
amnesia, in turn, perpetuates the myth of a happy, care-
free childhood. Societies such as our own, which have
created a radical discontinuity between childhood and
adulthood, can be expected to produce the most widespread childhood amnesia. This acute childhood amnesia
among people of western cultures makes their understanding of children less empathetic and more intellectual.

Greek mythology celebrates mnemosyne, the goddess of memory, as the mother of all art. She bore the nine muses to
Zeus.[1] Centuries after the origin of this myth Plato banned
poetry, the child of memory, from his ideal state as being
idle and seductive. While lawmakers, generals, and inventors
were useful for the common good, the fact that Homer was
nothing but a wandering minstrel without a home and without
a following proved how useless he was.[2] In the Odyssey the
voices of the Sirens tempt Ulysses.

> For never yet hath any man rowed past
> This isle in his black ship, till he hath heard
> The honeyed music of our lips, and goes
> His way delighted and a wiser man.
> For see, we know the whole tale of the travail
> That Greeks and Trojans suffered in wide Troy-land
> By heaven's behest; yea, and all things we know
> That come to pass upon the fruitful earth.

[1] The words "muse" and "mnemosyne" derive from the same root
μεν or μαν. Ludwig Preller, *Griechische Mythologie;* Berlin 1872; vol. 1,
p. 399, footnote 1. In German, too, the words "Gedächtnis" (memory)
and "Dichtung" (poetry) derive from the same root "denken" (think);
compare also "gedenken" (remember).

[2] Plato, *Republic*, 599, 600.

Their irresistible song, in evoking the past, promises a delight which will allow no future and will be the end of Ulysses' plans to return to an active life and to resume the rule of Ithaca. He prevents his shipmates from listening to the alluring voices by plugging their ears with wax, and he, too curious to renounce the pleasure, has himself chained to the ship's mast so that he will not be able to yield to their song and abandon the future.

This ambivalent attitude toward memory, especially toward its most potent form as embodied in the song, the epic, the tale, in poetry, music, fiction, and in all art, has accompanied the history of man. The modern, popular attitude, so widespread in the United States, the country of the most advanced industrial and technological civilization—that all art and poetry is "sissy"—is the latter-day implementation of the Platonic taboo. But with this difference: the contemporaries of Plato, and before them the shipmates of Ulysses, were susceptible to the promise of happiness that the song of the Sirens and of the muses contains, so that Ulysses and Plato, concerned with planning and not with the past, had to prevent their listening forcefully. Today the masses have internalized the ancient fear and prohibition of this alluring song and, in their contempt for it, express and repress both their longing for and their fear of the unknown vistas to which it might open the doors.

The profound fascination of memory of past experience and the double aspect of this fascination—its irresistible lure into the past with its promise of happiness and pleasure, and its threat to the kind of activity, planning, and purposeful thought and behavior encouraged by modern western civilization—have attracted the thought of two men in recent times who have made the most significant modern contribution to the ancient questions posed by the Greek myth: Sigmund Freud and Marcel Proust.

Both are aware of the antagonism inherent in memory, the conflict between reviving the past and actively participating in the present life of society. Both illuminate the nature of this conflict from different angles. Proust, the poet of memory, is ready to renounce all that people usually consider as active life, to renounce activity, enjoyment of the present moment, concern with the future, friendship, social intercourse, for the sublime happiness and profound truth recaptured in the most elusive of all treasures that man has hunted for, the "Remembrance of Things Past." He pursues this conflict be-

tween activity and memory into its most subtle manifestations. He knows that, as the awakening dreamer may lose
the memory of his dream when he moves his limbs, opens
his eyes, changes the position of his body, so the slightest
motion may endanger and dispel the deep pleasure of the
vision of the time in Combray, recaptured by the flavor of the
madeleine, or the image of Venice conjured up by the sensation and the posture which the unevenness of the pavement in
the court of the Guermantes town house brought to him as
the unevenness of the pavement of San Marco had years ago.[3]
He does not dare to stir, for fear that the exhilarating vision
may disappear. Bodily movement is the basic and simplest
form of all activity endangering memory. Action itself, the
attitude of activity, even the activity of enjoying the immediate
present are seen by Proust as the antagonists, the incompatible
alternative of memory.[4] From here it is only one step to the
insight that the memory which reveals the true vision of something past, the memory celebrated by Proust, is very different
from the voluntary, everyday memory, the useful instrument
needed by man every hour and every minute to recall a word,
a figure, a date, to recognize a person or an object, to think
of his plans, tasks, intentions, the eminently utilitarian memory characterized by the very fact that it serves the purposes
of active and conventionally organized life in society. Proust
speaks of the artificiality and untruth of the pictures that this
memory furnishes, of its flat and uniform quality which cannot do justice to the unique flavor and the true qualities of
anything remembered.[5]

While for Proust the antagonism between society and memory of the significant past can be resolved only by renouncing
either one or the other, Goethe seeks to reconcile the two.
When, at a party, a toast was proposed to memory he objected vehemently with these words: "I do not recognize memory in the sense in which you mean it. Whatever we encounter
that is great, beautiful, significant, need not be remembered
from outside, need not be hunted up and laid hold of as it
were. Rather, from the beginning, it must be woven into the
fabric of our inmost self, must become one with it, create a

[3] Marcel Proust, *À la recherche du temps perdu, VIII, Le temps
retrouvé;* Librairie Gallimard, Editions de la Nouvelle Revue Française,
Paris 1927; vol. 2., p. 8.
[4] Proust, p. 14.
[5] Proust, pp. 11–12.

new and better self in us and thus live and become a productive force in ourselves. There is no past that one is allowed to long for. There is only the eternally new, growing from the enlarged elements of the past; and genuine longing always must be productive, must create something new and better."[6]

Freud, not unlike Proust, approaches the problem of memory not from wondering what, or how well, or how much man remembers, but how hard it is to remember, how much is forgotten and not to be recovered at all or only with the greatest difficulty, and how the period richest in experience, the period of early childhood, is the one which usually is forgotten entirely save for a few apparently meaningless memory fragments. He finds this surprising since "we are informed that during those years which have left nothing but a few incomprehensible memory fragments, we have vividly reacted to impressions, that we have manifested human pain and pleasure and that we have expressed love, jealousy and other passions as they then affected us."[7] The few incomprehensible memory fragments left over from childhood, he considers as "concealing memories," (Deckerinnerungen)[8] and his painstaking work to decipher their language bears more than a superficial resemblance to Proust's attempt to decipher the hieroglyphic characters of the images of a cloud, a triangle, a belfry, a flower, a pebble—a most difficult undertaking, but the only way to the true memories enclosed in these signs which seemed to be only indifferent material objects or sensations.[9] It was Freud who made the discovery that a conflict, leading to repression, is responsible for the difficulty of this work of deciphering and for the difficulty of remembering the past. His well-known explanation of infantile amnesia is that the forgetting of childhood experiences is due to progressive repression of infantile sexuality, which reaches the peak of its manifestations in the third and fourth years of life. This repression is brought about by the "psychic forces of loathing, shame, and moral and

[6] Author's translation from *Goethe's Gespräche;* Herausgegeben von Flodoard Freiherr von Biedermann; Vol. 3, Leipzig 1910, p. 37 (November 4th, 1823). Compare with this Proust's *"Les vrais paradis sont les paradis qu'on a perdu."* Proust, p. 13.

[7] Sigmund Freud, Three Contributions to the Theory of Sex. In *The Basic Writings of Sigmund Freud;* Random House, New York 1938; p. 581.

[8] Sigmund Freud, Psychopathology of Everyday Life; see footnote 7; pp. 62–65.

[9] Proust, p. 24.

esthetic ideal demands."[10] These forces have the sanction of society, they are the product of society, they are part and serve the purposes of the same conventionally organized life of society which molds the functions of all social activity and of that "uniform" memory in which Proust saw the irreconcilable antagonists of the true remembrance of things past.

It is the purpose of this essay to explore further the dynamics of this conflict in memory which leads to the striking phenomenon of childhood amnesia as well as to the difficulty, encountered by Proust though more hidden to the average eye, of recovering *any* true picture of past experience. To speak of a conflict in memory is a convenient abbreviation. Formulated more explicitly and accurately, the intention of this presentation is to shed light on some of the factors and conflicts in man and his society which make it difficult if not impossible for him really to remember his past and especially his early childhood.

Obviously, the concept of memory which such an approach presupposes cannot be the impersonal, artificial, isolated, and abstract concept implied by experimentation on the recall of digits, nonsense syllables, and similar material, a concept which seems more appropriate for the testing of the capacity of some mechanical apparatus than for the understanding of the functioning of memory in the living person. Nor is such a concept fundamentally changed when logically meaningful phrases or perceptually organized "Gestalten" are substituted for nonsense syllables and memory is investigated for its capacity to reproduce those, rather than meaningless material. Nobody doubts that it is easier to remember meaningful than meaningless material and that the function of memory has not developed in order to make possible the recall of

[10] Freud, footnote 7; p. 583. Freud asserts that the development of these forces during the latency period is organically determined and that it "can occasionally be produced without the help of education." It is surprising that the man who discovered, explored, described, and emphasized over and over again the conflict between culture, society, and sexual instinct should have ascribed the ontogenetic origin of sexual inhibitions to organic factors as though he wanted to explain as natural those inhibitions which a culture, hostile to pleasure and to sex, has created, deepened, and strengthened in every imaginable way. The only explanation for such a strange and questionable hypothesis lies, to my mind, in Freud's and every great discoverer's tragic conflict between a powerful and lucid mind searching for truth and the person who never can entirely extricate himself from the thousand threads with which he is captured and tied to the prejudices, ideologies, falsehoods, and conventions of his time and society.

nonsense. Memory as a function of the living personality can be understood only as a capacity for the organization and reconstruction of past experiences and impressions in the service of present needs, fears, and interests. It goes without saying that, just as there is no such thing as impersonal perception and impersonal experience, there is also no impersonal memory. Man perceives and remembers not as a camera reproduces on the film the objects before its lens; the scope and quality of his perceptions and experiences as well as of their reproduction by memory are determined by his individual needs, fears, and interests. This is the more apparent the more significant an experience has been for the person.

With this concept of memory in mind, the puzzling problem of childhood amnesia seems to become more transparent and accessible to understanding. No greater change in the needs of man occurs than that which takes place between early childhood and adulthood. Into this change have gone all the decisive formative influences of the culture transmitted by the parents, laying the fundament of the transformation into the grown-up, "useful" member of society from the little heathen, who is helpless but as yet sees nothing wrong with following the pleasure principle completely and immediately and who has an insatiable curiosity and capacity for experience. An explanation of childhood amnesia that takes into account these changes leads to the following tentative hypothesis:

> The categories (or schemata) of adult memory are not suitable receptacles for early childhood experiences and therefore not fit to preserve these experiences and enable their recall. The functional capacity of the conscious, adult memory is usually limited to those types of experience which the adult consciously makes and is capable of making.

It is not merely the repression of a specific content, such as early sexual experience, that accounts for the general childhood amnesia; the biologically, culturally, and socially influenced process of memory organization results in the formation of categories (schemata) of memory which are not suitable vehicles to receive and reproduce experiences of the quality and intensity typical of early childhood. The world of modern western civilization has no use for this type of experience. In fact, it cannot permit itself to have any use for it; it cannot permit the memory of it, because such memory, if universal, would explode the restrictive social order of this civilization. No doubt the hostility of western civilization to pleasure, and to sexual pleasure as the strongest of all, is a most important factor operative in the transformation and education of the child into an adult who will be able to fulfill the role and the functions he has to take over in society and will be satisfied by them. Freud has not only called attention to the phenomenon of childhood amnesia but has also singled out a decisive factor in its genesis. I believe, however, that two points are important for a more adequate understanding of the phenomenon. First, it is not sufficiently clear why a repression of sexual experience should lead to a repression of all experience in early childhood. For this reason the assumption seems more likely that there must be something in the general quality of childhood experience which leads to the forgetting of that experience. Second, the phenomenon of childhood amnesia leads to a problem regarding the nature of repression, especially repression of childhood material. The term and concept of repression suggest that material which *per se* could be recalled is excluded from recall because of its traumatic nature. If the traumatic factor can be clarified and dissolved, the material is again accessible to recall. But even the most profound and prolonged psychoanalysis does not lead to a recovery of childhood memory; at best it unearths some incidents and feelings that had been forgotten. Childhood amnesia, then, may be due to a formation of the memory functions which makes them unsuitable to accommodate childhood experience, rather than exclusively to a censor repressing objectionable material which, without such repression, could and would be remembered. The adult is usually not capable of experiencing what the child experiences; more often than not he is not even capable of imagining what the child experiences. It would not be surprising, then, that he should be incapable of recalling his own childhood experiences since his whole mode of experiencing has changed. The person who remembers is the present person, a person who has changed considerably, whose interests, needs, fears, capacity for experience and emotion have changed. The two mechanisms of forgetting suggested here shade gradually and imperceptibly into one another. They are neither alternatives nor opposites, but rather the two ends of a continuous scale. It might be theoretically interesting to follow up this viewpoint to see how much it could clarify the much used but not too clear concept of repression and the processes underlying repression. However, this would lead too far away from

the immediate problem of a more concrete understanding
and testing of the suggested general theory of early childhood amnesia.

A closer examination and comparison of the content and
quality of adult and childhood memories may be helpful for
the purpose of such an understanding. Both Freud and Proust
speak of the autobiographical memory, and it is only with regard to this memory that the striking phenomenon of childhood amnesia and the less obvious difficulty of recovering any
past experience may be observed. There is no specific childhood amnesia as far as the remembrance of words learned
and of objects and persons recognized is concerned. This
type of material is remembered because, in contrast to the
autobiographical past, it is constantly re-experienced and used
and because it is essential for the orientation and adaptation
of the growing child to his environment. In the recall of this
type of material we have to deal with memory serving the
immediate, practical use of knowledge and perception (recognition) mainly. The memory of the personal past—of one's
past experiences, which also contain the material that has gone
into the formation of one's character—is a much less efficient
and reliable servant than the memory of learned material, on
the whole, seems to be. Yet the separation of the "useful"
from the "autobiographical" memory is, of course, an artificial abstraction. Actually this distinction of the content of remembered material is not clear-cut, and the two types of material indicated by it are continuously and everywhere
interrelated.

The autobiographical memory shows indeed in most persons, if not in all, the amnesia for their early childhood from
birth to approximately the fifth or sixth year. Of course, there
are considerable gaps in the memory of many people for later
periods of their lives also, probably more so for the period before than after puberty; but these gaps vary individually to a
much greater extent than does the ubiquitous early childhood amnesia. Freud's observation of this amnesia has not
stimulated others, as far as I can see, to significant investigations of the adult autobiographical memory. Yet it would
seem that an awareness of the main differences between the
type of material remembered from early childhood and that
remembered from later life might help in an understanding of
the phenomenon of childhood amnesia. If one believes Proust,
life after childhood is not remembered either, save for the elusive flashes of a vision given only to the most sensitive and

differentiated mind as the rare grace of a fortunate moment, which then the poet, with passionate devotion and patient labor, may try to transcribe and communicate.

Freud contrasts the presumable riches of childhood experience, the child's great capacity for impressions and experience, with the poverty or total lack of memory of such rich experience. If one looks closely at the average adult's memory of the periods of his life after childhood, such memory, it is true, usually shows no great temporal gaps. It is fairly continuous. But its formal continuity in time is offset by barrenness in content, by an incapacity to reproduce anything that resembles a really rich, full, rounded, and alive experience. Even the most "exciting" events are remembered as milestones rather than as moments filled with the concrete abundance of life. Adult memory reflects life as a road with occasional signposts and milestones rather than as the landscape through which this road has led. The milestones are the measurements of time, the months and years, the empty count of time gone by, so many years spent here, so many years spent there, moving from one place to another, so many birthdays, and so forth. The signposts represent the outstanding events to which they point—entering college, the first job, marriage, birth of children, buying a house, a family celebration, a trip. But it is not the events that are remembered as they really happened and were experienced at the time. What is remembered is usually, more or less, only the fact that such an event took place. The signpost is remembered, not the place, the thing, the situation to which it points. And even these signposts themselves do not usually indicate the really significant moments in a person's life; rather they point to the events that are conventionally supposed to be significant, to the clichés which society has come to consider as the main stations of life. Thus the memories of the majority of people come to resemble increasingly the stereotyped answers to a questionnaire, in which life consists of time and place of birth, religious denomination, residence, educational degrees, job, marriage, number and birthdates of children, income, sickness and death. The average traveler, asked about his trip, will tell you how many miles he has made (how many years he has lived); how fast he went (how successful he was); what places he has visited—usually only the well-known ones, often he visits only those that one "simply must have seen"—(the jobs he has held, the prestige he has gained). He can tell you whether the driving was smooth or rough, or whether somebody bumped his fender, but he will be quite unable to give you any real idea of the country through which he went. So the average traveler through life remembers chiefly what the road map or the guide book says, what he is supposed to remember because it is exactly what everybody else remembers too.

In the course of later childhood, adolescence, and adult life, perception and experience themselves develop increasingly into the rubber stamps of conventional clichés. The capacity to see and feel what is there gives way to the tendency to see and feel what one expects to see and feel, which, in turn, is what one is expected to see and feel because everybody else does.[11] Experience increasingly assumes the form of the cliché under which it will be recalled because this cliché is what conventionally is remembered by others. This is not the remembered situation itself, but the words which are customarily used to indicate this situation and the reactions which it is supposed to evoke. While this ubiquitous and powerful tendency toward pseudoexperience in terms of conventional clichés usually takes place unnoticed, it is quite articulate in some people and is used widely in advertising. There are people who experience a party, a visit to the movies, a play, a concert, a trip in the very words in which they are going to tell their friends about it; in fact, quite often, they anticipate such experience in these words. The experience is predigested, as it were, even before they have tasted of it. Like the unfortunate Midas, whose touch turned everything into gold so that he could not eat or drink, these people turn the potential nourishment of the anticipated experience into the sterile currency of the conventional phrase which exhausts their experience because they have seen, heard, felt nothing but this phrase with which later they will report to their friends the "exciting time" they have had. The advertising business seems to be quite aware of this. It does not have to promise a good book, a well-written and well-performed play, an entertaining or amusing movie. It suffices to say that the book, the play, the movie will be the talk of the town, of the next party, of one's friends. To have been there, to be able to say that one has been present at the performance, to have read the book even when one is unable

---

[11] Tolstoi gives a masterful description of how, in an adolescent girl during a visit to the opera, the experience of what happens on the stage changes from a genuine, naïve, and fresh view to the conventional "appreciation" of the opera habitué. His account of her initial perceptions, by the way, is a surrealist description of opera more than half a century before surrealism. Tolstoi, *War and Peace*, part 8, chapters 9 and 10.

to have the slightest personal reaction to it, is quite sufficient. But while Midas suffered tortures of starvation, the people under whose eyes every experience turns into a barren cliché do not know that they starve. Their starvation manifests itself merely in boredom or in restless activity and incapacity for any real enjoyment.

The burial and distortion of experience in the process of memory under the cliché of the conventionally accepted finds an interesting confirmation in Bartlett's experiments on memory.[12] In one of them he showed to his subjects, who were educated adults, five picture postcards, on each of which was the representation of the face of a naval or army officer or man. He asked them to look at each card for ten seconds "noting carefully as many of the characteristics of the faces as you can, so that later you may be able to describe the faces, and to answer questions about them." Half an hour after the exposure of the cards, each subject described them and answered questions about some of the details. This was repeated after a week and then after longer intervals. Reporting the outcome of this experiment, Bartlett says, among other things: "Obviously, complicating the perceptual pattern were all kinds of conventional notions about soldiers and sailors of a given rank. . . . A particular face often at once aroused a more or less conventional attitude appropriate to the given type. Thereupon, the attitude actively affected the detail of representation. Even in immediate memory the features of the face often tended to be made more conventional, while in subsequent recall they tended to approach yet more closely the conventional pattern." He summarizes the results of this experiment by saying that it "seems certain that attitudes may strongly influence recall and may tend in particular to produce stereotyped and conventional reproductions which adequately serve all normal needs, though they are very unfaithful to their originals."

In another experiment he used a North American Indian folk tale, "The War of the Ghosts." Each subject read the story twice. Then he reproduced it after 15 minutes and again, several times, after considerably longer intervals. In these reproductions a most important role is played by a factor which Bartlett calls "rationalization"; the function which he attributes to it is "to render material acceptable, understandable,

[12] F. C. Bartlett, *Remembering: A Study in Experimental and Social Psychology;* Cambridge University Press, Cambridge 1932; see especially pp. 53–54. 89. 125, 171–173.

comfortable, straightforward; to rob it of all puzzling elements." With one of his subjects all mention of ghosts disappeared in the very first reproduction of the story "in spite of the fact that special attention was called to the title. The same thing occurred at some stage in *every* series obtained with this story as a starting point. This omission illustrates how any element of imported culture which finds very little background in the culture to which it comes must fail to be assimilated."

However, conventionalization affects not only elements of "imported culture," but everything recalled. Bartlett gave newspaper reports of a cricket game and a passage from a review of Tilden's book *The Art of Lawn Tennis* to Cambridge undergraduates for repeated reproduction. In still another experiment he used a passage, "The intellect is vagabond," from Emerson's essay, *Self-Reliance*, with entirely similar results. In one chain of reproductions of the latter "every bit of general reasoning had disappeared. The whole point of the original is lost. All that is left is a bald record of a personal incident, and one general opinion. This opinion is the exact opposite to the original from which it is derived, but is no doubt more in accord with common views." In his summary of the experiments using stories and similar material, Bartlett comes to the conclusion that "all the stories tend to be shorn of their individualizing features, the descriptive passages lose most of the peculiarities of style and matter that they may possess, and the arguments tend to be reduced to a bald expression of conventional opinion. . . . Where the opinions expressed are individual they appear to tend to pass over into opposed conventional views; where the epithets are original they tend to become current, commonplace terms. The style gets flattened out and loses any pretensions it may have had to forcefulness and beauty."

The processes of memory thus substitute the conventional cliché for the actual experience. It is true that the original experience or perception usually is already, to a large extent, determined by conventional cliché, by what the person expected to see or hear, which means by what he has been taught to expect. However, everybody who has paid attention to these processes in himself and others can observe that there is, especially at first, some awareness of the discrepancy between the experience itself and the thought or words which articulate, preserve, and express it. The experience is always fuller and richer than the articulate formula by which we try to be aware of it or to recover it. As time passes, this formula comes to replace more and more the original experience and, in addition, to become itself increasingly flat and conventionalized. Memory, in other words, is even more governed by conventional patterns than perception and experience are. One might say that, while all human experience, perception, and thought are eminently social—that is, determined by the socially prevailing ways of experiencing, perceiving, and thinking—memory is even more socialized, to an even higher degree dependent on the commonly accepted categories of what and how one remembers. Bartlett's experiments confirm this. As time passes, the remembered story loses more and more of its original flavor until nothing remains of its essence and a banal cliché is substituted for it. "Rationalization," as psychoanalytic theory knows it, is but one type of such transformation of actual experience into individually and socially acceptable clichés. One important reason why memory is even more susceptible than experience and perception to such conventionalization is that experience and perception always are in *some*, however flimsy, immediate relation to the situation experienced, the object perceived, while memory is distant from it in time and space. The object of memory has less chance than the objects of experience and perception have to penetrate and do away with part of that glass, colored and ground by the social mores and viewpoints, through which man sees everything or fails to see it. Memory is a distance sense, as it were, and—to an even greater degree than the two other distance senses, vision and hearing—less immediately related to its objects than the proximity senses of smell, taste, and touch, and more influenced and molded by the categories of the mind. Also like sight and hearing, only more so, memory is a phylogenetically and ontogenetically more differentiated, later, and more "spiritual" development than smell, taste, and touch. All this predestines memory to lose contact with actual experience and to substitute preformed, conventional patterns of thought for it. And, as will be seen later, it has significant bearing especially on the problem of early childhood amnesia.

How well is the average highly conventionalized adult memory equipped to contain and recall the time and the experiences of early childhood? Very poorly or not at all. This will become more apparent through consideration of the quality of early childhood experience. The adult amnesia for this period prevents direct knowledge. Observation of little children and imagination are the only means of learning something about this subject. It is safe to assume that early childhood is the period of human life which is richest in experience. Everything is new to the newborn child. His gradual grasp of his environment and of the world around him are discoveries which, in experiential scope and quality, go far beyond any discovery that the most adventurous and daring explorer will ever make in his adult life. No Columbus, no Marco Polo has ever seen stranger and more fascinating and thoroughly absorbing sights than the child that learns to perceive, to taste, to smell, to touch, to hear and see, and to use his body, his senses, and his mind. No wonder that the child shows an insatiable curiosity. He has the whole world to discover. Education and learning, while on the one hand furthering this process of discovery, on the other hand gradually brake and finally stop it completely. There are relatively few adults who are fortunate enough to have retained something of the child's curiosity, his capacity for questioning and for wondering. The average adult "knows all the answers," which is exactly why he will never know even a single answer. He has ceased to wonder, to discover. He knows his way around, and it is indeed a way around and around the same conventional pattern, in which everything is familiar and nothing cause for wonder. It is this adult who answers the child's questions and, in answering, fails to answer them but instead acquaints the child with the conventional patterns of his civilization, which effectively close up the asking mouth and shut the wondering eye. Franz Kafka once formulated this aspect of education by saying that "probably all education is but two things, first, parrying of the ignorant children's impetuous assault on the truth and, second, gentle, imperceptible, step-by-step initiation of the humiliated children into the lie."[13]

Most children go through a period of endless questioning. While at first they desire an answer, gradually their search turns into an almost automatic repetition of the same seemingly senseless question or into the related ritual of countering every answer with a new question. It is as though the child no longer

[13] In view of the inadequacy of the author's translation, the German text is given here: "Wie ja allerdings wahrscheinlich alle Erziehung nur zweierlei ist, einmal Abwehr des ungestuemen Angriffs der unwissenden Kinder auf die Wahrheit und dann sanfte unmerklich-allmähliche Einfuehrung der gedemuetigten Kinder in die Luege." Franz Kafka, *Beschreibung eines Kampfes; Novellen, Skizzen, Aphorismen aus dem Nachlass;* Verlag Heinrich Mercy Sohn, Prag 1936; p. 317. The passage is taken from an earlier version of what probably was the last story Kafka wrote, "Forschungen eines Hundes" (Researches of a Dog).

really expected or perhaps wanted to obtain information by this type of questioning, but expressed only the last stubborn assault against the unbroken wall of adult "answers." The child has already almost forgotten what he wanted to know, but he still knows *that* he wanted to know and did not receive an answer. The automatic questioning may have the unconscious purpose of driving this point home to the adult. It is chiefly during the period of early childhood that the quality of the world around him changes for the growing child from a place where everything is new and to be explored—to be tasted, smelled, touched and handled, wondered about and marveled at—to a place where everything either has received a name and a label or is potentially capable of being "explained" by such a label, a process which will be pursued systematically in school. No experience, no object perceived with the quality of freshness, newness, of something wonder-full, can be preserved and recalled by the conventional concept of that object as designated in its conventional name in language. Even if, in modern western civilization, the capacity for such fresh experience has largely been deadened, most people, unless they have become complete automatons, have had glimpses of the exhilarating quality that makes fresh experience, unlabeled, so unique, concrete, and filled with life. They can realize, if their attention is called to it, the great difference between such experience and one which merely registers the label of things seen, of the furniture of the room, the familiar faces, the houses on the street. Yet this difference is small when compared with the difference that separates the young child's fresh experience and discoveries from the adult's recognition of the familiar clichés into which the automatic labeling of perception and language has transformed the objects around him. Since adult memory functions predominantly in terms of recalling clichés, the conventional schemata of things and experiences rather than the things and experiences themselves, it becomes apparent how ill-equipped, in fact incapable, such conventionalized memory is to recall the experiences of early childhood in their freshness, in the real significance which they had at that time. The age of discovery, early childhood, is buried deep under the age of routine familiarity, adulthood.

The incompatibility of early childhood experience with the categories and the organization of adult memory is to a large extent due to what I call the conventionalization of the adult memory. Conventionalization is a particular form of what one might call schematization of memory. Voluntary memory recalls largely schemata of experience rather than experience. These schemata are mostly built along the lines of words and concepts of the culture. Also the so-called visual or the auditory memory reproduces schemata of visual or auditory impressions rather than the impressions themselves. Obviously the schemata of experience as well as of memory[14] are determined by the culture which has developed a certain view of the world and of life, a view which furnishes the schemata for all experience and all memory. But the range and differentiation of a culture like that of Greece, India, China, or modern western civilization is of considerable scope. It offers highly differentiated and subtle as well as very conventional, banal, and commonplace schemata. By conventionalization of the memory (and experience) schemata I understand those memory processes which are subject to the most conventional schematization and which, therefore, are not capable of reproducing individual experience, but can only reproduce what John Doe is supposed to have experienced according to the Joneses' and everybody else's ideas of what people experience. Every fresh and spontaneous experience transcends the capacity of the conventionalized memory schema and, to some degree, of any schema. That part of the experience which transcends the memory schema as preformed by the culture is in danger of being lost because there exists as yet no vessel, as it were, in which to preserve it. Even if the schemata of experience have not prevented the person from becoming aware of or sensing that quality of his experience which transcended these schemata, this quality, if it is to be preserved and to become a productive part of the personality, has to overcome the second handicap of the memory schemata, which tend, as time goes on, to supplant this fresh and new element of experience with some preformed notion and thus to bury it. The process of schematization and conventionalization and

[14] The term memory schemata is taken from Bartlett (footnote 12) but used in a somewhat different sense. Bartlett rightly emphasizes that remembering is "an affair of reconstruction rather than mere reproduction." According to him, this reconstruction serves as a justification of the present attitude toward past experience. Such reconstructions he calls schemata, and these are determined by sense differences, appetites, instincts, and interests. In this essay, however, the concept of memory schemata is used only to designate socially and culturally determined patterns of reconstruction of the past, as contrasted to individually determined patterns. Obviously the greater part of all individual memory schemata in Bartlett's sense are culturally determined.

its effect on the raw material of experience, especially child-hood experience, can be well observed in two of its specific developments which take place as the child learns to make use of his senses and to speak.

Language, in its articulating and its obscuring function, may be considered first since the adult, too, encounters the problem of the incompatibility of experience with language and the consequent forgetting of experience or its distortion by the cliché of language. The fact that language is adult language, the language of an adult civilization, and that the infant and small child is molded only very gradually from its natural existence into a member of the civilization into which it is born makes the discrepancy between his precivilized, unsche-matized experience and the categories of civilized, conven-tional language much greater. Yet between this discrepancy and that existing between the adult's experience and his lan-guage, there is a difference of degree rather than of kind. Everyone who has honestly tried to describe some genuine experience exactly, however small and insignificant it may have seemed, knows how difficult if not impossible that is. One might well say that the greatest problem of the writer or the poet is the temptation of language. At every step a word beckons, it seems so convenient, so suitable, one has heard or read it so often in a similar context, it sounds so well, it makes the phrase flow so smoothly. If he follows the tempta-tion of this word, he will perhaps describe something that many people recognize at once, that they already know, that fol-lows a familiar pattern; but he will have missed the nuance that distinguishes his experience from others, that makes it his own. If he wants to communicate that elusive nuance which in some way, however small, will be his contribution, a widening or opening of the scope of articulate human ex-perience at some point, he has to fight constantly against the easy flow of words that offer themselves. Like the search for truth, which never reaches its goal yet never can be abandoned, the endeavor to articulate, express, and communicate an ex-perience can never succeed completely. It consists of an ap-proach, step by step, toward that distant vantage point, that bend of the road from which one hopes to see the real experience in its entirety and from where it will become visible to others—a point which is never reached. The lag, the dis-crepancy between experience and word is a productive force in man as long as he remains aware of it, as long as he knows and feels that his experience was in some way more than and different from what his concepts and words articulate. The awareness of this unexplored margin of experience, which may be its essential part, can turn into that productive energy which enables man to go one step closer to understanding and communicating his experience, and thus add to the scope of human insight. It is this awareness and the struggle and the ability to narrow the gap between experience and words which make the writer and the poet. The danger of the schemata of language, and especially of the worn currency of conventional language in vogue at the moment when the attempt is made to understand and describe an experience, is that the person making this attempt will overlook the discrepancy between experience and language cliché or that he will not be persistent enough in his attempt to eliminate this discrepancy. Once the conventional schema has replaced the experience in his mind, the significant quality of the experience is condemned to oblivion.

The discrepancy between concepts, language, and experience can be looked upon as a model and as part of the discrepancy between memory schemata and experience. This close relationship, of course, is not accidental since voluntary recall and communication of recalled experience are essentially dependent on conceptual thought and language. While there is also recall of experience without the vehicle of language, a great deal of what we recall, especially of what we recall voluntarily, is recalled already in terms of language and in concepts formed by language. This has considerable bearing on the problem of childhood amnesia. The infant and small child has to undergo and assimilate the comparatively greatest amount of new experience at a time when his language, his concepts, and his memory schemata are poorest or as yet entirely undeveloped. Only very gradually does he acquire the faculty of language, learn the conceptual schemata of his culture, and develop a memory and memory schemata. The experiences of the infant are inarticulate and complex. In a term coined by Sullivan, they are instantaneous records of total situations.[15] They are also as yet unformed and untainted by the experience schemata of the culture which, from the viewpoint of the culture, justifies Freud's remark that the small child is "polymorph perverse." He is a little animal, a little heathen, and his experiences are only gradually and in-

[15] Patrick Mullahy, A Theory of Interpersonal Relations and the Evolution of Personality, PSYCHIATRY (1945) 8:177–205; p. 183.

creasingly forced into the Procrustean bed of the culturally prevalent experience schemata which allow for certain experiences, forbid others, and omit a great many for which the culture has either no frame of reference or only an unsuitable one. It is true that only by learning and developing the schemata of language, conceptual thought, experience, and memory prevalent in the culture can the child progress from the phase of complex and inarticulate experience to that of specific and articulate experience. It is true that the complex and inarticulate experience of infancy and early childhood, because of the very lack of schemata for detailed articulation, is often prevented from reaching awareness or else soon removed from awareness and forgotten. But, on the other hand, the schemata provided by the culture and gradually acquired by the growing child cannot accommodate his experience in its entirety, but will distort and bias it according to the patterns of the culture. Two major trends thus operate in the direction of the eventual outcome of early childhood amnesia. First, the schemata for articulate experience and for recall of such experience are relatively slow and late in developing. They are entirely lacking in the earliest period of life and one could say generally that as they develop, experience gradually loses its character of newness and acquires the quality of familiarity and recognition. The tremendous amount of experience which the small child undergoes does not, therefore, find a proportionate variety of suitable vessels (schemata) for its preservation. Second, the quality of early childhood experience does not fit into the developing schemata of experience, thought, and memory since these are fashioned by the adult culture and all its biases, emphases, and taboos.

Both these trends become even more apparent if one considers them in connection with the development of the *senses* in the child. Such a consideration also shows how closely biological and cultural factors are interwoven in the causation of early childhood amnesia and how difficult, if not impossible, it is to draw a clear borderline between the two. What might have been a cultural factor in man's prehistory may well seem to the present observer like a biological development. Phylogenetically as well as ontogenetically the distance senses, sight and hearing, attain their full development later than the proximity senses, smell, taste, and touch. Sight and hearing are more highly differentiated and more closely linked up with the human mind than smell, taste, and touch. The latter senses, especially smell and taste, are neglected and to a considerable extent even tabooed by western civilization. They are the animalistic senses *par excellence.* Man, who has been engaged for thousands of years in a battle for control and mastery of nature outside and inside himself, especially western man, does not want to be reminded that he is not only man but also nature, also animal. Because of the cultural taboo on smell and taste—smell even more than taste, but the two are inseparable—it is even possible for the adult to realize clearly the effect which the discrepancy between experience on the one hand, and language and memory schemata, on the other hand, has on the capacity for recall, especially voluntary recall. English vocabulary, and equally the vocabulary of the other western languages, is conspicuously poor in words for the description of smells and tastes. Even when it comes to the flavor of wine or of a dish, in spite of the great material and historical role of drinking and eating, language is quite incapable of expressing any but the crudest differences in taste. A wine is said to be dry, sweet, robust, fine, full and so on, but none of these words enables one to imagine the flavor and bouquet of the wine. Compared with this poverty of words, the vocabulary for the description of the visible world and its forms and colors is much richer. Even poetry has never succeeded in conjuring the flavor of a smell or taste, although it sometimes enables the imagination to evoke a visual image. For these reasons, the experience schemata for smell and taste sensations are relatively undeveloped. This is true even more of the memory schemata. A taste or a smell is usually remembered only involuntarily; that is, the former experience may be recognized by renewed encounter with the same stimulus. But it is difficult or impossible for most people to recall voluntarily the taste of a particular wine or the smell of a particular flower, animal, or person. In fact, most people are hardly aware of the differences in smell of different people.

Both pleasure and disgust are more intimately linked with the proximity senses than with the distance senses. The pleasure which a perfume, a taste, or a texture can give is much more of a bodily, physical one, hence also more akin to sexual pleasure, than is the more sublime pleasure aroused by sound and the least bodily of all pleasures, the sight of something beautiful. No other sense produces the emotion of disgust more easily and violently and provokes reactions of nausea and vomiting more readily than the olfactory sense. The infant is not disgusted by his feces; he quite likes their smell. Very many, if not most adults do not have the reaction of disgust to the smell of their own excretions; many do not show it with regard to the body odor or the excretions of a beloved person. As everybody knows, animals, especially dogs, are best able to tell one person from another and one dog from another by body and excretion smell. The infant, long before he knows and remembers how his mother looks, knows how she smells and tastes. Very likely, angry or frightened mother tastes and smells rather different from good or comfortable mother to the infant, just as she will look very different to him as he grows older.[16] In his growing experience of the world around him, the proximity senses at first have primacy over the distance senses. He tastes and sniffs and touches earlier and better than he perceives with eye and ear. In order to get really acquainted with something or somebody, he has to touch it and to put it in his mouth as he first did with his mother's nipple. Only very gradually and slowly does the emphasis shift from the proximity to the distance senses. This partly biological and phylogenetically determined shift is helped along powerfully and the development of taste and smell discouraged by the stringent taboos of the significant adults, who do not want baby to take everything in his mouth and who drastically and persistently in cleanliness education show their disgust with the most important objects of smell, those of the body and its excretions, so that the child cannot but feel that he has to refrain not only from the pleasure given by body and excretion odors but even from the discriminating perception of them.[17] The proximity senses, which play such a great role in relations between animals and, if not repressed, in the sexual relations of man, are otherwise tabooed in interpersonal relations the more a culture or a group tends to isolate people, to put distance between them, and to prevent spontaneous relation-

[16] Groddeck, speaking about the paramount importance of the sense of smell in infancy and early childhood, asserts that, even more than the dog, the child judges people and objects largely by their smell and, since the child is small or is being held on the lap, this means chiefly the smell of legs, lap, sexual and excretory organs. G. Groddeck, *The World of Man;* The C. W. Daniel Company, London 1934; p. 132.

[17] Freud links fetishism with a repressed coprophilic smell desire; feet and hair become fetishes after the now unpleasant sensation of smell has been renounced. Reference footnote 7; p. 567, footnote 3. On another occasion he suggests that the sense of smell which attracts the male to the menstruating female animal became the victim of organic repression as man started to walk erect and that this was the origin of the emotion of disgust. *Das Unbehagen in der Kultur;* Wien 1930; p. 62 footnote.

ships and the "natural" animal-like expressions of such relations. The emphasis on distance and the taboo on smell in modern society is more outspoken in the ruling than in the laboring class, distance being also a means of domination and of imposing authority. Disgust arises where the repression has not succeeded completely and a powerful deterrent is needed in order to bolster it.[18]

Whatever the social and cultural reasons for the discouragement and neglect of the proximity senses, the shift from their initial predominance to that of the distance senses, which takes place progressively during infancy and early childhood and which is a result partly of these cultural factors and partly of biological and phylogenetical factors, necessarily entails for the child a far-reaching change in the whole way of perceiving and experiencing the people and the world around him, a change which the adult mind is quite unable to imagine concretely. Much less is the adult memory capable of recalling experience that had occurred before the shift in the organization of the senses was made, since this change altered the entire mode of perception and experience.

Together with and continuing after the shift in the organization of perception from the primacy of the proximity senses to that of the distance senses, a comprehensive development in the direction of specialization and differentiation takes place in the child's apparatus for experience. This, too, brings about considerable changes in the mode of experience. As ontogenetic development of the child from conception to adulthood repeats the phylogenetic development of man from his farthest ancestors in the most primitive living organisms to his present state, the development of consciousness is a relatively late stage in this process, beginning only some time after birth and continuing for a long period. Within the development of consciousness, the consciousness of self comes latest, and neither individually nor in the history of the race has man as yet ever reached anything approaching full consciousness of self. Memory, especially voluntary memory, is an important part of consciousness. It seems probable that in the infant and child the development of memory starts with a recognition of certain complex, undifferentiated states of his own body-feeling, primarily states of comfort, satisfaction and pleasure, and

[18] Something of the importance of the deeply rooted taboo on smell in western man comes to the surface in the vituperative and hateful use that is made of body odor in interracial conflicts.

states of discomfort, tension and displeasure. Since the infant
has as yet no cognition, one cannot properly speak of recognition either; rather one should speak of a re-sensing, a re-
experiencing of certain complex and dim states of his own
well-being or not well-being. The differentiation between body
and mind, body and psyche, also develops gradually and becomes more accentuated in the course of time. The infant,
at first, is probably not capable of distinguishing between himself and whatever persons or objects of his environment come
sufficiently close to him to affect him.[19] The mother's breast
is not, at first, part of "another person"; it belongs to the
undifferentiated little world of the infant, is part of his "own
cosmic entity," as Sullivan puts it.[20] The whole concept of
self and others does not make sense at this earliest period, and
nothing corresponding to this concept exists for the small infant. It is not chance, then, that much later in life those rare
instances of a whole vision recalled by involuntary memory
are often stimulated by some body-sensation, that is by the
re-sensing of a sensation of long ago. They are memories of
the body, as it were, or of the unexplored realm where body
and psyche are identical, and it is here that Proust's involuntary memory flashes, occasioned by the taste of the *madeleine*,
by the unevenness of the pavement, have their earliest origin.[21] The perception of the environment as something
separate, a changing configuration of various *objects*, develops
only very gradually in the infant and small child. Objects can
be handled and eventually controlled to some extent, but life
in the early stages of infancy as well as in the lower forms

[19] This was already the opinion of Descartes, who said: "In early
life the mind was so closely bound to the body that it attended to nothing beyond the thoughts by which it perceived the objects that made
impression on the body; nor as yet did it refer these thoughts to anything existing beyond itself, but simply felt pain when the body was hurt,
or pleasure when anything beneficial to the body occurred. . . . And
afterward when the machine of the body, which has been so fabricated
by nature that it can of its own inherent power move itself in various
ways, by turning itself at random on every side, followed after
what was useful and avoided what was detrimental, the mind, which
was closely connected with it, reflecting on the objects it pursued and
avoided, remarked, for the first time, that they existed out of itself. . . ." Descartes, *Principia Philosophiae*, I, 71, John Veitch's
translation.

[20] Harry Stack Sullivan, "Conceptions of Modern Psychiatry," PSY-
CHIATRY (1940) 3:1–117; p. 15.

[21] See also Ernest G. Schachtel, "The Dynamic Perception and the
Symbolism of Form: With Special Reference to the Rorschach Test,"
PSYCHIATRY (1941) 4:79–96; p. 85 and footnote 16.

of the fauna begins with a state in which the living organism is merely affected by his environment and experiences this as a change in his own bodily state, not—as the growing child and the adult will perceive it later—as the actions of people and objects outside himself. In this context it is significant that the olfactory sense, so important in infancy, throughout life is least, practically not at all, capable of objectifying stimuli, whereas the more spiritual and later developed sense of vision cannot but objectify the stimuli by which it is affected. In this respect also, the olfactory sense retains more of an earlier stage of development, a closer, less alienated, and less differentiated relationship to the environment than the distance senses and even the sense of touch. As the specialization and differentiation of the apparatus for experience continue—including the sensory apparatus and the slowly developing consciousness—the initial lack of distinction between organism and environment gives way more and more to the division that is of such fundamental importance in the history of man, that of subject and object, a division that comes about slowly and gradually, but one that the adult mind cannot possibly discard even in fantasy, and certainly not in perception and rational thinking. It becomes so predominant that it completely blots out the earlier kind of experience and whatever remains subterraneously, as it were, of this early way of experiencing the environment in later life. In the slow development of consciousness, the sharp differentiation between sleep and being awake also comes about only gradually. Memory is a relatively late product of this whole process of differentiation and specialization. Autobiographical memory—that is the ability for voluntary recall of one's past life—is one of the latest developments in childhood, which is not surprising since it is part of the awareness of self, a capacity found only in man, and even in adult man usually not very well developed. According to Stern,[22] memory up to the third year refers almost exclusively to the visible world of objects and events. The life of the small child is naturally oriented toward the present and the future, not toward the past. The concept of "I" hardly develops before the third year, which is but another expression of the fact that the division between subject and object is a gradual, relatively late development. Yet the significance of this division and its particular quality in a particular society,

[22] William Stern, *Psychologie der frühen Kindheit bis zum sechsten Lebensjahre;* Quelle & Meyer, Leipzig 1914; p. 166.

culture, and stage of historical development can hardly be
overestimated. It partakes of and is determined by all the
fundamental attitudes in the relation of man to his fellow men,
to nature, and to his material environment as they have developed in a specific society and culture.

The late development of the autobiographical memory and
of the concept of "I" or "self" as a subject preserving one's
identity in time is but another aspect of early childhood amnesia. The child lives much more in the present moment than
the average adult does. His life is so much more filled with
the exploration of the environment and of his own growing
capacities that the past has not much interest for him. And
even with the appearance of the first traces of autobiographical memory and of the concept "I" in the third year of life,
the quality of childhood experience is still so different from
that of the adult that the memory schemata of the adult cannot
accommodate the greater part of this experience.

The fact that autobiographical memory develops so late in
childhood should be considered also with the question in mind
of its usefulness for life, and especially for life in western
civilization. Considered from this angle it becomes apparent
that it is of much less immediate use for orientation in and
adaptation to the environment than the development of the
senses, of the mind, and of "useful" memory—that is, memory
in the service of the recognition of objects, the learning of
words, and similar functions important for survival. Biologically and culturally, autobiographical memory thus finds little
encouragement. In a culture oriented toward efficient performance of profitable activities, a society in which everybody has
to fit like a cog in a machine and where powerful pressure is
exerted to make people equal, in the sense of uniform, autobiographical memory is discouraged in its development and pre-
destined to atrophy. It is of no use for the reliable and efficient
performance of the worker at the machine, the clerk at his
desk, the surgeon at the operating table; in fact, it would interfere with their activities. It would stand in the way of the
process of equalization and uniformity since its very function
is to preserve individual experience rather than repeat cultural
and conventional schemata of experience. If Ulysses gives in
to the song of the Sirens, his active life will have reached its
end and his plans will come to naught. The pseudo-memory
of the adult, which reproduces not his real experience but the
experience schemata furnished by the culture, is a more re-

liable and conservative servant of the culture than the true memory which would preserve the real experience before it has been filtered through the memory schemata of the culture and thus cleansed from all that transcends the ubiquitous pattern.

In one other area of life, namely in the realm of *dreams*, one finds a general amnesia, although it is not quite so pervasive as that pertaining to early childhood. A closer study of the recall of dreams and especially of the period of awakening from a dream, when quite often one can observe its disappearance from memory or its transformation or fragmentation, may therefore add to, disprove, or corroborate the hypotheses developed so far for the phenomenon of early childhood amnesia and of adult forgetting of trans-schematic experience. It is probable that the majority of dreams are not remembered at all. A great many others are recalled in fragments only. Of those that are still remembered at the time of awakening, very many are forgotten in the course of the day, quite often in the first few minutes or the first hour of beginning the daily activities of rising, getting dressed, and so on. The relatively small proportion of dreams surviving in memory undergo a rapid transformation and fragmentation and usually they, too, are forgotten after a few days. If they are not forgotten, they are transformed in a way which is rather analogous to the transformation of the Indian story in Bartlett's experiment. That is to say, they lose increasingly their peculiar dream quality, and the peculiar language of the dream changes in the direction of conventionalization and rationalization. Even persons sensitized to awareness and recall of their dreams, for example psychoanalytic patients, find it difficult or impossible to counteract this powerful tendency toward forgetting or conventionalizing the dream unless they record their dreams as soon as possible after awakening. The dreams that make such a profound impression on the dreamer that they survive all these obstacles, although not without some damage, are rare indeed. Thus the question arises: What are the causes of this usual, general *dream-amnesia?* Why does one forget by far the greater part of his mental life going on during sleep, a life that in most people, judging from the fragments recalled, seems to be far more original, interesting, spontaneous, and creative than their waking life? It shares these latter qualities with early childhood which, from all one can observe, seems to be the most fascinating, spontaneous, original, and creative period in the life of most or perhaps of all people. Is it because of these qualities that the conventionalized memory schemata cannot reproduce the great majority of dreams and their real character?

Freud devotes a whole section of *The Interpretation of Dreams* to the problem of the forgetting of dreams.[23] His purpose in this section is to defend the validity of dream interpretation against the objection that one does not really know his dreams because he either forgets or distorts them. Freud's answer to the problem is that the "forgetting of dreams depends far more on the resistance [to the dream thought] than on the mutually alien character of the waking and sleeping states" and that the distortion of the dream in recalling or recounting it is "the secondary and often misunderstanding elaboration of the dream by the agency of normal thinking" and thus "no more than a part of the elaboration to which dream thoughts are constantly subjected as a result of the dream-censorship."[24] I think that the question should be raised whether "resistance" and "mutually alien character of the waking and sleeping states" are really, as Freud seems to assume, mutually exclusive and contradictory explanations of dream amnesia and dream distortion by waking thought. Or whether, as I believe, "resistance" is operative in the awake person, not only against the dream thought but against the whole quality and language of the dream, a resistance, to be sure, of a somewhat different character, yet fundamentally related to that which represses and censors those dream thoughts which are intolerable for consciousness.

In sleep and dream, man's activity in the outer world is suspended, especially his motor activity. Attention and perception are withdrawn from outer reality. The necessity to cope with the environment is interrupted for the duration of sleep. The stringent rules of logic and reason subside—rules which during waking life are geared to useful, rational, adaptative, conventional control of behavior and thought. The psyche receives leave, for the period of sleep, from the demands of active life in society. As Freud expresses it, endopsychic censorship is reduced. And the psyche makes good use of this short leave from the demands of reality. Its productions, seen from the usual, realistic viewpoint, seem utterly useless. It is true that other, older civilizations did not always share this viewpoint, but attributed considerable importance to dreams,

[23] Chapter VII, section A; Freud, footnote 7; pp. 470–485.
[24] Freud, footnote 23; pp. 476 and 472.

sometimes greater importance than to waking thought. But measured with the yardstick of modern western civilization with its emphasis on useful, efficient production and work, dreams are really quite useless.

During sleep motor activity, most essential for dealing with the outer reality of objects and people, is reduced to a minimum. Movements are not performed actively. But in the dream a world of movement is perceived. Rorschach has called attention to the fact that dreams are primarily kinesthesias, that is kinesthetic production.[25] Even in waking life Rorschach's experiment has demonstrated that kinesthetic perception, that is the most creative factor in perception, is invariably inhibited or made altogether impossible by an attitude of cramped attention, by the straining of willpower in the direction of control and good performance, and that it is facilitated by an attitude of giving in to one's ideas, to what will occur to one, without straining for ambitious performance. The dream, of course, is a mental production without any conscious effort and one in which the dreamer passively gives in to the images evoked by his fantasy. In that sense the dream is the opposite of *work* as it is known to western civilization, the opposite of efficiency. When awakening, it is often possible to catch hold of a dream, as Rorschach has pointed out, if one lies perfectly still and does not open his eyes. But the first movement, especially an active one like jumping out of bed, will very often chase the dream into oblivion. In other words, the return to the outer world through motor activity and reshifting of attention and perception to the environment leads to forgetting of the dream. This process is a quite general one and, as far as I have been able to observe, bears no relation to specific dream content. Therefore it seems to stem from the incompatibility of the extroversive attitude of waking with the introversive attitude of dreaming, rather than from resistance to specific strivings which are expressed in the dream thoughts. The antagonism between motor activity and dream recall brings to mind Proust's words, that he could recapture his former being only "dehors de l'action, de la jouissance

[25] Hermann Rorschach, *Psychodiagnostics: A Diagnostic Test Based on Perception* (English edition by Paul Lemkau and Bernard Kronenberg); Berne, Switzerland, Hans Huber, 1942; p. 72. Since dreams are the most creative mental production of the average person, this sheds an interesting light on one of Rorschach's significant findings, that of a close kinship between kinesthesia and mental creativity, and seems to corroborate this finding.

immediate"[26] and that in such a moment he did not dare to budge lest he lose the refound memory of the past.

But even without the described effect of the resumption of motor activity on the voluntary recall of dreams, it seems obvious that the experience and memory schemata developed and formed by man's life in his society are much less suitable to preserve the fantastic world of the dream than to recall conventional waking experience. The awakening mind has to cope again with outer reality, and to this end has to re-mobilize all the patterns and schemata useful for, and developed by, the conventional social forms of life and work. Attention has to be paid to the environment. And the attitude of attention is to the mind what purposeful motor activity is to the body.

In the forgetting and distortion of dreams during waking life it is important to distinguish between that which is due to the resistance to and repression of a specific dream thought or dream content and that which is due to the incapacity of the conventional memory schemata to retain the fantastic general quality and the strange language of dreams. The distortion of a dream thought which resistance wants to keep from awareness has to be distinguished from the process of conventionalization which, more or less, *all* dream elements undergo because the medium of the dream language is incompatible with the medium of the conventional world of waking life. In the degree of this incompatibility there are, of course, considerable variations between different people and, even more so, between different cultures. But modern western civilization with its streamlined efficiency, uniform mass culture, and emphasis on usefulness in terms of profitable, material production is particularly and strikingly at the opposite pole from the world of dreams.[27]

Dream amnesia and early childhood amnesia are due to related causes. Experience and thought transcending the conventional schemata of the culture are found in relatively few people. Yet they are universal in early childhood and in the dream: in early childhood because the spontaneity of the child has not yet been deadened or channelized into the conventional patterns of the culture; in the dream because the hold of these conventional patterns, the hold of reality, can be relaxed to some extent since the dreamer temporarily is cut off

[26] Proust, p. 14.

[27] Concerning the peculiar language of the dream, compare also Erich Fromm's "The Meaning of Dreams."

from active commerce with outer reality by the suspension of perception and motor activity. It is the trans-schematic quality of early childhood experience as well as of dreams which makes it difficult or impossible for the memory schemata to preserve and recall voluntarily such experience. Yet it is also this quality in which potentialities of progress, of going beyond the conventional pattern, and of widening the scope of human life are forever present and waiting to be released.

The main subject of my considerations so far has been to discover the causes of the forgetting of early childhood and other trans-schematic experience. What, then, are the qualities of that relatively rare remembrance by which the individual past, the lost experience is recalled, and what are the conditions favoring such recall? The veil of amnesia which hides former experience under the memory schemata of voluntary recall is sometimes lifted and the lost experience recovered. A dream, already forgotten, is suddenly remembered. A scene from childhood, buried under layers of years of a conventional life, reappears as though it had been yesterday. The recent age regression experiments in hypnoanalysis show in dramatic fashion how forgotten experiences of many years ago, secreted in the unconscious, are recalled and relived during hypnosis and again lost when amnesia returns after awakening from the trance. But this is a more striking demonstration only of the classical teaching of psychoanalysis about the memory traces of the unconscious which usually are immune to voluntary recall but may be approached by the special techniques of dream interpretation, free association, and recall under hypnosis or under the influence of resistance-reducing drugs.

The hidden quality of these lost memories, their separation from the rest of life, their inaccessibility, and their incompatibility with voluntary memory and with conventional, purposeful, daily activity are described lucidly by Proust. He compares the recesses of the lost memories to a thousand vases distributed on the various altitudes of the past years of one's life, filled with the particular atmosphere of that period of his life, and containing sometimes a gesture, a word, an insignificant act which, however, may be the key to the recapturing of the lost experiences, the lost past of his life. According to him, the very fact that the experience, the past time, has been *forgotten* and thus has remained isolated as at the bottom of a valley or on the peak of a summit, gives it an incomparable air of freshness and aliveness when it is re-

covered, *because it has not been able to form any link with
the present.*[28] In other words, it has not been distorted by
the memory schemata, by the needs and fears of the present,
by the routine of daily life. Proust's view, here, is almost
identical with that of Freud, whose theory of memory postu-
lates that *only* that which is unconscious can leave a permanent memory trace and that "becoming conscious and leaving behind a memory trace are processes incompatible with
each other in the same system."[29]

The memory trace that has been secluded from contact with
conscious present life thereby often acquires in the isolation
of the unconscious the character of *strangeness* to one's present life. Hence the surprise when it is recovered. Again, Proust
makes an illuminating contribution to the understanding of
this phenomenon. He describes how, in the library of the
Prince de Guermantes, he finds a book, *François le Champi,*
that his mother had read to him when he was a child.
The memory is painful at first. In the shock of sudden recall of the forgotten childhood scene he asks himself
angrily who causes him such pain, and in the same moment
he discovers that he sees *himself* as a child, he is the stranger.
In rereading the title of the book, *François le Champi,*
he suddenly finds himself transposed into the remote past and
he reads with the eyes of the child, of the person that he was
then, with the same reveries and the same fear of the next
day that he had felt then.[30] The reason for the strangeness of
such sudden and vivid recollections of hitherto forgotten experience is that such experience is in contrast to and alien
to one's present state and conscious preoccupations. The voluntary memory schemata accommodate the familiar and the
conventional only, in terms of the present life. The involuntary recovery of the forgotten past very often intrudes on this
present life like a strange, alien element. The person that one
was then, the child that Proust sees in the scene recalled,
has long since been buried under the years of social routine,
of changed needs and interests, of the preoccupations of the
present. He has become a stranger. But this stranger may also
assert a life and wishes which had been starved and suffocated by the time gone by and the pressures it brought.

[28] Proust, pp. 12–13.
[29] Freud, *Beyond the Pleasure Principle;* The International Psycho-
analytical Press, London 1922; p. 28. See also, The Interpretation of
Dreams; footnote 7; pp. 488–491.
[30] Proust, pp. 30–38.

In Proust's work the recovery of the forgotten past is characterized as the supreme satisfaction, carrying with it a sense of exhilarating happiness and constituting the very core of the work of art. This is not the place to discuss the profound meaning of his evaluation which, three thousand years after the Greek myth, again celebrates memory as the mother of art and poetry. Be it sufficient to say that in the conflict of modern society between efficient adaptation and activity, on the one hand, and the preservation and recovery of the total personality, which to him seems possible only by the fullest awareness of the individual past, Proust sides against his society and with the "lost paradises" of his own past. And it is true that each genuine recovery of forgotten experience and, with it, something of the person that one was when having the experience carries with it an element of enrichment, adds to the light of consciousness, and thus widens the conscious scope of one's life.

Such widening of the personality by the recovery of lost ground and its liberating and exhilarating effect has to be distinguished from what I propose to call the *possessive* attitude to memory, or to one's past, an attitude that occurs much more frequently than the instances of genuine recovery of the past. The possessive attitude to one's own past, particularly to past feelings, more often imagined than real, seems to me the essence of sentimentality. The person who has this attitude pats himself on the shoulder as it were and feels what a fine fellow he is for having had such feelings or such experience. It is the same attitude that leads also to a kind of proprietary satisfaction about one's character. Character, feelings, the past are looked upon as prized possessions enhancing the prestige of their owner. On closer analysis, it usually turns out that these treasures are spurious.[31] The possessive attitude toward the past prevents rather than furthers the gain in consciousness and the widening of the scope of life by the rediscovery of forgotten experience.

Since the lost experience is inaccessible to voluntary recall and incompatible with the conventional memory schemata, the

[31] The possessive attitude toward the (pseudo-) remembered past is closely related to and finds its counterpart in the acquisitive anticipation of (pseudo-) experience, already described, in which not some event is experienced, not some object perceived, but instead the motions are gone through and a preconceived cliché replaces actual experience because the performance of such pseudo-experience promises an increase in prestige.

question arises as to what the conditions are under which such forgotten experience may be recalled. Of course, a definite and complete catalogue of these conditions cannot be given. But it may be useful to consider some situations which typically favor the rediscovery of a past that has been forgotten. Proust attributes to bodily sensations and to perceptions the greatest importance, in fact exclusive importance, as carriers of such significant memories. The accidental recurrence of a bodily posture or of a sensory perception which he had experienced in the past, on some occasions brings with it the entire vision of that past, of the person he was then and of the way he saw things then. It is a sensation—feeling of a body posture or sensation of the perceptive apparatus—not a thought, as in willed recall, which revives the past. In Proust's account visual sensations are far outnumbered as carriers of such memories by those of the other, less spiritual, more bodily senses, such as the feeling of his own body in a particular posture, the touch of a napkin, the smell and taste of a flavor, the hearing of a sound—noise or melody, *not* the sound of words. All these sensations are far from conceptual thought, language, or conventional memory schemata. They renew a state of the psychosomatic entity, in some respect, that this entity had experienced before, felt before. It is as though they touched directly the unconscious memory trace, the record left behind by a total situation out of the past, whereas voluntary recall tries to approach and construct this past indirectly, coached and deflected by all those ideas, wishes, and needs which tell the present person how the past could, should, or might have been. Just as the infant's recall probably starts out as an automatic recognition or, rather, resensation of a certain state of his body—pleasurable or unpleasurable, satisfied or needy, comfortable or tense—and not as conscious recall of former experience, such resensation, more differentiated than in early infancy, seems to be one basis and one condition of involuntary recall of forgotten experience. By revival of a former sensation the attitude of the former self that first had this sensation is remobilized. And thus recall is made possible of the objects and feelings closely connected with the former sensation—objects and feelings which the present self would otherwise not perceive or experience in the same manner since it thinks, feels, behaves differently and since, therefore, the conscious memory schemata are not prepared for the ready reproduction of material stemming from a historical past in which the person was different, moved by needs, interests, and fears different from those that move him now, especially from those of which he is aware at present. But all experience leaves a record behind, as it were, a memory trace, inaccessible, as a rule, to the consciously, purposefully searching mind, revealed sometimes by the repetition of a sensation that had occurred at the time when the record was first made.

This hypothesis of one type of involuntary recall of forgotten experience seems to fit in with two data from psychoanalytic theory and therapy. One of them concerns Freud's "screen" or "concealing" memories ("Deckerinnerungen") from early childhood; the other, therapeutic findings of Wilhelm Reich. Freud calls attention to the "fact that the earliest recollections of a person often seemed to preserve the unimportant and accidental, whereas . . . not a trace is found in the adult memory of the weighty and affective impressions of this period."[32] He distinguishes regressive, encroaching, and contemporaneous or contiguous concealing memories. The indifferent, unimportant recollection, according to Freud, conceals the forgotten, significant emotional experience. If the image recalled has preceded the significant experience, he speaks of a regressive concealing memory; if it has succeeded the experience, he terms it an encroaching memory; if they belong to the same time, the concealing memory is a contemporaneous or contiguous one. To simplify matters I shall speak only of the contiguous screen memory. The question relevant for the problems presented in this essay concerns the nature of the associative connection between screen memory and forgotten, significant emotional experience. It is my impression that usually, if not always, this connection is very similar to the one described by Proust between the taste of the *madeleine* and the recall of his childhood, the sensation of uneven pavement and the recall of Venice, and all the other instances in which a seemingly quite indifferent object arouses most significant forgotten memories. In the analysis of such seemingly indifferent memories, such as the recall of a piece of furniture, a corridor, a stove in the parental home, of a piece of apparel worn by the child or by his parents, I have often found that it is possible, not only to rediscover the forgotten emotion "behind" this screen memory, but that what seemed merely a screen, an indifferent object, was not so indifferent after all. Quite often the feelings with which this par-

[32] Freud, Psychopathology of Everyday Life; footnote 7; p. 62.

ticular object was seen, the perceptive "aura" of the object was a condensation of significant emotions in the interpersonal relations of the child at that time. There was a time, in other words, when the way in which the now indifferent object was perceived, contained in a complex, condensed, inarticulate manner the essence of the life of the child at that time. That a simple perception should contain such condensed material is not as astonishing as it may seem. Rorschach's psychodiagnostic test is based on the fact that the way in which a person sees *is* the person and that it is possible to reach significant conclusions as to structure and conflicts of a personality by analyzing the processes of his visual perception. In many, possibly in all, cases of contiguous screen memories, the indifferent object is not so much the significant element as the perceptive aura of this object in childhood—the perception itself, its individual qualities and characteristics which contain the child, as it were, that once saw this object, the little stranger of whom the adult Proust speaks when the perception of the book *François le Champi* suddenly brings with it the whole atmosphere of the time when this book was read to him by his mother. In the course of growing up, the language label and the corresponding conventional memory schema replace the living perception of the object. Thus the significant individual perception is lost, the object loses its aura, and only its name remains; and its indifferent, conventional cliché or picture may be recalled voluntarily by the conventional memory schemata. But sometimes it is possible, by insisting, to revive the former alive perception, the childhood aura of the object, and in this way to arrive also at the significant emotional experiences of that time which endowed the object with its unique aura. Once the cliché quality of the object or scene recalled consciously in the screen memory is discarded, one can penetrate to the memory trace left behind by the living sensation, the individual perception of this object as experienced by this person in his past. The memory of the conscious, conventionalized mind thus gives way to the memory of the body, of the psychosomatic entity in which the old sensation left a record not only of this object but of the total emotional configuration in which the object was seen and which gave to it the aura that made it peculiarly fit to become a symbol for the period and event to which it refers.

The subjective element in perception, the individual perspective under which the seemingly indifferent object once was seen, thus turns out to be the associative link between

screen memory and significant experience. From this viewpoint, the screen memory loses its seemingly indifferent and
accidental character. The object of the screen memory and
the significant emotional experience belong together. The significant experience constituted the atmosphere in which the
object was perceived and which thus became part of that object. Significant experience and "accidental" object are no
longer separate; they belong together and often shade imperceptibly into one another. The perceptive attitude was
closely akin to, or identical with, the general attitude of the
child in his experiences.

If the screen memories show how this attitude may be recovered by reviving the former unschematic perception of
the object and by reviving therewith the attitude of the
child at that time, Reich's vegetotherapeutic technique has
shown how, starting not from an object recalled, but from
the bodily residua and encrustations of childhood attitudes in
posture, expression, and muscular armor, one can recover
forgotten experience.[33] Reich has found that "the dissolution
of a muscular rigidity . . . brings back into memory the very
infantile situation in which the repression had taken place."
According to him, the repressed affect and the defense against
this affect produce muscular fixations and changes in
the vegetative behavior. By analyzing and dissolving the muscular rigidity, it is possible to revive and bring to awareness
the defense against the repressed affect, the affect itself and
the memory of the experience which had originally produced
the affect. In other words, the body remembers as it were
what the mind has forgotten and repressed.

The discussed instances of recall of previously forgotten or
repressed material have in common that they all point to a
"location" of involuntary memory, not in the conscious, purposefully remembering mind and its memory schemata, but
in a sphere which is more adequately if vaguely described
as memory of the body or, rather, of the psychosomatic entity.
The forgotten experience is revived by the recurrence of a sensation which has left a record, a trace behind; or it is revived
by the understanding and reliving of the bodily attitudes, muscular and vegetative, which the forgotten experience produced.

Another condition favorable for the recovery of forgotten
experience which the conscious mind is unable to recall volun-

tarily is furnished by the psychoanalytic situation of free association. The relevant factor of this situation is indicated by the word "free." Three components may be distinguished in the freedom of association. One is the attempt, never entirely successful, to follow the fundamental rule of psychoanalysis: to eliminate rational, logical, and conventional control and censorship of one's thoughts in communicating them and to give in to whatever thought or feeling occurs. How well or how poorly one succeeds in this attempt is dependent chiefly on the two other factors important in free association, the general inner freedom of the person associating and the interpersonal relationship between him and the analyst. The more rigid, controlled, and automaton-like a person is, the more all his thinking is under the grip of the conventional schemata of thought, experience, and feeling, the less will he be able to associate freely, and the more difficult will it be for him to recover any experience that does not fit into the conventional patterns which govern his life. The same is true if he cannot relax from the purposeful, "useful" pursuit of some activity or thought and let his thoughts wander. In other words, the more a person is dependent on and a prisoner of the socially prevalent pattern of useful efficient activity—from which the usual highly uniform leisure-time pursuits are distinguished more by the fact that they are not profitable than by a fundamental difference of attitude—and the more his experiences and mode of living are conditioned by the conventional experience schemata of the culture, the less will he be able to escape the hold of these schemata, to relax and approach that state of relative freedom in which a forgotten experience may break through the armor of his conventionalized thought processes and memory schemata. As Alexander has pointed out, the recovery of memories is not the cause, but the result of therapeutic progress.[34] The loosening of rigid control and of defenses, the greater inner freedom brought about by the therapeutic process, gives the repressed and forgotten material a chance to reappear because the conventional thought and memory schemata have no longer such exclusive predominance in the mental life of the patient.

Freedom, which the psychoanalytic situation seeks to establish by controlled, purposeful procedure, is an essential con-

[34] Franz Alexander, Concerning the Genesis of the Castration Complex; *Psychoanalytic Rev.* (1935) 22:49–52. See also Franz Alexander and Thomas M. French, *Psychoanalytic Therapy;* The Ronald Press Company, New York 1946; pp. 20, 163.

dition for the possibility of true, that is nonschematic, recall
of experience. This freedom may be brought about in different ways. The relaxation of censorship in sleep brings
greater freedom. The memory schemata, which so largely
govern voluntary recall in a state of wakefulness, lose their
hold and relax their function during sleep, so that in dreams
experiences which otherwise have been forgotten may be recalled, usually in somewhat changed and distorted or in symbolic form. The artist, the writer, the poet, if they have any
real claim to their vocation, must be capable of nonschematic
experience. They must be perceptive; that is, they must experience, see, hear, feel things in a way which somewhere transcends the cultural, conventional experience schemata. The
relative freedom from these experience schemata is also freedom, to whatever extent, from the conventional memory
schemata. And memory, the Greek myth tells us, is the mother
of the muses.

Memory and forgetting partake of the nature of man, who
is both a biological and a cultural, social, historical being. In
memory and forgetting the conflicts between nature and society, as well as the dynamics and antagonisms of society, play
a determining role. To investigate abstract memory phenomena is to investigate an artifact, something that does not exist.
This has become apparent at each step of these considerations,
which now have led to a point where it is possible to formulate their main results.

Early childhood amnesia may be considered a *normal* amnesia. It shares this quality with most, though not all, of dream
amnesia and with the constant forgetting of those parts and
aspects of experience which do not fit into the ready patterns of language and culture—trans-schematic experience.
Normal amnesia is both akin to and different from pathological amnesia. Their likeness consists in their causation by a
conflict between nature and culture or by intercultural conflict. Their difference consists chiefly in the fact that the conflicts causing normal amnesia are ubiquitous in a culture and
their solution is part of the development of the personality in
that culture; whereas in pathological amnesia, by and large,
the conflict is due to individual traumatic experience which,
although caused too by the stresses and conflicts operative in
the culture, has become traumatic because of the particular
history of the individual person. One might say that the normal
amnesia, that which people usually are unable to recall, is an

illuminating index to the quality of any given culture and society. It is that which does not serve the purposes of that society and would interfere with the pattern of the culture, that
which would be traumatic to the culture because it would
break up or transcend the conventions and mores of that culture. Early childhood amnesia is the most striking and dramatic expression merely of a dynamism operative throughout
the life of people: the distortion or forgetting of trans-
schematic experience, that is of experience for which the culture provides no pattern and no schema.

Cultures vary in the degree to which they impose clichés
on experience and memory. The more a society develops in
the direction of mass conformism, whether such development
be achieved by a totalitarian pattern or within a democratic
framework by means of the employment market, education,
the patterns of social life, advertising, press, radio, movies,
best-sellers, and so on, the more stringent becomes the rule of
the conventional experience and memory schemata in the lives
of the members of that society. In the history of the last hundred years of western civilization the conventional schematization of experience and memory has become increasingly
prevalent at an accelerating pace.

Even within a culture the degree to which in different
groups conventional schemata of experience and memory prevent the recall of actual experience may show marked differences. Such a difference seems to exist, for example, between
European men and women. There is some reason to assume
that European men usually show a more extensive and pervasive amnesia for their early childhood than women.[35] A
plausible hypothesis for the explanation of this difference
would have to take into account the marked difference in the
social status of the two sexes in Europe and, specifically, the
difference in what one might call the social self-ideal of man
versus that of woman. This idea of what the grown-up person, the respectable citizen ought to be emphasizes the cleft
between childhood and adulthood much more in men than in
women. All things pertaining to the rearing of children and

[35] "Oral Communication" by Ruth Benedict. In interviewing a number of European men and women Benedict found consistently that the
women recalled quite a few details of their lives before they had reached
the age of 6 while the men hardly recalled anything. The people inter-
viewed by her did not constitute a representative sample of the population, yet the consistency of the phenomenon in all the people inter-
viewed seemed indicative of its more general significance.

to the home are the domain of the women and the average man would consider it beneath his "dignity" to know much about them or to be much concerned with them. Hence, to recall details of early childhood would be consistent with the social self-ideal of women whose interests are supposed to center around children, kitchen, and home. But to a man these things are not supposed to be sufficiently "important" to deserve much attention. To approximate the social self-ideal is important for his self-esteem; and the further removed from, and opposed to, the image of childhood the grown-up man's social self-ideal is the more difficult will it be for him to recall experiences showing that once he was an infant and little boy. In general, more extensive childhood amnesias are to be expected in those groups, cultures, and historical epochs which emphasize the belief that childhood is radically different from adulthood, than one is likely to find where the continuity between childhood and adult life is emphasized.[36]

Mankind's belief in a lost paradise is repeated in the belief, held by most people, in the individual myth of their happy childhood. Like most myths this one contains elements of both truth and illusion, is woven out of wishes, hopes, remembrance and sorrow, and hence has more than one meaning. One finds this belief even in people who have undergone cruel experiences as children and who had, without being or remaining aware of it, a childhood with hardly any love and affection from their parents. No doubt, one reason for the myth of happy childhood is that it bolsters parental authority and maintains a conventional prop of the authority of the family by asserting that one's parents were good and benevolent people who did everything for the good of their children, however much they may have done against it. And disappointed and suffering people, people without hope, want to believe that at least once there was a time in their life when they were happy. But the myth of happy childhood reflects also the truth that, as in the myth of paradise lost, there was a time before animalistic innocence was lost, before pleasure-seeking nature and pleasure-forbidding culture clashed in the battle called education, a battle in which the child always is the loser. At no time is life so exclusively and directly governed by the pleasure principle as it is in early infancy; at

[36] For the general significance of continuity and discontinuity between childhood and adulthood, see Ruth Benedict, Continuities and Discontinuities in Cultural Conditioning (also included in this collection—Editor).

no other time is man, especially civilized man, capable of abandoning himself so completely to pleasure and satisfaction. The myth of happy childhood takes the place of the lost memory of the actual riches, spontaneity, freshness of childhood experience, an experience which has been forgotten because there is no place for it in the adult memory schemata.

Childhood amnesia covers those aspects and experiences of the former personality which are incompatible with the culture. If they were remembered, man would demand that society affirm and accept the total personality with all its potentialities. In a society based on partial suppression of the personality such a demand, even the mere existence of a really free personality, would constitute a threat to the society. Hence it becomes necessary for the society that the remembrance of a time in which the potentialities of a fuller, freer, and more spontaneous life were strongly present and alive be extinguished. In memory's service of this purpose one may distinguish two processes which overlap and shade into one another. One process leaves the culturally unacceptable or unusable experiences and the memory thereof to starvation by the expedient of providing no linguistic, conceptual, and memory schemata for them and by channeling later experience into the experience schemata of the culture. As the person, in the process of education, gradually comes to live more and more exclusively within the framework of the culturally and conventionally provided experience schemata, there is less and less to remind him of the possibility of trans-schematic experience. As his memory schemata develop in accordance with the schematized experience, they become unfit to preserve and recall trans-schematic experience. Only if a person has escaped to some extent this process of schematization of experience and memory, only if he is more differentiated and more free than the average person, will he be in a position to break, at some point, the hold that the memory and experience schemata have on his life and his perceptiveness. But usually it needs special, fortunate circumstances to make possible the escape from the memory schemata and the recall of trans-schematic experience. In a highly developed culture this process resulting in amnesia for culturally undesirable or unacknowledged experience by means of providing memory schemata only for culturally acceptable experience is exceedingly complex, flexible, subtle, and all-pervading.

Compared with this process, the dynamism of the taboo and of repression of individually or culturally tabooed experience and strivings is like the nightstick of the policeman compared with the gradual, slow, insinuating process of education in which some things are just not mentioned and others said to be for the best of the child. But the dynamism active in normal amnesia is even more subtle than what is usually called education. It is an education of which the educators are not aware and of which the child is too helpless and too inarticulate to have more than the vaguest feeling that something is happening to him. On the other hand, those strivings, qualities, and potentialities of the child which are too strong to be left behind to die by the side of the road of education and which endanger the current social and cultural pattern have to be battled by the more drastic means of taboo and repression. In this sphere sexuality and the conflict with parental authority play central roles. One might say that taboo and repression are the psychological cannons of society against the child and against man, whereas in normal amnesia society uses the method of blockade and slow starvation against those experiences and memories which do not fit into the cultural pattern and which do not equip man for his role in the social process. The two methods of warfare supplement each other and, in the siege conducted by society against the human potentialities and inclinations which transcend the cultural pattern, the cannon helps to maintain the blockade, and the blockade and ensuing starvation make it less necessary to use the cannon.

Hesiod tells us that Lethe (Forgetting) is the daughter of Eris (Strife).[37] Amnesia, normal and pathological, is indeed the daughter of conflict, the conflict between nature and society and the conflict in society, the conflict between society and man and the conflict within man. Lethe is the stream of the underworld, of forgetting, the stream which constantly flows and never retains. In the realm of Lethe dwell the Danaïdes, who are condemned eternally to pour water into a leaking vessel. Plato interprets this as the punishment of those unwise souls who leak, who cannot remember and are therefore always empty.[38] But Mnemosyne is an older and more powerful goddess than Lethe. According to Hesiod she was one of the six Titanesses from whom all gods stem. And it

[37] Hesiod, *Theogony*, 227.

[38] Plato, *Gorgias*, 493 c 2. For the mythology of Mnemosyne and Lethe, see Karl Kerényi, Mnemosyne-Lesmosyne, in *Die Geburt der Helena*; Rhein Verlag, Zürich 1945.

was one of the world-founding deeds of Zeus that he begot the muses on her. Memory cannot be entirely extinguished in man, his capacity for experience cannot be entirely suppressed by schematization. It is in those experiences which transcend the cultural schemata, in those memories of experience which transcend the conventional memory schemata, that every new insight and every true work of art have their origin, and that the hope of progress, of a widening of the scope of human endeavor and human life, is founded.

The Magic Wand

JOSÉ ORTEGA Y GASSET

TRANSLATED BY TOBY TALBOT

(1921)

José Ortega y Gasset, the Spanish essayist and philosopher, deals impressionistically in this essay with the young
child's attitude toward reality, and the nature of his so-
called "loss of illusion" in passing from childhood to
maturity. Like Schachtel and Groddeck, Ortega indicates
how adult sensitivity to childhood can be blunted, in this
instance through failure to recognize the essence of the
childlike universe.

What is the landscape of childhood like? What is the general
character of the objects that dominate the juvenile scene? I
believe that every species relates to a limited domain of objects which, like the species itself, share a particular, unchang-
ing outline. A single structure on the broad Manchegan plain
is perceived by Don Quixote as a castle, whereas for Sancho
it represents an ordinary wayside inn.

If we compare the world of adults with that of children the
difference is promptly apparent. The objects which possess vital existence for a child, those which occupy and preoccupy
him, which capture his attention, unleash his desires, passions
and activity, are not real objects, but the objects that he desires. Upon occasion the object may happen to be real as well,
but the child's interest in it lies in its desirability rather than
in the fact that it is real. The reverse situation obtains with
grown-ups: things interest them by virtue of their reality,
though they may not be desirable.

It is customary to say of childhood, and of its extension,
youth, that it "thrives on illusion." The meaning implicit in
these words is I think somewhat erroneous; it would infer that
children imagine a delightful reality markedly unlike true reality, and that in the course of years they become disillusioned,
that is, the presumed reality is proven to be false. If a baby

were capable of understanding this statement, he would no doubt regard us with an utterly impish expression, as if to say: "My dear grown-up, you are grossly mistaken. You, precisely because you are grown-up, consider the question of whether something is real or imaginary as the paramount issue. For me and my friends, though, that hardly matters, and only in a vague, secondary fashion. What counts for us is whether something is beautiful. But let's drop this silly conversation and talk about something serious. Tell me a story."

The normal individual, on passing from childhood to manhood, does not suffer any disillusion. The "disillusioned" are abnormal and, consequently, pathological cases. The passage from childhood to maturity is simply a change in one's vital regime: whereas one heretofore gravitated toward the desirable, he now gravitates toward reality.* Allow some time to elapse and you will witness the individual's entry into a third psychological phase in which he tends to gravitate toward something that is neither real nor purely imaginary, to wit, the past. That is the final stage: old age. Have you ever noticed the heroic energy the elderly expend in order to shut out present reality? Disinterested in it, disassociated from it, liberated from it, their minds, like heliotropes, pathetically turn to the sunny days of their adolescence. Children, likewise, enjoy an extravagant capacity for eliminating things that are real, that is, things the way they are. Their little beings are like delicate filters which when placed in a stream intercept every solid particle and allow only the clear gurgling water to flow through and dance downstream. They too eliminate that which is real and retain only that which is desirable, that is, things the way they ought to be.

What is the origin of desirable objects? Every event, every phenomenon that penetrates the surface of our beings elicits in us two reactions, both in a sense mutually antagonistic. On the other hand, the mind begins to function in accordance with its own laws in relation to the new intrusive object, motivated completely by the desire to obtain an exact notion of the object, to elaborate a faithful transcription of it. This is the path by which knowledge is attained: our minds construct history. Conversely, fantasy emerges to comfort the new event and instead of being content with scrupulous reflection, as is the mind, fantasy boldly punctures it, fragments

* Cf. Ernest G. Schachtel, "On Memory and Childhood Amnesia" concerning the quality of the world of the child, pp. 17 ff. Also Georg Groddeck, "Man's Part as Child," pp. 65 ff. (Editor)

it, discards portions of it, retains others, possibly merges that which it keeps with elements of other things. In a word, fantasy decomposes reality and comes up with a fresh object composed solely of selected ingredients. In contrast to the real object discovered by the mind, a desirable object, or *desideratum* emerges, a product of fantasy oriented by desire. Our minds invent legend.

Nothing within our reach is immune from this dual reaction: history and legend. Sometimes one, sometimes the other dominates. Often the legendary halo that forms around an object or event as a result of contact with our fantasy is practically imperceptible. It is never absent. Moreover, legend occupies so large a portion of our scheme of things that in many instances we are unable to separate it from reality, and we are unaware in many instances that it is legend. The strictest notions of science are mulled over in the scientist's mind amid abundant legendary overtones. We must not forget that from a thing called "positivism" a religion emerged and, therefore, a myth. Finally, the very notion of science is a legend, a *desideratum* which has never been nor will ever be, strictly speaking, reality.

The world thus offers in its totality and in each of its parts, two sides: the historical and the legendary, the real and the desirable. Certain individuals have a greater capacity to perceive one over the other, *hyperpoetic* and *hypopoetic* temperaments. Although it is not commonplace in Spain, we all upon occasion have come across a man who, when discussing events and people, the present, the past, or the future, seems to endow each enumerated thing with a divine glow, thereby re-creating for us the most prosaic objects. Under the spell of such an exuberant spirit, we experience a feeling of seeing things for the first time, charged with evocative possibilities, awakening in our hearts unsuspected desires and a longing to fulfill them. Everything that comes in contact with our sensibilities in this way is magically embroidered and has a glowing aura of transformation. Yet, it possesses nothing of phantasmagoria, nor does it deal solely with noble things. Things humble remain humble, and things infirm remain infirm. However, the secret power of that voice suddenly endows humility and infirmity with unexpected grace, whereupon, without losing their original essence, they become congenial qualities and attractive powers. In the interim our world is delightfully ignited: everything impels us to life, everything incites us, everything awakens our effort. Shortly afterward, the fire is quenched, and the dull routine configuration makes its lack-luster reappearance, the way architecture gilded by the setting sun dissolves into ashen gray beneath the oncoming night. Such is the *hyperpoetic* temperament, which tears the mask of reality from the world and reveals its eternal desirable face.

Compared with grown-ups, children are heroic creators of legend. Everything they come in contact with is transformed, their landscape is composed almost exclusively of *desiderata*. Everything they see around them is the way it ought to be, and that which is not, they do not see. Even vices, death and crime, are purified by their mental alchemy and present only their attractive aspect. My son, who has the sensibility of a little Knight of the Round Table, prefers nonetheless among all his toys the one with which he plays robber. This is because his mind accepts only those qualities of the real thief that are truly desirable: audacity, aplomb, the urge for adventure. By the same token, death for children is a variation of hide-and-seek: man disappears only to reappear amid a bustling funeral. Hence in fairy tales death is regarded as an interlude prior to resurrection.

The latter authentically juvenile literature has unwittingly projected the secret of children's psychology regarding certain symbolic objects endowed with magical powers. "Little table to set," the magic wand, is endowed with the gift of transforming the universe into a landscape populated by desired things.

In fact, the real magic wand is the child's own mind.

Man's Part as Child

GEORG GRODDECK

(1934)

Georg Groddeck, a German analyst and contemporary
of Freud, pioneered the systematic study of psychosomatic
illness. He also coined the term *it* or *id,* later developed
as a basic element of Freud's theory of infantile sexuality.
In the following selection from his book *The World of
Man,* Groddeck traces the etymology and psychological
significance of the word "childhood" in different cultures. He discusses the childlike qualities man carries
with him into maturity, holding that a proper appreciation of these qualities in himself helps the adult to train
the child.

> *"Deare Childe."*
> EPITAPH IN THE CLOISTERS,
> WESTMINSTER ABBEY.

The third of the fundamental characters in human nature is
childlikeness, and according to the German language, at any
rate, the child (*das Kind*) is in existence from the moment
of its conception, since *Kind* derives from the great base *gen-.*
(English "child" is probably connected with the Gothic *kil-
thei,* womb, and this again with the Indo-Germanic *bhel,* to
swell.) In Greek the word *teknon* gives the same sort of association. The Latin word for children was *liberi,* and *Liber* was
the god of generation. All these connections, then, emphasize
the notions of propagation and origin, not the characteristics
of childhood, but the English infant and French *enfant* tell
us something about the child itself, for they come from the
Late Latin *infans, in*—not, *fari*—to speak. This fixes a definite
limit in time for childhood; it comes to an end when the
baby stops babbling and begins to talk.* English has kept

* Note in this connection M. M. Lewis's comments on babbling,
Froebel's observations on play-speech and Wolfenstein's remarks on
nicknames. (Editor)

that meaning in infancy, except in its legal usage, but the French *enfant* lives on through the kindergarten age, and the German *unmündig* is a minor, under age.

Infans, a creature who cannot speak, who is little more than an animal, a worm, a plant, or even a puppet. (My pretty poppet!) Most certainly a creature who knows nothing about right and wrong (Latin *fas* and *nefas,* from *fari,* to speak) is unknown to fame, makes no confession (*fateor,* to confess) and has no religious beliefs, or indeed, beliefs of any kind; who can no more conceive of fate and destiny than he can of Almighty God; who invents no moral stories because he can only babble (English baby, from the primitive *bha-,* to speak, German *babbeln,* Swedish *babbla,* to babble) and feed—(*bampfen* and *pampfen,* also from *bha-*). Thinking, I am told, can only be done with words, so the infant does not think. He neither thinks, *denken,* nor thinks too much of himself, *sich dünken,* from which, indeed, comes "thinking." (*Das Kind denkt nicht, es dünkt sich auch nicht, hat keinen Dünkel, woven sich ja das Wort denken herleitet.*) He is *arrhetos,* irrational (Greek *eiro,* to speak, to ask), while his elders are rational and rhetorical (*rhetor,* orator, *rhetos,* rational). Yet the nonrational has its own importance even in a scientific age: indeed, the wise men—not the learned merely—among the scientists have at all times recognized the nonrational side of human nature as the deepest source of life, and with wonder and reverence they have dared to speculate.

The irrational child cannot speak, *eiro,* yet he is by nature endowed with irony, *erioneia;* he is a jester, and his jokes are uttered in derision. For the great man he first has to deal with he has invented the stammer-word papa, *Pappler.* "You talk a great deal but why not give me my pap?" is what he means. Grave and reverend men of learning cannot be expected to understand an infant's joke; they believe that at the sight of his father a baby calls him papa because he recognizes the breadwinner of the family (pater, father, pope and patriarch are all derived from papa.) This is mere vanity, the arrogance of the male, the thinker, the orator, the fool (*fatuus,* from *fari*).

The Latin *verbum* and the English "word" are said to belong to the same family-group. The creative power of the word has been an article of belief from very ancient times; the first chapters of Genesis and the opening words of St. John's Gospel show that Jewish-Christian culture acknowledge it, at least. *En arche en ho logos*—In the beginning was the

Word. *Theos en ho logos*—God was the Word. God *said*, "Let there be light," and there was light. Now that the Scriptures are no longer the general basis of all learning, however, we have invented new phrases to indicate the power of the word, and we talk about the magic of words, spell-binding, and so forth. Magic, we are told, comes to us from Chaldea; *Zaubern* is the corresponding word in German, and this is said to be associated with the mystery of the written word, the sacred runes (cf. the double meaning of "spell"). In any case, we know that there are incalculable forces in the word (e.g. the hunt for a political formula); with a word we can be cast down in mind, with a word exalted. A word gives us power over what we have named. "We name a thing, and lo! the wonder flies—as in those profound myths where all goes well until curiosity comes to mar happiness—Psyche turns the light on Eros. Elsa must know Lohengrin's name. With what subtle instinct the Hebrew refuses to pronounce the name of his Deity! A name persuades that the unseizable is seized, that Leviathan is drawn out with a hook" (Zangwill). Words spare us the delay of continual representation by imagery, and so make for economy of thought, but the loss of that same imagery means that language is cut off from its roots in symbolic expression, and that we must go to the unconscious for evidence that the symbol is still operative in the depths of human nature. Now and again, however, one hears of people who are still consciously influenced by the magic power of words. In his *Fors Clavigera* Ruskin tells us that as a child the very sight of the word "crocodile" used to frighten him so much that he could not feel at ease again until he had turned over the page on which it occurred; and Christina Rossetti would never tread upon a piece of paper lest it should prove to have printed upon it the Holy Name. I have told elsewhere the story of a patient who could not bear to see the word "crucifix." Throughout all grades of culture, name-giving at birth is regarded as a serious matter, and few people are entirely objective about their own names. In fairy tales and folklore there are many stories which turn upon the secret name, the revelation of which brings about some sort of crisis (e.g. "Rumpelstiltskin"), and most of us feel happier if people with whom we are not intimate refrain from using our personal name. My professional colleagues may be interested to know that Walde relates *verbum* to *vraib*, physician, sorcerer, witch doctor. Alas, another derivative stands at its elbow, *vraka*, gossip. Verb. sap.! From this it might seem that the

child was neither a creator nor a sorcerer, yet who shall be
called creative if not the infant who, in his own person, builds
up body and mind, brain and heart, blood and water? And
who can so bewitch us as a baby; not with speech, it is true,
nor with writings, but by his very presence?

The Greeks had among the derivatives from *eiro* the word
eirene, which in German would be translated as *Frieden*,
peace, but this does not convey the essence of the word. What
a Greek meant by peace was the opportunity to talk, for his
keenest pleasure was to spend his time in gossip and argument.
(When Darius sent his messengers to find out what manner of
men the Athenians were, they brought him back the answer:
"They walk about the market-place gossiping.") The Latin
word *pax* (*papa, fari*) suggests the notion of conversation
and also of feasting (*pascor*). The German *Frieden* comes
from *frî*, to love, from which come also *Freiheit*, freedom,
and *Freundschaft*, friendship. Perhaps the Latin *liberi*, children, is connected with liberty; it is only infants who are
exempt from the moral law. *Eirene, pax?* No, *Frieden*. The
babbling infant is the center of a household's love; in his presence the world smiles and grows tender.

Not only is the child the symbol of love and devotion, he
is also that which both is and is becoming, wherein truth
lies. The childlike quality in man is in this being and becoming,
and the word "*wahr*," true, which has so much significance
in our lives and our quarrels, is derived by Kluge from the
base *wesro*, was. It must surely be clear to every thinking
mind that we can never know absolute truth, however we may
bandy the word about in our disputes, but only truth with the
human element in it, erring truth, truthful error.

In thus bringing together the being and the becoming with
the child, I am pursuing what the authorities would describe
as folk-etymology, little realizing how this term reflects upon
themselves. Science would not dream that any connection
existed between *Wesen* and *werden*, being and becoming, nor
allow *verus*, true, *verbum*, word, and *werden*, to become, to
be named in the same breath. The etymologists derive *werden*
from *vertere*, to turn, to turn over. At birth the child turns
from the downward position and for the first time assumes
his royal (*rex*, erect) status as a separate human being. In
different works I have on several occasions drawn attention
to the parallel between the rival theories of astronomy—the
Ptolemaic and the Copernican—and the different positions occupied by the child in the womb and the child on the lap.

This turning process is of fundamental importance in human ambivalence (i.e. duality of thought and of feeling) and it might be worth investigating the unconscious of those born normally as compared with those born in breech position, with special reference to ambivalent traits.

The relationship of *Kind*, child, and *König*, king, has been mentioned. History, as well as everyday experience, teaches us clearly enough that the essence of kingship is childlikeness. The more a king relies solely on his presence, the less he talks, the greater is the effect he produces and the greater he himself becomes. It was only after Frederick the Great had given up speaking and philosophizing, and was content to be silent, hoping nothing, desiring nothing, realizing his own child-like nature, that he became our truly great *"Alter Fritz."*

Close to king and *Kind* there are two other words, *können*, to be able, can, and *Kunde*, information. The lofty adult thinks the child incapable, that he must be taught everything. But quite apart from the fact that he is able to make the grown-ups serve his own ends, which we do not always find easy to do ourselves, the problems he sets himself, and often solves correctly, are such as we older people are too often inclined to ignore and repress into the unconscious because we no longer feel equal to them. If we allowed ourselves to realize once a day what a child is able to achieve we might gradually acquire some insight into the nature of children, gradually come to rejoice in what is fresh and childlike in our own natures, and even invent some better word in place of those thrice stupid terms, infantile, *"infantilismus."* We are all infantile, thank God! We could not even continue to exist, much less accomplish anything, were it not so. The essential life of any man depends upon the degree to which he has been able to remain childlike, infantile, in spite of the blunting influences of adult life.

Not only in achievement but in knowledge, *gnosis*, may this hold good. In the monasteries of Tibet, we are told, there are men who deliberately attempt by training to recover and develop in themselves the outlook of a child, and who, by means of the power thus obtained, can set at naught what we westerners are accustomed to regard as fundamental laws of physiology and psychology.

The Latin word *dicere*, to say, contained the meaning of "to show"; though the infant has not the power of speech, many other means of expression are always at his disposal, facial expression, gesture, temper, voice, pointing, staring, pricking up his ears, imitating other people, becoming ill. The Latin *vox*, voice, Greek *ops*, are narrower in application but still do not exclude the infant's babble, and *ops* leads us to think of that language of the eyes, which is of such importance in the realm of ophthalmology. I feel myself neither called upon nor qualified to encroach upon the specialist technique of the oculist, which has yielded results that are sufficiently great to need no further word of recognition. But since I believe that repression is as important a function of the eye as seeing; that the eye also serves a number of other functions beside these two, having nothing whatever to do with seeing; that it does not lead an independent existence detached from association with the organism, but as one of the most sensitive of the body's members may influence every side of life both in its owner and in other people, and in turn be subject to their influence; and that in addition to all these things and more important than any of them, it is a world-embracing symbol, I hold that ophthalmology has both the right and the duty of arranging for research on these wider lines and of acting in accordance with its findings. Sight is a function not of the eye but of human beings, and the oculist, like every other specialist, is the servant of humanity. "It is the soul that sees; the outward eyes present the object, but the soul descries." The specialist of any branch of medicine has to work on the plane of human nature if he is to be a worthy member of the medical profession.

When investigating the treatment of skin affection by hydroxylamine for my M.D. thesis in 1888, I came to the conclusion that this much-prized medium was in the majority of cases ineffective, in spite of the fact that previous research had given the verdict in its favor. In explaining this difference of opinion I had in the first place to point out that none of the earlier investigators had thought of trying the effect of hydroxylamine upon healthy skins. That is an omission which is all too frequent in the testing of new methods and media in medicine, and its importance cannot be overrated. . . . We had other means of treatment which proved more effective, so that hydroxylamine was unnecessary, and whatever is superfluous in medicine is harmful. We doctors boast that we are practical people, yet we offer the world the laughable spectacle of an endless succession of fashions in treatment which in the end prove fruitless. Even old Paracelsus reminded his contemporaries that it was not their usefulness which made an apothecary invest in all the apparatus, the glasses, pots, and oddments in his room. . . . My three main conclusions in regard to skin diseases were as follows:

(1) In many cases a man's illness is the result of the manner in which he lives, and if we are to heal him it is our business to get him to change the manner of his life, for only rarely will his disease be seriously affected by the employment of this or that specific.

(2) The choice of medicament matters less than the way in which it is used.

(3) The mental ascendancy of the physician over the patient is the most important factor in the success of his regimen.

If the oculist will bring his specialist's knowledge into action on the level of humanity he will use it fully and worthily, but so long as a training in optics ignores the unconscious and the world of symbols in which all of us are living, so long as it gives no heed to the fact that up till now every step forward in technique has been paid for in increasing blindness to human life, so long are we justified in saying that ophthalmology confuses technical dodges with medical art, and strives toward darkness, not toward the light. As matters stand at present, Schweninger's dictum still holds good, that medical specialists should be looked upon as no more than the living tools of the physician, servants with a certain technical ability. Of all medical specialities, however, ophthalmology stands in the greatest danger, because it is based entirely on physiological theory and optical laws, and in spite of repeated efforts made by individual oculists to enlarge its boundaries, it is still far removed from any concern with human nature.

The connection between speech and light is seen in the Greek *phemi*, to speak, cognate with *phaos*, light, and *phaino*, to show. The Swedish word for speech is *tal*, Dutch *taal;* in earlier times this had a wider application, as did also the English tell (Archaic, to count. "Every shepherd tells his tale," cf. German *Zahl*, number).

Various reasons may be suggested why language should have developed as a means of expression, but here I would merely call attention to the unconscious but purposeful ambivalence of words. "Language was given to men that they might hide their thoughts," said Talleyrand, but the hearer can often penetrate so superficial a disguise. Commonly enough, speech is accompanied by other methods of expression which give the lie to what is being said—stammering, changes of tone and pitch, pauses, hoarseness, posture, particularly of the hands, rate of breathing, etc. The proverb that speech is silver but silence golden only bears witness to the eloquence of silence. The Latin *tacere*, to be silent, is associated with such active verbs as Old Irish *taihtan*, to stifle, and Cymric *tagn*, to strangle. Silence may be the strangling of a word but it is none the less expressive of a meaning.

The infant, then, has these other means of expression just as the idiot (*fatuus*) has; indeed, there are still more which he can use from the time he is in his mother's womb until his third year of life. While I cannot agree with all that Freud says, I rejoice in reading everything he writes and in knowing that along my own lines I have reached the same conclusion as he, that childhood comes to an end round about the third year. Only I believe that his childish nature remains with man and rules him till the end of his life. As I see man, he is forever striving toward some blissful state which is what he was and what he had in infancy, and his only choice lies in becoming either childlike or childish. In old age he is sometimes one, sometimes the other; even those who die before they grow old do not escape this destiny, for all who have watched men die know that in dying every man becomes once more a child. In these days when all the world knows far more about Freud's discoveries than does Freud himself, it is unnecessary for me to expatiate on the sexual nature of children. So much nonsense is talked about it that it is better to keep away from the subject until people have got over their excitement and sanity returns. I shall, therefore, only mention the curious fact that newborn babies have the appearance of being unutterably old. And old they are in fact: "Before Abraham was. . . ." The embryo is as old as life itself, and whoever is given to paradox might well say that man grows younger, not older, as life goes on. Truly, many of life's problems would be clearer in the light of this assumption. Among other things we should understand why the child knows far better how to live than does the adult; he can still live in fullness of spirit because he has not come under the domination of the ego which distorts life, he is still infantile. He fears no king; even the majesty of death does not awe him. My mother often used to tell the story of my slipping into the room as she was showing her father's body to one of his friends, and jumping round and round the open coffin, clapping my hands and shouting: "My grandfather's inside there." And in this respect I have remained a child; death says nothing to me.

Indeed, I can only with difficulty bring myself to believe in other people's pain at the passing of their friends. In those words, "Let the dead bury their dead," the meaning is conveyed to me that those who mourn the dead and wish them back are dead themselves, spiritually dead.

The word *Kind*, child, gives no implication of a limit of age, and for a German mother, at any rate, her brood never cease to be children. The Roman *infans* grew into a *puer* when he could speak, and *puer* emphasizes the notion of sexual development, whereas the corresponding Greek *teknon* brings out that of growth, of building up. Another Greek word for child, *pais*, gives one the chance of a jest in connection with the great Grimm's Law, the law of sound-shift. Every German knows the lullaby, "*Eia popeia, eia popei*," but which of them dreams that this is a Greek verse with the sounds shifted? Yet so it is. A Greek nurse-girl sang it to an emperor's son—the mother was a Greek—and this is what she sang:

"eude mu paidion eude mu pai."

("Sleep then my baby, sleep then my child.")

And the other maids, listening, transformed it into "*eia popeia*."

The Greek *brephos* from *grebho*, to conceive, was used of the foetus and of the newly born. Words like baby, Swedish *barn*, the newly born and borne, are applied to babes in arms, before they have reached the walking stage. In German and elsewhere there is yet another term, *Säugling*, suckling, the child not yet weaned. I mention it particularly because among its verbal relations, Walde mentions, a little uncertainly, the word *Sau*, sow. He suggests that *sucus*, juice, *sugere*, to suck, and *sus*, sow, may all have come from a common base *su*, to give birth, to beget, to which Greek *hys* (hysteria), the womb, would also be related. This association, I imagine, has a parallel in the symbolizing fantasies of children which link up the images of mother, killing, and sow. Highly educated people like ourselves, of course, dismiss all such associations as absurd and revolting, but the fact remains that our own northern ancestors venerated the swine, while in certain religions and for certain races it is still tabu.

For a long time I have sought for any European word for child which should contain a reference to what I look upon as one of the most striking facts about childhood, that for some time after learning to speak the young child neither uses the word "I" nor seems to have any corresponding idea. I do not know what the philologists' views on this may be, and though ignorance is sometimes an advantage in that it enables one to pass boldly by many danger-points without anxiety, when one is at a loss the help of those who are better equipped would be a boon.[1]

The three points that I want to make clear—without meaning to rule out the conclusions reached by others who are working on a different line of approach—are that the infant is irrational, impersonal and amoral. It is his irrationality which gives us our unwarranted opinion of the child's inferior capacities. Actually he accomplishes far more than any adult both in his prenatal life and in the early years after birth. A good deal of energy is involved in learning to see, to hear, to suck, and to breathe, and the building up of his mental world through countless experiences and experiments is an achievement which can never be equaled by any later efforts. The child is indeed the maker of his world; he creates light and sound, tree and hill, house and man; everything is his work. What he does not create for himself out of his own experience is good and evil, right and wrong, conscious striving, self-plaguing. Nietzsche's immoralist was no illusion; he is alive in the child.

It is presumptuous to imagine that we can ever solve life's greatest riddle, the problem of good and evil, yet we are always obliged to talk about it. It is the sum and substance of our lives. "And ye shall be as gods, knowing both good and evil." So said the serpent, doomed to crawl upon his belly all the days of his life. Are we, then, as God? Do we know what is good and what evil?

Conscience tells us. Alas, conscience tells us nothing. Today we count that good which only yesterday seemed evil, and tomorrow what we now call evil may be blessed. The conscience of age is not the same as that of youth; the soldier lauds a deed abhorrent to the peaceful citizen; the Renaissance man despised what the Middle Ages adored; Chinese ideals are utterly different from European; our modern no-

---

[1] The great Danish philologist Jespersen alludes to the child's first use of "I" as the mastery of a mere verbal trick and pokes fun at the psychologists who hail it as a sign of awareness of self. Without entering into the discussion one may note that the author considered that psychological significance can be found in tricks or lies. As a doctor, for instance, he was interested not merely in uncovering the deception of a malingerer but in discovering what had led to the wish to malinger and to the choice of the particular symptoms simulated.

tions of good and evil would have revolted the ancient Greeks. And everywhere in the world there is one class of people without any conscience at all, the infants, the little children; yet of them it was said, "Of such is the kingdom of heaven."

As a youngster I kept a commonplace book, and in this my much-admired big brother once wrote for me a quotation from Shakespeare:

> "There's nothing either good or bad
> But thinking makes it so."

To me those words are essentially Christian: they accord well with that solemn injunction, "Judge not, that ye be not judged."

But the words might as well have been spoken to the wind for all the heed anyone pays to them. No one can live like that, no one can realize what a blasphemy it is to judge between good and evil, to condemn as a sin what happens by God's will and by His Will alone. It is only the child who knows no sin, although he practices everything we call vicious. Because he is irrational he is beyond good and evil, is amoral and therefore innocent, is unfettered by the ego and therefore shameless and pure. I purposely bracket those two words not because shameless people are necessarily pure, but because I am convinced that in his most glorious moments of purity man is entirely without shame. Shame comes from thinking too highly of one's ego, setting it up in opposition to the world of nature and taking oneself to be a whole instead of only a part of something infinitely greater than oneself. Purity demands that a man shall get rid of the self that he may live in harmony with human destiny. It is no more native to man than is shame, but is an occasional state which ensues only at such times as he is able to part with his ego. For this reason there may well be a state of purity which has nothing to do with virginity but is shared by two people who mutually give themselves the one to the other; the delight of such communion finds no cause for shame or consciousness of sin. When once it is realized that purity may involve the participation of others it is easy to understand that although the relationship of mother and child has more of erotism in it than has any other, it is none the less pure.

One sees this conception of purity in one of the chaste Uffizian pictures, a Memling Madonna with the Christ-Child and the angels. It is hardly necessary to say that this painting again shows us the one perfect symbolization of mankind, the mother with her son upon her lap. Art has everlastingly repeated this symbol, and continues to do so even in our own age, pitifully unchristian and rationalistic as it is. The Memling picture is a pure hymn in honor of the union of man and woman and of the ecstasy which accompanies this union. The figures are shown within a triangle, a common device and a symbol of deep import. This is emphasized by the fact that the Madonna's throne carries the eye upwards to the angle formed by the garland spread along the top. Six cherub angels hold the ends of the garland; the feminine six combines with the masculine three. On the pillars enclosing the picture are painted the lizard and the snail, both symbols of coitus.

The Christ-Child turns away from the woman who has been his mother, and toward the world beyond. That is human destiny. Life may indeed be regarded as one long process of getting free from the mother, beginning at the moment of conception, escaping from her body at birth, advancing step by step with the weaning from her breast, leaving her lap, going away from home, seeking a new mother in the beloved, resigning this mother to the claims of her son, returning to a second childhood in old age and closing finally with the committal of the body to the bosom of mother earth. There is something stranger than this, however, in the picture. The child is trying to grasp an apple held by one of the angels, and the apple stands for sin, for the desire to be as the gods, knowing good and evil. The two attendant angels also call for attention. The one on the left of the Child is playing the harp and bears a serious, almost melancholy look; the other has a strange smile, tender and enticing. It is he who proffers the apple to Christ who, like all the sons of men, is trying to get at it.

It is difficult to understand why religious people—as distinct from organized religion—should have repressed so completely their belief in the humanity of Christ. With the Church the case is different; though the doctrine was consciously incorporated in Christian dogma only after prolonged disputation, the Church's whole development is bound up with the teaching that Christ was sinless. No one now accepts Christ's word that he was the Son of Man, no one believes that God took on the nature of humanity, even though that belief is the beginning and the end of Christianity. Eccelesiastics will never admit that Christ was a man, with all the qualities of man's nature, even that which our little minds call sinfulness; they insist that even in his life on earth, Christ was a deity. Some teachers, on the other hand, deny him any divinity, saying that he was a man as other men, yet they claim to be Christians and toy with ideas that one would have supposed could hold no meaning for them. No, there is no one now who still believes in the Son of Man, in a God who, of his own free will, gave up the Godhead and came to earth as man to live a man's life, who lived and loved and hated with a man's stupidity, blessed this one and cursed that, idled away the time, was restless and unsettled, knew no better than any other man what was good and what was evil, yet was as ready as the rest of us to judge other people and call down eternal punishment upon them, who believed in God yet doubted his divinity at times, who was subject to every human limitation, and at the end died as a man to rise again as God. No one any longer believes all that, yet the faith lives on in the unconscious and nothing alters its conviction that Christ was human like ourselves, with human traits and feelings, human virtues and vices. He himself rebuked the mocking flatterer who called him "Rabbi, good Master," and Gospel stories make it plain that he was what we Pharisees would call a sinner. He could be pharisaic, too, just as we are. All this is known to the unconscious, and one of the results of that knowledge is that there is no representation of Christ in great art except as a child or as the crucified, the dead or dying man. We cannot live except in the belief that good and evil have a real existence, and because that belief has no foundation we must invent a perfect man and make Christ sinless; though he himself, whenever he is allowed to speak, repudiates this alleged perfection. Art, therefore, has no choice but to portray him as an infant or as a dead or dying man. Neither the infant nor the dead can protest when they are traduced, and not a single picture in the world that is worth seeing can show him as a man in all his strength.[2] Life's irony is shown in the fact that art chooses the infant because of men's belief in the sinlessness of infancy, whereas the unconscious knows full well that an infant surpasses everybody else as a conscienceless criminal, thief, murderer, blasphemer,

---

[2] There was recently in England a protest by Church dignitaries against the sentimentality of the religious pictures put before children. "Even the old masters whose great pictures so deeply satisfy many who revere Christ, often fail to meet the needs of children largely because they are apt to pass over all that lay between the Infancy and Passion Week."

pleasure-seeker. So it comes about that the pious painter brings forth from the unconscious the symbol of sin, and Memling's Christ-Child reaches for the apple. The angel who entices him has a bow and fiddle in his hand, and as soon as the Child bites into the apple, the angel will draw his bow across the fiddle. Over him we see inset the view of a fine castle, over the other angel, whom Christ ignores, a mill. In his left hand the Child holds a cherry. His mother clasps his feet in one hand, while her other hand recalls the symbolism of the apple. Every mother is bound to give her baby a sensation of erotic pleasure as she washes him, but it is doubtful whether any baby needs teaching. Since Adam and Eve did eat of the apple together, yet each for himself, every son of man has felt himself to be as God, has irretrievably separated his ego from the universe, the All, and has then become ashamed of his nakedness and denied his manhood.

People are forever asking me whether they should give up trying to train their children, adding as often as not: "You seem to think training is of no account." Ought we to train? There is no ought about it; we do train, and we cannot avoid training even if we would. If one acknowledges the "ought," it means that one fancies oneself Lord of the future. I see no meaning whatever in the question as it is put to me, but I see very clearly that everyone instructs and trains, that to give training is an essential quality of human beings just as much as having a skin or a heart. And just as man understands nothing about the essential nature of heart and skin, but only knows of their existence and of such facts about them as are accessible to his observation, and yet with the creative power of the mind is able to make up some sort of picture of them for his own satisfaction, so he sometimes muses upon his educative activities and makes up a picture of their effect upon other human beings, upon his "youngsters," in which category he puts all the people he meets. We really know nothing about the effect of our educational work, we cannot know anything about it, but we pursue it unceasingly. Whether it will bring good or evil to our "youngsters" we are quite unable to judge, no matter what trouble we take. We do not train because we want to be useful and do good, but because it is our nature, every man jack of us, to train.

Rightly put, the question should be not "How should one train?" but "How *am* I training, how is this ego of mine influencing another person at a given time in a given place?" And the answer which I can give to the question "Shall I train?" is the one and only answer that can be given: "Not my will but thine be done."

Know thyself! The form of the words indicates an admonition, a warning, that we should strive after self-knowledge, but in truth it is only an affirmation of the fact that he who knows himself is a special instrument in the hand of nature, of Gottnatur, that he has special powers of influence, which are like those of childhood. The best teachers are the children; "Unless ye become as little children ye shall in no wise enter into the kingdom of heaven . . ."

It is not given to everyone to be childlike, nor at every time. Be happy, then, if you have self-knowledge, even if only for moments now and then. The greatest monarch in the world is the infant. Whoever desires power—and which of us does not?—should go to little children and let himself be trained by them: "For of such is the kingdom of heaven."

II

EARLY STAGES OF INDIVIDUAL GROWTH

The Trauma of Birth

OTTO RANK

(1929)

In his controversial book *The Trauma of Birth,* Otto
Rank theorizes that the physical trauma of birth is the
ultimate biological basis of psychic disturbances in later
life. Anxieties, fears, notions of death, sibling rivalries,
even games are rooted in the initial anxiety of birth;
conversely, every later pleasure aims to re-create the
primal pleasure of the infant secure in the womb. According to Rank, birth trauma is the chief cause of neurosis, since all neurotic anxieties re-create and dramatize
the physiological phenomenon of birth. Rank considers
childhood as "the normal neurosis" during which children work out anxiety caused by the birth trauma.

. . . Before we can understand how the birth trauma can be
expressed in . . . various neurotic symptoms, we must first
trace its general human effect in the development of the normal individual, particularly in childhood. We shall take as our
guiding principle Freud's statement that all anxiety goes back
originally to the anxiety at birth (dyspnea).

If we look at the psychical development of the child from
this point of view, it may be said that the human being needs
many years—namely, his whole childhood—in which to overcome this first intensive trauma in an approximately normal
way. Every child has anxiety, and from the standpoint of the
average healthy adult, one can, with a certain amount of justification, designate the childhood of individuals as their normal neurosis. Only this may continue into adult life in the case
of certain individuals, the neurotics, who therefore remain
infantile or are called infantile.

Instead of numerous examples with the same simple mechanism, let us investigate the typical case of infantile anxiety which occurs when the child is left alone *in a dark
room* (usually the bedroom at bedtime). This situation reminds the child, who still is close to the experience of the pri-

mal trauma, of the womb situation—with the important difference that the child is now consciously separated from the mother, whose womb is only "symbolically" replaced by the dark room or warm bed. The anxiety disappears, according to Freud's brilliant observation, as soon as the child again becomes conscious of the existence (the nearness) of the loved person (contact, voice, etc.).[1]

From this example we can understand the anxiety mechanism, which is repeated almost unaltered in cases of phobia (claustrophobia, fear of railways, tunnels, traveling, etc.), as the unconscious reproduction of the anxiety at birth. And at the same time we can study the elements of symbol formation, and last but not least, the importance of the fact of being separated from the mother, and the calming "therapeutic" effect of the reunion with her, although only a partial or "symbolic" one.

Whilst reserving for later chapters more detailed discussion about these prospects which promise so much, let us look at a second situation, likewise typical of childish anxiety, which is nearer to the actual deeply repressed facts. We mean the universal childish *fear of animals*. We must not look for its explanation in an inherited human instinct of fear, in spite of its frequent relation to beasts of prey (carnivorous animals such as the wolf). For it is obvious that such a fear, could not relate to the domesticated animals, used thousands of years ago, whose harmlessness was experienced and met with by numerous generations of adults, in the same way as was the danger from beasts of prey. One would need to go further back to the primeval times of man—or even to his first biological stage (as do Stanley Hall and others)—and thence to the wild ancestors of our domesticated animals, in order to explain a typical anxiety reaction, which has its origin in our individual development. There are other, namely psychological (symbolic), factors, which are decisive for the choice of these objects of fear, which occurs originally according to the size of the animal (horse, cow, etc.), impressing the child. As the analysis of childish phobias has clearly shown, the size or fatness (circumference of the body) of the animals causing fear refers to the state of pregnancy of which the child, as we can show, has more than a vague memory. The beasts of prey, then, provide a rationalization, also sufficient, apparently, for grown-up psychologists, of the wish—through the desire to be

[1] See *Three Contributions to the Theory of Sex*, 1918, p. 84, footnote.

eaten—to get back again into the mother's animal womb. The significance of animals as a father substitute, which in the psychology of neuroses Freud has emphasized for the understanding of Totemism, remains not only undisturbed by this conception, but maintains a deepened biological significance, showing how, through the displacement of anxiety onto the father, the renunciation of the mother, necessary for the sake of life, is assured. For this feared father prevents the return to the mother and thereby the releasing of the much more painful primal anxiety, which is related to the mother's genitals as the place of birth, and later transferred to objects taking the place of the genitals.

The equally frequent anxiety about small animals, which, however, is usually accompanied by dread, has the same foundation, and the "uncanniness" of these objects clearly betrays this origin. From the analysis of such phobias or anxiety dreams, which have been found even in men, although less frequently than in women, it is clearly proved that the feeling of weirdness or uncanniness in the presence of these small creeping animals, such as mice, snakes, frogs, beetles, etc., can be traced to their peculiar ability completely to disappear into small holes in the earth. They therefore exhibit the wish to return into the maternal hiding-place as completely accomplished. And the feeling of dread which clings to them arises because they materialize one's own tendency, namely, to go back into mother, and one is afraid because they might creep into one's own body.[2] Whilst one is able to go into *large* animals, still in the meaning of the primal situation, although repressed (anxiety), the dread of *small* animals lies in the danger that they can enter one's own body. Moreover, all such small animals as insects, etc., were long ago recognized by Psychoanalysis as symbolic representations of children or embryos, not only on account of their small size, but also be-

---

[2] A little girl of three years, who feared small dogs just as much as if not more than large ones, was also afraid of insects (flies, bees, etc.). When asked by her mother why she was afraid of these small animals, which could not harm her, the little one replied without any hesitation, "Yet they can swallow me!" But at the approach of small dogs, she makes the same characteristic movements of defense that a grown-up person makes with a mouse; she bends her knees so low, at the same time pressing her legs close together, that her little dress touches the ground, and she can cover herself as if she wanted to prevent them from "creeping in." Another time, when directly asked by her mother as to the cause of her fear of bees, she explained with many contradictions that she wanted to go into the bee's body and yet again not to go in.

cause of the possibility of their growing bigger (symbol of fertility).[3] But they become a penis symbol or rather a penis ideal just because of their capacity *completely* to go in and disappear into holes, etc., whereby their essential peculiarity, the special smallness, which has led to their being interpreted even as spermatozoa or ova, directly indicates the womb as their place of abode. Thus the (large) animal represents at first the pleasure-laden, then the anxiety-laden, mother symbol. Later, by displacement of the anxiety into a phobia, the animal becomes an inhibiting father substitute. Finally, by means of observation of the sexuality of animals and of small animals, which symbolize the foetus as well as the penis, it again becomes invested with maternal libido.

This explains why a number of small animals become *soul-animals* in popular beliefs. The best-known example is that of the snake, whose phallic significance can undoubtedly be traced back to the ease with which it can completely enter and disappear into a hole (in the earth).[4]

This is shown in the well-known belief in animal-spirits of the Australians and certain Central Asiatic tribes. According to this belief, children go into the mother, mostly through the navel, in the form of little animals. Thus the natives of Cape Bedford believe "that boys go into the mother's womb in the form of a snake, and girls in the form of snipe."[5] The

[3] Recently in Freud's *History of an Infantile Neurosis*, p. 569, *Collected Papers*, vol. iii., he shows that in the fear of butterflies the opening and shutting of the wings is the disturbing factor, which again clearly reminds one of the opening in the body (*cf.* the widespread mythical motive of symplegades, or closing rocks).

The spider is a clear symbol of the dreaded mother in whose net one is caught. *Cf.* the "unconscious birth phantasy" which Ferenczi quotes from the description in a diary of a patient's attack of anxiety ("Introjection and Transference," p. 70 in *Contributions to Psychoanalysis*): "Hypochondria surrounds my soul like a fine mist, or rather like a cobweb, just as a fungus covers the swamp. I have the feeling as though I were sticking in a bog, as though I had to stretch out my head so as to be able to breathe. I want to tear the cobweb, to tear it. But no, I can't do it! The web is fastened somewhere—the props would have to be pulled out on which it hangs. If that can't be done, one would have slowly to work one's way through the net in order to get air. Man surely is not here to be veiled in such a cobweb, suffocated, and robbed of the light of the sun."

[4] That the peculiarity, especially in large snakes, of swallowing their prey alive and whole, thus causing their body to swell up, belongs to this circle of ideas, appears to me just as certain as in the case of the other remarkable fact of their shedding their skin (rebirth).

[5] See F. Reitzenstein's article "Aberglaube" in *Handworterbuch der Sexualwissenschaft*, edited by Max Marcuse, 1923, p. 5.

quite primitive identity of child and phallus—the phallus goes
completely into the woman and there grows into a child—
appears later in popular beliefs and in fairy tales, as a soul
endowed with a body, where the soul of a sleeping or dead
person creeps out of the mouth in the form of such animals
as mouse, snake, etc. Then after a while it enters again through
the mouth into the same human being (dream) or into
another one (fertilization, new birth).[6] Here may be added
the very ancient popular practice of picturing the womb as
an animal. This belief hitherto has found no explanation,[7]
but presumably is also connected with the idea of the animal
which has crept into the womb and has not come out again,
and thus finally refers to the *content* of the impregnated uterus.
In Braunschweig it is the custom not to let the child during
the first twenty-four hours after its birth lie by the mother's
side, "otherwise the uterus can find no rest and scratches about
in the woman's body, like a large mouse."[8] "It can also creep
forth during sleep through the mouth, bathe, and return in the
same way," as in the legend recorded by Panzer of a woman
pilgrim who lay in the grass for rest. If it cannot find the way
back the woman becomes sterile.

The reference to these typical childish situations of anxiety
and their parallels in folklore should suffice to show what we
mean. In thoroughly investigating the conditions under which
the child's anxiety arises, we find that the anxiety experienced
at parturition really continues, undisposed of, to influence the
child. And every opportunity, which somehow "reminds" the
child—mostly in a "symbolic" way—of the birth trauma is used
again and again for the abreaction of the undisposed-of affect

[6] In the Malay Fanany-fairy tale, the East African snake of death develops into a soul-worm, which appears from the grave, after about
six or eight months, by means of a bamboo reed stuck in the earth (according to H. L. Held, *Schlangenkultus Atlas Africanus*, vol. iii. Mün-
chen, 1922).

[7] That this animal is most frequently a toad, which creeps (*verkrie-
chen, kröte*) into dark and inaccessible holes, would seem to agree
with this idea. See "Die Kröte, ein Bild der Gebärmutter," by Karl
Spiess (*Mitra*, i., column 209 ff., 1914, No. 8). Even in ancient Egypt
the goddess of birth was thought of as frogheaded (see Jacoby and
Spiegelberg, "Der Frosch als Symbol der Auferstehung bei den Ägyp-
tern," *Sphinx*, vii.); on the other hand, the head of the "uterus-toad"
shows at times human characteristics (see picture in Spiess, *l.c.*, column
217). *Cf.* Ernest Fuhrmann on the same significance of the toad in
ancient Mexico: *Mexiko*, iii., p. 20 ff. (*Kulturen der Erde*, vol. xiii.
Darmstadt, 1922).

[8] See article "Aberglaube," *l.c.*

(*cf.* for instance the frequency of *pavor nocturnus* in children). If one ventures to accept literally and seriously the origin of the anxiety-affect which Freud recognized as arising in the process of birth—and one is forced to do so by a number of experiences—then it is easy to realize *how every infantile utterance of anxiety or fear is really a partial disposal of the birth anxiety.*

We will approach later, in the discussion of the pleasure-pain-mechanism, the pressing question as to how the tendency to repeat so strong an affect of pain arises. But we wish to dwell for the moment on the equally indubitable analytic fact that, just as the anxiety at birth forms the basis of every anxiety or fear, so *every pleasure has as its final aim the re-establishment of the intrauterine primal pleasure.* The child's normal functions, the assimilation of nourishment (sucking) and the expulsion of the product assimilated, both of which functions analysis recognizes as libidinal, betray the tendency to continue as long as possible the unlimited freedom of the prenatal state. As we know from the analyses of neurotics, the Unconscious never gives up this claim, which the Ego has to set aside in favor of social adjustment, and the Unconscious, in its predominating states, which approach the primal condition (dream, neurosis, coma), is ready every time to come forward with this regressive tendency.

More clearly still do the "childish faults," resulting from a too persistent clinging to these sources of pleasure, show the origin and tendency of this libido gratification. I mean such "faults" as sucking on the one hand, and wetting and dirtying themselves on the other, when these go beyond a certain length of time or to a certain degree of intensity (for instance, in the exquisite "neurotic" symptom of enuresis nocturna). In the consciously uncontrollable and apparently automatic ejection of urine and discharge of feces ("as proof of love" for the mother) the child behaves as if it were still in the womb; *inter faeces et urinas.*[9] The proverbial connection between fear and defecation rests on a similar mechanism. The temporary (or, after weaning, the complete) substitution of a finger for the mother's breast shows on the other hand the child's first attempt to replace the mother's body by its own ("identification"), or by a part of its own. And the enigmatic preference for the toes clearly betrays the tendency to re-establish the

---

[9] The water closet appears in dreams as a typical representation for the womb (Stekel, *Die Sprache des Traumes,* 1911).

intrauterine position of the body.[10] From sucking as well as from the pleasurable discharge of the urine (enuresis), the way discovered by Psychoanalysis leads to the "childish fault" *par excellence,* masturbation of the genitals (*cf.* also the later replacing of enuresis by pollution). This leads to and helps to prepare for the final and sublimest substitution for the re-union with the mother, namely, the sexual act. The attempt to associate with sexuality the mother's genitals, originally invested with anxiety, causes the guilt feeling, because the mother anxiety became attached to the father according to the mechanism of the phobia. In this way the partial change of the primal anxiety into the (sexual) guilt feeling occurs. One can observe clearly how the fear of animals originally referring to the mother changes into fear of the father, resting on sexual repression. Then it can become perfectly rationalized through displacement to robbers, criminals, black men, etc., according to the phobia mechanism. Here the so-called real fear arising from danger comes into existence as a connecting link and as an outlet for the displaced primal anxiety. Thus the change of the claustrophobia referring to the mother into the anxiety of something entering oneself referring to the father completely corresponds to the (child's) attitude to the large (motherly) and to the small (phallic) animals.

At this point we anticipate from the psychoanalytic side an objection which we hope easily to dispose of. The general validity of the experience that the child's every anxiety consists of the anxiety at birth (and the child's every pleasure aims at the re-establishing of the intrauterine primal pleasure) could be called in question in view of the so-called *castration anxiety,* which has recently been so strongly emphasized. Yet it seems to me quite intelligible that the childish primal anxiety, in the course of its development, should cling more especially to the genitals just on account of their vaguely imagined (or remembered) actual biological relation to birth (and procreation). It is conceivable, indeed obvious, that precisely the female genitals, being the place of the birth trauma, should soon again become the chief object of the anxiety-affect origi-

---

[10] According to a verbal communication, the Viennese child specialist, J. K. Friedjung, was able on many occasions to observe children who came into the world with a finger in the mouth. This shows the tendency to an immediate substitution of the mother in *statu nascendi.* Recent experiments on the reflex excitability of the foetus have been able to show that already in the sixth or seventh month sucking reflexes can be produced.

nally arising there. Thus the importance of the castration fear is based, as Stärcke thinks,[11] on the primal castration at birth, that is, on the separation of the child from the mother.[12]

But it does not seem quite appropriate to speak of "castration" where, as yet, there is no clearer relation of anxiety to the genitals, than is given by the fact of birth from the (female) genitals.[13] This conception finds a strong heuristic support in that it solves the riddle of the ubiquity of the "castration complex" in a natural way by deriving it from the indisputable universality of the act of birth. This is a point of view which proves to be of the greatest importance for the complete understanding and also for the real foundation of other primal fantasies. We believe that we are now better able to understand why the castration threat should cause such a stupendous and lasting effect on the child—and, moreover, why childish anxiety and the guilt feeling brought on by birth and arising from it cannot be avoided by any kind of educational measure or removed by the usual analytic explanations.[14] The threat of castration hits not only the vaguely remembered primal trauma and the undisposed-of anxiety representing it, but also a second trauma, consciously experienced and painful in character, though later obliterated by repression, namely weaning, the intensity and persistence of which falls far short of that of the first trauma, but owes a great part of its "traumatic" effect to it. Only in the third place, then, does there appear the genital trauma of castration *regularly fantasied* in the history of the individual and, at most, experienced as a threat.[15] But this, just on account of its unreality, seems predisposed

[11] A. Stärcke, "Psychoanalysis and Psychiatry," *The Internat. Journal of Ps.A.*, vol. ii., 1921.

[12] In dreams at the end of the analytic cure I found the phallus often used as "symbol" of the umbilical cord.

[13] See also Freud, "The Infantile Genital Organization of the Libido," *Collected Papers*, vol. ii. (quoted only after the conclusion of this work).

[14] See in addition Melanie Klein, "The Development of a Child," *Internat. Journal of Ps.A.*, vol. iv., 1923.

[15] The typical duality, which as symbol of defense and consolation for castration should compensate the loss of one irreplaceable member (often by a multiplicity), seems originally to belong to the weaning trauma, and to go back to the possibility of obtaining nourishment at both breasts, whereby actually the one breast replaces the "loss" of the other. Also the "symbolic" use of the testicles proves to be not infrequently a point of transition between the breasts and the penis, like the udder of a cow (*cf.* Stekel's symbolic equation of "pairs of organs"). On another level, the duality of the castration defense seems to serve infantile irony in face of the lies of the grown-ups (see also *infra*, pp. 21–2).

to take upon itself the greatest part of the natal anxiety-affect as guilt feeling, which, as in the meaning of the biblical fall of man, actually proves to be connected with the differentiation of the sexes, the difference in the sexual organs and the sexual functions. The deepest Unconscious which always remains sexually indifferent (bi-sexual) knows nothing of this and knows only the first primal anxiety of the universal human act of birth.

In comparison with the painfully experienced actual traumata of birth and weaning, a real threat of castration seems even to make easier the normal discharge of the primal anxiety as genital guilt feeling, in so far and just as soon as the child has discovered the insincerity of the castration threat as of all other untruths of adults. In contrast to the primal trauma, then, the castration fantasy, which is soon unmasked as an empty threat, can occur rather as a consolation since the severance cannot take place.[16] From this point we are led directly to the infantile sexual theories which refuse to recognize "castration" (the female genitals), obviously so as to be able to deny along with it the trauma of birth (primal-separation).

It should be noticed, moreover, that every playful use of the tragic primal motive, which occurs with the consciousness of unreality, works in a pleasurable way in that it advantageously denies the reality of any trauma. Examples of this are the typical children's *games* from the earliest "hiding" (hide-and-seek) to the games of swinging, trains, dolls, and doctor,[17] which, moreover, as Freud very soon recognized, contain the same elements as the corresponding neurotic symptoms, only with positive pleasurable signs. The game of hiding (also conjuring), which children tirelessly repeat, represents the situation of separation (and of finding again) as not of a serious kind; the rhythmic games of movement (swinging, hopping, etc.) simply repeat the rhythm felt in the embryonic state. This rhythm shows, in the neurotic symptom of dizziness, the other side of the Janus head. Soon the child's every game will somehow be subordinated to the viewpoint of its unreality. And Psychoanalysis has been able to show how, from the

[16] The same mechanism of solace or consolation is again to be found in the faulty acts of losing things, recognized as actions of sacrifice. One cuts oneself off from a valuable part of one's ego instead of being completely "cut off" ("the ring of Polycrates," which is thrown into the sea, but which comes to light again in the fish's belly).

[17] The last two with direct reference to childbirth (doll = fetus in dream).

child's game, the higher and the highest pleasure-giving un-
realities, namely, fantasy and art, emerge.[18] Even in the highest forms of these pretended realities, as, for example, in the
Greek tragedies, we are in a position to *enjoy anxiety* and
horror because we abreact these primal affects, in the meaning of Aristotle's catharsis, just as the child now works off the
separation from the mother, originally full of dread, in its
game of willing concealment,[19] which can easily and often
be broken off and repeated at the child's pleasure.

The child's constant proneness to anxiety, which originates
in the birth trauma and is transferable to almost anything, is
expressed in a more direct, and so to speak, a more biological
way in the child's characteristic attitude toward death, important also from a general point of view. What astonished us
at first was not the fact that the child knows nothing at all of
the idea of death, but that here also, as in the sexual realm,
it is, for a long time, not in a position to accept the facts and
explanations as to its real significance. It is one of Freud's
greatest merits that he has called our attention to the child's
negative idea of death, which is expressed, for example, in
the fact that it treats a dead person as one temporarily absent.
It is well known, also, that the Unconscious never gives up
this idea, to which not only the ever-reviving belief in immortality bears witness but also the fact that we dream of
the dead as living.

It would be quite wrong, too, to suppose, according to our
intellectualist attitude, that the child cannot accept the idea of
death on account of its painfulness and its unpleasant character; this is not the case for the reason that the child turns
away from the idea of it *a priori,* without having any understanding of its content. In general the child cannot be said
to have any abstract idea of death, and reacts only to cases
that have been actually experienced or to those that have
been described (explained) to it in connection with the persons well known to it. To be dead has the same meaning for
the child as to be away (Freud)—that is, to be *separated*—
and this directly touches on the primal trauma. The child
thus accepts the conscious idea of death by unconsciously identifying it with the primal trauma. It may, therefore, seem
brutal to adults that the child should want the death of an

[18] Freud, *Der Dichter und das Phantasieren,* 1908.

[19] In fairy tales also, as, for example, in the Seven Kids, the concealment has the significance of birth and rescue, that is, return to
the mother's womb in the case of external danger.

unwished-for rival, a new little brother or sister whose intrusion is not pleasing to it: this is much the same as when we ourselves say to someone, he can go to the devil—that is, leave us alone. Only the child betrays a far better knowledge than the adult of the original meaning of this "manner of speech," when, for example, it advises the intruding little brother or sister to go back to where he came from. The child means this quite seriously and can do so again on the strength of those dim memories of the place whence children come. And so with the thought of death is connected from the beginning a strong unconscious sense of pleasure associated with the return to the mother's womb. This pleasurable affect has been maintained undiminished through the whole history of mankind, from the primitive customs of cremation to the spiritual return in the form of an astral body.

But it is not merely the human *idea* of death that has this libidinal background, for man also unconsciously plays the trump card of prenatal existence—the only condition of which we have any experience apart from our conscious life—against the idea of destruction in death, consciously recognized as real. When the child wants to remove a competitor disturbing to his peace, and therefore wishes he were dead, he can do this only by means of his own pleasurable memory of the place he came from and whence the little brother or sister also came—from the mother. One could also say that he wishes himself back again in the place where there is no kind of disturbance from outside. In the childish wish for the death of others, the justification for emphasizing their own unconscious wish element is made clear from the understanding of the self-reproaches with which neurotics regularly react at the accidental realization of such a wish. When one loses a closely connected person of either sex, this loss reminds one again of the primal separation from the mother; and the painful task of disengaging the libido from this person (recognized by Freud in the process of *mourning*) corresponds to a psychical repetition of the primal trauma. In the different human customs of mourning it is undoubtedly clear, as recently shown by Reik in a lecture,[20] that the mourner tries to identify himself with the dead, showing how he envies him the return to the mother. The marked impressions, which the premature death of a brother or sister leaves in the Unconscious of the

[20] "Tabnit, König von Sidon" (Wiener Psychoanalytic Association, March, 1923).

survivors, who later often become neurotic, clearly show the strange aftereffects of this identification with the dead. This not seldom expresses itself in the fact that the person in question spends his life, as it were, in perpetual mourning, that is, in a state which is adapted in a bewildering way to the dead person's supposed place of abode. Many neuroses, taken as a whole, can be understood as such an embryonal continuance of the prematurely cut-off existence of a brother or sister. And melancholy frequently shows the same mechanism as a reaction to an actual death.[21]

As one clearly sees in analyses, the child envies the dead the happiness of return to the mother and so links his real jealousy to the new brother or sister, generally at the period of pregnancy, that is, at the time of the abode in the mother. The well-known adjustment to the fact of the new competitor, on the other hand, begins soon after its birth (the child as a living doll) by identification with the mother (the child from the father). In the child's unconscious tendency to identify itself in the mother's womb with the child whose imminent arrival has been sufficiently announced lies the decisive factor, which in the meaning of psychoanalytic investigations might be described as the *Trauma of the Second Child* (brother or sister trauma). Its essential factor consists in the fact that the later coming child materializes the deepest wish tendency of the already present child to be again in the mother, and, as it were, spoils once and for all the chances of ever returning there. This can become a determining factor for the whole further attitude and development of the first or previously born (see *The Psychology of the Youngest,* p. 107, "Heroic Compensation"). From this many otherwise unintelligible traits in adult love life (neurotic limitation of children, etc.), as also certain neurotic organic sufferings of women, become analytically accessible (pseudo-sterility, etc.).

The identification of death with the return to the mother also explains why the dead must not be disturbed in their rest and why such a disturbance is regarded as the greatest punishment. This proves the secondary nature of the whole rebirth fantasy, which has no other meaning than to re-establish the original condition and remain there. This is shown also by various biological facts which lead to the exclusion of the ethical-anagogic element of the rebirth idea, held er-

[21] It would be worth while in the anamneses of melancholics to find out whether they had experienced a death in the family in their childhood.

roneously by Jung to be essential.[22] A certain species of *Cichlides* (mouth-brooders) forms a particularly instructive example. The female carries the spawn till their maturity in a pouch in her throat.[23] In the existing North African species, *Haplochromis strigigena,* which fasten their eggs to plants and stones, the mother's throat-pouch is a receptacle and protection *only for the hatched-out young ones.* Should any danger threaten, or when night comes, the mother opens her mouth and a whole brood of young Haplochromes creep into it and stay there till the danger is past or the morning dawns. This behavior is especially interesting, not only because it proves that physiological sleep throughout the whole animal kingdom is a temporary return to the mother's womb but because in this species the real incubation takes place on stones or plants outside the mother's body; this is compensated for later by these animals because they apparently cannot do without it.

Other animals, differing from the pouched animals (kangaroo) in that they have no partial return to the mother's body for protection, replace this in a way that can only be called "symbolic," as, for example, the birds by building their nests[24] (which Jung has already referred to). We want here to draw attention to the fact that what we call animal *instinct* contains in its essence the adjustment of the prenatal libido to the outer world, and also the tendency to make this outer world resemble as faithfully as possible the previously experienced primal state; whilst man, because of his long period of pregnancy and with the help of later-developed and higher capacities for thought, attempts, in every conceivable way, to re-establish,

[22] Jung has here blindly passed over the biological facts, because he seeks to protect himself from the "analytic" tendency to regression, and thereby overlooks the biological. So he has slipped into the opposite ethical anagogic direction, which places in the center the idea of rebirth, which is only an intellectualized ramification. *Psychology of the Unconscious,* p. 251.

[23] The brood hatched in the mouth is found in numerous bony fishes, and in isolated cases even among the higher vertebrate animals. S. Meisenheimer, *Geschlecht und Geschlechter im Tierreich,* Jena, 1921, vol. i., chap. 20; "Die Verwendung des elterlichen Körpers im Dienst der Brutflege," viii., Stufe, p. 566 f. Here belong also the wonderful homing instincts of birds of passage and migrating fish, which return to *their place of birth* from every strange place to which *they have been taken or to which they themselves have migrated.*

[24] An American kindergarten teacher once told me that little children, when playing with plasticine, mostly spontaneously formed birds' nests.

as it were, creatively the real primal condition. He succeeds in doing this with a great amount of pleasure in the socially adjusted fantasy products of art, religion, mythology; whereas he fails piteously in the neurosis.

The ground for this lies, as Psychoanalysis has shown, in a psycho-biological arrest in development, which we shall discuss . . . from the point of view of the *sexual trauma*. The essential factor in the development of neuroses seems to be that man, in the biological as in the cultural overcoming of the birth trauma, which we call adjustment, comes to grief at the crossroad of sexual gratification, which most nearly approaches the primal situation, yet does not completely re-establish it in the infantile meaning.

Infancy: The Role of Anxiety in the Beginning Differentiation of Experience

HARRY STACK SULLIVAN

(1946–1947)

Harry Stack Sullivan viewed psychiatry as the study of interpersonal relations, regarding psychosis, neurosis, and normalcy as being largely defined in terms of one's power to communicate his needs and emotions. In the following selection, originally a lecture later incorporated in his book *The Interpersonal Theory of Psychiatry* (1953), he demonstrates the magical significance of a hungry infant's cry and shows that, if untended, it is one of life's first experiences of unexpected powerlessness. Similarly, anxiety contracted from the mother is repeated and ramified in later forms of anxiety.

Crying is adequate and appropriate action of the hungry infant in that it frequently "produces" the lips-nipple experience and its satisfaction-giving consequents of sucking, swallowing, and so on. Now crying is adequate and appropriate action for the relief of the infant's hunger, not because it *invariably* gets him fed, but because it *frequently*, so far as he is concerned, leads to that change which is the nipple between his lips, which is the instituting or initiating step in the procedure of sucking and swallowing, which in the end relieves or at least diminishes the hunger. This lips-nipple experience, which we are sure the infant has, generally produces the fluid sucked and swallowed, the arrival of which is closely related to the relaxation or reduction of the tension of need for water and food.

Now one of the things I most detest in the German language is the production of words that take a printed line, by compounding other words. Unhappily, in trying to throw some light on the essentially simply inferable living of the infant, I have had to resort to compound hyphenated words. The one which provokes my distress at the moment is crying-when-hungry. Crying-when-hungry has no necessary relatedness, in the infant's experience, with crying-when-cold, crying-when-pained, or crying-under-any-other-circumstances. If crying-when-hungry frequently initiates the necessary circumstances for the relief of hunger and thirst, it comes to mean, in a primitive, prototaxic way, something like what I may suggest by the word sequence: "Come, nipple, into my mouth." It is a vocal gesture with reasonably dependable power of so manipulating what will later be called reality that the nipple complies. In other words, crying-when-hungry, so far as infantile experience can go, has power to manipulate quite ungraspable aspects of something-or-other, later lumped as reality, so that the nipple dutifully appears.

The most refined study of the sound waves which make up crying-when-hungry need show no "objective difference" whatever from the sound waves making up crying-when-cold, for example. The two may not only sound alike, but in the physical acoustic sense may be the same, may have a one-to-one correspondence in every measurable sense; that is, the pattern of progression of sound waves, if duly recorded on a cathode-ray oscillograph, may be absolutely identical in every characteristic that can be measured through such a devise. And yet, from the infantile standpoint, crying-when-hungry and crying-when-cold will not be in any sense the same thing.

The same kind of physical acoustic correspondence often appears when one says *whole* and *hole*. The so-called objective facts do not have significance with respect to the meaning, to the speaking person, of the (as we say) two different words. He may never have discovered that his two words are homonyms or homophones. We may say, under these circumstances, that he has not differentiated the homophonous character of the two words. As long as the use of either of these two homophones generally proves adequate to his needs, it is of no great importance to his living to discover that the two words, very different in dictionary meaning, sound alike—that is, are experienced by the hearer as quite exactly the same. Until something has called for such differentiation, our person may well believe that he "sounds different," as he might put it, when he utters "hole" from the way he sounds when he says "whole." In general, the matter will never have occurred to him, never have been the subject of what I shall later discuss as *observation, identifying,* and *valid formulation* of two different, but acoustically identical, verbal acts. I trust that I have illustrated, by this discussion of two homonymous or homophonous words, how, from the standpoint of the physics of sound, or from the study of linquistic process in actual operation, two very different words are utterly the same. Their difference, which comes out nicely when written words are substituted for them (remember that written words are symbols for spoken words) is a difference in the use to which they are put—that is, their usefulness as tools, their meaning to the user, what they are good for.

In the same way, the infant's crying-when-hungry, however utterly indistinguishable outside, you might say, it is from crying-when-cold, is an entirely different performance so far as the infant and his experience go. Thus one's actions, however they may impress the observer, are most importantly defined by what they are "intended" for—that is, they are determined by the general pattern of motivation that is involved, by what is significant to the person concerned, quite irrespective of any impressions an observer may have.

A great many mistakes are made in psychiatry as a result of overlooking this fact. Some of these mistakes are very devastating indeed, such as the ancient superstition that the performances of the schizophrenic are essentially unpsychological. Few more sad combinations of words could be spouted. The truth is that however the performance of a Javanese head-hunter might look to a clerk in a Wall Street financial institution, the clerk's opinions would have only recreational or conversational value; they would be of exceedingly little importance with respect to head-hunters in Java.

The infant's experience of crying-when-hungry comes very early to relate backward and forward—that is, as recall and as foresight—to the "producing" of the lips-nipple experience with its desired consequents of sucking and swallowing. I have said that crying-when-hungry *frequently* produces the nipple and the possibilities of relief. I want now to discuss two special instances in which this very early magical potency of vocal behavior goes wrong, as it were. Before I do that, I wish that you could rid yourself of any preconceptions about magic. I would like to suggest that when we speak of *magical potency* we are likely to mean—I think it may be adequately stated this way—that we have an exceedingly inadequate grasp on all that is actually happening. When you do something that works, it is like turning on the electric lights by flipping a switch. The lights come on magically because you flipped the switch—that is, if you don't know anything in particular about electricity and electric circuits, it seems magical; if the lights don't come on, that's extraordinary, indicating that something must be wrong somewhere. But if you know enough to guess *where* something may be wrong, you are pretty well acquainted with reality. I might add—perhaps slightly to parallel the relationship of the infant's crying-when-hungry and getting food—that even though sometimes when you flip a switch the lights don't come on, the fact that they generally have will probably lead you to flip switches in the future when you want light; and you will remain convinced that there is considerable potency in flipping a switch when you want light, even though it hasn't always worked. And so it is with a great deal in life.

I want particularly now to discuss very early experience of this sort of *infrequent* event. The first is the failure of the crying-when-hungry, arising from (as we see it) the absence of the necessary, more adult person who actually (in our sense) is the provider of the nipple. To digress for a moment, it is well to remember that the very young infant has no grasp on those phases of reality which we call independent persons, with or without nipples, and with or without milk to run through those nipples; this is utterly exterior to any reasonable supposition about very young infants. Now let us assume that the infant happens to be surrounded only by male persons —perhaps the mother is out doing some shopping or whatever. Crying-when-hungry therefore does not produce, in its usual magical fashion, the nipple in the mouth, which is the initiatory stage of infantile activity which satisfies hunger and thirst. In this case crying-when-hungry is continued until the nipple is produced, or until mounting fear has called out apathy and the infant finally sleeps. Crying-when-hungry then recurs as soon as the infant awakens. Now this is the beginning of a very important train of events with which we have dealings throughout life.

The other special instance which I wish to discuss is that in which anxiety is a complicating factor. We shall take a case in which the crying-when-hungry has produced the nipple, but this success, preliminary to sucking and the satisfaction of hunger and thirst, is complicated by the interference of the anxiety which has been induced in the infant because of or by anxiety in or pertaining to the person who carries the nipple in actuality. The satisfaction-giving consequents on the production of the nipple under these circumstances do not follow. Investing the nipple with the lips, sucking, swallowing, or any or all of these and other parts of the accessory behavior of nursing may be disordered by the coincidence of anxiety in the infant, induced by the mothering one's anxiety, with the infant's crying-when-hungry. The infant may produce the nipple in the magical fashion that has become frequent enough to be the normal expectation, as you might describe it—the proof of the power of crying-when-hungry—but this time something is very wrong.

The first of the special instances which I have mentioned—that is, crying-when-hungry when there is nobody to rally around tenderly—is a very early experience of the occasional inadequacy or powerlessness of otherwise generally appropriate and adequate behavior for the manipulation of what later will be called reality. The infant cries when hungry, and nothing happens except the development of processes in the infant which culminate finally in apathy and sleep, with the recurrence of crying on awakening. As I have said, this is a very early instance of a type of situation which recurs more or less frequently throughout life, in which a generally appropriate and adequate series of acts—that is, behavior—proves to be inadequate, and proves to have no power to bring about that which this behavior is ordinarily entirely sufficient to produce. This sort of experience, the experience of unexpected powerlessness, as we may call it, is an event infrequent enough to be quite exterior to expectation; in other words, it is an exception to something to which we are accustomed, an exception to the many times we have done something and the right result has come of it.

The accompaniments of these experiences of powerlessness are various. The significance of such experiences of powerlessness probably increases for some time after birth, until one has developed adequate ways of handling such experiences, and by adequate I mean personally adequate in the sense of avoiding very unpleasant emotion. The very early experiences would, if they continued long enough, unquestionably produce very marked effects on the developing personality of the infant, but here the intervention of the dynamism of apathy tones off, as it were, these instances of powerlessness, somewhat after the fashion that the old magic lanterns produced vignettes—you remember, something would fade out gradually, and later something would gradually come in. And so the intervention of the apathy processes, to which I have already referred, prevents a serious complicating effect from the relatively infrequent instances of the infant's powerlessness to produce the nipple by the cry.

I hope that I have made it clear that, even very early in life, frequent success has a very powerful influence in determining the character of foresight. I believe that I will not mislead you if I talk quite loosely and say that, given a pressing need which is increasing, it is not strange that the extremely young infant does not accumulate negative instances; and in any case the accumulation of negative instances is less apt to be significant because apathy has a sort of fade-out effect on things, and the chances of success upon the resumption of crying after sleep are pretty fair. Thus the relatively frequent, rather consistent success stamps in the magical power of the cry; and the occasional failures, due to the absence of the mother, and so on, do not greatly impair this growing conviction of what we would much later call a cause-and-effect relationship, which could be expressed—putting a great many words into the mouth of a very early infant—as, "I cry when I suffer a certain distress, and that produces something different which is connected with the relief of the distress."

This relief need not absolutely always occur for such convictions of relationship in the universe to become firmly entrenched in the infant. If this seems doubtful, let me say that one of the most conspicuous things we see, in the intensive study of personality, is the fantastic ease with which unnumbered negative instances can be overlooked for years in the area of one's more acute personal problems. It may even be that under certain circumstances, although not in very early infancy, a success which is purely an accident—that is, which is so exceedingly complex that it may be regarded as pure chance—may give rise to firm conviction that there is a vital causal relationship involved, and that if one could only do the right thing again it would produce the desirable result with which it was originally associated only by the merest and most terribly complex chance. So the erasing effect of negative experience is not very impressive, even from extremely early in life.[1]

[1] Note by Sullivan's original editors: The preceding three paragraphs are taken from Sullivan's 1948 lecture series, which was interrupted by his death. Earlier he had discussed these experiences of powerlessness as belonging generically to the field of the uncanny emotions—awe, dread, loathing, and horror. Sullivan remarked in his 1948 lecture, "Since this lecture series was originally prepared, I have changed my mind about uncanny emotion, about which I have done some fairly active thinking in the recent past. . . . It used to be very depressing to discover that I didn't agree with myself from one year to another, but ultimately I have found it rather encouraging. At least it gives me a

Now what I have said thus far concerns the first of the special instances in which the infant's crying-when-hungry fails —the instance in which the provider of the nipple is absent. The second of the special instances, on the other hand, the case where anxiety is induced in the infant along with the showing up of the nipple, is to the infant an utterly different sort of experience. The adequate and appropriate crying-when-hungry has produced the nipple, but in the process has evoked anxiety; I am talking entirely from the standpoint of the infant, who is unable to discriminate anxiety as induced by the mother's anxiety—in fact, all of this is exterior to the clear understanding of the infant. But as mother draws near with her nipple—in other words, as from the infantile standpoint this mighty power of crying-when-hungry is about to bring results—lo, there comes the very severe drop in euphoria, in the general feeling of well-being, which is anxiety. Thus in this instance, while crying-when-hungry has produced the first step in the business, the nipple in the mouth, it has also brought anxiety—very severe tension which interferes with behavior activity in satisfaction of the need for water and food. What this must be like in infantile experience is suggested when I say that under these circumstances crying-when-hungry has produced a *different* nipple; the nipple now produced is not the same nipple, so far as the infant is concerned. The lips-nipple configuration is something new, and is anything but the satisfying lips-nipple configuration ordinarily produced; in fact, it is one that will not work, that is anything but relieving. It is, to use an exceedingly broad term in one of its exceedingly early relevancies, an evil eventuality which has arisen in connection with the oral zone of interaction, although we, in contradistinction to the infant, know that the anxiety has no primary or necessary relationship to the oral zone. On the contrary, the first time anything like this happens, it is perfectly certain that the anxiety in the mother which induced anxiety in the infant did not have any relation to the infant's taking nourishment. Afterward her anxiety may have something to do with the difficulties about feeding that characterized the first time she was anxious with her infant. But this is utterly outside the experience of the infant, and a matter of no consequence whatever in thinking about his experience,

---

chance to reemphasize to you that psychiatry is a developing field, in which, perhaps, it is not to one's vast discredit that one does not become entirely and rigidly crystallized in the defense of what is an archaic idea. . . ."

because the infant cannot differentiate the source of the anxiety. The anxiety is just there, and is extremely unpleasant; nothing that generally went right *does* go right, and the experience which unquestionably occurs—that is, the conjunction of nipple and lips—may actually be so clearly different that the infant rejects this particular nipple, will not hold it in his mouth, and therefore does not suck it.

Anxiety relates to the whole field of interpersonal interaction; that is, anxiety about *anything* in the mother induces anxiety in the infant. It doesn't need to have anything to do with the infant or the nursing situation. For example, as I mentioned before, a telegram announcing something of very serious moment to the prestige or peace of mind of the mother may induce a state of anxiety in her which induces anxiety in the infant; the infant's anxiety shows, so far as she is concerned, in this unexpected and exceedingly unsatisfactory difficulty in getting the infant to nurse. Now looking at it from the infant's standpoint, we can infer with certainly only that in this particular circumstance the outcome of ordinarily appropriate and adequate behavior when hungry—namely, crying-when-hungry—has produced the wrong nipple, a very evil situation with very unpleasant and unsatisfactory consequences

Now oral rejection, in which the infant will not invest and hang on to the nipple, is not an appropriate and adequate way to deal with this particular evil or bad nipple. It does not in any way diminish or favorably affect the anxiety, which is induced by the mother's anxiety. In fact, if the mother is capable of noticing what's going on, and observes that the infant now rejects the nipple, avoids it, and will not hold and suck it, this will probably aggravate the mother's anxiety, adding a new anxiety, which will tend to aggravate the infant's anxiety. So mere rejection (you will remember that when first I spoke of the oral zone, I suggested that it accepted and rejected certain things) of this bad or anxiety-toned nipple is not adequate or appropriate: it doesn't reduce the anxiety, it certainly doesn't satisfy the need for food, and therefore it is a very perduring instance of the relationship of anxiety to living.

Now let me invite your attention briefly to something which I hope to express better later on. Even though anxiety is experience, and, as such, is total, and even though it has no necessary relationship to any particular zone of interaction, anxiety can be, as we put it, erroneously associated with a particular zone of interaction. For example, it may be erroneously associated with the mother's nipple, and consequently with the oral zone, since the nipple is significant to the infant only in connection with the oral zone at this very early stage—the infant has no interest in nipples except the nipple in the mouth or in the immediate proximity of the mouth. If the circumstances are something like those I have just discussed in my example of the mother made anxious by a telegram, there is no possibility of the infant's discriminating the irrelevance of his behavior in the oral zone of interaction, in rejecting the nipple, from something quite properly related to that zone of interaction as profitable experience—that is, extending backward and forward as recall and foresight. Now if you begin to grasp this aspect of anxiety-laden, or anxiety-colored, details of behavior, you will begin to have a hint of what a devastating complication of development frequent experiences of anxiety can be.

Here we have inferred what I believe perfect logical necessity requires: beginning discrimination by the infant of an actual nipple as two very different nipples, one conventional and desirable, the other evil and connected with, you might almost say, unending trouble. The more I talk about anxiety, the more you will see that this first appearance of anxiety which I have discussed is not so very different from an enormous number of the very troublesome results of anxiety in human living.

Early Stages of the Oedipus Conflict

MELANIE KLEIN

(1928)

One of the most ambitious systematic attempts to analyze children was that of Melanie Klein, the English psychoanalyst, who used play technique to treat children's neurosis. Her work was made possible by Freud's, although she ascribed to the mother a more important role in the instinctual life of the infant. Klein concentrated on the infant's fantasy life—his preoccupation with the interior of his body, especially the mouth (the first link to reality), his fear of being incorporated and of incorporating, his guilt feelings and desires to make reparation. The following controversial piece, an early work, touches on these themes.

In my analyses of children, especially of children between the ages of three and six, I have come to a number of conclusions of which I shall here present a summary.

I have repeatedly alluded to the conclusion that the Oedipus complex comes into operation earlier than is usually supposed. In my paper, "The Psychological Principles of Infant Analysis," I discussed this subject in greater detail. The conclusion which I reached there was that the Oedipus tendencies are released in consequence of the frustration which the child experiences at weaning, and that they make their appearance at the end of the first and the beginning of the second year of life; they receive reinforcement through the anal frustrations undergone during training in cleanliness. The next determining influence upon the mental processes is that of the anatomical difference between the sexes.

The boy, when he finds himself impelled to abandon the oral and anal positions for the genital, passes on to the aim of *penetration* associated with possession of the penis. Thus he changes not only his libido-position, but its *aim,* and this enables him to retain his original love-object. In the girl, on the other hand, the *receptive* aim is carried over from the oral to the genital position: she changes her libido-position, but retains its aim, which has already led to disappointment in relation to her mother. In this way receptivity for the penis is produced in the girl, who then turns to the father as her love-object.

The very onset of the Oedipus wishes, however, already becomes associated with incipient dread of castration and feelings of guilt.

The analysis of adults, as well as of children, has familiarized us with the fact that the pregenital instinctual impulses carry with them a sense of guilt, and it was thought at first that the feelings of guilt were of subsequent growth, displaced back on to these tendencies, though not originally associated with them. Ferenczi assumes that, connected with the urethral and anal impluses, there is a "kind of physiological forerunner of the super-ego," which he terms "sphincter-morality." According to Abraham, anxiety makes its appearance on the cannibalistic level, while the sense of guilt arises in the succeeding early anal-sadistic phase.

My findings lead rather further. They show that the sense of guilt associated with pregenital fixation is already the direct effect of the Oedipus conflict. And this seems to account satisfactorily for the genesis of such feelings, for we know the sense of guilt to be in fact a result of the introjection (already accomplished or, as I would add, in process of being accomplished) of the Oedipus love-objects: that is, a sense of guilt is a product of the formation of the super-ego.

The analysis of little children reveals the structure of the super-ego as built up of identifications dating from very different periods and strata in the mental life. These identifications are surprisingly contradictory in nature, excessive goodness and excessive severity existing side by side. We find in them, too, an explanation of the severity of the super-ego, which comes out specially plainly in these infant analyses. It does not seem clear why a child of, say, four years old should set up in his mind an unreal, fantastic image of parents who devour, cut and bite. But it *is* clear why in a child of about *one year old* the anxiety caused by the beginning of the Oedipus conflict takes the form of a dread of being devoured and destroyed. The child himself desires to destroy the libidinal object by biting, devouring and cutting it, which leads to anxiety, since awakening of the Oedipus tendencies is followed by introjection of the object, which then becomes one from which punishment is to be expected. The child then dreads a punishment corresponding to the offense: the super-ego becomes something which bites, devours and cuts.

The connection between the formation of the super-ego and the pregenital phases of development is very important from two points of view. On the one hand, the sense of guilt attaches itself to the oral- and anal-sadistic phases, which as yet predominate; and, on the other, the super-ego comes into being while these phases are in the ascendant, which accounts for its sadistic severity.

These conclusions open up a new perspective. Only by strong repression can the still very feeble ego defend itself against a super-ego so menacing. Since the Oedipus tendencies are at first chiefly expressed in the form of oral and anal impulses, the question of which fixations will predominate in the Oedipus development will be mainly determined by the degree of the repression which takes place at this early stage.

Another reason why the direct connection between the pregenital phase of development and the sense of guilt is so important is that the oral and anal frustrations, which are the prototypes of all later frustrations in life, at the same time signify *punishment* and give rise to anxiety. This circimstance makes the frustration more acutely felt, and this bitterness contributes largely to the hardship of all subsequent frustrations.

We find that important consequences ensue from the fact that the ego is still so little developed when it is assailed by the onset of the Oedipus tendencies and the incipient sexual curiosity associated with them. The infant, still undeveloped intellectually, is exposed to an onrush of problems and questions. One of the most bitter grievances which we come upon in the unconscious is that these many overwhelming questions, which are apparently only partly conscious and even when conscious cannot yet be expressed in words, remain unanswered. Another reproach follows hard upon this, namely, that the child could not understand words and speech. Thus his first questions go back beyond the beginnings of his understanding of speech.

In analysis both these grievances give rise to an extraordinary amount of hate. Singly or in conjunction they are the cause of numerous inhibitions of the epistemophilic impulse: for instance, the incapacity to learn foreign languages, and, further, hatred of those who speak a different tongue. They are also responsible for direct disturbances in speech, etc. The curiosity which shows itself plainly later on, mostly in the fourth or fifth year of life, is not the beginning, but the climax and termination, of this phase of development, which I have also found to be true of the Oedipus conflict in general.

The early feeling of *not knowing* has manifold connections. It unites with the feeling of being incapable, impotent, which soon results from the Oedipus situation. The child also feels this frustration the more acutely because he *knows nothing* definite about sexual processes. In both sexes the castration complex is accentuated by this feeling of ignorance.

The early connection between the epistemophilic impulse and sadism is very important for the whole mental development. This instinct, activated by the rise of the Oedipus tendencies, at first mainly concerns itself with the mother's body, which is assumed to be the scene of all sexual processes and developments. The child is still dominated by the anal-sadistic libido-position which impels him to wish to *appropriate* the contents of the body. He thus begins to be curious about what it contains, what it is like, etc. So the epistemophilic instinct and the desire to take possession come quite early to be most intimately connected with one another and at the same time with the sense of guilt aroused by the incipient Oedipus conflict. This significant connection ushers in a phase of development in both sexes which is of vital importance, hitherto not sufficiently recognized. It consists of a very early identification with the mother.

The course run by this "femininity phase" must be examined separately in boys and in girls, but, before I proceed to this, I shall show its connection with the previous phase, which is common to both sexes.

In the early anal-sadistic stage the child sustains his second severe trauma, which strengthens his tendency to turn away from the mother. She has frustrated his oral desires, and now she also interferes with his anal pleasures. It seems as though at this point the anal deprivations cause the anal tendencies to amalgamate with the sadistic tendencies. The child desires to get possession of the mother's feces, by penetrating into her body, cutting it to pieces, devouring and destroying it. Under the influence of his genital impulses, the boy is beginning to turn to his mother as a love-object. But his sadistic impulses are fully at work, and the hate originating in earlier frustrations is powerfully opposed to his object-love on the genital level. A still greater obstacle to his love is his dread of castration by the father, which arises with the Oedipus impulses. The degree to which he attains the genital position will partly depend on his capacity for tolerating this anxiety. Here the intensity of the oral-sadistic and anal-sadistic fixations is an important factor. It affects the degree of hatred which the boy feels toward the mother; and this, in its turn, hinders him to a greater or lesser extent in attaining a positive relation to her. The sadistic fixations exercise also a decisive influence upon the formation of the super-ego, which is coming into being while these phases are in the ascendant. The more cruel the super-ego the more terrifying will be the father as castrator, and the more tenaciously, in the child's flight from his genital impulses, will he cling to the sadistic levels, from which levels his Oedipus tendencies, too, in the first instance, take their color.

In these early stages all the positions in the Oedipus development are cathected in rapid succession. This, however, is not noticeable, because the picture is dominated by the pregenital impulses. Moreover, no rigid line can be drawn between the active hetero-sexual attitude which finds expression on the anal level and the further stage of identification with the mother.

We have now reached that phase of development of which I spoke before under the name of the "femininity phase." It has its basis on the anal-sadistic level and imparts to that level a new content, for feces are now equated with the child that is longed for, and the desire to rob the mother now applies to the child as well as to feces. Here we can discern two aims which merge with one another. The one is directed by the desire for children, the intention being to appropriate them, while the other aim is motivated by jealousy of the future brothers and sisters whose appearance is expected, and by the wish to destroy them in the mother. (A third object of the boy's oral-sadistic tendencies inside the mother is the father's penis.)

As in the castration complex of girls, so in the femininity complex of the male, there is at bottom the frustrated desire for a special organ. The tendencies to steal and destroy are concerned with the organs of conception, pregnancy and parturition, which the boy assumes to exist in the mother, and further with the vagina and the breasts, the fountain of milk, which are coveted as organs of receptivity and bounty from the time when the libidinal position is purely oral.

The boy fears punishment for his destruction of his mother's body, but, besides this, his fear is of a more general nature, and here we have an analogy to the anxiety associated with the castration-wishes of the girl. He fears that his body will be mutilated and dismembered, and this dread also means castration. Here we have a direct contribution to the castration complex. In this early period of development the mother who takes away the child's feces signifies also a mother who dismembers and castrates him. Not only by means of the anal frustrations which she inflict does she pave the way for the castration complex: in terms of psychic reality she *is* also already the *castrator*.

This dread of the mother is so overwhelming because there is combined with it an intense dread of castration by the father. The destructive tendencies whose object is the womb are also directed with their full oral- and anal-sadistic intensity against the father's penis, which is supposed to be located there. It is upon this penis that the dread of castration by the father is focused in this phase. Thus the femininity phase is characterized by anxiety relating to the womb and the father's penis, and this anxiety subjects the boy to the tyranny of a super-ego which devours, dismembers and castrates and is formed from the image of father and mother alike.

The incipient genital positions are thus from the beginning crisscrossed by and intermingled with the manifold pregenital tendencies. The greater the preponderance of sadistic fixations, the more does the boy's identification with his mother correspond to an attitude of rivalry toward the woman, with its blending of envy and hatred; for, on account of his wish for a child, he feels himself at a disadvantage and inferior to the mother.

Let us now consider why the femininity complex of men seems so much more obscure than the castration complex in women, with which it is equally important.

The amalgamation of the desire for a child with the epistemophilic impulse enables a boy to effect a displacement onto the intellectual plane; his sense of being at a disadvantage is then concealed and overcompensated by the superiority he deduces from his possession of a penis, which is also acknowledged by girls. This exaggeration of the masculine position results in excessive protestations of masculinity. In her paper ("Die Wurzel des Wissbegierde"),[1] Mary Chadwick, too, has traced the man's narcissistic overestimation of the penis, and his attitude of intellectual rivalry toward women, to the frustration of his wish for a child and to the displacement of this desire onto the intellectual plane.

[1] *Internationale Zeitschrift für Psychoanalyse,* vol. xi, 1925.

A tendency in boys to express excessive aggression, which very frequently occurs, has its source in the femininity complex. It goes with an attitude of contempt and "knowing better," and is highly asocial and sadistic; it is partly determined by an attempt to mask the anxiety and ignorance which lie behind it. In part it coincides with the boy's protest (originating in his fear of castration) against the feminine *role,* but it is rooted also in his dread of his mother, whom he intended to rob of the father's penis, her children and her female sexual organs. This excessive aggression unites with the pleasure in attack which proceeds from the direct, genital Oedipus situation, but it represents that part of the situation which is by far the more asocial factor in character-formation. This is why a man's rivalry with women will be far more asocial than his rivalry with his fellow-men, which is largely prompted through the genital position. Of course the quantity of sadistic fixations will also determine the relationship of a man to other men when they are rivals. If, on the contrary, the identification with the mother is based on a more securely established genital position, on the one hand his relation to women will be positive in character, and on the other the desire for a child and the feminine component, which play so essential a part in men's work, will find more favorable opportunities for sublimation.

In both sexes one of the principal roots of inhibitions in work is the anxiety and sense of guilt associated with the femininity phase. Experience has taught me, however, that a thorough analysis of this phase is, for other reasons as well, important from a therapeutic point of view, and should be of help in some obsessional cases which seem to have reached a point where nothing more could be resolved.

In the boy's development the femininity phase is succeeded by a prolonged struggle between the pregenital and the genital positions of the libido. When at its height, in the third to the fifth year of life, this struggle is plainly recognizable as the Oedipus conflict. The anxiety associated with the femininity phase drives the boy back to identification with the father; but this stimulus in itself does not provide a firm foundation for the genital position, since it leads mainly to repression and over-compensation of the anal-sadistic instincts, and not to overcoming them. The dread of castration by the father strengthens the fixation to the anal-sadistic levels. The degree of constitutional genitality also plays an important part as regards a favorable issue, *i.e.* the attainment of the genital level. Often the outcome of the struggle remains undecided, and this gives rise to neurotic troubles and disturbances of potency.[2] Thus the attainment of complete potency and reaching the genital position will in part depend upon the favorable issue of the femininity phase.

I will now turn to the development of girls. As a result of the process of weaning, the girl-child has turned from the mother, being impelled more strongly to do so by the anal deprivations she has undergone. Genital trends now begin to influence her mental development.

I entirely agree with Helene Deutsch,[3] who holds that the genital development of the woman finds its completion in the successful displacement of oral libido onto the genital. Only, my results lead me to believe that this displacement begins with the first stirrings of the genital impulses and that the oral, receptive aim of the genitals exercises a determining influence in the *girl's turning to the father*. Also I am led to conclude that not only an unconscious awareness of the vagina, but also sensations in that organ and the rest of the genital apparatus, are aroused as soon as the Oedipus impulses make their appearance. In girls, however, onanism does not afford anything like so adequate an outlet for these quantities of excitation as it does in boys. Hence the accumulated lack of gratification provides yet another reason for more complications and disturbances of female sexual development. The difficulty of obtaining full gratification by masturbation may be another cause, besides those indicated by Freud, for the girl's repudiation of onanism, and this may partly explain why, during her struggle to give it up, manual masturbation is generally replaced by pressing the legs together.

Besides the receptive quality of the genital organ, which is brought into play by the intense desire for a new source of gratification, envy and hatred of the mother who possesses the father's penis seem, at the period when these first Oedipus impulses are stirring, to be a further motive for the little girl's turning to the father. His caresses have now the effect of a seduction and are felt as "the attraction of the opposite sex."[4]

[2] Cf. here W. Reich: "Die Funktion des Orgasmus," reprinted in *The Discovery of the Orgone* (New York, 1942).

[3] H. Deutsch: *Psychoanalyse der weiblichen Sexualfunktion.*

[4] We regularly come across the unconscious reproach that the mother has seduced the child while tending it. This reproach goes back to the period when genital desires come to the fore and the Oedipus tendencies are awakening.

In the girl identification with the mother results directly from the Oedipus impulses: the whole struggle caused in the boy by his castration anxiety is absent in her. In girls as well as boys this identification coincides with the anal-sadistic tendencies to rob and destroy the mother. If identification with the mother takes place predominantly at a stage when oral- and anal-sadistic tendencies are very strong, dread of a primitive maternal super-ego will lead to the repression and fixation of this phase and interfere with further genital development. Dread of the mother, too, impels the little girl to give up identification with her, and identification with the father begins.

The little girl's epistemophilic impulse is first roused by the Oedipus complex; the result is that she discovers her lack of a penis. She feels this lack to be a fresh cause of hatred of the mother, but at the same time her sense of guilt makes her regard it as a punishment. This embitters her frustration in this direction, and in its turn, exercises a profound influence on the whole castration complex.

This early grievance about the lack of a penis is greatly magnified later on, when the phallic phase and the castration complex are fully active. Freud has stated that the discovery of the lack of a penis causes the turning from the mother to the father. My findings show, however, that this discovery operates only as a reinforcement in this direction: it is made at a very early stage in the Oedipus conflict, and penis-envy succeeds the wish for a child, which again replaces penis-envy in later development. I regard the deprivation of the breast as the most fundamental cause of the turning to the father.

Identification with the father is less charged with anxiety than that with the mother; moreover, the sense of guilt toward her impels to overcompensation through a fresh love-relation with her. Against the new love-relation with her there operates the castration complex which makes a masculine attitude difficult, and also the hatred of her which sprang from the earlier positions. Hate and rivalry of the mother, however, again lead to abandoning the identification with the father and turning to him as the object to love and be loved by.

The girl's relation to her mother causes her relation to her father to take both a positive and a negative direction. The frustration undergone at his hands has as its very deepest basis the disappointment already suffered in relation to the mother; a powerful motive in the desire to possess him springs from the hatred and envy against the mother. If the sadistic fixations remain predominant, this hatred and its overcompensation will also materially affect the woman's relation to men. On the other hand, if there is a more positive relation to the mother, built up on the genital position, not only will the woman be freer from a sense of guilt in her relation to her children, but her love for her husband will be strongly reinforced, since for the woman he always stands at one and the same time for the mother who gives what is desired and for the beloved child. On this very significant foundation is built up that part of the relation which is connected exclusively with the father. At first it is focused on the act of the penis in coitus. This act, which also promises gratification of the desires that are now displaced onto the genital, seems to the little girl a most consumate performance.

Her admiration is, indeed, shaken by the Oedipus frustration, but unless it is converted into hate, it constitutes one of the fundamental features of the woman's relation to the man. Later, when full satisfaction of the love-impulses is obtained, there is joined with this admiration the great gratitude ensuing from the long-pent-up deprivation. This gratitude finds expression in the greater feminine capacity for complete and lasting surrender to one love-object, especially to the "first love."

One way in which the little girl's development is greatly handicapped is the following. While the boy does in reality *possess* the penis, in respect of which he enters into rivalry with the father, the little girl has only the *unsatisfied* desire for motherhood, and of this, too, she has but a dim and uncertain, though a very intense, awareness.

It is not merely this uncertainty which disturbs her hope of future motherhood. It is weakened far more by anxiety and sense of guilt, and these may seriously and permanently damage the maternal capacity of a woman. Because of the destructive tendencies once directed by her against the mother's body (or certain organs in it) and against the children in the womb, the girl anticipates retribution in the form of destruction of her own capacity for motherhood or of the organs connected with this function and of her own children. Here we have also one root of the constant concern of women (often so excessive) for their personal beauty, for they dread that this too will be destroyed by the mother. At the bottom of the impulse to deck and beautify themselves there is always the motive of *restoring* damaged comeliness, and this has its origin in anxiety and sense of guilt.[5]

It is probable that this deep dread of the destruction of internal organs may be the psychic cause of the greater susceptibility of women, as compared with men, to conversion-hysteria and organic diseases.

It is this anxiety and sense of guilt which is the chief cause of the repression of feelings of pride and joy in the feminine *role*, which are originally very strong. This repression results in depreciation of the capacity for motherhood, at the outset so highly prized. Thus the girl lacks the powerful support which the boy derives from his possession of the penis, and which she herself might find in the anticipation of motherhood.

The girl's very intense anxiety about her womanhood can be shown to be analogous to the boy's dread of castration, for it certainly contributes to the checking of her Oedipus impulses. The course run by the boy's castration anxiety concerning the penis which *visibly* exists is, however, different; it might be termed more *acute* than the more chronic anxiety of the girl concerning her internal organs, with which she is necessarily less familiar. Moreover, it is bound to make a difference that the boy's anxiety is determined by the paternal and the girl's by the maternal super-ego.

Freud has said that the girl's super-ego develops on different lines from that of the boy. We constantly find confirmation of the fact that jealousy plays a greater part in women's lives than in men's, because it is reinforced by deflected envy of the male on account of the penis. On the other hand, however, women especially possess a great capacity, which is not based merely on an overcompensation, for disregarding their own wishes and devoting themselves with self-sacrifice to ethical and social tasks. We cannot account for this capacity by the blending of masculine and feminine traits which, because of the human being's bisexual disposition, does in individual cases influence the formation of character, for this capacity is so plainly maternal in nature. I think that in order to explain how women can run so wide a gamut from the most petty jealousy to the most self-forgetful loving-kindness, we have to take into consideration the peculiar conditions of the formation of the feminine super-ego. From the early identification with the mother in which the anal-sadistic

[5] Cf. Hárnik's paper at the Innsbruck Psycho-Analytical Congress: "Die ökonomischen Beziehungen zwischen dem Schuldgefühl und dem weiblichen Narzissmus."

level so largely preponderates, the little girl derives jealousy and hatred and forms a cruel super-ego after the maternal imago. The super-ego which develops at this stage from a father-identification can also be menacing and cause anxiety, but it seems never to reach the same proportions as that derived from the mother-identification. But the more the identification with the mother becomes stabilized on the genital basis, the more will it be characterized by the devoted kindness of a bountiful mother-ideal. Thus this positive affective attitude depends on the extent to which the maternal mother-ideal bears the characteristics of the pregenital or of the genital stage. But when it comes to the active conversion of the emotional attitude into social or other activities, it would seem that it is the paternal ego-ideal which is at work. The deep admiration felt by the little girl for the father's genital activity leads to the formation of a paternal super-ego which sets before her active aims to which she can never fully attain. If, owing to certain factors in her development, the incentive to accomplish these aims is strong enough, their very impossibility of attainment may lend an impetus to her efforts which, combined with the capacity for self-sacrifice which she derives from the maternal super-ego, gives a woman, in individual instances, the capacity for very exceptional achievements on the intuitive plane and in specific fields.

The boy, too, derives from the feminine phase a maternal super-ego which causes him, like the girl, to make both cruelly primitive and kindly identifications. But he passes through this phase to resume (it is true, in varying degrees) identification with the father. However much the maternal side makes itself felt in the formation of the super-ego, it is yet the *paternal* super-ego which from the beginning is the decisive influence for the man. He too sets before himself a figure of an exalted character upon which to model himself, but, because the boy *is* "made in the image of" his ideal, it is not unattainable. This circumstance contributes to the more sustained and objective creative work of the male.

The dread of injury to her womanhood exercises a profound influence on the castration complex of the little girl, for it causes her to overestimate the penis which she herself lacks; this exaggeration is then much more obvious than is the underlying anxiety about her own womanhood. I would remind you here of the work of Karen Horney, who was the first to examine the sources of the castration complex in women in so far as those sources lie in the Oedipus situation.

In this connection I must speak of the importance for sexual development of certain early experiences in childhood. In the paper which I read at the Salzburg Congress in 1924, I mentioned that when observations of coitus take place at a later stage of development they assume the character of traumata, but that if such experiences occur at an early age they become fixated and form part of the sexual development. I must now add that a fixation of this sort may hold in its grip not only that particular stage of development, but also the super-ego which is then in process of formation, and may thus injure its further development. For the more completely the super-ego reaches its zenith in the genital stage, the less prominent will be the sadistic identifications in its structure and the more likely will be the securing of mental health and the development of a personality on an ethically high level.

There is another kind of experience in early childhood which strikes me as typical and exceedingly important. These experiences often follow closely in time upon the observations of coitus and are induced or fostered by the excitations set up thereby. I refer to the sexual relations of little children with one another, between brothers and sisters or playmates, which consist in the most varied acts: looking, touching, performing excretion in common, fellatio, cunnilingus and often direct attempts at coitus. They are deeply repressed and have a cathexis of profound feelings of guilt. These feelings are mainly due to the fact that this love-object, chosen under the pressure of the excitation due to the Oedipus conflict, is felt by the child to be a substitute for the father or mother or both. Thus these relations, which seem so insignificant and which apparently no child under the stimulus of the Oedipus development escapes, take on the character of an Oedipus relation actually realized, and exercise a determining influence upon the formation of the Oedipus complex, the subject's detachment from that complex and upon his later sexual relations. Moreover, an experience of this sort forms an important fixation-point in the development of the super-ego. In consequence of the need for punishment and the repetition-compulsion, these experiences often cause the child to subject himself to sexual traumata. In this connection I would refer you to Abraham,[6] who showed that experiencing sexual traumata is one part of the sexual development of children. The analytic

[6] Karl Abraham, *Selected Papers*, International Psycho-Analytical Library, No. 13.

investigation of these experiences, during the analysis of adults as well as of children, to a great extent clears up the Oedipus situation in its connection with early fixations, and is therefore important from the therapeutic point of view.

To sum up my conclusions: I wish first of all to point out that they do not, in my opinion, contradict the statements of Professor Freud. I think that the essential point in the additional considerations which I have advanced is that I date these processes earlier and that the different phases (especially in the initial stages) merge more freely in one another than was hitherto supposed.

The early stages of the Oedipus conflict are so largely dominated by pregenital phases of development that the genital phase, when it begins to be active, is at first heavily shrouded and only later, between the third and fifth years of life, becomes clearly recognizable. At this age the Oedipus complex and the formation of the super-ego reach their climax. But the fact that the Oedipus tendencies begin so much earlier than we supposed, the pressure of the sense of guilt which therefore falls upon the pregenital levels, the determining influence thus exercised so early upon the Oedipus development on the one hand and that of the super-ego on the other, and accordingly upon character-formation, sexuality and all the rest of the subject's development—all these things seem to me of great and hitherto unrecognized importance. I found out the therapeutic value of this knowledge in the analyses of children, but it is not confined to these. I have been able to test the resulting conclusions in the analysis of adults and have found not only that their theoretical correctness was confirmed but that their therapeutic importance was established.

Origins of Love and Hate

IAN SUTTIE

(1952)

The following selection: "Benevolence, Altruism and Hedonism" is from Suttie's work *Origins of Love and Hate*. While the cornerstone of Freud's analysis of children is infantile sexuality, in Suttie's system it is "love." He believes that from the beginning "the germ of goodness or love" is present in the infant, though frustrated in its spontaneous benevolence by tradition. In attributing to the mother the significance in rearing that Freud attributed to the father, he follows Melanie Klein. The individual's development must overcome the anxiety about separation from one's mother produced by the child-rearing customs of our culture, particularly as we wean and toilet-train children. In social activities the individual seeks to restore or reincarnate the intimacy with his mother which he lost in infancy.

If we postulate the existence from infancy of a social need, then the "pilgrimage to maturity" assumes for us an aspect different from that which we obtain by looking backward from an anxious, competitive adulthood. The greed and hate, "the ape and the tiger within us," "original sin," proclaimed by Freudians and the theologians alike as characteristically human, appear as fictions of their own social maladjustments and of their "forced" or "false" maturation. In the beginning of life none of the transactions between mother and infant could be distinguished *by the latter* (even were it endowed with adult mind and power of expression) as "giving" or as "getting" in the sense of "losing" or "gaining." The mother gives the breast, certainly, but the infant *gives the mouth*, which is equally necessary to the *transaction* of suckling. The fact that there is a transfer of substances from the mother's to the child's body is immaterial to the child's mind, *if the milk comes "willingly."* It never thinks of this as "the mother's sacrifice" or feels under a burdensome obligation. (From now on I will use the word "gift" in a wide sense to cover not merely material offerings but also such "gifts" as approbation, attention, interest, etc.) There should be no conflict and even no separation of the "interests" of mother and child. Still less is it possible for the child to *offend* the mother; all its acts are absolutely acceptable; it is both "free" and "good" in a sense that has given rise to the myth of the golden age (though there may be some historical truth behind this) and has contributed much to the idea of Paradise, and the aspirations after Utopias.

In this ideal state anxiety is at a minimum and resentments are only transient. There is no abiding sense of insecurity or of grievance. But the exigencies of life itself—(for example the advent of a second baby), or of culture (e.g. cleanliness-training), or of civilization (e.g. the working mother who must leave her babies), interrupt this happy symbiotic relationship. The baby finds its acts *occasionally* unacceptable, and the mother's "gifts" to it conditional or even unpleasant. Until these conditions are understood and a satisfactory habit adjustment has been made, the infant must feel insecure and irritable.

The infant now appears to feel for the mother a mixture of love-longing, apprehension and anger that is called *ambivalence*. It is extremely uncomfortable because obviously none of these emotions can get free expression; even the enjoyment of suckling may be seriously interfered with. The "separation-anxiety" is in full force, and henceforth all effort (not directly concerned with survival and appetite-gratification) is devoted to "the Mastery of Anxiety." Freudians still talk as if this process were one of "resolution of endopsychic conflict," or even of an immunization to the feeling of anxiety, i.e. an acquired tolerance. They employ also the phrase "overcoming hate with love," which, since they believe hate to be a separate instinct, independent of love, must mean *repression*. This again seems inconsistent with their other view that life is a struggle to attain peace by the release of impulse (the so-called "detensioning function of the psyche" as expounded in "Beyond the Pleasure Principle"). These inconsistencies—as they appear to me—seem to arise because of the Freudians' obstinate determination to leave out of account social situations and hypothetical social motives. They wish to account for the whole process of mental development in terms of what goes on within the individual mind itself, with a minimum of reference to any stresses of adjustment between one mind and another and involving the interplay of both. I, on the contrary, would say that "mastering anxiety" and "overcoming hate with love" refer to the *situation* between the child and the mother and later to its substitute relationships with its whole social environment. The child's attempt is *primarily not* to secure an endopsychic adjustment of conflicting feelings, but to remove the *cause* of the anxiety and hate by restoring harmonious social relationships. When the social disagreement is removed the feeling rapport can *change back from anxiety and hate into love and security*, not "overcoming" the former by the latter, but *retransforming them into the latter*. The "release of impulse" *in some measure* is necessary to this; but the aim of the anxious psyche is not merely the peace and sensory, selfish gratification of self-expression by detumescence but the *direction of these pleasurable activities upon lines that will be acceptable to others* (i.e. responded to favorably) and the control of the resentments that are aroused by frustration. Thus purposes that might be called moral, or at least "guilt sensible," are present from the very beginning of directed behavior. It is true that infantile guilt cannot contain the elements of shame, remorse and pity, which characterize the adult consciousness of guilt. Primitively it is much more personal, more closely allied to anxiety, though tinged with grief and longing and tending more directly than anxiety to reconciliation. Thus I put a social interpretation upon these three processes, "mastery of anxiety," "overcoming hate with love" and "release of impulse," which Freudians regard as the characteristic master-motives of human mind. By so doing I not only overcome the inconsistency between these formulae themselves, showing how they are but different aspects of the same purpose (the love quest), but I avoid two fallacies which have seriously disturbed the development of Psychoanalytic theory. The first of these is already *admitted by them to have been an error*—namely, the idea that anxiety is nothing but frustrated sexual desire. The second—the theory of Death-aggressive Instinct—is admittedly a very unsatisfactory explanation of sadism and masochism (which is its only empirical justification), while it has caused serious dissensions among psychoanalysts themselves.

The social interpretation I put upon early child strivings, brings my view very much more closely in line with Adler's than with Freud's. I disagree with the former, however, in his view that the quest for power is a primary and universal

characteristic of human nature. I regard the struggle to ex-
cel as an *anxiety-reaction to a particular mode of upbringing*
and hence *contingent* upon certain cultural influences. I further consider that Adler's conceptions, like Freud's, are influenced by the materialistic and aggressive character of our
own tradition. They concentrate attention upon the material
services of which the child is deprived (or threatened to
be deprived) without regard to the probability that some of
these material services, e.g. washing, are accepted by the child
more in the light of a caress than as a practical utility. In
their emphasis upon "mastery" and "excelling" too, Adlerians
seem to accept the Freudian idea of aggressiveness and egoism
as fundamental, whereas I regard this as merely one mode,
and secondary at that, of recovering the sense of social security which is lost on the emergence from the unconditional
love of (indulged) infancy into disciplined childhood. I feel,
in fact, that both Freud and Adler accept the traditional
view that the child is a "bad" animal that is forced in its own
interests, by external threats and compulsions, to become "social" or "good." (The Adlerians of course do recognize a
"community feeling"; but I have seen no definition of this or
suggestion of its origin and genetic and other relationships to
other instincts.) I on my part have come to regard the desire to love, to give, and "to be good" or "co-operative" as
influencing the appetites from their very first thwartings.
Doubtless the tendency of this social feeling is, to begin with,
toward a continuance of infantile parasitism; but there is
neither greed nor malice, "the ape or the tiger," in this, for
the infant is helpless to give *in our material sense*. It has only
its pleasure and goodwill, and these it gives freely.

Be that as it may, it is not to be doubted that very early in
life the infant in our culture discovers that the benevolence
of others is whimsical or conditional and that its own gifts
in turn are apt to be criticized and rejected. This I call the
Crisis of Anxiety and I agree with Adler that the child's
"choice" of adaptation, its character, its "neurosis" (or, if any,
its "psychosis") depends upon the role in life which *at this
time* seems to it preferable to itself and more acceptable to
others.

Automatically, as a matter of its inborn constitution, the
child's frustrated social love turns to anxiety (at a later age it
may turn directly to guilt as the child feels it ought not to have
asked for what the mother has refused or offered what she

rejected), and then to hate if the frustration is sufficiently severe. But hate of a loved object (ambivalence) as I have said, is intolerable; the love relationship must be preserved as a matter of life or death, and there are various means of doing this. First, it may be done by the preservation of the lovability of the first loved object—the mother (see later). An alternative is to abandon the mother, *as she now appears in reality,* for the mother as she once appeared and as she is remembered. This involves the technique of *taking refuge from reality in fantasy,* to which reference has already been made. It is true that the child may seek a "good" substitute for the "bad" mother in the nurse or in the father; but toward this substitute the same demands will be put forward and the same struggle renewed. Yet it is true that to the progressive transference of dependency to others than the mother, the normal person owes much of his success. A fourth alternative is found in the Adlerian technique of power (or in possession), which involves aggression, coercion, anger and love-protests on the part of the child. These alternatives might be restated as imaginary explicit declarations of the child's own intentions by itself.

I. The *Preservation* of the lovableness of the mother. "Mother *is* good and kind; if she does not love me that is because *I* am bad." From this starting point is developed what is called by some people "inferiority complex." The ultimate extreme is "melancholia," where the patient has a sense of utter unworthiness. We find the same developmental motive in the Augustinian Theory that unbaptized infants go straight to Hell forever and that God is *right* to ordain this. On the other hand this feeling is the stimulus to idealisms and to the wish to become "what mother loves."

II. The *regression* to the pre-moral infancy might be expressed thus: "I *will* be a baby again, because mother is only kind to babies," or, as a variant, suggested by experience of illness in childhood, "Kiss it and make it well," or "Mother nurses sick people *like* babies."

The former *regression* (to babyhood) under fantasy leads to a great deal of infantility of character in adult life, and, where it involves the *complete turning away from reality,* we find the condition of Dementia Praecox which is responsible for the filling of perhaps one-third of all asylum accommodation. The lesser degree of regressiveness, namely the utilization of illness, its exaggeration or manufacture—produces hysterical invalidism. Here fantasy flourishes *but does not obscure reality*. The patient still craves and intrigues to obtain the attentions of *real* people, and does not withdraw into a dream world of her own.

III. The third technique of renouncing mother might be stated thus: *"You* are bad; I will get a better mother than you."* (The Paranoiac says in effect to his *social environment*, "You have denied me the rights I was born with, you hate and conspire against me, *I am good* and you are bad.")

It leads to the adoption (by the child) of the father as *the* parent, whereas he had previously had little significance. If it does not interfere with sexual attitude in the boy or produce excessive "father fixation" in the woman, it can be looked on as normal, as it ultimately leads on to the adoption of the whole social environment in lieu of mother.

IV. The fourth mode of dealing with the separation anxiety is that of seeking security by substituting the *power to exact* services for the spontaneous, "free," love of infancy. The child who adopts it might be imagined as saying, "You *must* love me or *fear* me; I will bite you and not love you until you do." "Delinquency" is largely a product of this technique, which, carried to its highest point, plays an important part in producing "Paranoia."

This disease is characterized by the retention of an excessive egoism and self-importance along with a suspicious and overbearing attitude toward other people. The paranoid combines the naïve egocentricity of the child with the arbitrary power and irresponsible privilege of the "bad" parent *as known to the child mind*. Apart from producing abnormality, however, it is true that the reliance upon power in lieu of love characterizes and perhaps vitiates our whole culture and tradition.

One other mechanism that operates at this early and critical phase of life is what is called "phobic substitution." Another is the impulse to earn love by *becoming what is wanted*. A particular form of phobic substitution has already been mentioned, namely the desire to exonerate the mother by condemning the self. Hate and fear, however, can be displaced in other ways from the loved object, for example, the whole blame may be put upon "the rival," perhaps the father or the younger baby. The more constructive way of earning love by becoming what is wanted is the strongest incentive to character development, though it is capable—*if directed by childish misunderstanding*—of producing lamentable results, e.g. of turning a girl into a would-be boy, or vice versa. The failure of other techniques for obtaining love leads to the defensive technique I have described as "tenderness taboo."

This account of the directing forces which start human development along so many different lines is much nearer an Adlerian than a Freudian interpretation. Freud considers that the whole vital force motivating appetite and social behavior alike is of a sexual nature—libido. At least he frequently writes in this sense, though occasionally and inconsistently he makes casual references to "ego instincts," love, etc.—conceptions to which, however, he gives no real functional place in his theory of mind—using them only as descriptive conveniences. Freud considers that the character of a person develops from his psycho-sexual attitude and that the form of his mental illness (if any) can be explained by the manner in which this diffuse and primitive sexual urge organizes and directs itself. At first, as I have already explained, it is imagined as directed upon the self in narcissism, later it is directed upon others as object love, but still with a view to the attainment of sensory or fantasy gratification or the avoidance of material danger. Libido is also supposed to undergo transformations *in its mode of expression.* To begin with, it is supposed to be dominated by *sucking* interests, or rather by sucking and then by biting. These are therefore called the Oral Phases. Next the libidinal development is dominated by excretory impulses, "expulsive" and "retentive," and this period is termed accordingly the Anal Phase—First and Second. By degrees genital feelings and impulses get control of the developing libido so that sexuality proper (as we know it and use the term) appears—the Phallic Phase.

On this theory of human development a certain amount of libido was supposed to remain arrested at each level of development, so that the resultant character was a composite of all these fixations. A heavy fixation at the first oral level is supposed to produce Dementia Praecox; if it occurs at the second oral, Melancholia results. Paranoia was due to this happening at the First Anal Phase and Obsessional Neurosis to fixation at the Second Anal. Hysterics were supposed to have reached the genital level, but not to have emerged into the normal object-choice of adult sexuality and so on. So little reason, however, could be given for incidence of these hypothetical "fixations" that they were supposed to be largely determined *by heredity.* Consequently the theory could neither *explain the mechanism of treatment* nor suggest any effective means of preventing these fixations. In fact it seems that analysts are just quietly allowing these conceptions to fall into disuse or at least into the background of theory, while laying more and more stress upon the *overcoming of separation-anxiety* as being the directing motive of human development (i.e. social purpose is tacitly displacing mechanistic cause as fundamental motive). Now I have suggested that this conception is only a clumsy psychological way of describing the child's efforts to retain or regain pleasant relations with the mother; that is to say separation-anxiety is merely the felt discomfort at an inadequate social adaptation. These supposed phases of libidinal development would then appear to be merely means of adjusting to the mother's demands in regard respectively to sucking and weaning, to excretory pleasures and prohibitions and finally to the growing prominence of genital feelings. The supposed "phases of libido development" on this view would *no longer* appear as stages determined by inborn forces in the same way as bodily development is determined. They would rather appear as *responses* on the child's part to a changing relationship between itself and the mother; and this relationship in turn is largely determined by the rearing customs imposed by culture and civilization. Character and mental disease would then appear not as the automatic expression of internal developmental forces operating with little regard to the environment, but as responses on the part of the mind to the social situation in which it finds itself.

This difference in theory is really highly characteristic of the different attitudes to life of Freud and Adler respectively. The former endeavors always to treat the indvidual as a self-contained and self-determining entity—the latter regards him always as dependent upon his society. That is to say, Adler, in contrast to Freud, always frames his explanations to account for a changing or strained rapport between the subject and some other person or persons. There can be no question but that in this matter Adler's conception of his problem is truer—less artificial—than that of Freud as the recent trend of Freudian theory is showing. My criticism of Adler is that, having stated his problem correctly, he does not push his inquiry more closely into the true nature and beginning of mind, but accepts the "competitive ego" and "community feeling" as universal and elemental—the starting point of all development and incapable of analysis—and henceforth confines himself to practical interests. He is in fact *wiser* than Freud but less scientific—less given to scrutinize supposedly fundamental conceptions.

It appears indisputable that an understanding of the nature, origin and relations of love and hate is the key not only to the interpretation of psychopathy and of individual character but to the understanding of culture. You will observe that in both the Freudian and the Adlerian theories, *the root-motive of human life is taken to be the "advantage of the individual."* While Adler explicitly allows the importance of "the other person," he sees the latter only as the "subject" or minister to the egoistic individual. For him socialization is a *keeping in check* of egoism, a restriction of self-assertion enforced from the outside (i.e. by the remonstrances of other people), not by any natural goodwill or altruism inherent in the individual. The conception of community feeling is only employed "ad hoc." Freud's outlook upon life is even more egocentric, since his idea of ultimate enjoyment (and hence purpose) is merely that of sense-gratification and the *exhaustion* of impulse. He also makes much of the power-quest; for him this is the attempt to recover the infantile omnipotence, the reduction of all other individuals to the service of the self. In the last resort, then, the philosophy of life of these two thinkers is agreed that the goal of life is self-assertion and self-seeking, limited only by fear of unpleasant consequences or retaliation. Both think gain is the essential appeal of the "reality-sense," that is to say the reason why it becomes an actual motive directing or inhibiting natural impulse.

It seems to me that an alternative view is possible—in fact, that we can turn this whole philosophy outside in and still use all its formulae with increased effect. Instead of seeking other peoples' love for the sake of the power it confers upon us of getting them to do things for us (i.e. making them our servants) it often comes to be the other way about. We get them to do things, perhaps needless things, for us in order to be assured of their love. That is to say, it is possible that we seek to influence, impress or please other people for the sake of demonstrating to ourselves that we are loved. In other words we seek power as a means to love (through neurotic anxiety), not love as a means to power. The primal state is not one of omnipotence, for omnipotence implies the consciousness of self as distinct from mother, which differentiation (as is known) cannot exist in early infancy. Prior to this differentiation of the self from the not-self, as I have shown, there can be no question of power, nor of a conflict of interest or wish nor any awareness of the distinction between gain or loss. The interactions between mother and infant are entirely pleasurable or unpleasurable and convey no sense of advantage or defeat to either side. Displeasure and anger therefore are not at this stage transformed into hates or grudges. Even after the differentiation has been made and the infant begins to know its mother as a separate, independent, being or agency, there are still *moments of reunion or at-one-ment in which interaction is in no way competitive*. In these moments there is no question of a "balance of trade" of benefits conferred or *obligations incurred*. It is not even *"more blessed to give than to receive,"* for every *gift is* in fact a gain; every transaction liquidates itself immediately; the baby is *solvent* and there is literally *no occasion* for anxiety. Power at this moment is as meaningless as *credits and debits*. There is no *criticism*, so that "goodness" and "badness" are nonexistent. This is the age (or the "moment") of innocence.

It is important to realize that the emergence from this paradise is not felt merely as the refusal of the mother to *give* the breast, caresses, attention, etc. Just as the original intercourse with the mother was at once both a giving and a getting without distinction between the two, so the anxious sense of separation seems to the infant as much a *rejection of its own gifts* as a refusal of the mother to give. The rejection of the child's "gifts," like any failure to make adequate response, leads to a sense of badness, unlovableness in the self, with melancholia as its culminating expression.

The refusal of the mother to give to the child leads to anxiety, hate, aggression (which Freud mistakes for a primary instinct), and the quest for power which Adler mistakes for an equally fundamental and inevitable characteristic of human nature. The abstraction of the *responsive state* of love into giving and getting, with a possible balance of gain and loss, is an artificiality of our anxiety-ridden minds which cannot get away from the analogy with *material transactions*. Both Freud and Adler appear to regard aggressive and even antipathetic feeling as welling up spontaneously within the individual irrespective of its environment. I regard it as a product of a particular relationship to environment, namely one of refusal *and rejection* by the mother or, more generally, nonresponsiveness. In practice the emergence from primitive infancy and the consequent anxiety and anger reactions may not be entirely avoidable, but there is no doubt from a comparison of upbringing and its results under different culture conditions that it is variable within wide limits.

Now many people would argue that it makes no difference whether we regard aggressiveness and antagonism as inherent in human nature (as supposed by Freud and Adler), or whether we regard it as merely a *potentiality, evoked by almost inevitable circumstances.* In any case (they would argue) it *will* appear, and in any case it does so because man is born with the capacity for reacting in this way. This is quite true, but it is always necessary to have our *theory* correct, irrespective of whether *we can* see at present that it makes any *practical* difference or not. I think further that it does make both practical and theoretical differences (even in the present state of our knowledge), whether we regard aggressiveness as an *appetite* like hunger, which must assert itself in all circumstances in response to *internal* processes, or as a merely *reflex response* like fear which (theoretically) need never have been evoked at all as it is contingent upon environmental stimuli.

As an example of the difference it makes to assume a primary appetite of aggression I would say that this assumption has led Freud to accept hatred and violence as inevitable, and to suppose that the wisest possible human policy can do no better than find socially harmless targets for this unavoidable hatred. The same philosophy of life has led Adler to feel that the baby must be forced into "co-operation from the earliest possible moment," so that I suggested to him (without evoking any protest on his part) that his ideal of upbringing was that the child should receive the minimum of unconditional love which was compatible with its survival! In other words he would introduce the child to the anxiety of *conditional* love at the earliest possible moment. Both Freud and Adler therefore regard the infant as "bad" by nature and as having to be made "good" or "social" by external compulsion, or else allowed outlet for its badness. I considered that the germ of goodness or of love is in the individual (of every species which has evolved a nurtured infancy) from the very beginning, and that our traditional method of upbringing frustrates this spontaneous benvolence and substitutes a "guilt-anxiety" morality for natural goodness. I consider further that the traditional attitude is so deeply ingrained in Freud and Adler's outlook on life that they cannot admit the existence of love as other than a prudent avoidance of the anger of others. Theoretical results of these views will be further considered in the chapters on Psychotherapy, etc.

I hope, therefore, you will be willing to try out the supposition that the infant brings the power and will to love with it; and that, even in the separation-anxiety and angry protests, it pursues one or other of two courses,—either it aims to recover that love rapport in which there was no competition, no grudging, no suspicion, no balancing of advantage and disadvantage; or on the other hand it renounces the pursuit of this kind of spontaneous love relationship for the substitute one of power. These are the two strands of development, the latter of which has almost exclusively absorbed the attention of Freud and Adler. I call them "strands," for both aims are present in the thread of life from the first moment of self-consciousness. They do not lead toward different goals as do those to which reference has already been made. On the one hand we have the "strand" or factor of egoistic dominance, which mainly occupies psychoanalytic attention, on the other hand we have the attempt to overcome anxiety, not by gaining power over the love object, but by restoring reciprocal relations with its object; not by enforcing claims but by making oneself lovable. It is true that Freud now and then refers to the morality-enforcing fear as "fear of losing love"; but it is only very slowly that this social point of view is affecting the originally individualistic standpoint of Analytic Psychology.

The baby then not only starts life with a benevolent attitude, but the Need-to-Give continues as a dominant motive throughout life, and, like every other need, brings anxiety when it is frustrated. Our adult, grudging, materialistic minds have decided that the baby gets the best of the partnership with the mother, and we talk of the mother's sacrifice! The mother-child relationship however (to the child's mind) is a true, "balanced," Symbiosis; and the *need to give* is as vital, therefore, as the *need to get*. The feeling that our gifts (love) are not acceptable is as intolerable as the feeling that others' gifts are no longer obtainable. Yet one or other of these two feelings may dominate an individual life. The former feeling (of unwantedness) plays a dominant part in anxiety and frustration symptoms, the latter likewise contributes to aggression. To some extent the two anxiety ridden impulses might be respectively equated with the "repressor" and the "repressed," so that the process of psychotherapy appears from the point of view as nothing but the *overcoming of the barriers to loving and feeling oneself loved,* and not as the removal of fear-

imposed inhibitions to the expression of innate, anti-social, egoistic and sensual desires.

Cleanliness and Ethics

In our culture one of the most important (because earliest
enforced) adaptations is that to cleanliness, etc. Interference
with evacuatory impulses has most important repercussions
both upon interest development and upon social-moral attitudes. Of course this field has been systematically explored
by psychoanalysts (notably E. Jones in this country), but, I
consider, with a prepossession attributing greater importance
to sensual values than to associative needs, and with an insufficient appreciation of the significance of the priority in development of this adaptation over that concerned with genital taboos.

The baby feeds because it must—it has no option of long
delay. It feeds to please and satisfy itself; and normally its
feeding is uniformly encouraged by those in contact with it.
With the evacuatory function it is different in two respects.
The baby has a certain choice and control; and the exercise of this volition early affects the reactions of those who
are "training" it. Here then is its *first* experience of power—
and that power the all-important one of pleasing or displeasing.
With that sense of power and significance comes also the rudi-
ment of responsibility, anxiety and hostility. This experience
first elevated the infant into a moral being open to reward or
blame. The earlier experiences of power—the "magic cries"
and gestures of Freud, are subjectively I believe more automatic techniques than this; they are not based upon a clear perception of the difference between "the self" and "the others";
they belong to the "solipsist" phase, and are therefore not
concerned with the love (or hate) of others.

I do not think that at this stage the infant has a sense of
pride or of "property" in his evacuations, nor do I attribute
the same significance as most Freudians to the sensory gratification or "creative significance" of the act as affecting the
child's *primary* interest in excreta. If we take the view—to
which I have no objection—that these are the first "property"
and incentive to possession then we must also admit (as I
have argued elsewhere) that in our culture the Institution of
Property is social (i.e. other-regarding) *ab initio*—in other
words that individual possessions were not only to use and
enjoy but *to give away to* or withhold from others.

It is difficult for anyone but a nurse or a practicing psycho-therapist to realize the importance to the infant of these functions, which for us have become so much a matter of course and so little a matter of pleasure, reflection or *serious* discussion. Yet we ought to remember the smallness of the baby's world in which quite a little matter may loom large. We ought to remember that these are *first* impressions of life and the *foundation* therefore of organized experience. The only infantile experience of comparable sensory and affective value is that of feeding *which is followed by sleep*. Evacuation is much more a waking function and is followed by *washing*, etc., an experience which must convey the most vivid possible realization of the separate existence and independent activities of *other people*.

We are naturally averse to allowing such significance in mental development to a function which plays so little part in *our* social, cultural and economic system. Yet, without postulating repression, we can account for the difference between adult and (alleged) infantile interests very clearly. There is no "hush hush" convention in the early rearing. The "good" nurse or mother is not merely tolerant; she is genuinely interested in these functions and freely shows anxiety and approval to the child, *never* disgust for the legitimate function. There is nothing to suggest to the child that the mother's interest in these matters at this period is not equal to (and on some occasions greater than) its own, or that it has any radically disapproving quality. How could the child imagine any aesthetic-conventional ideals superior to its mother's?

But a change takes place in the mother's attitude, a change which—if too sudden and unexplained—is shattering to the infant's confidence in what it has learned and to its feelings of importance to other people. The mother professes disgust for the very functions upon which the infant had relied to hold and cultivate her liking. This change in the very basis of the child's love-worthiness as felt by itself, must be shattering to its confidence (*a*) in other people, and (*b*) in its own acceptability to them. This is the "crisis of anxiety."

Summing up, we may say that cleanliness training and washing are therefore more important factors in the development of social disposition and interest than even feeding for the following reasons:

(1) Evacuation is critical, orgastic in fact, whereas feeding brings a *gradual* detention of hunger.

(2) Evacuation is followed by the interesting and sensual experience of handling, washing, attention, and, to begin with, by approval. Feeding, by contrast, is not accompanied by attention to the outside world (which indeed is all but invisible during feeding) and further it leads quietly and insensibly to sleep and not to the vivid waking experience of washing.

(3) As a rule, until weaning, the breast is always given willingly, whereas in our culture the maternal attitude to excreta is more equivocal, and the baby must feel her original appreciation change into intolerance—which must be anxiety-provoking in the highest degree.

(4) In the matter of suckling the baby has little power to choose; hunger drives effectively, or death eliminates the recalcitrant. The experience of maternal pleasure-displeasure however can teach it sphincter-control quite early, and this control affords the *very first experience of social power*. With this (limited and, to begin with, uncertain) power of affecting other people's *favor* expressions, there must go a sense of responsibility. Love is no longer unconditional, but it is "up to" the baby itself to "earn" it. Food as stated in (3) is never conditional in this sense until the period of sweet-giving or withholding.

For all these reasons I judge the functions of excretion to have an enormous influence on the very foundation of (social) character. This in no way denies the sensual significance of the functions, called "anal" and "urethral" erotisms by the Freudians; but it does shift the main emphasis from its organic and sensual meaning to its *social* significance.

Psychic Conflicts in a Child

CARL JUNG

(1916)

The following paper by Carl Jung, the Swiss psychiatrist, is the case history of a little girl's enlightenment about the act of birth. It is interesting to compare Anna's conflicts, fantasies, dreams and awareness with those of Little Hans in Freud's "Analysis of a Phobia in a Five-year-old Boy," the famous case in which a small boy was cured of his fear that a horse—which symbolized his father—would castrate him. Jung concludes that children seek more than clear, factual answers to their questions about sex. The biological facts do not totally gratify their sense of mystery and wonder about birth. Characteristically Jungian is the speculation here that fairy tales are childhood's equivalent to myth: the child is a mythmaker, among whose myths are those concerning sexual processes.

About the time when Freud published his report on the case of "Little Hans,"[1] I received from a father who was acquainted with psychoanalysis a series of observations concerning his little daughter, then four years old.

These observations have so much that bears upon, and supplements, Freud's report on "Little Hans" that I cannot refrain from making this material accessible to a wider public. The widespread incomprehension, not to say indignation, with which "Little Hans" was greeted, was for me an additional reason for publishing my material, although it is nothing like as extensive as that of "Little Hans." Nevertheless, it contains points which seem to confirm how typical the case of "Little Hans" is. So-called "scientific" criticism, so far as it has taken any notice at all of these important matters, has once more proved overhasty, seeing that people have still not learned first to examine and then to judge.

[1] "Analysis of a Phobia in a Five-year-old Boy," *Collected Papers*, Vol. III (London, 1925; first published in 1909).

The little girl to whose sagacity and intellectual sprightliness we are indebted for the following observations is a healthy, lively child of emotional temperament. She has never been seriously ill, nor had she ever shown any trace of "nervous" symptoms.

Livelier systematic interests awakened in the child about her third year; she began to ask questions and to spin wishful fantasies. In the report which now follows we shall, unfortunately, have to give up the idea of a consistent exposition, for it is made up of anecdotes which treat of one isolated experience out of a whole cycle of similar ones, and which cannot, therefore, be dealt with scientifically and systematically, but must rather take the form of a story. We cannot dispense with this mode of exposition in the present state of our psychology, for we are still a long way from being able in all cases to separate with unerring certainty what is curious from what is typical.

When the child, whom we will call Anna, was about three years old, she had the following conversation with her grandmother:

"Granny, why are your eyes so dim?"

"Because I am old."

"But you will become young again?"

Oh dear, no. I shall become older and older, and then I shall die."

"And what then?"

"Then I shall be an angel."

"And then you will be a baby again?"

The child found here a welcome opportunity for the provisional solution of a problem. For some time she had been in the habit of asking her mother whether she would ever have a real live doll, a baby brother, which naturally gave rise to the question of where babies come from. As such questions were asked quite spontaneously and unobtrusively, the parents attached no significance to them, but responded to them as lightly as the child herself seemed to ask them. Thus one day she was told the pretty story that children are brought by the stork. Anna had already heard somewhere a slightly more serious version, namely that children are little angels who live in heaven and are then brought down by the said stork. This theory seems to have become the point of departure for the little one's investigating activities. From the conversation with the grandmother it could be seen that this theory was capable of wide application; for it solved in a comforting manner not only the painful thought of dying, but at the same time the riddle of where children come from. Anna seemed to be saying to herself: "When somebody dies he becomes an angel, and then he becomes a child." Solutions of this sort, which kill at least two birds with one stone, used to be tenaciously adhered to even in science, and cannot be undone in the child's mind without a certain amount of shock. In this simple conception there lie the seeds of the reincarnation theory, which, as we know, is still alive today in millions of human beings.[2]

Just as the birth of a little sister was the turning point in the history of "Little Hans," so in this case it was the arrival of a baby brother, which took place when Anna had reached the age of four. The problem of where children come from, hardly touched upon so far, now became topical. The mother's pregnancy had apparently passed unnoticed; that is to say, Anna had never made any observations on this subject. On the evening before the birth, when labor pains were just beginning, the child found herself in her father's room. He took her on his knee and said, "Tell me, what would you say if you got a little brother tonight?" "I would kill him," was the prompt answer. The expression "kill" looks very alarming, but in reality it is quite harmless, for "kill" and "die" in child language only mean to "get rid of," either actively or passively, as has already been pointed out a number of times by Freud. I once had to treat a fifteen-year-old girl who, under analysis, had a recurrent association, and kept on thinking of Schiller's "Song of the Bell." She had never really read the poem, but had once glanced through it, and could only remember something about a cathedral tower. She could recall no further details. The passage goes:

> From the tower
> The bell-notes fall
> Heavy and sad
> For the funeral. . . .
> Alas it is the wife and mother,
> Little wife and faithful mother,
> Whom the dark prince of the shadows
> Snatches from her spouse's arms. . . .

[2] In the light of Professor Jung's later researches these theories can be understood as based upon the archetype of rebirth, in the unconscious. Several other examples of archetypal activity are to be found in this essay.—JUNG'S EDITORS

She naturally loved her mother dearly and had not thought of her death, but on the other hand the present position was this: she had to go away with her mother for five weeks, staying with relatives; the year before, the mother had gone by herself, and the daughter (an only and spoiled child) was left at home alone with her father. Unfortunately this year it was the "little wife" who was being snatched from the arms of her spouse, whereas the daughter would greatly have preferred the "faithful mother" to be parted from her child.

On the lips of a child, therefore, "kill" is a perfectly harmless expression, especially when one knows that Anna used it quite promiscuously for all possible kinds of destruction, removal, demolition, etc. All the same this tendency is worth noting. (Compare the analysis of "Little Hans.")

The birth occurred in the early morning. When all traces of the birth had been removed, together with the bloodstains, the father went into the room where Anna slept. She awoke as he entered. He told her the news of the arrival of a little brother, which she took with a surprised and tense expression on her face. The father then picked her up and carried her into the bedroom. Anna threw a rapid glance at her rather wan-looking mother and then displayed something like a mixture of embarrassment and suspicion, as if thinking, "What's going to happen now?" She evinced hardly any pleasure at the sight of the new arrival, so that the cool reception she gave it caused general disappointment. For the rest of the morning she kept very noticeably away from her mother; this was the more striking, as normally she was always hanging around her. But once, when her mother was alone, she ran into the room, flung her arms round her neck and whispered hurriedly, "Aren't you going to die now?"

Something of the conflict in the child's soul is now revealed to us. The stork theory had obviously never caught on properly, but the fruitful rebirth hypothesis undoubtedly had, according to which a person helps a child into life by dying. Mama ought therefore to die. Why, then, should Anna feel any pleasure over the new arrival, of whom she was beginning to feel childishly jealous anyway? Hence, she had to assure herself at a favorable opportunity whether Mama was going to die or not. Mama did not die. With this happy issue, however, the rebirth theory received a severe setback. How was it now possible to explain little brother's birth and the origins of children in general? There still remained the stork theory, which, though never expressly rejected, had been implicitly waived in favor of the rebirth hypothesis.[3] The next attempts at explanation unfortunately remained hidden from the parents, as the child went to stay with her grandmother for a few weeks. From the latter's report, however, it appears that the stork theory was much discussed, there being of course a tacit agreement to support it.

When Anna returned home she again displayed, on meeting her mother, the same mixture of embarrassment and suspicion as after the birth. The impression was quite explicit to both parents, though not explicable. Her behavior toward the baby was very nice. Meantime a nurse had arrived, who made a deep impression on little Anna with her uniform—an extremely negative impression at first, as she evinced the greatest hostility toward her in all things. Thus nothing would induce her to let herself be undressed in the evenings and put to bed by this nurse. The reason for this resistance soon became clear in a stormy scene by the bedside of the little brother, when Anna shouted at the nurse, "That's not your little brother, he is mine!" Gradually, however, she became reconciled to the nurse and began to play nurse herself; she had to have her white cap and apron, nursing her little brother and and her dolls in turn. In contrast to her former mood the present one was unmistakably elegiac and dreamy. She often sat for hours crouched under the table singing long stories to herself and making rhymes, partly incomprehensible, but consisting partly of wishful fantasies on the "nurse" theme ("I am a nurse of the green cross"), and partly of distinctly painful feelings which were struggling for expression.

Here we meet with an important new feature in the little one's life: reveries, the first stirrings of poetry, moods of an elegiac strain—all of them things which are usually to be met

[3] One might ask at this point why one is justified in supposing at all that children of this age worry their heads about such theories. The answer is that children are intensely interested in all the sensuously perceptible things going on around them. This also shows itself in the well-known endless questions concerning the why and wherefore of everything. One has to put off the dun-colored spectacles of our culture for a moment if one wants to understand the psychology of a child. For everybody the birth of a child is quite the most important event there can possibly be. For our civilized thinking, however, birth has lost much of its biological uniqueness, just as sex has done. But somewhere or other the mind must have stored up the correct biological valuations impressed upon it all through the ages. What could be more probable than that the child still has these valuations and makes no bones about showing them, before civilization spreads like a pall over his primitive thinking?

with only at a later phase of life, at a time when the youth or maiden is preparing to sever the family tie, to step forth into life as an independent person, but is still inwardly held back by aching feelings of homesickness for the warmth of the family hearth. At such a time they begin weaving poetic fancies in order to compensate for what is lacking. To approximate the psychology of a four-year-old to that of the boy or girl approaching puberty may at first sight seem paradoxical; the affinity lies, however, not in the age but in the mechanism. The elegiac reveries express the fact that part of the love which formerly belonged, and should belong, to a real object, is now *introverted,* that is, it is turned inward into the subject and there produces an increased fantasy activity.[4] Whence comes this introversion? Is it a psychological manifestation peculiar to this period, or does it come from a conflict?

On this point the following episode is enlightening. Anna disobeyed her mother more and more often, saying insolently, "I shall go back to Granny!"

"But I shall be sad if you leave me."

"Ah, but you've got baby brother."

The mother's reaction shows us what the child was really getting at with her threats to go away again: she obviously wanted to hear what her mother would say to her proposal, what her attitude was in general, and whether the little brother had not ousted her altogether from her mother's affection. One must not, however, fall for this transparent piece of trickery. The child could see and feel perfectly well that she was not stinted of anything essential in her mother's love, despite the existence of her baby brother. The veiled reproach she levels at her mother on that score is therefore unjustified, and to the trained ear this is betrayed by the slightly affected tone of voice. One often hears similar tones even with grown-up people. Such a tone, which is quite unmistakable, does not expect to be taken seriously and obtrudes itself all the

---

[4] This process is altogether typical. When life comes up against an obstacle, so that no adaptation can be achieved and the transference of libido to reality is suspended, then an introversion takes place. That is to say, instead of the libido working toward reality there is an increased fantasy activity which aims at removing the obstacle, or at least removing it in fantasy, and this may in time lead to a practical solution. Hence the exaggerated sexual fantasies of neurotics, who in this way try to overcome their specific repression; hence also the typical fantasy of stammerers, that they really possess a great talent for eloquence. (That they have some claims in this respect is brought home to us by Alfred Adler's thoughtful studies on organ inferiority.)

more forcibly for that reason. Nor should the reproach be taken to heart by the mother, for it is merely the forerunner of other and this time more serious resistances. Not long after the conversation narrated above, the following scene took place:

Mother: "Come, we'll go into the garden."

Anna: "You're lying to me. Watch out if you're not telling the truth!"

Mother: "What are you thinking of? Of course I'm telling the truth."

Anna: "No, you are not telling the truth."

Mother: "You'll soon see whether I'm telling the truth: we are going into the garden this minute."

Anna: "Is that true? You're quite sure it's true? You're not lying?"

Scenes of this kind were repeated a number of times. But this time the tone was more vehement and insistent, and also the accent on the word "lie" betrayed something special which the parents did not understand; indeed they attributed far too little significance at first to the child's spontaneous utterances. In this they were only doing what all official education does. We do not usually listen to children at any stage of their careers; in all the essentials we treat them as *non compos mentis* and in all the unessentials they are drilled to the perfection of automatons. Behind resistances there always lies a question, a conflict, of which we hear soon enough at another time and on another occasion. But usually we forget to connect the thing heard with the resistances. Thus, on another occasion, Anna faced her mother with the awkward questions:

"I want to be a nurse when I grow up."

"That's what I wanted to be when I was a child."

"Why aren't you a nurse, then?"

"Well, because I am a mother instead, and so I have children of my own to nurse."

Anna (thoughtfully): "Shall I be a different woman from you? Shall I live in a different place? Shall I still talk with you?"

The mother's answer again shows where the child's question was leading.[5] Anna would obviously like to have a child to

[5] The somewhat paradoxical view that the aim of the child's question is to be sought in the mother's answer requires a little discussion. It is one of the greatest of Freud's services to psychology that he opened up again the whole questionableness of *conscious* motives. One consequence of repressing the instincts is that the importance of conscious

nurse, just as the nurse has. Where the nurse got the child from is quite clear, and Anna could get a child in the same way when she grew up. Why then wasn't Mama such a nurse —that is, how did she get the child if she didn't get it in the same way as the nurse? Anna could get a child just as the nurse had done, but how all that was going to be different in the future, or rather how she was going to be like her mother in the matter of getting children, was not so easy to see. Hence the thoughtful question "Shall I be a different woman from you?" Shall I be different in every way? The stork theory is evidently no good, the dying theory no less so, therefore one gets a child as the nurse, for example, got hers. In this natural way she, too, could get one; but how about the mother, who is no nurse and yet has children? Looking at the matter from this angle, Anna asks, "Why aren't you a nurse?"—meaning: why haven't you got your child in the plain, straightforward, natural way? This strangely indirect mode of interrogation is typical and may be connected with the child's hazy grasp of the problem, unless we are to assume a certain "diplomatic vagueness" prompted by a desire to evade direct questioning. Later we shall find evidence of this possibility.

Anna is therefore confronted with the question "Where does the child come from?" The stork did not bring it; Mama did not die; nor did Mama get it in the same way as the nurse. She has, however, asked this question before and was informed by her father that the stork brings the children; but this is definitely not so, she has never been deceived on this point. Therefore Papa and Mama and all the others lie. This readily explains her mistrustful attitude at the birth and the reproaches leveled against her mother. But it also explains another point, namely the elegiac reveries which we have attributed to a partial introversion. We now know the real object from which love had to be withdrawn and introverted for lack of an aim: it was withdrawn from the parents who deceived her and refused to tell her the truth. (What can this be which must not be uttered? What goes on here? Such are the parenthetic questions which the child later formulated to her-

---

thinking for action is boundlessly overestimated. According to Freud, the criterion for the psychology of the act is not the conscious motive, but the *result* of the act (the result being evaluated not physically but psychologically). This view sets the act in a new and biologically revealing light. I refrain from examples and shall content myself with observing that this view is extremely valuable for psychoanalysis both in principle and as regards interpretation.

self. Answer: It must be something that needs hushing up, perhaps something dangerous.) Attempts to make the mother talk and to draw out the truth by means of artful questions were futile, so resistance meets with resistance and the introversion of love begins. Naturally the capacity for sublimation in a four-year-old child is still too meagerly developed for it to render more than symptomatic service; hence she has to rely on another compensation, that is, she resorts to one of the already abandoned infantile devices for securing love by force, preferably that of crying and calling the mother at night. This had been diligently practiced and exploited during her first year. It now returns and, in keeping with her age, has become well motivated and equipped with recent impressions.

We should mention that the Messina earthquake had just occurred, and this event was much discussed at table. Anna was extraordinarily interested in everything to do with it, getting her grandmother to tell her over and over again how the earth shook and the houses tumbled down and how many people lost their lives. That was the beginning of her nocturnal fears; she could not be left alone, her mother had to go to her and stay with her, otherwise she was afraid that the earthquake would come and the house fall in and kill her. By day, too, she was intensely occupied with such thoughts; when out walking with her mother she would pester her with such questions as "Will the house be standing when we get home? Will Papa still be alive? Are you sure there's no earthquake at home?" At every stone in the road she would ask whether it was from the earthquake. A house under construction was a house destroyed by the earthquake, and so on. Finally she used to cry out at night that the earthquake was coming, she could hear it rumbling. Every evening she had to be solemnly promised that no earthquake would come. Various ways of calming her were tried, for instance she was told that earthquakes only occur where there are volcanoes. But then she had to be satisfied that the mountains surrounding the town were not volcanoes. This reasoning gradually led the child to an intense and, at her age, unnatural craving for knowledge, until finally all the geological pictures and atlases had to be fetched from her father's library. For hours she would rummage through them looking for pictures of volcanoes and earthquakes, and asking endless questions.

We see here an energetic attempt being made to sublimate fear into a desire for knowledge, which strikes us as decidedly premature at this age. But how many gifted children, suffering from exactly the same problem, do we not see being spoon-fed on this untimely sublimation, and by no means to their advantage. For if one fosters sublimation at this age one is only strengthening a neurosis. The root of the child's desire for knowledge is fear, and the fear is the expression of converted libido, that is, of an introversion that has become neurotic and is neither necessary nor favorable to the development of the child at this age. Where this desire for knowledge is ultimately leading is made clear by a series of questions which arose almost daily: "Why is Sophie [a younger sister] younger than I? Where was Freddie [her little brother] before? Was he in heaven and what was he doing there? Why did he only come down now, why not before?"

Such being the state of affairs, the father decided that the mother ought to tell the child the truth about her little brother at the first favorable opportunity.

This presented itself when, soon afterward, Anna again inquired about the stork. Her mother told her that the story of the stork was not true, but that Freddie grew inside his mother as the flower grows out of the earth. At first he was very little, and then he grew bigger and bigger like a plant. The child listened attentively without the least surprise and then asked:

"But did he come all by himself?"

"Yes."

"But he can't walk yet!"

Sophie: "Then he crawled out."

Anna (overhearing Sophie's remark): "Is there a hole here" —pointing to her chest—"or did he come out of the mouth? Who came out of the nurse?"

At this point she interrupted herself and exclaimed, "No, I know the stork brought him down from heaven!" Then, before the mother could answer her questions, she dropped the subject and again asked to see pictures of volcanoes. The evening following this conversation was calm. The sudden explanation had evidently produced in the child a whole chain of ideas, which announced themselves in a spate of questions. New and unexpected vistas were opened, and she rapidly approached the main problem: "Where did the baby come out? Was it from a hole in the chest or from the mouth?" Both suppositions qualify as acceptable theories. We even meet with young married women who still entertain the theory of the hole in the abdominal wall or of Caesarean section; this is supposed to betray a very unusual degree of innocence. As a matter of

fact it is not innocence; in such cases we are practically always dealing with infantile sexual activities which in later life
have brought the *vias naturales* into ill repute.

It may be asked where the child got the absurd idea that
there is a hole in the chest, or that the birth takes place
through the mouth. Why did she not pick on one of the natural
openings in the pelvis, from which things come out daily? The
explanation is simple. It was not so very long since our little
one had challenged all the educative arts of her mother by her
heightened interest in both these openings and their remarkable
products—an interest not always in accord with the demands
of cleanliness and decorum. Then for the first time she became acquainted with the exceptional laws relating to these
bodily regions and, being a sensitive child, she soon noticed
that there was something taboo about them. Consequently
this region had to be left out of her calculations, a trivial
error of thought which may be forgiven in a child when one
considers all those people who, despite the most powerful
spectacles, can never see anything sexual anywhere. In this
matter Anna reacted far more docilely than her little sister,
whose scatological interests and achievements were certainly
phenomenal and who even misbehaved in that way at table.
She invariably described her excesses as "funny," but Mama
said no, it was not funny, and forbade such fun. The child
seemed to take these incomprehensible educational sallies in
good part, but she soon had her revenge. Once when a new
dish appeared on the table she categorically refused to have
anything to do with it, remarking that it was "not funny."
Thereafter all culinary novelties were declined on the ground
that they were "not funny."

The psychology of this negativism is quite typical and is
not hard to fathom. The logic of feeling says simply: "If you
don't find my little tricks funny and make me give them up,
then I won't find your tricks funny either, and won't play
with you." Like all childish compensations of this kind, this
works on the important infantile principle "It serves you right
when I'm hurt."

After this digression, let us return to our theme. Anna had
merely shown herself docile and had so adjusted herself to
the cultural demands that she thought (or at least spoke) of
the simplest things last. The incorrect theories that have
been substituted for the correct ones sometimes persist for
years, until brusque enlightenment comes from without. It is

therefore no wonder that such theories, the formation of and adherence to which is favored even by parents and educationists, should later become determinants of important symptoms in a neurosis, or of delusions in a psychosis, as I have shown in my "Psychology of Dementia Praecox."[6] Things that have existed in the psyche for years always remain somewhere, even though they may be hidden under compensations of a seemingly different nature.

But even before the question is settled as to where the child actually comes out a new problem obtrudes itself: children come out of Mama, but how about the nurse? Did someone come out of her too? Then follows the abrupt exclamation, "No, I know the stork brought him down from heaven!" What is there so peculiar about the fact that nobody came out of the nurse? We recall that Anna has identified herself with the nurse and plans to become a nurse later, for she too would like to have a child, and she could get one just as easily as the nurse had done. But now, when it is known that little brother grew in Mama, what is to be done?

This disquieting question is averted by a quick return to the stork-angel theory, which had never really been believed and which after a few trials is definitely abandoned. Two questions, however, remain in the air. The first is: where does the child come out? and the second, a considerably more difficult one: how is it that Mama has children while the nurse and the servants do not? Neither question is asked for the time being.

The next day at lunch, Anna announced, apparently out of the blue, "My brother is in Italy and has a house made of cloth and glass and it doesn't fall down."

Here always it was impossible to ask for an explanation; the resistances were too great, and Anna would not have let herself be pinned down. This unique and rather officious announcement is very significant. For some three months the children had been spinning a stereotyped fantasy of a "big brother" who knew everything, could do everything, and had everything. He had been to all the places where they had not been, was allowed to do all the things they were not allowed to do, was the owner of enormous cows, horses, sheep, dogs, etc.[7] Each of them had such a big brother. The source of this fantasy is not far to seek: its model is the father, who

[6] *Coll. Works,* Vol. 3.
[7] This is a primitive definition of God.

seems to be rather like a brother to Mama. So the children too must have an equally powerful brother. This brother is very brave, he is at present in dangerous Italy and lives in an impossibly fragile house which does not fall down. For the child this is an important wish-fulfillment: the earthquake is no longer dangerous. In consequence the fear and anxiety were banished and did not return. The fear of earthquakes now entirely disappeared. Instead of calling her father to her bedside every evening to conjure away the fear, she now became more affectionate and begged him to kiss her good night. In order to test this new state of affairs, the father showed her more pictures of volcanoes and earthquakes, but Anna remained indifferent and examined the pictures coldly: "Dead people! I've seen all that before." Even the photograph of a volcanic eruption no longer held any attractions for her. Thus all her scientific interest collapsed and vanished as suddenly as it had come. However, during the days that followed her enlightenment Anna had more important matters to attend to, for she had her newly found knowledge to disseminate among her circle of acquaintances. She began by recounting, at great length, how Freddie had grown in Mama, and herself and her younger sister likewise; how Papa grew in *his* mother and Mama in *her* mother, and the servants in their respective mothers. By dint of numerous questions she also tested whether her knowledge was firmly founded in truth, for her suspicions had been aroused in no small degree, so that repeated corroboration was needed to dissipate all her misgivings. In between times the children brought up the stork-angel theory again, but in a less believing tone, and even lectured the dolls in a singsong voice.

The new knowledge, however, obviously held its ground, for the phobia did not return.

Only once did her certainty threaten to go to pieces. About a week after the enlightenment her father had to spend the morning in bed with an attack of influenza. The children knew nothing of this, and Anna, coming into her parents' bedroom, saw the unexpected sight of her father lying in bed. She made an oddly surprised face, remained standing far away from the bed, and would not come nearer, evidently feeling shy and mistrustful again. Suddenly she burst out with the question "Why are you in bed? Have you got a plant in your inside too?"

Naturally her father had to laugh, and assured her that children never grew in their fathers, that as a matter of fact men did not have children, but only women, whereupon the child instantly became friendly again. But though the surface was calm the problems went on working in the depths. A few days later Anna again announced at lunch, "I had a dream last night about Noah's Ark." The father then asked her what she had dreamed, to which Anna only let out a stream of nonsense. In such cases one must simply wait and pay attention. Sure enough, after a few minutes Anna said to her grandmother, "I had a dream last night about Noah's Ark and there were lots of little animals in it." Another pause. Then she began the story for the third time: *"I had a dream last night about Noah's Ark and there were lots of little animals in it and underneath there was a lid which opened and all the little animals fell out."* Knowledgeable persons will understand the fantasy. The children really did have a Noah's Ark, but the opening, a lid, was in the roof and not underneath. This is a delicate hint that the story about children being born from the mouth or chest was wrong, and that she had a pretty good idea of where they did come out—namely, from underneath.

Several weeks now passed without any noteworthy occurrences. There was one dream: *"I dreamed about Papa and Mama, they were sitting up late in the study and we children were there too."*

On the face of it this is just the well-known wish of children to be allowed to stay up as long as the parents. This wish is here realized, or rather it is used to mask a much more important wish, the wish to be present in the evenings when the parents are alone, and—naturally and innocently enough— in the *study* where she had seen all those interesting books and had satisfied her thirst for knowledge. In other words, she was really seeking an answer to the burning question of where little brother came from. If the children were there they would find out.

A few days later Anna had a nightmare, from which she awoke screaming. "The earthquake is coming, the house is beginning to shake!" Her mother went to her and comforted her, saying that there was no earthquake, everything was quiet and everybody was asleep. Then Anna said in an urgent tone, "I'd just like to see the spring, how all the little flowers come out and how all the fields are full of flowers; I want to see Freddie, he has such a dear little face. What is Papa doing —what did he say?" Her mother told her he was asleep and hadn't said anything. Anna then remarked, with a sarcastic smile, "He will probably be sick again in the morning!"

This text must be read backward. The last sentence is not intended seriously, as it was uttered in a sarcastic tone of voice. The last time father was sick Anna suspected him of having "a plant in his inside." The sarcasm therefore means "He will probably have a child in the morning!" But this is not intended seriously, for Papa cannot have a child, only Mama has children; perhaps she will have another tomorrow, but where from? "What is Papa doing?" Here we have an unmistakable formulation of the difficult problem: what does Papa do if he does not produce children? Anna would very much like to find the clue to all her problems; she would like to know how Freddie came into the world, she would like to see how the flowers come out of the earth in the spring, and these wishes all hide behind her fear of earthquakes.

After this intermezzo Anna slept peacefully until morning. In the morning her mother asked her what was the matter with her last night. Anna had forgotten everything and thought she had only had a dream: *"I dreamed I could make the summer and then someone threw a golliwog down the toilet."*

This singular dream is made up of two different scenes, which are separated by the word "then." The second part derives its material from a recent wish to have a golliwog, i.e., to have a masculine doll just as Mama has a little boy. Someone throws the golliwog down the toilet—but usually one lets quite other things drop down the toilet. The inference is that children come out just like the things into the toilet. Here we have an analogy to the *Lumpf*-theory of Little Hans. Whenever several scenes are found in one dream, each scene ordinarily represents a special variation of the working out of the complex. Thus the first part is only a variation of the theme found in the second part. We had noted above what is meant by "seeing the spring" or "seeing the flowers come out." Anna now dreams that she *can make the summer,* i.e., can cause the flowers to come out; she herself can make a little child, and the second part of the dream represents this as analogous to the making of a motion. Here we put our finger on the egoistic wish which lies behind the seemingly objective interest of the previous night's conversation.

A few days later the mother received a visit from a lady who was looking forward to her confinement. The children apparently noticed nothing. But the next day they amused themselves, under the guidance of the elder girl, by taking all the old newspapers out of their father's waste-paper basket and stuffing them under their frocks in front, so that the imitation was unmistakable. That night Anna again had a dream: *"I dreamed about a lady in the town, she had a very fat stomach."* As the chief actor in a dream is always the dreamer himself under a definite aspect, the game of the day before finds complete interpretation.

Not long after, Anna surprised her mother with the following performance: she stuck her doll under her clothes and slowly pulled it out head downwards, saying, "Look, the baby is coming out, now it is all out." Anna was telling her mother: thus I conceive the problem of birth. What do you think of it? is it right? The game is really meant as a question, for, as we shall see later, this conception still had to be officially confirmed.

Rumination on the problem by no means ended here, as is apparent from the ideas Anna conceived during the following weeks. Thus she repeated the same game a few days later with her Teddy bear, which had the function of a specially beloved doll. Another day, pointing to a rose, she said to her grandmother, "Look, the rose is getting a baby." As the grandmother did not quite take her meaning, the child pointed to the swollen calyx: "Don't you see, it's all fat here!"

One day she was quarreling with her younger sister, when the latter exclaimed angrily, "I'll kill you!" Whereupon Anna replied, "When I am dead you will be all alone, and then you'll have to pray to God for a live baby." And immediately the scene changed: Anna was the angel, and the younger sister had to kneel down before her and beg her to send a living child. In this way Anna became the child-giving mother.

Once they had oranges for supper. Anna impatiently asked for one and said, "I'll take an orange and I'll swallow it all down into my stomach, and then I shall get a baby."

This instantly reminds us of the fairy tales in which childless women finally make themselves pregnant by swallowing fruit, fish and the like.[8] Anna was here trying to solve the problem of how children actually get into the mother. In so doing she takes up a position of inquiry which had never been formulated before so precisely. The solution follows in the form of an analogy, which is characteristic of the archaic thinking of the child. (Thinking in analogies is also found in the adult, in the stratum lying immediately below consciousness.

[8] Cf. Franz Riklin *Wishfulfillment and Symbolism in Fairy Tales* (trans. by W. A. White, Nervous and Mental Disease Monograph Series, No. 21, New York, 1921).

Dreams bring the analogies to the surface, as also does dementia praecox.) In German and numerous other foreign fairy tales one frequently finds such childish comparisons. Fairy tales seem to be the myths of childhood and they therefore contain among other things the mythology which children weave for themselves concerning sexual processes. The poetry of fairy tales, whose magic is felt even by the adult, rests not least upon the fact that some of the old theories are still alive in our unconscious. We experience a strange and mysterious feeling whatever a fragment of our remotest youth stirs into life again, not actually reaching consciousness, but merely shedding a reflection of its emotional intensity on the conscious mind.

The problem of how the child gets into the mother is a difficult one to solve. As the only way of getting things into the body is through the mouth, it stands to reason that the mother ate something like a fruit, which then grew inside her. But here another difficulty presents itself: one knows what comes out of the mother, but what is the use of the father? Now, it is an old rule of the mental economy to connect two unknowns and to use one to solve the other.

Hence the conviction rapidly fastened on the child that the father is somehow involved in the whole business, particularly in view of the fact that the problem of where children come from still leaves the question open of how they get into the mother.

What does the father do? This question occupied Anna to the exclusion of all else. One morning she ran into her parents' bedroom while they were still dressing, jumped into her father's bed, lay flat on her face, and flailed with her legs, crying out, "Look, is that what Papa does?" Her parents laughed and did not answer, as it only dawned on them afterward what this performance probably signified. The analogy with the horse of Little Hans, which made such a commotion with its legs, is surprisingly close.

Here, with this latest achievement, the matter seemed to rest; at any rate the parents found no opportunity to make any pertinent observations. That the problem should come to a standstill at this point is not really surprising, for this is the most difficult part. The child knows nothing about sperms and nothing about coitus. There is but one possibility: the mother must eat something, for only in that way can anything get into the body. But what does the father do? The frequent comparisons with the nurse and other unmarried people were obviously to some purpose. Anna was bound to conclude that the existence of the father was in some way significant. But what on earth does he do? Anna and Little Hans are agreed that it must have something to do with the legs.

This standstill lasted about five months, during which time no phobias or any other signs of a working through of the complex appeared. Then came the first premonition of future events. Anna's family were at that time living in a country house near a lake, where the children could bathe with their mother. As Anna was afraid to go more than knee-deep into the water, her father once took her right in with him, which led to a great outburst of crying. That evening, when going to bed, Anna said to her mother, "Papa wanted to drown me, didn't he?"

A few days later there was another outburst. She had continued to stand in the gardener's way until finally, for a joke, he picked her up and put her in a hole he had just dug. Anna started to cry miserably, and declared afterward that the man had tried to bury her.

The upshot was that Anna woke up one night with fearful screams. Her mother went to her in the adjoining room and quieted her. Anna had dreamed that *"a train went by overhead and fell down."*

Here we have a parallel to the "stage coach" story of Little Hans. These incidents show clearly enough that fear was again in the air, i.e., that there was some obstacle preventing the transference of love to the parents and that therefore a large part of it was converted into fear. This time the mistrust was directed not against the mother, but against the father, who she was sure must know the secret, but would never let anything out. What could the father be doing or keeping up his sleeve? To the child this secret appeared to be something very dangerous, so obviously she felt that the worst might be expected of the father. (This childish fear of the father is to be seen particularly clearly in adults in cases of dementia praecox, which takes the lid off many unconscious processes as though it were acting on psychoanalytical principles.) Hence Anna arrived at the apparently nonsensical notion that her father wanted to drown her.

Meanwhile Anna had grown a little older and her interest in her father took on a special tinge which is rather hard to describe. Language has no words for the peculiar kind of tender curiosity that shone in the child's eyes.

It is probably no accident that the children began playing

a pretty game about this time. They called the two biggest dolls their "grandmothers" and played at hospital with them, a toolshed being taken over as a hospital. There the grandmothers were brought, interned, and left to sit overnight. "Grandmother" in this connection is distinctly reminiscent of the "big brother" earlier. It seems very likely that the "grandmother" deputizes for the mother. So the children were already conspiring to get the mother out of the way.[9] This intention was assisted by the fact that the mother had again given Anna cause for displeasure.

It came about in the following way: The gardener had laid out a large bed which he was sowing with grass. Anna helped him in this work with much pleasure, apparently without guessing the profound significance of her childish play. About a fortnight later she began to observe with delight the young grass sprouting. On one of these occasions she went to her mother and asked, "How did the eyes grow into the head?"

Her mother told her she didn't know. But Anna went on to ask whether God knew, or her father, and why God and her father knew everything? The mother then referred her to her father, who might be able to tell her how the eyes grew into the head. Some days later there was a family gathering at tea. After the meal had broken up, the father remained at the table reading the paper, and Anna also stayed behind. Suddenly approaching her father she said, "Tell me, how did the eyes grow into the head?"

Father: "They did not grow into the head; they were there from the beginning and grew with the head."

Anna: "Weren't the eyes planted?"

Father: "No, they just grew in the head like the nose."

Anna: "But did the mouth and the ears grow like that? And the hair?"

Father: "Yes, they all grew the same way."

Anna: "Even the hair? But the baby mice come into the world all naked. Where was the hair before? Aren't there little seeds for it?"

---

[9] This tendency to get rid of the mother also showed itself in the following incident: The children had requisitioned the toolshed as a house for themselves and their dolls. An important room in any house is, as we know, the toilet, which obviously cannot be lacking. Accordingly, the children went to the toilet in a corner of the toolshed. Their mother naturally could not help spoiling this illusion by forbidding such games. Soon afterward she caught the remark, "When Mama is dead we'll do it every day in the toolshed and put on Sunday clothes every day."

Father: "No. The hair, you see, comes out of little granules which are like seeds, but they are already in the skin and nobody sowed them there."

The father was now getting into a fix. He guessed where the little one was leading him, therefore he did not want to upset, on account of a single false application, the diplomatically introduced seed theory which she had most fortunately picked up from nature; for the child spoke with an unwonted earnestness which compelled consideration.

Anna (visibly disappointed, and in a distressed voice): "But how did Freddie get into Mama? Who stuck him in? And who stuck you into your mama? Where did he come out?"

From this sudden storm of questions the father chose the last for his first answer:

"Think, now, you know that Freddie is a boy; boys grow into men and girls into women, and only women can have children. Now, just think, where could Freddie have come out?"

Anna (laughing joyfully and pointing to her genitals): "Did he come out here?"

Father: "But of course. Surely you must have thought of that before?"

Anna (overlooking the question): "But how did Freddie get into Mama? Did anybody plant him? Was the seed sown?"

This extremely precise question could no longer be evaded by the father. He explained to the child, who listened with the greatest attention, that the mother is like the soil and the father like the gardener; that the father provides the seed which grows in the mother and thus produces a baby. This answer gave her extraordinary satisfaction; she immediately ran to her mother and said, "Papa has told me everything; now I know it all." But what it was she knew, she never told to anyone.

The new knowledge was, however, put into practice the following day. Anna went up to her mother and said brightly: "Just think, Mama, Papa told me that Freddie was a little angel and was brought down from heaven by the stork." Her mother was naturally astounded, and said, "I am quite certain your father never told you anything of the sort." Whereupon the little one skipped away laughing.

This was her revenge. Her mother evidently would not or could not tell her how the eyes grew into the head; she didn't even know how Freddie had got into her. Therefore she could easily be led up the garden path with that old story about the stork. She might believe it still.

The child was now satisfied, for her knowledge had been enriched and a difficult problem solved. An even greater advantage, however, was the fact that she had won a more intimate relationship with her father, which did not prejudice her intellectual independence in the least. The father of course was left with an uneasy feeling, for he was not altogether happy about having passed on to a four-and-a-half-year-old child a secret which other parents carefully guard. He was disquieted by the thought of what Anna might do with her knowledge. What if she was indiscreet and exploited it? She might so easily instruct her playmates or gleefully play the *enfant terrible* with grown-ups. But these fears proved to be groundless. Anna never breathed a word about it, either then or at any time. The enlightenment had, moreover, brought a complete silencing of the problem, so that no more questions presented themselves. Yet the unconscious did not lose sight of the riddle of human creation. A few weeks after her enlightenment Anna recounted the following dream: She was "*in the garden and several gardeners stood making wee-wee against the trees, and Papa was also doing it.*"

This recalls the earlier unsolved problem: what does the father do?

Also about this time a carpenter came into the house in order to repair an ill-fitting cupboard; Anna stood by and watched him planing the wood. That night she dreamed that the carpenter "sliced off" her genitals.

The dream could be interpreted to mean that Anna was asking herself: will it work with me? oughtn't one to do something like what the carpenter did, in order to make it work? Such an hypothesis would indicate that this problem is particularly active in the unconscious at the moment, because there is something not quite clear about it. That this is so was shown by the next incident, which did not, however, occur until several months later, when Anna was approaching her fifth birthday. Meantime the younger sister, Sophie, was taking a growing interest in these matters. She had been present when Anna received enlightenment at the time of the earthquake phobia, and had even thrown in an apparently understanding remark on that occasion, as the reader may remember. But in actual fact the explanation was not understood by her at the time. This became clear soon afterward. She had days when she was more than usually affectionate with her mother and never left her skirts; but she could also be really naughty and irritable. On one of these bad days she tried to tip her little brother out of his carriage. Her mother scolded her, whereupon she set up a loud wailing. Suddenly, in the midst of her tears, she said, "I don't know anything about where children come from!" She was then given the same explanation that her elder sister had received earlier. This seemed to allay the problem for her, and for several months there was peace. Then once more there were days when she was whining and bad-tempered. One day, quite out of the blue, she turned to her mother with the question "Was Freddie really in your inside?"

Mother: "Yes."

Sophie: "Did you push him out?"

Mother: "Yes."

Anna (butting in): "But was it down below?"

Here Anna employed a childish term which is used for the genitals as well as for the anus.

Sophie: "And then you let him drop down?"

The expression "drop down" comes from that toilet mechanism, of such absorbing interest to children, whereby one lets the excreta drop down into the bowl.

Anna: "Or was he sicked up?"

The evening before, Anna had been sick owing to a slightly upset stomach.

After a pause of several months Sophie had suddenly caught up and now wished to make sure of the explanation previously vouchsafed to her. This making doubly sure seems to indicate that doubts had arisen concerning the explanation given by her mother. To judge by the content of the questions, the doubts arose because the process of birth had not been adequately explained. "Push" is a word children sometimes use for the act of defecation. It tells us along what lines the theory will develop with Sophie, too. Her further remark, as to whether one had let Freddie "drop down," betrays such a complete identification of her baby brother with excrement that it borders on the ludicrous. To this Anna makes the singular remark that perhaps Freddie was "sicked up." Her own vomiting of the day before had made a deep impression on her. It was the first time she had been sick since her earliest childhood. That was one way in which things could leave the body, though she had obviously not given it serious thought until now. (Only once had it occurred to her, and that was

when they were discussing the body openings and she had
thought of the mouth.) Her remark is a firm pointer away
from the excrement theory. Why did she not point at once to
the genitals? Her last dream gives us a clue to the probable
reasons: there is something about the genitals which Anna still
does not understand; something or other has to be done there
to make it "work." Maybe it wasn't the genitals at all; maybe
the seed for little children got into the body through the
mouth, like food, and the child came out like "sick."

The detailed mechanism of birth, therefore, was still puzzling. Anna was again told by her mother that the child really
does come out down below. About a month later, Anna suddenly had the following dream: *"I dreamed I was in the
bedroom of Uncle and Auntie. Both of them were in bed. I
pulled the bedclothes off Uncle, lay on his stomach, and jog-
gled up and down on it."*

This dream came like a bolt from the blue. The children
were then on holiday for several weeks and the father, who
had been detained in town on business, had arrived on that
same day for a visit. Anna was especially affectionate with
him. He asked her jokingly, "Will you travel up to town with
me this evening?" Anna: "Yes, and then I can sleep with you?"
All this time she hung lovingly on her father's arm as her
mother sometimes did. A few moments later she brought out
her dream. Some days previously she had been staying as a
guest with the aunt mentioned in the dream (the dream, too,
was some days old). She had looked forward particularly to
that visit, because she was certain she would meet two small
cousins—boys—in whom she showed an unfeigned interest. Unfortunately, the cousins were not there, and Anna was very
disappointed. There must have been something in her present
situation that was related to the content of the dream for it to
be remembered so suddenly. The relation between the manifest
content and the conversation with her father is clear enough.
The uncle was a decrepit old gentleman and only known to
the child from a few rare encounters. In the dream he is
patently a substitute for her father. The dream itself creates a
substitute for the disappointment of the day before: she is in
bed with her father. Here we have the *tertium comparationis*
with the present. Hence the sudden remembrance of the
dream. The dream recapitulates a game which Anna often
played in her father's (empty) bed, the game of joggling about
and kicking with her legs on the mattress. From this game
stemmed the question "Is this what Papa does?" Her immedi-

ate disappointment is that her father answered her question with the words, "You can sleep by yourself in the next room." Then follows the remembrance of the same dream which has already consoled her for a previous erotic disappointment (with the cousins). At the same time the dream is essentially an illustration of the theory that "it" takes place in bed, and by means of the aforementioned rhythmical movements. Whether the remark that she lay on her uncle's stomach had anything to do with her being sick cannot be proved.

Such is the extent of our observations up to the present. Anna is now a little over five years old and already in possession, as we have seen, of a number of the most important sexual facts. Any adverse effect of this knowledge upon her morals and character has yet to be observed. Of the favorable therapeutic effect we have spoken already. It is also quite clear from the report that the younger sister is in need of a special explanation for herself, as and when the problem arises for her. If the time is not ripe, no amount of enlightenment, it would seem, is of the slightest use.

I am no apostle of sex education for schoolchildren, or indeed of any standardized mechanical explanations. I am therefore not in a position to offer any positive and uniformly valid advice. I can only draw one conclusion from the material here recorded, which is, that we should try to see children as they really are, and not as we would wish them; that, in educating them, we should follow the natural path of development, and eschew dead prescriptions.

Supplement

Our views have undergone a considerable change since this paper was first published. There is, in the observations, one point in particular which has not been sufficiently appreciated, namely the fact that again and again, despite the enlightenment they received, the children exhibited a distinct preference for some fantastic explanation. Since the first appearance of the present work this tendency, contrary to my expectations, has increased: the children continue to favor a fantastic theory. In this matter I have before me a number of incontestable observations, some of them concerning the children of other parents. The four-year-old daughter of one of my friends, for instance, who does not hold with useless secrecy in education, was allowed last year to help her mother decorate the

Christmas tree. But this year the child told her mother, "It wasn't right last year. This time I'll not look and you will lock the door with the key."

As a result of this and similar observations, I have been left wondering whether the fantastic or mythological explanation preferred by the child might not, for that very reason, be more suitable than a "scientific" one, which, although factually correct, threatens to clamp down the latch on fantasy for good. In the present instance the latch could be unclamped again, but only because the fantasy brushed "science" aside.

Did their enlightenment harm the children? Nothing of the sort was observed. They developed healthily and normally. The problems they broached apparently sank right into the background, presumably as a result of the manifold external interests arising out of school life, and the like. The fantasy activity was not harmed in the least, nor did it pursue paths that could be described as in any way abnormal. Occasional remarks or observations of a delicate nature were made openly and without secrecy.

I have therefore come to hold the view that the earlier free discussions took the wind out of the children's imagination and thus prevented any secretive fantasy from developing which would have cast a sidelong glance at these things, and would, in consequence, have been nothing but an obstacle to the free development of thinking. The fact that the fantasy activity simply ignored the right explanation seems, in my view, to be an important indication that all freely developing thought has an irresistible need to emancipate itself from the realism of fact and to create a world of its own.

Consequently, however little advisable it is to give children false explanations which would only sow the seeds of mistrust, it is, so it seems to me, no less inadvisable to insist on the acceptance of the right explanation. For the freedom of the mind's development would merely be suppressed through such rigid consistency, and the child forced into a concretism of outlook that would preclude further development. Side by side with the biological, the spiritual, too, has its inviolable rights. It is assuredly no accident that primitive peoples, even in adult life, make the most fantastic assertions about well-known sexual process, as for instance that coitus has nothing to do with pregnancy.[10] From this it has been concluded that these peo-

[10] Cf. Bronislaw Malinowski, *The Sexual Life of Savages* (3d ed., London and New York, 1932).—EDITORS.

ple do not even know there is such a connection. But more accurate investigation has shown that they know very well that with animals copulation is followed by pregnancy. Only for human beings is it denied—not *not known*, but flatly *denied*—that this is so, for the simple reason that they prefer a mythological explanation which has freed itself from the trammels of concretism. It is not hard to see that in these facts, so frequently observed among primitives, there lie the beginnings of *abstraction,* which is so very important for culture. We have every reason to suppose that this is also true of the psychology of the child. If certain South American Indians really and truly call themselves red cockatoos and expressly repudiate a figurative interpretation of this fact, this has absolutely nothing to do with any sexual repression on "moral" grounds, but is due to the law of independence inherent in the thinking function and to its emancipation from the concretism of sensuous perceptions. We must assign a separate principle to the thinking function, a principle which coincides with the beginnings of sexuality only in the polyvalent germinal disposition of the very young child. To reduce the origins of thinking to mere sexuality is an undertaking that runs counter to the basic facts of human psychology.

III

FIRST CONTACTS WITH THE WORLD AND OTHERS

Babbling

M. M. LEWIS

(1930)

In this selection from his classic work, *Infant Speech*, M. M. Lewis compares the child's babbling to a work of art. Babbling is play with the toy of language and, like other forms of play, it reveals the child's desire for mastery and his delight in pattern. It contains the rudimentary features of an aesthetic sense of language. It transcends satisfaction of primary needs—that is, expressing these to an adult—as elaborated above by Georg Groddeck and Harry Stack Sullivan.

The Incentive in Babbling. What kind of delight is it that the child finds in uttering either isolated sounds or strings of them? Although we may say that play movements in general are made for the mere sake of making them, this is inadequate as an explanation of babbling.

For speech, even at the rudimentary level we are considering, is already a very special kind of activity. It is expressive, and expressive both of comfort and discomfort. Our problem then is this, under what conditions is the child likely to engage in the utterance of sounds not as expression, but for the mere pleasure of uttering them?

If it were only a matter of repeating sounds which have been expressive of comfort, one might be tempted to say that it is their association with a pleasant state which now brings about their repetition. It might be said that something of this pleasantness would tend to be reinstated whenever the sound were uttered; the back consonant **g**, for instance, or the labial **b**, would carry with it something of the pleasant feeling that follows a good meal. Then we might suppose that the child, "when he had nothing better to do," that is, when all his primary needs were satisfied, might try in a vague way to make those noises that bring such a pleasant feeling with them. Or alternatively, we might suppose that the child, when quite comfortable, might utter one or other of these sounds "at random," and then, something of the original pleasant condition being reinstated, he would seek to prolong this by repeating the sound.

But this, although it may cover some cases, is certainly not a complete explanation, for it leaves out of account the fact, mentioned above, that sounds primarily expressive of *discomfort* also become transformed into babbling. No theory of babbling can be regarded as adequate unless it embraces this transformation.

It is therefore worth pointing out that this kind of transformation in other forms of play has recently received some attention, although as far as I know it has not hitherto been demonstrated in the case of babbling. Thus Freud finds great significance in the fact that in play the child often repeats experiences that were unpleasant in the first instance. Guillaume, without referring to Freud, records several examples from the behavior of his year-old son; the child, having pricked his finger with a pin, repeated the action several times with a tiny shriek; on another occasion he tried to replace his finger in a door where it had been pinched. Guernsey tells us that a child of 0;11, having accidently struck his head so hard against a bed that he cried, proceeded then to repeat the experience several times in rapid succession. And Bekhterev mentions the case of a child of 2;0 who, having been hurt in stumbling over a threshold, then amused herself by stepping backward and forward over it a dozen times.

Freud's explanation of such facts is well known. The child, he tells us, by repeating what was in the first instance an unpleasant experience thereby gains mastery over it; an unpleasant impression—which, when it occurred, had to be endured —now becomes something that the child freely wills, something under his control. C. and K. Bühler have applied this theory in a thoroughgoing way to the early play of children; but nobody has hitherto, I think, shown that it also applies to their babbling.

For there can be no doubt that here we have a hypothesis that provides adequately for all the facts of babbling, especially if we couple with it—as the Bühlers do—some reference to the form or pattern of the activity. The view that pleasure may arise from the mere pattern of an experience is accepted as a hypothesis by divergent schools of psychology, although it has perhaps been stated with most insistence by the Gestalttheorists. As Koffka says, an experience of a sequence of events forms itself into a pattern, which becomes more definite by repetition. Then if an adequate portion of this pattern is experienced, it will tend to arouse an expectation of the complete pattern, and satisfaction will only arrive when completion takes place.

Now there can be no doubt that repetitive play in general, and babbling in particular, is characterized by having a regular pattern. The most obvious feature of babbling is the reduplication of sounds; but in addition to this phonetic pattern there is frequently a pattern of intonation—a "tune"—which, though it may not be exactly repeated, has certainly a definite form. Further, in any series of babbling there is a marked rhythm; Guernsey found in her observations of two hundred children up to the age of twenty-one months that the rhythmical character of babbling contrasted most strongly with the formlessness of the child's imitation of adults uttering the same sounds.

We may well say, therefore, that the desire for "mastery" and the delight in a pattern are the two fundamental incentives in babbling as in other kinds of play. We must, however, go further and again point out that babbling is different from all other play by the very fact that it is play with the medium of language. For since language is expressive, when the child utters a cry in the course of any experience, a double pattern is formed for him: the pattern of the experience and the pattern of the accompanying cry. And when in babbling he recalls his earlier cry he not only is mastering this, but at the same time reinstating and also thereby mastering the experience which accompanied it. We might say, in fact, that when a child who has cried *mama* while hungry later says it in babbling, he is both playing at crying and playing at being hungry, and obtaining a "mastery" over both experiences.

The significance of this, both for the understanding of babbling itself and of its place in the development of language appears when we come to our next question: In what sense may babbling be regarded as rudimentary art?

Babbling as a Form of Art. As soon as we recognize that babbling is a function of language standing by itself in the child's development we are recognizing that he is occupied with a form of art, rudimentary indeed though this may be. To what extent can this view be justified? Certainly it is a commonplace of aesthetics that there is a close relation between art and play. In the case of babbling this is generally covered by the statement that babbling is a form of art, or that it represents the beginning of the art of language in the life of the child.

But the acceptance of a vague general resemblance is not enough. It is not enough to say that babbling is play, that play gives rise to art, hence babbling is rudimentary art. We need to make a closer comparison, for the importance of recognizing the aesthetic character of babbling is twofold. First, it enables us to complete our picture of the child's early linguistic activity, and secondly it gives us further insight into the later aesthetic function of language by enabling us to trace its development from the beginnings.

We are not, of course, called upon to make any analysis of "art" in general, if indeed any such analysis be possible. We need only make a summary of the broad characteristics of the aesthetic use of language, as contrasted with its scientific or practical uses.

Characteristics of Language with an Aesthetic Intention. Language—whether the intention of the writer be aesthetic, scientific or practical—is used to symbolize experience. Are there any special characteristics in the nature of the experience, and in the nature of the symbolization, which enable us to distinguish the aesthetic from the other uses of language?

It will be agreed that the main difference between the artist —as we may call him—and the practical or scientific writer lies in the *intention* of his activity. The practical or scientific use of language is a means to an end, whereas aesthetic activity is self-sufficing: this of course is one of its affinities with play. And this difference between the aesthetic and other uses of language is found to exist both in the nature of the experience symbolized, and in the manner of its symbolization.

(i) *The Experience Symbolized.* All instances of utterance with an aesthetic intention involve the reinstatement of experience. So too does the use of language either with a practical or with a scientific intention. But we may contrast these with the aesthetic use in that here the reinstatement of experience is for the sake of the satisfaction which this very reinstatement brings; whereas in the practical or the scientific use previous experiences are reinstated as a means to an end—the reinstatement is brought to bear upon the situation in hand.

Where the experience—"actual" or "imagined"—is pleasurable, it is easy to understand why it should be reinstated. This covers a large proportion of descriptive and narrative verse and prose, and much of the drama.

It is more difficult to understand why we should seek to reinstate an experience—actual or imagined—which is not pleasurable, which is perhaps even painful in itself. This is the problem of much lyrical poetry and of tragedy. What is the motive that causes Shakespeare to bring up before us the events of *King Lear?* Here we are not called upon to do more than mention this ancient problem; we have only to notice that when an experience is symbolized with an aesthetic intention, it is for the satisfaction which the reinstatement brings, a satisfaction which arises irrespective of the pleasant or painful nature of the original experience in itself.

(ii) *The Language that Symbolizes the Experience.* Turning now from the experience to the language in which it is symbolized, we may say that this has a twofold function: referential and expressive—the words not only call up a situation, but they also express the writer's emotion. But does this emotion arise from the original situation in itself: is poetry primarily the expression, as Wordsworth says, of emotion recollected in tranquillity? We may follow Alexander in doubting this, for although in some forms of poetry the emotion aroused in the writer by the original situation may be expressed, in other forms—the drama, for instance—it may be almost entirely absent.

But this does not mean, continues Alexander, that poetry is not born of emotion; there is another source of affect which is not only legitimate in art but indeed its distinguishing feature. Following Clive Bell, he calls this "aesthetic emotion"; the delight engendered by the act of aesthetic symbolization. There is a joy in the manipulation of the material, and it is this joy—more than the emotion aroused by the original experience —which drives the artist to creation, and which he communicates to some extent in his work of art.

Here is to be found one source of our delight in tragedy. The painful qualities of the original experience are not only transformed by the present reinstatement, but also subordinated to the pleasure which arises in the course of the work of symbolization, so that while we might shun the mere repetition of the actual experience in itself, we find pleasure in the aesthetic symbolization of it.

Presence of These Characteristics in Babbling. It may seem ludicrous to attempt to trace the presence of these features of the aesthetic use of language in the babbling of an infant. But their existence is certainly implied in all comparisons made between babbling and art. To what extent, then, are these features actually to be found?

It is clear from our discussion in the earlier part of this chapter that they certainly exist in a rudimentary form in babbling. Such differences as there are arise necessarily from the immaturity of the child. Thus there is as yet no question of the symbolization of experience, there is only the expression of affect: but insofar as in babbling the child must partly revive bygone affective states when he repeats the sounds which once expressed them, we have the rudiments both of the reinstatement of an experience and the symbolization of it—the two aspects of the aesthetic process.

In both respects babbling is rudimentary art. With regard to the experience reinstated we have seen that in babbling the child may come not only to repeat sounds originally expressive of pleasant states—possibly because they were pleasant—but also sounds expressive of an unpleasant state. We find that in order to explain this latter fact we had to invoke the hypothesis of "mastery"; the problem is, at its own primitive level, exactly parallel to that of the nature of tragedy in dramatic art. The poet who makes the tragic verse of *King Lear* an embodiment of human suffering is, at an immeasurable distance, like the child who in a moment of play repeats his own cry of hunger.

Again, we find a similar parallel when we compare the child's attention to his sounds in babbling with the artist's attitude to the language he uses in symbolizing experience. In some measure the sounds uttered in babbling may still express the emotion which they originally expressed: but undoubtedly this is subordinated to the emotion now present—the joy of babbling, the joy of manipulating the material: spoken sounds. In a word, the affective attitude, "aesthetic emotion," which Alexander finds peculiarly characteristic of the artist, we find present in a rudimentary form in the babbling child.

Thus even in this brief comparison it is evident that babbling presents in a rudimentary form the features of the aesthetic use of language. We must recognize therefore that there is much more than a vague general similarity between the two activities: the child's babbling is actually the beginning of his aesthetic use of words; so that almost from the very outset the practical and the aesthetic functions of language develop side by side. Thus there are twin impulses in the development of language in the child's life: on the one hand, the

satisfaction of his primary needs, and, on the other, the satisfaction of aesthetic tendencies which, arising in the first instance out of his expression of these needs, soon become an
independent activity.

Identification

ALICE BALINT

(1931)

Alice Balint regarded childhood as the period during which the child is transformed from a primitive into a civilized being, and she thought inevitable the frustrations caused by a child's adaption to postponement and prohibition of satisfaction for his wishes. But education, she maintained, can minimize the toll of coming to terms with the external world. In the following selection from *The Early Years of Life,* first published in Hungarian in 1931, Alice Balint shows that identification is decisive in adapting the child to external reality and overcoming his anxiety and helplessness. In her view, identification extends a portion of the child's ego to span the distance between narcissism and object love, the vital gap between the self and other people.

1. *The Conquest of the External World*

So far we have been mainly concerned with the *content* of the conflicts of childhood and we have said very little of the ways in which those conflicts are dealt with. And, now that we are approaching that side of the problem, we must for the time being leave the firm ground of direct observation and turn to a more theoretical consideration of the means adopted by children for the solution of their conflicts. I have already referred in passing to a few of these methods: repression, for instance, and displacement, and (something that is akin to the latter) sublimation. Repression enables us to blot out of our consciousness any wishes that have proved incapable of fulfillment, while displacement and sublimation enable some of our instincts to pursue their existence in a new and legitimate sphere. In the course of my remarks upon displacement I hinted at the existence of another method—namely, identificatory thought. I mentioned that displacement is closely related to this peculiarity of primitive thought, to the fact, that is, that children from the very first get to know the external world by means of "identifications." For instance, a small child will regard any thick mass of material as feces, and any liquid as urine, because feces and urine are things that are already familiar to it. One advantage of these identifications is that they enable the child to find substitutes for primitive sources of pleasure that have to be given up under the pressure of education. Thus identificatory thinking is employed for the purpose of avoiding what is unpleasurable and obtaining what is pleasurable, and it aims at transforming a strange and consequently frightening external world into one that is familiar and enjoyable. This is the only way (apart from direct gratification) in which we can approach the external world. And since the relation between the ego and the external world is after all the main problem of all educative measures, it is worth while examining the phenomenon of identificatory thought in all its details.

The ego, and more particularly the primitive "pleasure ego," plays the principal part in identificatory thinking to a much greater degree than it does subsequently, after the development of what is called "objective" thinking. For the basis for the earliest identifications is not resemblance to the object (though naturally this plays its part) but the manner in which the object in question enters into relation with the child's instincts. Indeed, this is self-evident: since whatever does not belong to our ego is alien to us, and thus the starting point for identification must necessarily be our own body or our own instincts.[1]

Thus, for instance, a piece of brown paper will remind a four-year-old boy not of a parcel or of anything connected with paper, but of feces—which is bound to strike an adult as an exceedingly forced comparison. In the same way a running tap usually reminds children of micturating. I have . . . given the instance of a four-year-old boy who identified a soldier's saber with a penis. So, too, the very widespread infantile theory of birth through the anus is essentially an identification of the process of birth with the familiar process of defecation.

[1] After we have taken mental possession of a portion of the external world by means of identification, mental material which has thus been assimilated can itself serve as a basis for further identifications. So there would seem to be no essential distinction between ego-identification (i.e. identification of the ego with an object) and object-identification (i.e. identification of one object with another). For it is only objects which have already been identified with ourselves that can become the starting point for further identifications.

(This explains how it is that this theory so often makes its appearance even when children have been given precise information upon the facts.)

It is obvious that an external world that has been discovered and conquered in such a fashion will be to the last degree egocentric. And this remarkable picture of the world, with the pleasure-ego as its center, persists in our unconscious all through our lives and constitutes the basis of the anthropomorphism which always lurks in the background even of the most objective and scientific thought.

It is by means of identification that a child makes the acquaintance even of its own body. Here the basis for the identification is afforded by those organs or parts of the body which are at the moment playing the largest part in the attainment of pleasure, either because some particular stage of development has been reached or because some external influences have been at work.

A four-year-old girl, for instance, had formerly derived her greatest pleasure from sucking her fingers. She then experimented with genital masturbation, and had recently practiced it more frequently. She explained it with the words: "I'm feeding my bottom." This strange explanation shows that, even in the case of a pleasurable, and therefore self-explanatory, activity like masturbation, the process requires to be made more familiar by means of identification. (It seems likely that behind the equation of masturbation with feeding, or eating, there lay an earlier comparison between sexual tension and hunger.) It is of course possible that the sense of guilt involved in masturbation also played a part in the child's explanation. If so, she would have been using the identification to pacify not so much herself as her inquiring elders, as though she were saying: "There's nothing in it really, it's only the same sort of thing as eating." A very similar, though simpler, example is provided by the little boy who, as was appropriate to his age, was, like her, devoted to sucking his fingers, and called his penis a "little finger." On the other hand, a girl used to call the genitals of a boy she played with a "little nose," and was thus comparing it with an organ that she herself also possessed. In this case the girl was using identificatory thinking to try to soothe the unpleasurable feelings caused by her lack of a penis.

From all of this it seems as though identificatory thinking were in its nature allied to narcissism. But, whereas narcissism never extends beyond the subject's own ego, identification constitutes the bridge that leads across from naked self-love to getting to love reality.

Nevertheless, identification is not yet object-love. The attachment that we form with the external world by means of identification is far better described as a kind of incorporation or assimilation or, inversely, as an extension of the ego. This can be demonstrated very clearly from a child's relation to its toys. It is a remarkable fact, for instance, that the essence of a small child's play consists in the child itself becoming a dog or a motorcar or a railway train though the corresponding toys are close at hand. Until this mental incorporation has been achieved, the toy remains something alien and frightening. The preference felt by children for a piece of paper or wood, for an empty box or a bit of string, is easily explained by the fact that these things can assume a greater diversity of shape and consequently afford wider possibilities for identification.

A boy I know was positively terrified of toys that have to be wound up and that then move automatically. He only enjoyed playing with them if he himself moved his whole body in unison with the toy. Most instructive in this connection was the way in which a child of about two and a half came to be on friendly terms with a new toy. He was presented with a red india-rubber elephant, but received it with violent dislike and pushed it away with screams and tears. The function of an elephant's trunk was then demonstrated to him by use of his own arm; he was shown how the end of the trunk worked like his own fingers; and was told how the elephant could squirt water with its trunk, put food into its mouth, and so on. Not until he himself had imitated these various movements for some time could he at last be prevailed upon to look at the toy and take it in his hands. It is worth trying to find the meaning of the various details of this everyday episode. The boy's throwing away of the toy and refusal to look at it may without any exaggeration be regarded as the destruction of a strange and troublesome object. Next followed the game with his own arm and fingers, which opened the way to an identification. After this process of mental "digestion" had been successfully achieved, the object that had been so repellent only a short time before could now be held in the child's hands and felt as something friendly and familiar.

Processes of an exactly similar kind are taking place in an adult when he says that he must "digest" a new idea before he can "get on friendly terms" with it; and to "explain" something means in fact to facilitate this process of digestion. The game which the child was shown with his arm was an explanation of the elephant's body given in a form appropriate to a child's understanding. But the "appropriate" form of this explanation lay, as we have seen, in the fact that it made possible an identification with the child's ego. Thus, on the one hand, children's play can be regarded partly as a summation of primitive explanations; and, on the other hand, the intellectual working over of a problem would seem probably always to be a process of identification. This would constitute the inevitable libidinal foundation of knowledge or understanding in general. If this close connection between knowledge and identification in fact holds, it implies that knowing is always *re*-knowing, that is, that we are able to know the external world only as something akin to the ego.

Thus, as we have seen, in the last resort a child wishes to meet only its own beloved self.

A story of a three-year-old boy will serve to exemplify this. He was afraid of thunderstorms; and one morning after a thundery night it was found that he had wetted his bed. Since he had been trained for some time, this event required a special explanation. The child told his mother what had happened in these words: "I didn't want to do it. But the sun said I *was* to do it in the bed. I said I wouldn't. But the sun said it does it too." "How's that?" asked his mother. "When it rains, of course." Here the little boy was trying to get on friendly terms with the frightening rainstorm by identifying the rain with micturition, which at the same time allowed him to indulge in a pleasure which had long been forbidden.

A child can only get on friendly terms with toys, with animals, with natural phenomena, as well as with the grown-up people living with him, if he can succeed in identifying himself with them. Identification can accordingly be regarded as a flight from the external world—this flight being carried out by means of our making a larger and larger portion of the external world into a portion of our ego. The further a child advances along this path, with the more things must he become acquainted which were at first disagreeable. This is an instructive instance of the way in which the pleasure principle itself leads to adaptation to reality. A child's one aim is to feel contented. But he is hindered in this by the external world which, by means of constant stimuli, is constantly confronting him with new problems. His way out is identification, by the help of which he takes the external world into himself, or, as we may say, assimilates it.

All this leads us to what will undoubtedly seem a paradoxical conclusion, namely, that a child is driven to have recourse to identification above all when he is overcome by painful impressions from which he has no other means of escape. And since running away or getting rid of a disturbing phenomenon is the least practicable method of defense in earliest childhood, identification is incomparably more important at that period of development than at any other time of life. If, therefore, we wish to be quite accurate, we must say, not that a child gets on friendly terms with something because it reminds him of something else of which he is already fond or which he already knows, but that a child can only become fond of something unknown if he can succeed, by the help of one of his instincts, in identifying it with something known. The common basis of loving and of understanding is identification, and without it both would be impossible.

Loving is not, of course, merely synonymous with identification; on the one hand it is the result of direct instinctual satisfaction, while on the other hand it presupposes a certain degree of sense of reality, which makes it possible to distinguish the ego from the external world. But what does that mean? We must above all not forget that the separation of ego from non-ego is originally effected by the help of painful experiences. We are taught, for instance, that our mother's breast is not a part of our own body by the painful experience that it is not always there when we need it. Loving is thus preceded by anger or, more precisely, by the discovery that what gives us satisfaction is an alien and hostile object belonging to the external world. This means that when a child is hungry he is not fond of his mother's breast but angry with it. In order to love it, the child must be able to remember the pleasure which the breast was the means of giving him. Thus loving is essentially gratitude, that is, the maintenance of affectionate feelings even at a time at which direct gratification has ceased.

A good example of a contrary state of things is afforded by the following anecdote, of which the hero is a boy of about six. He was out somewhere on a visit and had been playing very happily with a small dog, so that finally he could not bear the idea of parting with it. When he saw that all was in vain and that he *must* go home without it, he suddenly said: "Horrid dog! I don't love you!" Here we can see plainly that the child was angry with the bad dog that was the cause of his sorrow at parting.

It commonly happens that on such occasions a child will console himself with the help of identification. He will, for instance, turn himself into a dog and to such good effect that he no longer has the smallest need of the real animal. Thus identification can not only promote the development of loving but can just as easily hinder it: for if we are scared at the suffering which is involved in loving we can turn back to identification, as though to a more primitive form of relationship. But in setting up this secondary identification we have to fight not only against the alien nature of the object but also against an especially evil characteristic that it possesses, namely, the fact that it is not invariably or unconditionally at our disposal. In this case the aim of identification is no longer getting to know something that is unknown but replacing something that is missing. I no longer need the bad dog which I had to part with, if I can myself become a dog and so get satisfaction from myself.

The capital distinction between loving and identification lies in the fact that identification is the transforming of a painful, disturbing state of affairs into a pleasurable one, whereas loving is linked to gratification (that is, to something pleasurable) and in such a way that from the gratification we can find strength to tolerate the suffering that is bound up with it. The greater the direct gratification, the less need there is for identification. The other great distinction between identification and loving is that identification tends to do away with the separation between the ego and the external world, while it is a necessary condition of loving that we should recognize the fact that something else exists outside ourselves.

The first important gratification which we obtain through the agency of another person is sucking. Sucking comprises three different kinds of relation: first, an actual incorporation of a portion of the external world; secondly, narcissistic pleasure (since the process occurs at an age at which the separation of ego from non-ego has not yet been completely effected); and, finally, it contains the germ of the first love-relation. During sucking complete peace still reigns between the ego and the external world, between narcissism and object-love. It is the prototype of complete happiness. When we reflect, therefore, that it is precisely in the sphere of oral erotism that a child experiences not only its first great happiness but also its first great shocks (such, for instance, as weaning, teething and—last but not least—hunger), we shall more readily understand the great importance of the part played in mental life by identification, which is so closely related to the impulse of oral incorporation. It is common knowledge that small children seek to allay every pain, whether mental or physical, in one and the same way: by taking something into their mouth. The prototype of this mechanism of consolation is the assuaging of hunger—that is to say, sucking. If milk is not in a child's mouth when he becomes hungry, he has a high degree of unpleasurable feeling; and this painful event leads to a sharp differentiation between his ego and the external world. If milk then enters his mouth, this disharmony ceases and the integrity of his ego is re-established. This process, which is in part physiological, is a complete counterpart to the purely mental process which we term identification. Thus identification serves the pleasure principle in two sorts of ways: on the one hand, it removes the tension between the ego and the external world, and, on the other hand, its mechanism brings a recollection of the happiness which we enjoyed as sucklings.

Our relation with our own self develops in a manner precisely similar to what we have already described in the case of the ego and the external world. Let us take as our starting point those cases in which a child feels as something alien to him a part of his body which is causing him pain. We see children holding an injured finger far away from them, being angry with it and not wanting to look at it. Or they talk about the organ that is tormenting them in the third person—"that naughty tummy"—and wish someone would buy them another one, and so one. It is as though this behavior meant: "I'm fond of myself; but what hurts me is naughty and I don't like it; that's not me at all." On the other hand, therefore, everything that is not part of the ego is, to begin with, bad and alien, while, on the other hand, there is an inclination to project into the external world everything in the ego that is disturbing. Here, too, in other words, the separation of the ego from the external world proceeds according to the rule: what is good is ego, what is bad is non-ego.

Children will endeavor to get rid of disturbing emotions in the same way, by means of projection. For instance, a child of four said to his playmate: "If you don't leave my toy alone, a man'll come out and be angry." The child was asked why he did not simply say that he himself would be angry. His answer was: "Because I don't want to be angry any more."

Since in the case of physical pains being angry or repudiating the aching part does not, of course, lead to the desired end, the child is once more obliged to take refuge in identification. The result of this process of identification is that he nurses and caresses the aching part. But to this we shall return later.

A similar situation also occurs in the case of psychological injuries. We have already mentioned in connection with the castration complex how easily small children feel insulted, precisely because of their narcissism. After narcissistic injuries of this kind it may happen that a child will so to speak abandon his own self, since he no longer feels any pleasure in his ego. A very common sign of this is that the child assumes a new name and declares that his old ego is dead and exists no longer. If after this we call him by his old name the result is usually a bitter outburst of crying or a fit of rage; so that I have found as a rule that people give way to "strange whims" of this kind on the part of a child. We often find, for instance, that little girls, as soon as they have noticed that they lack something that little boys possess, want to stop being girls. The effect of this is intensified by remarks which they often hear preferring boys to girls. A snub or a sign of dislike may entirely take away a little girl's pleasure in herself. And the same thing may happen to a little boy if he is too bluntly reminded of his weakness and smallness compared with grown-up people. The impenetrable armor which we also call narcissism and which affords the individual his most effective protection against the opinion of others is already something secondary and is already in its essentials the product of a process of identification. When a child finds that he cannot get free from his own imperfect ego, he identifies himself with the people who are fond of him in spite of his imperfections. This origin of secondary self-love gives us a satisfactory explanation of the invulnerability of those who are protected by its armor.

The child's original attitude to the external world may be formulated in these words: "if you are fond of me, then make me as perfect as I myself feel I am." At first, for instance, a little girl will be angry because people are fond of her as a little girl and endeavor to use that as a means of inducing her to submit to her lot. Strange as it may seem, she feels this love as hostility. (We frequently come across this same conflict in the pages of modern love stories, where the mainspring of the plot consists in a woman feeling her self-respect injured because she is loved "merely as a woman" and "not as a human being.")

Something precisely similar is to be observed in physical suffering. A man who is ill abandons himself in just the same way as a child whose self-respect has been injured. It is as though he were surrendering his now worthless ego to his environment: "I don't need it any more; please do whatever you like with it." For the sick adult is, like the child, angry with his environment, as though he were making it responsible for his suffering. Just as a child is angry because she has been brought into the world so small, or because she has been made a girl and not a boy, so does the sick man (or child) nourish a hostile feeling against his environment because it has made him fall ill. This anger is a direct derivative of the mechanism of projection of which I have already spoken in connection with physical pain. We are unwilling to regard as part of our ego anything that is painful or imperfect—anything of which we must feel ashamed; and we therefore do our best to locate either the evil itself, or at least its causes, outside ourself.

The following anecdote offers an amusing example of this. A small boy of five fell down off a piece of furniture. He burst into sobs and tears and complained that his grandfather, who happened to be in another corner of the room, had pushed him over. Instead of admitting his own clumsiness, he looked for a scapegoat with whom he could be heartily angry, whereas, if he had had an understanding of the situation, he would have had to be angry with himself.

Anger with the environment is, as we can see, a protection against abandoning the self, or, more correctly, against the narcissistic injury which would be the consequence of understanding. This anger with the environment, on the one hand, and the inclination to self-abandonment, on the other, are the justification for special spoiling in case of illness or other mischance. For it is only by the help of identification with his environment that a person can contrive to love himself even though he is small or ill or humiliated.

Of course we must not forget that the impulse to self-abandonment is counteracted most strongly by—what is the actual basis of primary narcissism—the gratification which a person obtains from his own body: from masturbation in the widest sense of the word. From this point of view masturbation must be regarded as a positively lifesaving agency. We shall also understand why it is that masturbation increases at the period at which children have to go through a series of disappointments and humiliations in connection with the Oedipus and castration complexes. Masturbation prevents complete self-abandonment; it assures us, even in times of need, of our love for ourself, which, like all other love, is built up upon gratification.

Thus we see that, in the process of establishing the relation between an individual and the external world, the decisive part is played by identification and love. Loving stands furthest away from the original aim. It demands the greatest possible adaptation to the external world and at the same time makes the greatest breach in primary narcissism. Identification is the most primitive method of recognizing external reality; it is, in fact, nothing less than mental mimicry. Its necessary preconditions are an unbroken narcissism, which cannot bear that anything should exist outside itself, and the weakness of the individual, which makes him unable either to annihilate his environment or to take flight from it.

2. *The Child and His Educators*

From a practical point of view there is one exceedingly important special case of the relation between an individual and the external world, namely the relation between a child and his educators. For small children their parents and educators represent an immense power, the loss of whose love and goodwill is almost the same thing as the gravest mortal danger. It is easy to see why this is so, for it is a self-evident implication of children's complete physical and mental dependence. If a child were not helpless, he might, for instance, if his parents refused to give him something he wanted, say to himself: "I'm going away: I don't like it here." Since this solution is impossible for him, anger becomes a forbidden luxury, and he is obliged instead to resort to the same method in relation to his prohibiting and hence disagreeable parents as he has previously been able to use against the hostile and mighty external world—namely, to the method of identification. On the other hand, however, we know that these same parents are also a source of intense gratification for him and for that very reason are his first and most important love objects. Thus it is that parents come to bear the weight of the most vital, because the strongest and most permanent, attachments. We love them because they bring us pleasure and we identify ourselves with them as being the powerful representatives of the frustrating external world. Accordingly, in relation to parents, love and identification are so much intermingled that any clear differentiation between the two seems hopeless. And the position is made still more difficult by the fact that these two types of relation, which are so fundamentally different in their essence, make use for the most part of the same forms of expression. Love toward parents is not only something that is felt spontaneously but also something that is strictly forbidden. An educator is as a rule very little concerned as to the manner in which a child is attached to him; it is enough for him to know that such an attachment exists and is utilizable for the purposes of education. And yet, as we shall see presently, even from the practical point of view the distinction between the two forms of relation is not a matter of indifference. But I will first endeavor to draw a rough outline picture of the way in which love and identification are intermixed, and of how they alternate in the course of a child's development.

According to the schematic formula of the Oedipus complex, a small boy should love his mother and identify himself with his father. And this is in general the case. The boy's mother is after all the source of gratification and his father is the powerful rival against whom he cannot defend himself successfully either by attack or by flight, so that he is eventually obliged to resort to identification. The most familiar form taken by this identification is where the boy tries to do whatever his father is doing, imitates his father's movements and little habits, etc. It is true, of course, that the repressed Oedipus wish also re-emerges in this identification: the little boy is becoming his father—that is, he is becoming his mother's husband. The hostile intention which was the precursor of the identification finds its expression in such remarks as: "if I was Daddy, Daddy'd be a baby and I'd push him in the carriage." What I have said applies also, *mutatis mutandis,* to little girls. A girl is happy if she can imitate her mother in respect of her clothes or in the way she wears her hair; and it appears too that she would like to have a husband just like Mummy's. I once heard a young woman doctor say of her parents: "Getting married wasn't much of a job for Mummy, she got married to Daddy."

Differences in family circumstances, in the character of the parents, in their educational methods and in the possibilities of gratification open to a child can of course lead to the most various consequences. But, besides these, there are other factors of a much more general nature that can alter the picture to a greater or less extent. For instance, the mother or nurse is the chief source of pleasure for children of *both* sexes in their earliest years. Yet during the processes of weaning and of training in cleanliness the same person becomes a most disagreeable creature from the child's standpoint. At that period the child withdraws his love from her and directs it instead to his father, who as a rule has no share in this early education. One often hears a mother complaining of her baby's ingratitude because he prefers his father, although he only spares an occasional leisure moment to him, whereas he has not the least regard for his mother, who devotes the whole day to him. For older children, on the contrary, their father as a rule once again becomes the representative of harsh reality, while their mother is affectionate and indulgent. Alterations of this kind in the part played by parents bring about now an intensification, now a diminution in the effect of the Oedipus and castration complexes. These two complexes, moreover, do not operate entirely in the same sense. As we have seen, for instance, a little boy will usually associate his father with prohibition but his mother with failure. This applies equally to little girls. Her mother appears as a prohibiting force, but, since she has been disappointed by her father, she had no alternative but to turn away, to a greater or lesser extent, from *both* her parents. And in fact we find that after the climax of the Oedipus complex there follows a calming-down of the feelings that have been raging around the parents. Under the pressure of its various disappointments the child withdraws its love in part from its parents and turns to the external world—in a wider sense of the word. Then follows the period in which friendships begin, the desire for knowledge increases and the personality develops.

The child's "psychological emigration" from his parents' house is occasionally expressed in attempts at an actual emigration. I myself once witnessed something of the sort in the case of a boy of three. The child lived near me and I only knew him by sight. One night his mother gave birth to a baby. Next morning the little boy came across from the neighboring garden and spent the whole day with me, as though we had always been old friends. His parents were especially astonished because he was a rather nervous child and they had never before known him do anything like it. But, when we consider that the appearance of a new rival was far from being an agreeable event in the child's life, we shall understand his bold attempt at flight.

Another observation showed me that "going for a walk by oneself" means for a child "going away from Mummy." A six-year-old boy went into the street by himself for the first time because he was angry with his mother for refusing him something he wanted. A few weeks later a strange little episode occurred in connection with the same child, who in the meantime had gone for a number of short walks by himself without any particular excitement. As he was going out, his mother saw him out of the window and called out a friendly word to him. The little boy stopped, answered, made a lot of nonsensical remarks, danced about impatiently where he was standing, and finally shouted angrily: "I want to go off now!" "Well, go off then!" said the mother. To which he replied: "But I can't so long as I see you!" And it was not until his mother had gone away from the window that he was able to start for his walk.

The fact that toward the beginning of school age parents are thrown into the background by no means implies any diminution of their influence upon the development of a child's character. Physical, mental and social ties continue to bind him to his parents and so it is that the "mental emigration" that I have just mentioned takes place for the most part along paths prescribed or sanctioned by the parents (as, for instance, when a child is sent to school). This means that the climax of the Oedipus complex is succeeded by the period of educability. The stormy and contradictory feelings are replaced by identification with the parents. We know from what has gone before that identification disposes of an aggressive, rebellious feeling and does so by making a powerful external impression into a part of our own ego. That is precisely what a child does with commands and prohibitions which he is obliged to obey, so that he ends by being able to believe that he is following his own will. This procedure can easily be observed in quite small children. A child who cries bitterly if an attempt is made to carry him forcibly out of the room will calm down if he is given an opportunity of going out "of his own accord." It is possible in this way to get most children to want things that are the exact opposite of what they wanted originally. The protest which children raise against orders comes clearly to light in a number of very common childish habits. For instance, everyone knows that children are more inclined to obey if we tell them to do the opposite of what we want. Indeed, they will often say straight out: "Tell me not to do it and I'll do it."[2] The meaning is much the same, too, when a child amuses himself by using words in the sense opposite to their real one and says "yes" instead of "no," etc.

All these games are in reality attempts at preserving self-esteem in the face of superior power; and it becomes clear from this that giving way is painful to a child, irrespective of what it is that he is ordered to do. He even dislikes doing under orders something that he would otherwise be glad to do. This violent protest is in the end the cause of the child's defeat. Since his narcissism is incapable of tolerating a command, he becomes prepared at last, rather than obey, to will the same thing that the adults require him to do. The child who gets out of the room "of his own accord" is giving up his own will for the sake of preserving a fictitious "free will."

The outcome of the struggle round an individual's narcissism is one of the most important events of his development. As a result of identification with the various commands and prohibitions, his ego undergoes a decisive transformation. Since obedience takes place not through understanding but through identification, the command becomes a part of the child's ego, which he defends henceforward just as much as his own will. This is the explanation of the remarkable, rigid conservatism with which a child clings to regulations when he has once accepted them. To be sure, we must not forget at this point that, just as repression is unable to destroy the instinct from which a forbidden wish arises, so identification with the will of the adults does not do away with the wishes that are in contradiction to that will. The consequence is a splitting of the ego into two parts, of which one is the vehicle of the original instinctual wishes while the other is the vehicle of the wishes that have been incorporated by means of identification. This second, transformed part of the ego is called by Freud the "super-ego." The super-ego behaves toward the instinctual ego precisely as a child's educators originally behaved to the child. The child feels the educatory origin of the super-ego as his conscience. Yet conscience, however disagreeable it may be upon occasion, is no longer an external but an internal compulsion, in obeying which the child can feel as though he were acting in accordance

[2] Among the North American Indian tribes there used to be societies whose members were young warriors who, according to their rules, always did the opposite of what they were told. During a battle, for instance, if someone called out to them "Retire!", they would advance even if it meant certain death.

with a wish of his own. We may often observe that it is precisely the most self-willed children who become the most conscientious. Those children who can least tolerate punishment are inclined to anticipate it with remorse or even with self-punishment. In such a case a child is behaving like a hero who, rather than fall into the hands of his enemies, puts an end to his own life or who (as we know from historical instances), if he is to be executed, will not let himself be bound, but ascends the scaffold "free" and as though the decision to do so were his own. In moments of critical danger adults are themselves in the same situation as a child in relation to his parents: in both cases the sense of complete surrender leads to similar measures of defense.

Some people will certainly think it exaggerated to compare a child who is undergoing his education with a man in mortal danger. Nevertheless, from the point of view of the instinctual ego, the comparison comes very close to reality. The coming into existence of the super-ego can be regarded as a sentence of death upon the primitive life of the instincts. We can see this most clearly in children's behavior. In any nursery a child who is asked who did this or that forbidden act may be heard answering that *he* was not the guilty one but some other, naughtier person. This other person is often given a name and becomes a permanent guest in the nursery. Many suppose that this is merely a lie and that the child simply wants to deny his misdemeanor for fear of being punished. But there is something in the form taken by the denial that catches our attention. The child does not deny the misdemeanor but only that it was he who committed it. He is trying to regard the part of his mind that has become disagreeable to him owing to the threats (or merely prohibitions) of his educators as something alien and outside himself. And he is perfectly ready to join with the adults in jeering at this naughty other person or in beating him or even in destroying him. Of course we also learn from time to time that this other person is very powerful and clever, so that it is not so easy to get rid of him. But if on an occasion like this we try to make it clear to the child that this naughty other person is himself, then the understanding between us breaks down and violent protests ensue. The child's behavior in this connection is exactly like. his behavior toward physical pains: he attempts by means of projection to get rid of the disturbing portion of his ego.

Rasmussen, in his *Child Psychology*, writes: "At the age of 4 years and 1 month Ruth used occasionally to vomit a little after her midday meal. I corrected her and told her it was not nice. By way of excuse Ruth remarked: 'Yes, but *I* didn't do it; I didn't want to, but my tummy did it.'—A fortnight later she wanted to be naughty and began to stamp her foot. But she soon stopped, stamped once more very gently and said: 'One of my legs is rather naughty.' " In the second of these examples the splitting of the ego takes place before our very eyes. The first angry stamping still shows the individual undivided: then comes the recollection of the prohibition and the repudiation of the naughty portion of the ego.

Thus in the splitting of the ego two forces play a part, forces which are closely interrelated but which are clearly to be distinguished: one of these is identification with the behavior of the environment and the other is projection of the portion of the ego which has become disagreeable precisely owing to that identification. It is probably only later, in connection with the development of the sense of reality, that there sets in repression—that is, a complete elimination from consciousness—of the affects and wishes which were in the first instance projected. For to begin with a child makes no distinction between his world of fantasy and reality. At that stage of development he is quite content with the fiction that the guilty foot does not belong to him. It is not until this notion becomes untenable that he is obliged to have recourse to repression. For something of which I know nothing can surely not be "I": even the grown-ups must see that. Accordingly, it would be a necessary precondition of repression that we should have identified ourselves with the adult idea of reality.

The process of super-ego formation discovered by Freud, which I have been so far discussing, is in general represented as a method of adaptation to the prohibitions and commands of the environment. That, however, is only one side of this immensely important psychological phenomenon. Ferenczi's experiences in adult analyses, and particularly in character analyses, show that super-ego formation, though originally a form of adaptation to external reality, can none the less become an obstacle to subsequent adaptations. According to Ferenczi, the splitting of the ego as a result of identification with a prohibition involves serious damage to the ego. The first sign that a splitting of the ego is setting in is a child's protest against the assumption that he himself is "the guilty person." The disadvantage of this method of dealing with the situation is obvious. It is true that it may lead to the child (taking the last example) no longer stamping her foot; but we

can no longer discuss with the child *why* she stamped. Henceforward she will always put us off by saying that it was her
foot and not she herself that was "naughty." The fact that
the "why" remained hidden in Rasmussen's instance as well
is shown by the typical way in which the account of the whole
episode is worded: "one day she wanted to be naughty."
The educators lay the stress upon the rule of conduct: "you
must not stamp your foot at your parents." Any impulses that
cause the emergence of a wish to stamp are therefore to be
dreaded, and the child will have nothing to do with them. In
this way, however, after the super-ego formation has been
effected, both parts of the ego cease to be susceptible to influence: one because it is split off and no longer recognized as
a portion of our self, and the other, which has already been
made rigid by identification with the prohibition, because it
only admits of a strictly circumscribed method of behavior.
Any lifting of the rigid regulation is guarded against by the
anxiety which made the identification (the splitting of the ego)
necessary. Thus we see that every adaptation by means of
identification is at the same time a limitation upon the free and
elastic capacity for adaptation which rests upon an understanding judgment of the situation. In place of that capacity
we only too often find a rigid, automatic character which,
though it is a product of practical acts of adaptation, can nevertheless find itself in gross conflict with the demands of reality.[3]
In what follows I shall return to the consideration of how
educational methods can be adapted so as to reduce to a
minimum the development of automatisms of character.

This discussion must inevitably raise the question of how
the part played by identification can be reconciled with the
domination of the pleasure principle in mental life. It is true
that, as we have seen, identification always operates in the
interest of narcissism and does what it can to defend narcissism; yet it may well seem that the price paid for that defense
is far too high. The child takes over the adults' desires and
tastes and makes them his own; following their example, he
is ready to condemn what has previously been pleasurable

[3] The removal of the splitting of the ego by recollecting its causative
experiences can enable a person to submit his automatisms to conscious control. Such conscious control and the accompanying reduction of anxiety is of course not the same thing as a reduction of the
inhibitions of instinct that are necessary to civilization. What happens
is simply that anxiety is replaced as the basis for the restriction of
instinct by love and reason.

to him and ultimately he goes so far as to remove the forbidden feelings and thoughts entirely from his consciousness.

Children will not infrequently tell us how hard it is for them to fulfill these requirements. A little girl of seven once said to me: "I'm not allowed to do anything nice and I have to do everything nasty." And here is the heart-rending complaint made to his mother by a six-year-old boy: "I'd no idea when I was born that I should have such a bad time." When his mother asked him in astonishment what had happened to him that was so terrible, he enumerated all those apparently trivial prohibitions and restrictions which *we* scarcely notice but which embitter a child's life.

And in this connection we must not forget that complaints of this kind are only made by children who are in a relatively good state, that is to say, who retain some degree of freedom of thought. The most tactful education cannot protect a child from the sufferings necessarily involved in the process of putting a rein upon the instincts—partly because education begins at an age at which it is too early for us to be able to count on understanding and partly because the measures in question are not always of a kind where understanding is possible. For the requirements imposed upon small children are to a great extent a matter of convention and the only ground for obeying them is fear of losing the parents' love. Yet it follows from the narcissistic nature of young children that the love which they receive from their environment, essential though it is to them, cannot compensate them for the loss of their primitive instinctual gratifications. A child depends upon us to a high degree, but he does not love us enough to be able to make so great a sacrifice for our sake. That is to say, we can only force him to make the renunciation, without being in a position to offer him a full compensation for it. But against all this there is the fact that a human being is only able to make a renunciation in return for some substitute gratification, which, indeed, follows from our inability to extinguish the instincts by any defensive measures. But it is in the very nature of an instinct to strive to find its way by some path or other to its inevitable discharge. The question thus arises in what manner a child gratifies the instincts with which, on the basis of his identification with his educators, he has repudiated any kind of association.

When I was speaking of the education of the instincts, I mentioned that the various inhibitions divert an instinct from its original direction. It is true, of course, that a diversion of this kind is not possible in the case of every instinct: for instance, hunger can only be satisfied by eating. Susceptibility to diversion is primarily a quality of the sexual instincts. This peculiarity, coupled with identificatory thinking, affords them an almost unlimited possibility of making their way through. And in this, the opportunities for gratification that are offered by identification with adults play a particularly important part, since they facilitate considerably a child's social adaptation.

At a first glance this assertion may seem strange: for identification with his elders brings a child little else than a restriction of his instincts. But the apparent contradiction can be explained by an example. Let us take an event that occurs in the life of every child. Uncle Doctor arrives and looks down the child's throat with a spoon. On the first such occasion most children react violently against the assault and make it absolutely clear that the whole thing is very far indeed from pleasing them. But, strange to say, instead of forgetting the unpleasant business as quickly as possible, they almost without exception begin soon afterward to play at doctor. Thus the child behaves after the doctor's visit just as he does after parting from an object that he likes. This is all the more peculiar because, according to what we have hitherto found, a child identifies himself with an absent object in order to replace it and so get rid of his longing for it. But children do not long for the doctor: so what can be the meaning of the identification here? The child dislikes what the doctor does to him but he is compelled to submit to it. Then, afterward, the child becomes the doctor, looks down everyone's throat, applies compresses, gives medicine, and so on. Thus he does actively what he suffered passively. We know how much it injures a child's narcissism if he is obliged to put up with something against his will. By means of the identification he brings about the interchange of roles which he so much desires. Moreover, in playing at doctor the child is able to express his anger. This is shown by the fact that the whole procedure is as a rule repeated in the game in a more merciless fashion than the child himself actually experienced. We find the same thing happen when children play at Mummy and Daddy or at School. Children who have never been hit will beat their dolls black and blue for the sort of offenses that they themselves commit. The splitting of the ego, which I spoke of above, makes it possible for a child to abreact his aggressiveness not only upon his dolls or upon other objects but also upon himself. The severity toward our own self which we call conscience is indeed nothing but a turning back of our sadism upon our own ego.

We have already discussed the narcissistic pleasure which a child obtains from its identification with a command. To this we may now add that by falling in with the command the child becomes more like the adult and that anything that diminishes the gap between the two of them soothes the injury suffered by the child's narcissism. In order to be like adults, children will put up with the boredom of being good, will consent to dress in uncomfortable clothes—in short, will think anything in the world desirable merely because it forms part of the adults' system of life. This narcissistic advantage still further increases the conservative way in which, as I have already remarked, a child clings to a command when once he has obeyed it. Incidentally, this conservatism is also a good method by which to abreact his aggressiveness. In every nursery we can see the way in which from time to time the adults become the slaves of their own commands. There is no one more critical than a child: he perceives the slightest inconsistency in his parents' behavior and makes them pay for it.

For instance, a little boy was promised by his father that he would take him for a walk on Sunday. Some visitors came, however, and the promise was forgotten. In the middle of the lunch the child suddenly declared in deadly serious tones: "Daddy tells lies too!" Since obedience (in the present instance the love of truth) is not the result of understanding but of identification, the child knows neither compromise nor consideration. So it can come about that by means of identification a code of laws is established in the child, which brings him into a growing opposition to his own parents and that he turns against his parents the commands which he took over from them.

A good example of this is offered by daughters. We may often find that, if a daughter who has been brought up on extremely moral lines discovers that her mother is in fact living in sexual relations with a man, she will either feel a profound contempt for her or pity her as a poor, weak woman who is compelled to humiliate herself. For the severe daughter, by identification with her educative prohibitions, has long ago blotted out of her mind the fact that she herself once had longings for a sexual life and that all her wishes took the direction of wanting, like her mummy, to be loved by her daddy, to have children and to feed them. Along with all the rest of the commands, she has obeyed the one which told her that a girl must not have such thoughts; but her old grudge reappears in the severity with which she now condemns her mother. In this highly typical case the mother's behavior intensifies the child's impulse to identify herself with her commands instead of loving and comprehending. Love is made more difficult by the fact that the mother permits herself what she forbids to the child; and comprehension is wrecked by the contradictory discovery that an adult is quite free to do what in a child is regarded as a piece of naughtiness or even as a sin.

The educational methods adopted determine whether a child identifies itself with the command or with the real parents. In either case the result may be an estrangement between parents and children. If the education is strict, then the child (as in the previous example) will identify himself with the commands and, from the height of his superior self-control, will look down with contemptuous condemnation upon his parents and the whole of adult society. If the pressure of education is less severe, then the child will identify himself with the parents, will do what they do and will come into conflict with the prohibitions and commands, which will be constantly insisted upon—even though unsuccessfully—by his wider environment. In that case it will be made impossible for the child to be "good." He does everything like his parents and none the less is met with nothing but reproofs. The uncertainty in which such a child finds himself makes love for his parents no less difficult than in a straightforward character formation based upon identification. Here, too, the final result will be estrangement. A person who has remained under the sway of his instincts will come into conflict with his parents, who preach morality but have given him neither the strength for self-control nor a true freedom.

In this way, then, it comes about that identification itself may in the long run separate children from their parents. The most effective countermeasure is that, in educating a child, we should seek from the very first to work as much as possible upon his reason—in other words, to replace identification, so far as we possibly can, by understanding. This can be achieved in a variety of ways. In the first place, we must give up any attempt at producing records in the direction of early training. For what we gain by that means in rapid adaptation we lose in flexibility of thought. Thus many things which a child of one or two can only accomplish by means of identification can without too much trouble be made intelligible to a child of three or four. Of course we must not imagine that by measures of this kind we can get rid of identification altogether. To begin with, it sets in at a stage long before explanations of any sort are possible, and, in the second place, as we are already aware "understanding" and "explaining" are also based upon identification. Nevertheless, we can avoid producing too great a rigidity in identification, too gross a subjugation of the child's ego. If he is not obliged to condemn his own wish in addition to obeying the educatory command, much less of his aggressiveness toward his parents will be worked into the identification.

Another effective way in which it is possible to avoid blind adaptation based upon identification lies in adults being ready openly to admit, even to quite small children, any occasional mistakes of their own.[4] We mean, of course, such mistakes as the child himself might make and can himself as a rule detect. Admitting a mistake encourages him to use his powers of criticism and to dare to think for himself. It is instructive to watch a child when a mistake or a piece of ignorance has been admitted to him by his parents. On the one hand he is delighted by the event since it brings him closer to them, but on the other hand he protests against it and insists that they should not makes mistakes but should remain omniscient and omnipotent. For if parents too can make mistakes, there is a risk of losing the substitute gratification which the child has tried to achieve by means of identification. A child begins by regarding himself as omnipotent; then, when he is compelled to obey a command, he abandons this omnipotence, but at the same time attributes it to his parents whom, by means of identification, he seeks to resemble.

Numbers of children's sayings prove that in their fantasy nothing is impossible to their parents. Here is one example out of many. A girl of six was refused something she wanted on the ground that her father had no money. The child: "Then, why don't you make some, Daddy?" The father: "Only the King can do that." The child (greatly disappointed): "But aren't you a King?" The following episode shows how deeply

---

[4] This way of behaving to children agrees precisely with Ferenczi's advice upon the behavior of analysts in character analyses. He recommends the admission by the analyst of any occasional slips or errors that he may make as being one of the most valuable helps in the difficult work of demolishing what has become an automatic method of behaving on the part of the patient.

a child's narcissism is injured when it turns out that someone (his father, for instance) with whom he has identified himself is not the most important person in the world. The father was mountaineering, and the little boy heard on this occasion that someone else and not his father was acting as leader. He found the fact quite incredible and it was hardly possible to make him understand that his father was not always first—the one position that he himself wanted to occupy.

What children so often sigh for—"when I'm grown up"—means, as we all know, "when I can do everything I want to." Thus identification is a means by which they seek to recapture their old position of autocracy; and this hope is increased by parents who, while being strict with their children, allow themselves every sort of indulgence. Most parents believe that they are educating their children for the tasks of life by exacting unquestioning obedience and limitless faith from them. But the facts are just the other way, and children are brought into closer contact with reality if they learn that even their parents are neither onmipotent nor infallible.

By way of summary, it may be said that identification never fails to reveal itself as a direct derivative of narcissism. Even though it sometimes looks as though it were a means toward doing without something and making an adaptation, it turns out in the end that it is clinging obstinately to its original aim, the defense of narcissism. In contrast to narcissism, love and understanding are the two factors by whose help we enter into a true relation with reality. From this it follows that in education we must attach the greatest importance to these two motive forces. Capacity to love and understanding (or reason) are the two genuine weapons for the conquest of the external world. For, while through identification we yield to external force by way of a kind of mimicry, love and reason enable us to influence the external world in the direction of our wishes.

The Art of Children

SIR HERBERT READ

(1943, 1956)

In his book *Education through Art,* Sir Herbert Read, like
Plato, advocates that art be the basis of education. Like
Dewey, he believes we should try to balance intellect
and feeling in some more organic system of education,
encouraging aesthetic sensibility to preserve the integrity
of human personality. In this selection he relates children's art to early play, their spontaneity to the quality
we later term "inspiration." The growth of content in
the art of children, which is at first non-representational,
shows Read that children first record their feelings, only
later their perceptions.

The art itself is nature.—Froebel

1. *Free Expression*

The child begins to *express* itself from birth. It begins with
certain instinctive desires which it must make known to the
external world, a world which is at first represented almost
exclusively by the mother. Its first cries and gestures are, therefore, a primitive language by means of which the child tries
to communicate with others.

But already in the first few weeks of its life we can distinguish between expression which is directed to a specific
end—namely, securing the satisfaction of some appetite, such
as hunger; and expression which is undirected and has no
other object but to exteriorize a more generalized feeling, such
as pleasure, anxiety or anger. It is true that these two modes
of expression are related: the satisfaction of hunger, for example, induces a state of pleasure which is then expressed in
a smile; or the prolongation of hunger induces a state of displeasure or pain which is then expressed in angry cries. But
as often as not the states of pleasure and displeasure are not

immediately or directly connected or associated with instinctive needs, and the expression is *apparently* disinterested.

We may say, therefore, that the state of feeling which is expressed varies in definiteness, even in an infant. In popular language we already distinguish between a *feeling* and a *mood*. The one is concentrated, the other diffuse. But what is diffuse is not necessarily less urgent; indeed, the very diffuseness of a mood may give rise to a very positive need of expression, for we feel the need to define what is indefinite. For example, the existence in us of "a vague feeling of anxiety," which is a mood in our sense of the word, will inspire activities of quite a general, and apparently unrelated nature. The child, no less than the adult, has such moods, and desires to express them. Such expression is, of course, ultimately controlled by the somatic (particularly the glandular) and psychological disposition of the child, but because it is relatively indirect and apparently not designed to secure the satisfaction of an immediate need, we call it *"free expression."* We may perhaps anticipate a later discussion by remarking here that it is not implied that "free" expression is necessarily "artistic" expression.

2. *Play or Art?*

Free expression covers a wide range of bodily activities and mental processes. Play is the most obvious form of free expression in children and there has been a persistent attempt on the part of anthropologists and psychologists to identify all forms of free expression with play. The play theory has, indeed, a very respectable ancestry, going back to Kant and Schiller on the philosophical side, and to Froebel and Spencer on the psychological side. Froebel went so far as to claim that "play is the highest expression of human development in the child, for it alone is the free expression of what is in the child's soul. It is the purest and most spiritual product of the child, and at the same time it is a type and copy of human life at all stages and in all relations."[1] In this wide sense we should have no difficulty in describing as a form of play those plastic modes of expression with which we are now concerned; but the tendency since Froebel's time has been to give a much

[1] *Chief Writings on Education*, trans. by S. S. F. Fletcher and J. Welton (London, 1908), p. 50. For a more general survey of the play element in culture, see J. Huizinga, *Homo Ludens* (London, 1949).

narrower interpretation to play activity. Spencer, for example, regarded children's play as the discharge of surplus energy, a biological theory which was further developed by Karl Groos and Stanley Hall. It is not part of my present purpose to give a critical account of the play theory—this, indeed, has been done fairly recently and very adequately by Dr. Margaret Lowenfeld[2]—but it must be stated quite generally that the biological or genetic point of view fails to make the distinction, which from our point of view is essential, between free and functional modes of expression. Dr. Lowenfeld provides a very necessary corrective to this functional bias. For example, she criticizes Groos for failing "to distinguish between movements made by the child in the effort to gain control over his body, which are to the child purely functional in purpose, and movements and activities made by the child for the sake only of the pleasure they bring."[3] In her own view "play in children is the expression of the child's relation to the whole of life, and no theory of play is possible which is not also a theory which will cover the whole of a child's relation to life. Play . . . is taken as applying to all activities in children that are spontaneous and self-generated; that are ends in themselves; and that are unrelated to 'lessons' or to the normal physiological needs of a child's own day." This is a point of view almost identical with the one to be put forward here: the only difference being that while Dr. Lowenfeld regards art as a form of play, we regard play as a form of art. This is not a merely verbal distinction, because our order of words does in effect restore a teleological element which Dr. Lowenfeld has altogether rejected. Art we have already defined as mankind's effort to achieve integration with the basic forms of the physical universe and the organic rhythms of life. All forms of play (bodily activity, repetition of experience, fantasy, realization of environment, preparation for life, group games—these are Dr. Lowenfeld's categories) are so many kinaesthetic attempts at integration, and from this point of view are akin to the ritual dances of primitive races and like them are to be regarded as rudimentary forms of poetry and drama, with which are naturally associated rudimentary forms of the visual and plastic arts.[4]

[2] *Play in Childhood* (London, 1935).
[3] *Op. cit.*, p. 34.
[4] Hartlaub (*Der Genius im Kinde;* Breslau, 1922, p. 23) suggests that play becomes art the moment it is directed to an audience or spectator. Cf. Sully, quotation given on pages 116–7.

3. *Spontaneity and Inspiration*

Perhaps what we need, as a first step in this discussion, is a definition of *spontaneity,* especially in relation to such terms as *inspiration, creation* and *invention.* The opposite term to spontaneity is *constraint,* and negatively spontaneity may be defined as doing something or expressing oneself without constraint. The notion is always of an inner activity or volition, and of the absence of obstacles to this inner activity in the external world.[5]

Obviously inner activity may be different kinds of degrees. It may be what Spencer and Groos describe as an accumulation of "energy," the release of this pressure taking the form of bodily activity. The mechanism of this process is presumably sensation, but the energy may equally well be emotional, or rational, or intuitional—that is to say, it may be an activity of any one of the four mental functions, and ideally it would be desirable to have a separate term for the spontaneous or unconstrained expression of each of these forms of mental activity.

In the natural course of growth these mental activities are expressed without constraint, or with only so much constraint as is implied in the act of communication. In that sense the whole of our lives, if they are happy, are spontaneous. But what is implied in the Spencer-Groos theory of play, and in various theories of inspiration and "free" expression, is that such day-to-day natural expression of mental activity does not take place—that there is in effect a constraint on such activity, a damming of physical or psychical energy, and that a sudden release of the condition of tension becomes necessary. Spontaneity seems to be too wide a term for such a limited and occasional event. Indeed, if we do not live spontaneously, that is to say, freely exteriorizing our mental activities, then something much worse than a state of mental tension or accumulation arises, namely, a neurosis.

The word "inspiration" might be reserved for the occasional release of mental tension, especially if we do not insist too much on the etymological meaning of the word "inspiration," and if by "mental tension" we imply something far more super-

[5] The problem of spontaneity in relation to the wider problems of social and political freedom is discussed by Erich Fromm: *The Fear of Freedom,* pp. 258–64.

ficial than the state of unconscious repression. At the conclusion of her book on the subject which we have already referred to, Dr. Harding defines inspiration as: "the result of
some unknown factor accidentally met with operating on the
mind of the man of science or artist at that particular moment
when it is pent up to a certain tension either by accumulation of 'visions, colors, forms,' or by facts and pondering over
them in the unsuccessful attempt to solve a problem. Although inspiration can occur to anyone it will only be manifested in its highest degree in those persons who are capable
of this emotional tension."

This definition we may accept as accurate as far as it goes,
but though it does implicitly distinguish between the thinking
activity (pondering over an accumulation of facts in the unsuccessful attempt to solve a problem) and the feeling activity
(the emotional tension produced by an accumulation of visions, colors, forms, etc.[6]), it should for the sake of completeness have covered the accumulation of energy (the sen-
sational aspect) and the much more difficult problem of
intuition. But extended in this sense, the definition would serve
to distinguish clearly between spontaneity and inspiration. Free
or spontaneous expression is the unconstrained exterioriza-
tion of the mental activities of thinking, feeling, sensation and
intuition. Where, however, for some reason these mental activities cannot achieve immediate expression, and a state of tension is produced, the tension may be suddenly and perhaps accidentally released, and then the expression takes on an
inspirational character. The supposition is that unconscious
processes of organization are possible, and that the tension induced in the higher nervous centers of the brain by the given
elements of a problem may of itself "inspire" a solution, which
solution emerges into consciousness the moment the relevant
aesthetic organization is achieved. We shall offer direct evidence of such unconscious processes in a later chapter.

[6] Dr. Harding's definition owes some of its terminology to a striking
description of Alphonse Daudet's views, which she quotes from Léon
Daudet's book on his father (*Alphonse Daudet*, trans. by C. de Kay,
London, 1898). The following passage from the book (pp. 156–7) is
the most significant: his father, Léon says, believed "that in the case of
all creators there are accumulations of sentient force made without
their knowledge. Their nerves, in a state of high excitation, register
visions, colors, forms, and odors in those half-realized reservoirs which
are the treasuries of poets. All of a sudden, through some influence or
emotion, through some accident or thought, these impressions meet each
other with the suddenness of a chemical combination."

It follows that inspiration should have a fourfold character, and indeed there is no difficulty in distinguishing these modes. The sudden solution of the intellectual problem, the "automatic" or lyrical expression of feeling in poetry, the improvised dance or play activity as a release of suppressed energy, the intuitional apprehension of new relations of form in mathematics, music and architecture—these are the inspired moments upon which human progress in the arts and sciences ultimately depends.

The terms "invention" and "creation" may perhaps be incorporated in this definition. The Oxford English Dictionary should be consulted for the various meanings which have at various times been given to the word invention: they range from "to come upon, or find"—the meaning embodied in the name of the church festival known as the Invention of the Cross—to the current sense of devising or originating a new method or instrument. But all the meanings imply previously existing objects or facts, with the mind as merely an agent that arranges or combines them in a new order. Here is no question of accumulation or tension: only the spontaneous exercise of normal mental processes is involved, and their expression in constructive activity.

"Creation," on the other hand, should imply the calling into existence of what previously had no form or feature. It is an anomalous word, for strictly speaking there can only be creation out of nothing, as in the myth of the Creation. Otherwise, creation always involves the use and adaptation of existing materials, and therefore the difference between invention and creation can only be one of degree. It would seem best, therefore, to avoid the words create, creative and creation unless the context makes it clear that we are not using them in a literal sense.

4. Montessori on Spontaneous Expression

These considerations are not without relevance to our immediate subject, the nature of the activity carried on by children when they get hold of a pencil or a brush and proceed to draw or paint. Obviously, in so far as such children act of their own free will, their activity is spontaneous. But is the product of their activity in any sense inspired—can it in any sense of the word be described as artistic? Or is it, as Dr. Lowenfeld suggests, merely one form of play?

We may best approach this question, which has many implications, by quoting a passage from one of Dr. Montessori's books:

"There can be no 'graduated exercises in drawing,' leading up to an artistic creation. That goal can be attained only through the development of mechanical technique and through freedom of the spirit. That is our reason for not teaching drawing directly to the child. We prepare him indirectly, leaving him free to the mysterious and divine labor of producing things according to his own feelings. Thus drawing comes to satisfy a need for expression, as does language; and almost every idea may seek expression in drawing. The effort to perfect such expression is very similar to that which the child makes when he is spurred on to perfect his language in order to see his thoughts translated into reality. This effort is spontaneous; and the real drawing teacher is the inner life, which of itself develops, attains refinement, and seeks irresistibly to be born into external existence in some empirical form. Even the smallest children try spontaneously to draw outlines of the objects which they see; but the hideous drawings which are exhibited in the common schools, as 'free drawings,' 'characteristic' of childhood, are not found among our children. These horrible daubs so carefully collected, observed and catalogued by modern psychologists as 'documents of the infant mind' are nothing but monstrous expressions of intellectual lawlessness; they show only that the eye of their child is uneducated, the hand inert, the mind insensible alike to the beautiful and the ugly, blind to the true as well as to the false. Like most documents collected by psychologists who study the children of our schools, they reveal not the soul but the errors of the soul; and these drawings, with their monstrous deformities, show simply what the uneducated human being is like. Such things are not 'free drawings' by children. *Free drawings* are possible only when we have a *free child* who has been allowed to grow and perfect himself in the assimilation of his surroundings and in mechanical reproduction; and who, when left free to create and express himself, actually does create and express himself.

"The sensory and manual preparation for drawing is nothing more than an alphabet; but without it the child is an illiterate and cannot express himself. And just as it is impossible to study the writing of people who cannot write, so there can be no psychological study of the drawings of children who have been abandoned to spiritual and muscular chaos. All psychic expressions acquire value when the inner personality has acquired value by the development of its formative processes. Until this fundamental principle has become an absolute acquisition we can have no idea of the psychology of a child as regards his creative powers.

"Thus, unless we know how a child should develop in order to unfold his natural energies, we shall not know how drawing as a natural expression is developed. The universal development of the wondrous language of the hand will come not from a 'school of design,' but from a 'school of the new man' which will cause this language to spring forth spontaneously like water from an inexhaustible spring. To confer the gift of drawing we must create an eye that sees, a hand that obeys, a soul that feels; and in this task the whole life must cooperate. In this sense life itself is the only preparation for drawing. Once we have lived, the inner spark of vision does the rest."[7]

This passage is evidently written with an unusual degree of feeling, which may account for what appear to be certain confusions of thought. Drawing cannot, or should not, be taught, says Dr. Montessori. It should be a spontaneous activity, a free expression of the child's own self, own thoughts. Thus far Dr. Montessori is obviously conforming to the definition of spontaneity we have just given. But then she goes on to condemn, in violent language, children's drawings which are certainly the product of a spontaneous activity. She applies to these drawings a certain aesthetic standard—condemns them because they are monstrous, ugly, deformed, etc. That is to say, she judges them by some standard of "beauty" which is assumed rather than stated, but which we may in our turn assume to be the standard of a classical idealism, or perhaps of a naïve naturalism.

To ensure that the child should produce drawings which conform to this standard, we gather that its "inner life" must first be developed, refined, inspired with some vision of "eternal existence"; and that at the same time the hand of the child should be trained in muscular ability, so that it can reproduce its spiritualized feelings. There are three preliminary conditions which must be satisfied before the child is allowed to express itself by plastic means—"an eye that sees, a hand that obeys, and a soul that feels."

[7] *The advanced Montessori Method* (London, 1918), Vol. II, pp. 304–6.

I have no wish to question the idealism which inspires the whole of Dr. Montessori's teachings: it has been one of the most significant and valuable contributions to modern education theory and practice. But to reject all "graduated exercises in drawing" and "schools of design" with a view to liberating the child's powers of expression and then to substitute "the development of mechanical technique" and "the development of the formative processes of the inner personality" is merely to substitute one form of discipline for another, without making clear in what the superiority of the new system consists. That is to say, it is by no means clear why a mechanical technique should not be developed by graduated exercises in drawing; and the development of the inner personality of the child is certainly not restricted by the production of drawings which, though natural and spontaneous, fail to satisfy the canons of "beauty." It is perhaps only a question of priority, but before we can proceed with this discussion it is obvious that we must have some clear conception of what actually happens when a child begins to draw spontaneously It is a question to which psychologists and educationalists have given much attention, but without, in my opinion, coming to any very satisfactory conclusion.

5. *What Happens When the Child Begins to Draw?*

Let us first glance at the history of this problem. It begins with Ruskin. In 1857 *The Elements of Drawing* was published, and in this and subsequent works (e.g., *The Laws of Fésole*, 1877–9) Ruskin first drew attention to what might be called the educational possibilities of drawing. It would be fair to say that Ruskin's ultimate object was the production of artists; even when he was teaching at the Working Men's College, he was sustained by the hope that he might discover a Giotto among his pupils. But some remarks of his in the *Elements of Drawing*[8] inspired an English teacher, Ebenezer

[8] Ruskin: *Elements of Drawing*, 1857. Preface, § 11: "I do not think it advisable to engage a child (under the age of twelve or fourteen) in any but the most voluntary practice of art. If it has talent for drawing, it will be continually scrawling on what paper it can get; and should be allowed to scrawl at its own free will, due praise being given for every appearance of care, of truth, in its efforts. It should be allowed to amuse itself with cheap colors almost as soon as it has sense enough to wish for them. If it merely daubs the paper with senseless stains, the color may be taken away till it knows better; but as soon as it be-

Cooke, to reconsider the principles of art-teaching in the schools, and two articles which Cooke contributed to the *Journal of Education* at the end of 1885 and beginning of 1886 are the first documents in a long and increasingly complicated process of research.

Even before this time, Cooke had established relations with the leading English psychologist of the period—James Sully, and together they discussed the significance of children's drawings. The subject was beginning to awaken interest in other countries. In 1887 Corrado Ricci published *L'arte dei bambini* at Bologna, and the following year *L'art et la poésie chez l'enfant* by Bernard Perez appeared in Paris. These works already approached the subject from the point of view of child-psychology, but it was Sully's *Studies in Childhood* (1895) which first attempted to give a coherent theoretical explanation to the gathering volume of evidence. As was perhaps inevitable at that time, the theory was evolutionary. Sully deals with several aspects of the child's mind, and when he comes to deal with the child as artist, he traces a typical line of development from selected drawings and makes a first attempt to relate this development to the "phenomena of primitive race-culture." Art-activity he regards as continuous but not identical with play-activity. "The play impulse becomes the art-impulse (supposing it is strong enough to survive the play-years) when it is illumined by a growing participation in the social consciousness, and a sense of the common worth of things, when, in other words, it becomes conscious of itself as a power of shaping semblances which shall have value for other eyes or ears, and shall bring recognition and renown."[9]

In tracing the evolution of children's drawings, Sully con-

gins painting red coats on soldiers, striped flags to ships, etc., it should have colors at command and, without restraining its choice of subject in that imaginative and historical art, of a military tendency, which children delight in (generally quite as valuable, by the way, as any historical art delighted in by their elders), it should be gently led by the parents to draw, in such childish fashion as may be, the things it can see and likes—birds or butterflies, or flowers or fruit."

[9] *Studies of Childhood*, p. 327. Cf. the following definition of play by a modern psychologist: "Play is a necessity, not merely to develop the bodily and mental faculties, but to give to the individual that reassuring contact with his fellows which he has lost when the mother's nurtural services are no longer required or offered. . . . Cultural interests do ultimately form a powerful antidote to loneliness even where there is no participator present in person; that is to say, cultural pursuits have a social value even where 'the other person' is imagined or left unspecified." Ian D. Suttie, *The Origins of Love and Hate* (1935), p. 18.

fined himself to delineations of the human figure and of animals, especially the horse, and with a few exceptions he did not go outside the age-range from two or three to about six. He wisely gave preference to drawings made by children in elementary schools, "as these appear to illustrate the childish manner with less of parental interference than is wont to be present in a cultured home."

Sully then distinguishes the various stages of development, beginning with aimless scribbling, passing through primitive design "typified by what I have called the lunar scheme of the human face," and reaching at about the age of six a more sophisticated treatment of the human figure. We shall not review Sully's classification in detail, because it was made the basis of all subsequent classifications and it is better to give a more complete elaboration. But this process of elaboration can be traced stage by stage through Levinstein (1905), Kerschensteiner (1905), Stern (1910), Rouma (1913), Luquet (1913), Krötzsch (1917), Burt (1922), Luquet (1927), Wulff (1927), and Eng (1931). This does not altogether exhaust the list, but it represents a structure built upon the foundations laid by Cooke and Sully.

6. *The Stages of Development in Children's Drawing*

We may take, as the most schematic summary of this genetic theory of the evolution of children's drawings, the stages distinguished by Sir Cyril Burt in his *Mental and Scholastic Tests* (pp. 319–22). They are as follows:

(i) *Scribble*—age 2–5 with peak at 3. Subdivided into:
  (a) purposeless pencilings—purely muscular movements from the shoulder, usually from right to left.
  (b) purposive pencilings—the scribble is a center of attention and may be given a name.
  (c) imitative pencilings—the overmastering interest is still muscular, but wrist movements have replaced arm movements, and finger movements tend to replace wrist movements, usually in an effort to mimic the movements of an adult draftsman.
  (d) localized scribbling—the child seeks to reproduce specific parts of an object—a stage transitional to:
(ii) *Line*—age 4.
  Visual control is now progressive. The human figure becomes the favorite subject, with circle for head, dots

for eyes, and a pair of single lines for legs. More rarely a second circle may be added for body, and more rarely still, a pair of lines for the arms. It is usual for feet to be represented earlier than arms or body. A complete synthesis of parts is unobtainable and often unattempted.

(iii) *Descriptive Symbolism*—age 5–6.

Human figure now reproduced with tolerable accuracy, but as a crude symbolic schema. The features are localized in the roughest way and each is a conventional form. The general "schema" assumes a somewhat different type with different children, but the same child clings pretty closely, for most purposes and for long periods, to the same favorite pattern.

(iv) *Descriptive Realism*—age 7–8.

The drawings are still logical rather than visual. The child "sets down what he knows, not what he sees; and is still thinking, not of the present individual, but rather of the generic type." He is trying to communicate, express, or catalogue all that he remembers, or all that interests him, in a subject. The "schema" becomes more true to detail; items, however, are suggested more by the association of ideas than by the analysis of percepts. Profile views of the face are attempted, but perspective, opacity, foreshortening, and all the consequences of singleness of viewpoint are still disregarded. There is a gathering interest in decorative details.

(v) *Visual Realism*—age 9–10.

The child passes from the stage of drawing from memory and imagination to the stage of drawing from nature. There are two phases:

(a) two dimensional phase—outline only is used.

(b) three-dimensional phase—solidity is attempted. Attention is given to overlapping and perspective. A little shading and occasional foreshortening may be attempted. Landscapes are attempted.

(vi) *Repression*—age 11–14.

This stage sets in most commonly about the age of 13. Burt (and his view was representative at the time he wrote) regards this stage as part of the child's natural development. Progress in the attempt to reproduce objects is now at best laborious and slow, and the child becomes disillusioned and discouraged. Interest is transferred to expression through the medium of language, and if drawing continues the preference is for conventional designs, and the human figure becomes rare.

(vii) *Artistic Revival*—early adolescence.

"From about the age of 15, drawing for the first time blossoms into a genuine artistic activity." Drawings now tell a story. A clear distinction between the sexes is now evident. Girls show a love of richness in color, of grace in form, of beauty in line; youths tend to use drawing more as a technical and mechanical outlet.

But by many, perhaps by most, this final stage is never reached. The repression at the previous stage has been too complete.

Such is the generally accepted account of the development of children's drawings.[10] It has been criticized in some of

[10] From a more formal point of view *eleven* stages of development have been distinguished by Dr. Ruth Griffiths (*Imagination in Early Childhood*, London, 1935, pp. 190–209). She summarizes these stages as follows:

(i) *Undifferentiated scribble.*

(ii) *Rough geometrical shapes appear,* usually circles and squares.

(iii) The making of further objects by the *combination of lines and squares,* and separately of circles. The circles and squares are not yet combined together.

(iv) *Combination of circles and lines* to make many other objects, of which one of outstanding interest is the human figure.

(v) *Juxtaposition of many objects* rapidly drawn and named, but often unrecognizable.

(vi) *Tendency to concentrate on one object at a time,* bolder work, care taken, a degree of detail present.

(vii) *Further juxtaposition,* but clear subjective association usually present, work recognizable.

(viii) *Partial synthesis.* Some items are shown in definite relation to each other.

(ix) *The pure picture.* A tendency also to draw one picture only.

(x) *Multiplication of pictures.* Pure joy of representation.

(xi) *Development of a theme* by means of a series of pictures.

In an accompanying table (p. 211) Dr. Griffiths shows a definite correlation between these stages of development and the mental ages of fifty children. (Binet-Simon scale, Stanford Revision.)

More recently Mrs. Rhoda Kellogg has made a study of more than 100,000 drawings and paintings by children of two, three and four years of age in the Golden Gate Nursery Schools in San Francisco (*What Children Scribble and Why,* 1955). She found that "beginning with the first stroke of the pencil and continuing to the time when the child can make the finished drawing in which there is a pictorial likeness to the objects drawn, there is evidence of sequential unfolding of drawing ability." She discovered that the scribbles could be classified into twenty basic types (dot, vertical line, horizontal line, diagonal line, curved line, zigzag line, loop line, spiral line, etc.). Out of various combinations of these basic scribbles emerge six basic designs (Greek cross, square, circle, triangle, odd shaped areas and diagonal cross). These are then combined or aggregated, and representation features are gradually attached to, or associated with, these combines and aggregates. One of these basic designs seems to predominate—the circle combined with the cross, which is the magic circle or "mandala," "the dominant religious image of the whole Oriental world." Mrs. Kellogg shows, in an its aspects, particularly by Wulff. Our own criticism will be directed to three fundamental points:

A The concept of the "schema."
B The genetic theory in general—the neglected correlation of expression and temperament.
C The supposed inevitability of a stage of "repression."

7. The "Schema"

So far as I can discover, the word schema was first used casually, and without particular significance, by Sully in the following context (*Op. cit.*, pp. 352–3). He has been describing the earliest attempts of children to represent hands and fingers, and after discussing various radial arrangements, he remarks that an important advance on these crude devices is seen where an attempt is made to indicate the hand and the relation of the fingers to the hand. "One of the earliest of these attempts takes the form of the well-known toasting-fork or rake hand. Here a line at right angles to that of the arm symbolically represents the hand, and the fingers are set forth by the prongs or teeth. . . . Number is here as little attended to as in the radial arrangements. It is worth noting that this *schema* seems to be widely diffused among children of different nationalities, and occurs in the drawings of untaught adults."

The word thus innocently used on this occasion by Sully was taken up by Kerschensteiner and given portentous significance by him and by subsequent German psychologists.[11] The

ingenious chart, how a variety of pictorial representations can be gradually evolved from this single basic design.

These researches would seem to prove that the schema is not arbitrary in its origin: there is in the child's scribbling activity an inherent tendency to form, and even to a specific form that has primordial significance for the unconscious.

[11] It is amusing to observe that thirty-six years later, the translator of Helga Eng's *Psychology of Children's Drawings* (London, 1931, p. 109n) deliberates on how this German word *Schema* should be translated into English, and decides on "formula" as an English equivalent. "Dr. Eng pointed out that, although 'schema,' 'schematized,' etc., are very rarely used in English, some English psychologists have adopted them(!) . . . In spite of this, it was decided to use 'formula,' etc., as these terms are already in common use in the same sense in connection with drawing and painting generally. It seems unnecessary to introduce a new term, which has the grave disadvantage of being closely similar to a common word, 'scheme,' having an allied meaning."

general meaning of the word, however, is clear enough. Apart
from certain rare exceptions, when children first begin to draw
intentionally, they apparently make no attempt to translate
their visual images into plastic equivalents (imitative or naturalistic representations), but are fully satisfied with certain
graphic signs which they identify with their images. These
graphic signs may vary from a mark or scribble which has
no recognizable relation to the object associated with it, to a
linear outline in which all the main features of the object
are economically indicated. With their passion for a unitary
genetic pattern, all previous writers on the subject have attempted to trace the evolution of the schema, from the first
chance recognition of a resemblance in the child's purposeless
scribblings, to the first attempt to give such arbitrary discoveries some coherence (Schema der lokalen Anordnung),
and soon to a deliberate *linear* or one-dimensional schema,
and then to an *outline* or two-dimensional schema. Variations
in the rate at which different children develop along these lines
is accounted for by supposing that some children are more
"visually gifted" than others.

My own observations do not altogether support such a neat
evolutionary theory. In the first place, I have not found that
the first recognizable representational drawings necessarily
emerge by chance from the scribble stage. The drawings by a
boy of three years one month were contemporary with the
child's first scribbling, but were a separate activity, and
clearly indicated a separate intention. They were drawn with
great deliberation, and care was taken to connect the limbs
to the body "securely." But the same child would give a
name to a completely non-representational scribble. From
the beginning the child finds it possible to invest both an
abstract symbol (any mark or object whatsoever) and a
summary "schema" with all the vitality or reality of an image,
and in this, of course, he conforms to the animism of primitive man. Under the influence of this environment (the "naturalistic" taste of his parents and teachers) the modern child
sooner or later discards the abstract symbol, but I find that
some children persist with it, not only longer than others, but
in conjunction with their more representational schemas.
What Luquet, for a later stage of development calls a "dupli-
cité de types," is, in my view, present from the beginning, and
this fact has a fundamental bearing on any psychological
analysis of the child's activity.

Luquet[12] is discussing the drawings of children of about eight years old when he arrives at what he describes as "an almost incredible fact, liable to disturb all preconceived ideas based on a too simple conception of the child's mind, but the truth of which cannot be denied. Not only does the child recognize that other people draw in a style different from his; not only does he expect such people to observe the same fidelity to their style as he does to his; but further, when he draws for another person, he adopts for that occasion the style of that person instead of his own. . . . The universality of this curious fact, which one might call 'duplicity of styles,' is put beyond doubt by looking at the drawings which we find on walls and pavements. These 'graffiti' emanate from children of all ages; sometimes even from adolescents and adults; most of the artists have had schooling, and many of the drawings are done in the interval between two lessons. Now, among them we find a considerable number of those figures without a body, none of which would be acceptable to a teacher. It is necessary then to admit that the child artist uses simultaneously for the same subject two different styles of representation: one for his own personal satisfaction, the other for the satisfaction of other people."

This duplicity, which may be observed from the very beginning of the child's graphic or plastic activity, may be explained as a distinction between (a) what the child does for the satisfaction of his own inner needs, and (b) what he does as a social gesture, as a sign of sympathy with or emulation of, an external person or persons.

The second activity is *imitative,* and all authorities are agreed that from the first scribble onwards, a large element of imitation of the adult enters into the child's drawing. He imitates, not only what the adult draws, but the muscular actions of the adult's hand and fingers. There can be no doubt that this imitative instinct plays a large part in the development of a child's drawing in the direction of realism. There is evidence to show that if a child is accustomed to abstract patterns or paintings, or if the parents are themselves abstract painters, the child will develop an abstract style: it has not been proved that the normal child has an irresistible desire to make naturalistic representations of objects. There are historical periods during which a non-figurative art prevailed (the

[12] *Le Dessin enfantin* (Paris, 1927), pp. 65–6.

Neolithic age, the Celtic and Arabic civilizations), and such periods prove that a non-representational tradition can be "natural" or "normal" at all stages of individual development. There is no reason to suppose that an infant of the New Stone Age drew humpty-dumpties, and the little Moslem child would presumably not be allowed to indulge in any such naturalistic "schemas."

So far as I am aware, no one has ever made the experiment of bringing up a child in complete immunity from all types of representational art other than its own, and from all adult examples of graphic activity. Such an experiment, if it were possible, would provide valuable evidence. The nearest approach to such evidence is that provided by Münz and Loewenfeld in their observations of the art of weak-sighted and blind children.[13] Unfortunately the evidence for the totally blind relates to subjects already fairly advanced in age, whose haptic experience is already sufficiently coherent for naturalistic representation, and who, moreover, have been subjected to a training with a strong representational bias. I see no reason to suppose that such subjects, if urged to express themselves in abstract symbols, would not have developed a plastic language of a non-representational type.

We may certainly conclude that the graphic activity in the child may be devoid, not merely of any representational intention, but equally of any imitative instinct. Whatever the child may draw under influence or instruction, he does also draw for his own obscure purposes, and it is the nature of this independent activity which must first be established.

8. Kinaesthetic Imagination

But before we proceed to our analysis, let us distinguish a separate activity which might be confused with this graphic activity. We have already seen that Burt describes a stage (i) (b) of "purposive penciling." It arises from the pleasure the child takes in its arm movements, and in the visible trace of the movements left on the paper. Krötzsch[14] has given a

---

[13] V. Loewenfeld: *The Nature of Creative Activity*, and L. Münz and V. Loewenfeld: *Die plastische Arbeiten Blinder* (Brunn, 1934).

[14] *Rhythmus und Form in der freien Kinderzeichnung* (Leipzig, 1917). I have been unable to consult this work, but it is summarized by Wulff, Stern and other writers on the subject. For a more recent and

careful analysis of the development of this purely kinaesthetic activity which he regards as mainly a spontaneous one of the muscles, the expression of an innate bodily rhythm, but for our present purpose we need only note the fact that it does gradually become controlled, repetitious and consciously rhythmical. The line becomes the zigzag, the zigzag a wavy line, the wavy line returns on itself and becomes a loop, and from the loop develops the spiral and the circle. At this point the rhythmical activity is interrupted, for the child, so it is assumed, suddenly recognizes in the circle the outline of an object—the human face. The kinaesthetic activity is supposed to end and the representational activity to begin.

We have already criticized this evolutionary theory, but it may be further objected, that the kinaesthetic activity does not actually end. A closer observation of the child shows that it continues as an independent activity. In one case which I observed (a boy of 3), I noticed that when "cars" were drawn at his request, he would sometimes take the pencil and scribble thickly and fastly over the wheels. When he drew his own first cars, he would repeat this performance. What he was doing was to associate the kinaesthetic activity of scribbling with his motor image of the revolving wheels. The same child would draw long lines and describe them as "cars going along the road."[15]

Another objection to this theory of "sudden recognition" is that long before the child evolves the schema, he will give a name to his scribble. Krötzsch assumes that this is due to

---

extreme theory of the motor origin of children's drawing see R. Arnheim, *Art and Visual Perception* (London and Berkeley, California, 1956). Cf. p. 135, "Drawing, painting, and modeling are a part of human motor behavior, and they may be assumed to have developed from two older and more general kinds of such behavior—physiognomic and descriptive movement."

[15] This observation was anticipated by Froebel—cf. *The Education of Man*, p. 36: "The ball that is rolling or has been rolled, the stone that has been thrown and falls, the water that was dammed and conducted into many branching ditches—all these have taught the child that the effect of a force, in its individual manifestations, is always in the direction of a line.

"Thus the representation of objects by lines soon leads the child to the perception and representation of the direction in which a force acts. 'Here flows a brook,' and saying this, the child makes a mark indicating the course of a brook. . . . Very significantly the child says, 'Here comes a bird flying,' and draws in the direction of the supposed flight a winding line." Cf. also Arnheim, *op. cit.*, p. 138.

adult influence, a view adopted by Wulff.[16] But like Loewen-feld[17] I have frequently observed that children quite spontaneously give names to their scribbles; I do not, however, find that they always subsequently discover some similarities in the scribble to justify the name. There seems to be general agreement that at first naming takes place *after* the scribble has been completed, and that only at a later age does the child announce what his scribble is going to represent. The age at which naming just begins seems to vary widely: Margaret, the child observed in such detail by Dr. Eng, began at the age of 1, ix, 10 (1 year, nine months, ten days). There does not seem to have been the slightest adult suggestion in this case. She began to name her scribbles *before* making them only a few days after first naming the scribbles *after* making them.[18]

9. *The Image and the Sign*

We shall never be able to determine exactly what does happen at this stage of the child's development, but the hypothesis I wish to put forward can be supported by certain analogies from the history of art. I think it might be also supported by considerations drawn from the origin of writing, but I would rather ignore this evidence, which would, even if I were competent to present it, be highly speculative.

I suggest that we have three terms at our disposal: the image, the sign or symbol, and the representation.

We have already considered the nature of the image, and its function in the process of thinking. We found reason to believe that in young children the image is of unusual vividness, and may in a large number of cases be eidetic. But during the course of the child's maturation, the image gradually loses its intensity and individuation, and is replaced by concepts, whose function it is to facilitate the process of thought and reasoning. But we found that in the higher processes of reasoning, where intuition and the perception of pattern or wholeness of relationships is called for, the image still plays an important part.

If we desire to represent an image, so that the image in our mind can be seen and appreciated by other people, we

[16] *Die Kunst des Kindes*, p. 2.
[17] *Op. cit.*, p. 19.
[18] *Psychology of Children's Drawings*, pp. 5–8.

must translate it into a medium of communication. Such media are either aural, visual or kinetic. The principal aural medium is speech, which has evolved from representational or imitative sounds, but in addition to this purely functional medium man has elaborated the arts of song and music, which we may regard as a more subtle kind of language. Kinetic communication is made through the medium of gesture, elaborated into the arts of ritual and dance. Visual communication, with which we are more particularly concerned, aims at a representation of the formal features of the image—its outline, mass and color—in a plastic material like paint or clay, or a glyptic material like stone. The success of this method of communication is usually judged by the *verisimilitude* of the representation, though various stylistic mannerisms are permitted.

But in addition to these forms of communication, mankind has elaborated various *signs* or *symbols,* which may be aural or kinetic, but are more usually graphic or plastic. These signs or symbols are not imitative, avoid verisimilitude, and only become media of communication by agreement between two or more persons. The word "tree" is a sign. It is a sound, or some marks made on paper with ink to represent this sound, which by common agreement and tradition, have come to mean, among the limited number of people who understand the English language, "a perennial plant with single woody self-supporting stem or trunk usually unbranched for some distance above ground." When I speak or write the word "tree" I may or may not bring to mind a memory-image of a particular or a generic tree—that is a psychological problem which does not concern us now. The point is that I can, if required, communicate an image of a tree by the use of a purely abstract sign, the word "tree."

Signs or symbols can be still more arbitrary (for words have an evolutionary history, and are only rarely invented *ad hoc*). If I make the mark * (an asterisk) in the course of writing this page, the reader knows, by previous agreement, that I intend to draw his attention to something outside the normal course of the text—to a footnote, for example. The symbol then stands for a verbal statement or command such as "Look down at the bottom of the page." If I see a cross on a building, I know at once that the building is, or has been, associated with the Christian religion, a vast complex of emotions, images and ideas all reduced to this convenient and economical sign. The field of art is strewn with such symbols, some of them representing images or concepts which we can no longer identify, or can only identify by acquiring special knowledge. If, for example, a peasant were to dig up a gem of the third century A.D. engraved with a fish, he would see a fish and nothing more. But a scholar would be able to tell him that the fish was one of the earliest symbols for the person of Jesus Christ, and that it was based on the fact that the letters of the Greek word for fish make an acrostic for the five Greek words meaning "Jesus Christ, Son of God, Savior"; and the psychologist and ethnologist could further inform him that long before the time of Christ the fish was used as a sexual or fertility symbol in various parts of the world.

Signs or symbols, therefore, vary in their degree of esotericism or obscurity, and the more primitive or repressed the tribe or religion may be, the most esoteric its symbols tend to be, *even to the point of being entirely non-representational or abstract*. From a general aesthetic standpoint I have dealt with such symbols in another book,[19] but I must refer to them again, for their significance is of fundamental importance for an understanding of children's drawings. One of the best examples of this abstract symbolism comes from the native tribes of Central Australia, and since I wrote *Art and Society*, additional material of great value has been collected by Mr. C. P. Mountford, of the South Australian Museum.[20] In Mr. Mountford's words: "The drawings of the Central Australian aborigines are peculiar in that, instead of depicting the particular animal, human being or object in a naturalistic manner, a conventional symbol is used. For example, the U within U design is often used to indicate a human or semi-human ancestor; the circle or spiral, a waterhole, hill or totemic place; the tracks of certain creatures, the animal itself."[21] Mr. Mountford then warns the reader against "attempting to interpret aboriginal rock paintings or carvings without the help of the artist who produced them, or alternatively, an aboriginal who knows their meanings intimately.

[19] *Art and Society* (London, 2nd ed., 1945), pp. 30 ff., and Plates 16 and 17.

[20] See *Transactions of the Royal Society of South Australia*, Vol. LXI (1937), pp. 30–40, 84–95, 226–40; LXII (1938), pp. 241–54. *Records of the South Australian Museum*, Vol. VI (1937–8), pp. 1–28, 111–4.

[21] Cf. the case, quoted on p. 203, of the boy of three who represented cars by lines, i.e. by their tracks.

Symbols, which in one drawing represent a waterhole, will in another illustrate a hill or a camp. It is obvious that the exact meaning cannot be even guessed at, although, in general, certain symbols are used extensively to illustrate the same or similar objects." This agrees with the earlier observations of Spencer and Gillen, quoted in *Art and Society* (pp. 34–5).

What is more significant for our present purpose is that this description of the savage's artistic activities agrees with our observations of the child's earliest artistic activities. He, too, draws lines and spirals and other geometrical marks and gives them a name; and he too will at different times attribute different meanings to the same scribble. It may, of course, be argued that the savage's drawings express a religious symbolism, if only of a primitive magical order, and their abstraction is determined by their magical purpose; and Mountford, indeed, quotes a case of an aboriginal whose drawings, formerly of a conventional "primary" school type and, as a result of his contact with civilized people and schools, quite undistinctive, became abstract and symbolic after he had returned to his tribe and undergone an initiation ceremony.[22] What happened here, in effect, was that the aboriginal exchanged the graphic language of one society for the graphic language of another, the difference being that the first language was diffused and naturalistic, the second arcane and abstract. Both had for him a comparable significance in relation to the societies of which they were characteristic.

I am not suggesting that the young child creates a systematic symbolism: his symbols may be arbitrary and disconnected, but nevertheless, they are a social language of a rudimentary kind, and for adults it is a language which must be interpreted. Incidentally, in reply to a query I addressed to him, Mr. Mountford tells me that the children of the Australian aborigines also draw from an early age, and that their drawings, in general, resemble those of the adults.

The point I wish to make by this comparison is that a child's first drawings, which may at first be quite abstract or nonfigurative, and which then become recognizable symbols or "schemas," have no basis in immediate *visual* experience.[23]

[22] *Records of the S. A. Museum*, VI (1938), pp. 111–4.
[23] Further evidence of this fact is provided by the Rorschach "inkblot reactions," a stimulus to fantasy formation which has been used by several investigators in attempts to measure temperament and personality. Cf. H. Rorschach: *Psychodiagnostik: Methodik und Ergebnisse eines wahrnehmungsdiagnostichen Experiments* (2nd ed., Berne, 1932).

They are not an attempt to translate an image into graphic or plastic form: they are objects with imaginary associations. They are only representational in the sense that a geometrical sign may stand for a visual image or for some other mental element—just as, in the case of the aboriginal, a spiral may stand for a waterhole (or equally for a gum-tree) or parallel lines for a range of hills (or equally for the track of an animal).

10. *Three Hypotheses*

The exact relation of the schema to the image in the child's mind is admittedly difficult to determine. We have a choice of three hypotheses:

(i) The generally accepted theory that the child's drawings, from the first stroke to the final stage of visual realism, represent progressive efforts to achieve the accurate imitation of memory images or percepts. This theory we have already found to be inconsistent with the observed facts.

(ii) The child, unable to translate his images into adequate graphic or plastic representations, is satisfied with a merely associative relationship between a mark he makes (sign or symbol) and an image. This would account for the variability of the images associated with one particular symbol, but it does not explain the child's progressive attempts to elaborate his symbols, nor the persistence of the schema long after an ability to imitate the object in a naturalistic manner has been acquired.

(iii) The child is seeking to escape from the vividness of his eidetic images, from an omnipresent realism. He wants to create something relatively fixed and personal, an escape from reality, something which is "his own," and not an uncalled image. He has a feeling or "affect" which is independent of his conceptual thought (in so far as this has been developed) and of his perceptual images. It is no doubt a residue

Dr. Griffiths, in her experiments with this test, found that the analogy which the child finds almost immediately "is so strong upon him in some cases, that it becomes almost of the nature of identity. Thus the blot does not merely resemble a horse, or a rat, or an airplane, it *is* such. . . . So much is this so, that many children having given the blot a name, and imbued it with all the characteristics of the fancied object, are unable to break free from this idea to find a second association. . . . There are degrees in the strength and force of this identity as observed in different subjects, and in the same subject on different occasions." *Imagination in Early Childhood*, p. 237.

of his perceptual and other bodily (proprioceptive) experiences, but it is not yet communicable. He is "charged" with this feeling or affect, for which images are inadequate, or perhaps too adequate, and for which he has not yet evolved the sophisticated machinery of conceptual thought. He therefore creates—and it is here if anywhere that the use of this word is justified—a visual symbol, a cipher in this language of line, which will express his feelings, communicate its quality to others, fix it in the shifting world of appearances.

Normally, as the child acquires the machinery of conceptual thought, the vividness of his images declines: concurrently, the realism of his drawings increases. There would seem to be something in the nature of a law of compensation, vividness of expression becoming more and more necessary or tolerable as abstractness of thought increases, abstractness of expression becoming less and less necessary as a foil to the vividness of the spontaneous images which until then have crowded the mind.[24] From this point of view we may agree with Hartlaub[25] that the schema or symbol is a natural product ("Naturprodukt") of the child's mind rather than a special faculty of abstraction called into being by special circumstances.

It is this third hypothesis which I propose to adopt, and for which I shall seek further support. But the revolutionary significance of such a theory should be realized. Writing in the light of the first and still too "logical" interpretation of these facts ("the child draws what he means, thinks, knows—not what he sees"), and before their exact nature had been analyzed, William Stern observed that they threw "a dazzling searchlight on the insufficiency of older theories concerning the beginnings of human apprehension and experience. The belief that contemplation, pure and simple, forms the beginnings of all apprehension, and that, from it, abstract knowledge and judgment slowly develop, can no longer be maintained. . . . It is found that, to begin with, the pictorial representation is only looked upon as the symbol of something meant, something thought of, and that it is only after much effort that the power develops of keeping the pictorial representation of things as they appear to the senses free from all

[24] For the distinction between voluntary and spontaneous imagery, see G. H. Betts, *Distribution and Functions of Mental Imagery*, p. 5.
[25] *Op. cit.*, p. 81.

'intentional' features, i.e. those that correspond to the drawer's knowledge and ideas."[26] We may add that this power develops *pari passu* with the control of the mental process of imagining; when the mind can call up images at will (and suppress them at will) then it can bear to represent things "as they appear to the senses." Meanwhile, up to the age of adolescence, nothing could be more unnatural than a naturalistic mode of expression.

[26] *Psychology of Early Childhood*, pp. 352–3. It is odd that such a careful psychologist as Stern should have been so ready to ascribe "knowledge and ideas" to the child of three or four years.

The Ball: First Plaything of Childhood

FRIEDRICH FROBEL

(1907)

In this selection from *Pedagogies of the Kindergarten* Friedrich Froebel, the German educator who founded the kindergarten system, explains the educational impact of a ball on the susceptible infant intellect. Here, as in his other work, Froebel stresses the importance of play in the development of the child, an aspect of childhood subsequently emphasized by psychoanalysts and philosophers of education. He points out how play with the ball stimulates the child's play-speech, encourages him to use play as speech and connects him conversationally with parents and surroundings. Like Dewey, Froebel believes learning progresses from "existence to sensation and thought."

Even the word ball, in our significant language [German-Ed.], is full of expression and meaning, pointing out that the ball is, as it were, an image of the all (*der B-all ist ein Bild des All*); but the ball itself has such an extraordinary charm, such a constant attraction for early childhood, as well as for later youth, that it is beyond comparison the first as well as the most important plaything of childhood especially. The child loyal to its human nature—at whatever incomplete and dim stage of observation it may be—perceives in the ball the general expression of each object as well as of itself (the child) as a self-dependent whole and unity. It is above all important for the child, as a human being destined to become and in the future to *be* conscious, to perceive that which is inclosed in itself, indeed complete (*vollendeten*), and so, as it were, the counterpart of himself and his opposite; for man seeks even as a child to develop himself as well as everything in Nature by means of that which is its opposite yet resembles it; and so the child likes to employ himself with the ball, even early in life, in order to cultivate and fashion himself, though unconsciously, through and by it, as that which is his opposite and yet resembles him. Indeed, the ball in the totality of its properties, as will be clearly shown in the course of our considerations, is in manifold respects as instructive a type for the child, as the All (the universe), with its phenomena, is for the adult.

There is yet another thing which gives to the ball not only a great charm for the children but likewise deep significance as a plaything, and so as a means of education; this is, that the child, feeling himself a whole, early seeks and must seek in conformity with his human nature and his destiny, even at the stage of unconsciousness, always to contemplate, to grasp, and to possess a whole, but never merely a part as such. He seeks to contemplate, to grasp, and to possess a whole in all things, and in each thing, or at least, by means of and with them. This can be abundantly proved in the history of the development of the individual human being as well as of whole nations, and of all humanity. Many phenomena in child-life, on the bright side of life as well as on the dark, can also be explained thereby. This whole for which the child seeks is also supplied to him by the ball.

Only we further notice in the life of the child how he—like the man in the fairy story—would like to *perceive* all *in* all, and also to make all from each. The ball is well adapted to fulfill this desire also of the child, being (as a whole inclosed in itself) the image of all in general, and also the particular image of individual things; as, for example, the apple, as well as all things which are spherical in form, and from which such manifoldness again develops, such as seed grains and the like. The ball—or, what is the same, the sphere—is actually the foundation, the germ, as it were, of all other forms which can therefore logically be developed from it in conformity with fixed simple laws; this fact will later be proved in the course of presenting the plays and the means of employment for children. Indeed, the sphere takes up immediately into itself all surrounding objects, since they are mirrored in it, as is justly said. Thus all which the child needs in the expressions of his life and activity, in the earliest beginning as well as in the later course of his development, are afforded by the ball; for, as it is a whole in itself, it is, as it were, the representative, the general expression of each whole. The child can see each whole and himself in it, as he makes each whole or each object from it, can repeatedly impress upon it his own image and thus stand face to face with himself.

In fostering the development of the child special attention must be given to these expressions of his life and activity, as these expressions are the foundation and means of the recognition of individual oneness, of unity as such, and of the accord of all things to which man is destined. Attention should also be given to that which clearly follows from the preceding, and which on account of its great importance must be brought forward here at the beginning of a play—namely, that the spirit in which a play is conceived and originated, as well as the spirit in which the plaything is treated and the play played, give to the play its significance and its worth, its efficient value to humanity. So also if the spirit by which Nature is created is comprehended by man, and if Nature is observed and treated in accordance with that comprehension, this spirit gives to Nature the significance which it has for man—a significance as true as it is deep and full of life, producing life as well as fostering and unfolding life.

But now how is the ball to be considered and used, especially for the first strengthening of the child as a whole, for the first exercise of his bodily powers, the development of the activity of his limbs and senses, as well as for the arousing and nourishing of his attention and of his free independent action?

This is wholly in accordance with the needs of the child and the nature of the ball.

We see how the little child likes so much to seize and grasp everything, even its own thumb or its other hand or fist if it has nothing else. We also see—which is certainly worthy of earnest consideration—how each hand by itself is well adapted to enclose a ball, as are also both hands together.

Therefore a ball is early given into the child's little hand, though at first only for grasping, for him to lay his little fingers round like rings, in order to comprehend its roundness and thus come to possess and hold it fast.

Even this clasping will soon strengthen the muscles of the child's fingers, hand, and arm, and also develop hand and fingers so as to fit them first of all for voluntary handling of the ball, and later for the right handling of other things. Every one knows how much in the life of man, and even in the life of the child, depends on the proper grasping and the right handling of each thing in the actual as well as in the figurative sense. It is therefore inexpressibly important for the whole future life of the child that he should early learn to actually handle even one extraneous object on all sides.

This now requires that, as the child's use of limbs and senses increases, the ball may show itself to the child more as a thing separate from him; for at first the ball seems to be, as it were, one with the hand of the child himself, and seems to grow together with it like his fist; and this is well, as thus all future recognition of the child's surroundings and of the outer world come to the child by means of the ball.

As soon as the child is sufficiently developed to perceive the ball as a thing separate from himself, it will be easy for you, the mother, and you, the nurse, having previously fastened a string to the ball which you give into the child's little hand, to draw the ball gently by the string as if you wished to lift it out of the child's little hand. The child will hold the ball fast, the arm will rise as you lift the ball, and as you loosen the string the hand and arm will sink back from their own weight and through holding the ball fast; the feeling of the utterance of force, as well as the alternation of the movement, will soon delight the child; and the use of the arm in this activity gives dexterity to the arm and strengthens the arm and hand.

Now, mothers, here is the beginning of your play and playing with your child through the mediation of the ball. From this, however, soon springs a quite new play, and thus also something new to the child, when, through a suitable drawing and lifting by the string, the ball escapes from the child's hand, and then quietly moves freely before him as an individual object. Through this play is developed in the child the new feeling, the new perception of the object as a something now clasped, grasped, and handled, and now a freely active, opposite something.

One may say with deep conviction that even this simple activity is inexpressibly important for the child, for which reason it is to be repeated as a play with the child as often as possible. What the little one has up to this time directly felt so often by the touch of the mother's breast—union and separation—it now perceives outwardly in an object which can be grasped and clasped, and which has actually been grasped and clasped. Thus the repetition of this play confirms, strengthens, and clears up in the mind of the child a feeling and perception deeply grounded in and important to the whole life of man—the feeling and perception of oneness and individuality, and of disjunction and separateness; also of present and past possession.

It is exceedingly important for the child which is to be developed, as well as for the adults who are to develop him (therefore, first of all, for the father and mother), that they (the adults) should not only perceive but should also suitably foster the awakening individual power and individual activity, and the awakening spirit of their child in the traces and slightest expressions found in the almost imperceptible beginning, so that the development of these qualities and this spirit may not be carried on by accidental, arbitrary, and disconnected exercises. It is also important to observe the progressive development of the strength as well as of the activity by means of a measuring object, for which also the play with the ball is in manifold ways the most suitable means for parents and child.

The idea of return or recurrence soon develops to the child's perception from the presence and absence; that of reunion, from the singleness and separateness; that of future repossession, from present and past possession; and so the ideas of being, having, and becoming are most important to the whole life of man in their results, and are therefore the dim perceptions which first dawn on the child.

From these perceptions there at once develop in the child's mind the three great perceptions of object, space, and time, which were at first one collective perception. From the perceptions of being, having, and becoming in respect to space and object, and in connection with them, there soon develop also the new perceptions of present, past, and future in respect to time. Indeed, these ninefold perceptions which open to the child the portals of a new objective life, unfold themselves most clearly to the child by means of his constant play with the one single ball.

As we now find that all the development of the child has its foundation in almost imperceptible attainments and perceptions, and as we see that its first evanescent perceptions (almost imperceptible in the beginning) are fixed, increased, and clarified by innumerable repetitions—that is, by change—so we also remark that when two different and separate perceptions have been once received by the child, the third and the following perceptions necessarily proceed from them.

It is highly important for the careful and faithful fostering of the child that the fosterer should devote her whole attention to this truth early in the life of the child. It is also important early to observe, to retain, and therefore to connect with the objective, the linking together of the apparent and of the existent life, though this linking together is at first but dimly perceptible. For the future sure attainment of the earthly destiny of man not only depends on the comprehension of the nature of being, having, and becoming, of object, space, and

time, as well as on the correct comprehension and consideration of present, past, and future, but man himself will, even in
early childhood, in his triune nature and in conformity with
the qualities combined in him in a manner corresponding to
his nature, claim the attainment of this destiny. The more
clearly you perceive this, parents and fosterers of childhood,
and the more definitely you employ it in your fostering, the
richer in results will be your education of children.

True, the natural and unspoiled feeling of the mother often
hits upon the right thing to do; but this right thing is done by
her too unconsciously and too unconnectedly, it is not repeated
continuously enough; still less is it constantly and progressively
developed, and so it is not logically enough built up. The
mothers themselves, and yet more the nurses who undertake
the mothers' business at a later time, only too easily abandon the path correctly pointed out by the pure motherly feeling, as could be easily demonstrated in many places; but we
wish and endeavor to have that which the natural motherly
feeling correctly though unconsciously suggests clearly recognized and constantly and progressively fostered, and so that
life may become by this, for parents and child, a whole, the
parts of which constantly, progressively, and reciprocally
train one another—a whole which is consciously and progressively formed.

Thus the mother, guided by human feelings, connects the
mute action, the becoming and become, with that which is
perceptible only to the sight and touch—as, for instance, the
action is connected with a definite place and object, and then,
almost without exception, is connected with the audible word,
the sign vanishing again almost as soon as it arises.

From the connection of opposites and the duality of the silent and the soundings, of the abiding and the vanishing, of the
visible and the invisible, of the corporeal and the spiritual
object, there goes forth to the child (who also bears this
duality within himself in its unity) the object as recognized
by the mind, and thus held fast, and the consciousness of the
object; in this way consciousness itself develops in the child.

But consciousness itself belongs to the nature of man and
is one with it. To become conscious of itself is the first task in
the life of the child, as it is the task of the whole life of man.
That this task may be accomplished, the child is even from
his first appearance on earth surrounded by a definite place,
and by objects: by the air blowing around all living creatures,
as well as by the arousing, human, spiritual language of words;

and so the animating word, at least the animating song, belong to each voluntary employment, and hence to playing with the child. Genuine, childlike human beings, mothers especially, as we have before seen, know this very well of themselves, therefore they undertake nothing with the child which they do not accompany with words spiritually exhaled and inhaled, even if obliged to confess that there can be no understanding of the spoken words by the child, as the general sense of hearing is not yet developed, still less the special hearing of words.* So we find the mother, soon after the child's birth, caressing and talking to the little one; for that which can develop and originate, and is intended to do so, begins and must begin when as yet nothing exists but the conditions; the possibility, and, especially with human fostering, the dim anticipation of it. Thus is it with the attainment of man to consciousness, and the speech required and conditioned by that attainment to consciousness.

But now, how shall this word accompanying the play with the child, the play-speech of the child, be formed?

As childlike, as motherly, as playfully as possible; so motherly, that the mother creates it herself in the instant of using it with the child; that, quite unconsciously to herself, she creates it afresh in her own mind and from life so that it passes away as the word dies away; for this speech is to express the highest personal and most directly felt motherly life with the child; it is therefore impossible to put it down in black and white and represent it in its individuality, in its life-awakening and life-ravishing fullness, which is caused by momentary emotions of the mind and mind-union, by gaze, movement, and tone, as well as by song, etc.

Yet, in order as much as possible to come to an understanding with the fosterers of childhood, a hint at least, may be permitted to us.

Just as soon as the child's first capacity for speech is somewhat developed, we note how it follows out the sound in and by means of the movement which it remarks, and that it tries to imitate that sound with its own organs. "Tic, tac," we hear it say, an imitation of the movement of the pendulum and the striking of the clock. We hear it say, or sing, "Bim, bom," when the sound of the movement is more audible, or is comprehended as a sound. In the words *in* and *out* (*Innen und*

* Cf. Georg Groddeck selection regarding the usefulness of childlike qualities in adults for training children. [Editor]

Aussen), it is worthy of note that the child uses the vowel scale ē–ah–oo, which symbolizes the movement from within (ē) to the outward (oo) . . .

We must perceive that the child, in the beginning of its use of speech, comprehends, designates, and retains through the words "tic, tac" rather the physical part of the movement; but by "bim, bom" he comprehends the movement more from the feeling, if one might so say, in the mind. And (if I may be permitted to express myself thus) through the "there, here," which comes later, the child follows the movement more as a thing of comparison, of recognition, and, in his dawning thought, more intellectually.

A further treatment of this subject must come later; now, we can only remark that it is highly important for the nurse to observe even the first and slightest traces of the articulate connection of the corporeal, intellectual, and spiritual nature of the child, and to observe it in its development from existence to sensation and thought, so that none of these directions of the child's nature should be arrested, or cultivated, in the development of the child at the expense of the others; but neither should any be repressed and neglected for the sake of the others. It appears important to us here, and we believe that all who quietly consider the first development of the child have already remarked, or will yet remark, that children, even from the first stage of development at the point to which they have arrived, are apt to indicate the swinging movement, "bim, bom," in a singing tone which approaches to song, and serves as such the emotional nature and its cultivation. They thus early and definitely point out that the center, the real foundation, the starting point of human development, and thus of the child's development, is the heart and emotions; but the training to action and to thought, the corporeal and spiritual, goes on constantly and inseparably by the side of it; and thought must form itself into action, and action resolve and clear itself in thought; but both have their roots in the emotional nature.

After these remarks, which are necessary for the knowledge, fostering, and protection of the primitive course of development, and of the laws of development of the human being, let us return to our childish play, but now with a presentiment of its deep significance.

By a slow and constant pull, the ball, hanging to a string, escapes from the child's hand, and "Bim, bom; bim, bom; tic, tac; tic, tac; here, there; here, there" sounds immediately from the mother's mouth, and indicates the movement of the ball.

This quite simple play admits of many changes by connecting it with different tones and words.

"See, child, see the ball—there, here; there, here."

The ball resting, "Here hangs the ball."

Slowly raising and lowering the ball by the string, "Up, down."

Letting it swing over an object (for example, the other hand placed crosswise): "There, here; there, here; over there, over here." Or, considerably lengthening the string, that the ball may swing slowly now toward the child, now away from him, "Near, far; near, far"; or, "Now comes the ball; off goes the ball," or "The ball comes; the ball goes away"; or as a general indication, "Here it comes, there it goes."

Swinging the ball slowly in a circle: "Around, around; round to the right, round to the right; round to the left, round to the left."

Or, playing with the ball on a firm surface on the table before the child, "Tap, tap, tap," letting the ball fall on different parts of the surface, especially in a vertical direction.

"Jump, ball, jump!" "See, now the ball jumps! Jump! jump! jump!" letting the ball, held by the string, fall quickly and rebound by its own elasticity.

Or, helping it by a quick, short drawing of the string, "The ball jumps high"; "The ball can jump no more; it is tired; it lies down to sleep."

Quickly lifting the ball from the surface of the table on something, for example, the ball's box, "Hop up high"; or, raising it quickly over the box, "Hop over."

Twirling the ball on a surface in a horizontal position by the string, and then around a center, and imitating with the voice the more outward movement "r r r r" or merely "Around, around."

And now raising the ball quickly by the string in a vertical direction into the air, and now hanging it, letting it twirl quietly and quickly backward, and now imitating more its inner movement by "l l l l" or "Turn, turn; swiftly, swiftly," or, pointing out the increasing speed of the movement, "Faster and faster."

The rolling on the surface can now be repeated, "Now to the right, now to the left"; and so also can the turning of the ball hanging by the string be changed, "Now to the left, now to the right."

Then drawing the ball on a surface, "Pull, pull, pull." The string may at this point be laid in the child's hand, and string and hand grasped by the mother's hand and the ball drawn off the support: "Ah, there falls the ball!" This, which appears to the child an effect of his own action, delights him exceedingly.

Now the swinging movement may be again made with the ball in the air, either out from the middle, "Always wider," or from the outside toward the center "Always narrower."

As the child before perceived the circling movement, so it sees here the spiral widening and narrowing. So the movement of the ball can also be made in an oval line, "Lengthen out," or "Widen out."

In the same way, winding the ball on a string up and down round a stick in the form of a screw, "Always higher, always lower."

Or, merely drawing the ball on a string slowly up and letting it down, "High, low; high, low."

Now, the ball free from the string is allowed to roll on the surface. "Roll, roll, roll, roll; there the ball runs!"

Or the ball can be made to recoil from a surface—for example, the ball box or a book: "Come, ball, come again to baby"; "Here comes the ball"; "Catch the ball"; "The ball has fallen"; "Go for the ball"; "Look for the ball." The mother may lift the child to the place where the ball lies, in order that the little one may itself pick it up. If the child has attained to any degree of intellectual and physical development and strength, he must be allowed to pick up the ball himself when he throws it to the ground; and if the child is as yet too small and helpless to move himself for that purpose, he must be lifted to the place where the ball lies, especially if he himself has thrown the ball away; so that he may early experience the consequences and requirements of his own action, and discover that he must himself fulfill the requirements and bear the consequences. Effort should be early made not only to have the child make many and definite discoveries, but to have it retain them, as well in respect to their connections with each other as in respect to their results.

"Where is the ball?" "There is the ball again." "Ball, stay now with baby."

Or, closing the hand over the ball, "Where is the ball?" Opening the hand again, "There is the ball."

A beautiful exercise, which is particularly pleasing to the child, is this: to make the ball turn constantly around its own center in the hollowed hand by a constant alteration of its center of gravity, or rather its point of support. This play can be well performed by moving the ball in a saucer in the same manner, by which the ball can be made to run around almost on the rim without falling. This representation can be accompanied by—"Dance prettily," or "See, the ball dances!" etc.

Or, raising the ball again by the string behind the other hand, placed crosswise, "Off!" etc. "Where!" etc. Bringing it again before the hand, "There!" etc.

Each of these exercises can now be repeated by itself as often as it gives the child pleasure. Through this repetition these exercises become just as important for the extension of the horizon of experience as for the greater clearness, definiteness, and distinctness of the child's experiences.

Thoughtful and attentive mothers and nurses can, however, perceive that all this proceeds from the play and the exercises themselves.

Then, lowering the ball into some enclosed space—for example, into the ball box—"Deep in!"

Shutting the ball up in the box again: "The ball is gone!" "It wants to sleep!" "My child is tired; yes, it is tired; it wants to sleep too!"

These and many other observation exercises offer in their connections innumerable changes for the employment of the child and for the awakening and nourishing of his intellectual as well as of his bodily activity; especially when the limbs of the child are so strengthened and developed in power that the ball can be given up to him, at least partly, and he can, by his capacity for speech, which is equally developing, already enter into a kind of conversation with his mother; and yet we have here in the employment with the ball a whole side of childish employment and play to consider, namely, *the fact that the child likes so much to see all in each object, and to make all from each.* Many kinds of objects, inanimate and animate, can not fail to appear in the neighborhood of the child, in his surroundings; to the latter especially his attention is called involuntarily by their coming and going, or, intentionally, by his nurse. Life generally attracts life, as it awakens life. The child sees the coming of the dog and cat; in one case of the poodle or Spitz, in the other of the cat or kitten. The child notices the bird, the birdie in the cage, the sparrow at the window; the dove, the cock, and hen, the hen and chicken in the yard; he sees the carriage, and the horse, etc.

In conformity with this quality and requirement of the child, the swinging ball can now become a birdie: "See how the birdie flies, now here, now there!"

Now the springing ball can become a kitten: "There springs the kitty on the bench."

Now a dog: "Hop goes the dog over the hedge."

Now the ball becomes a chicken: "Tip, tap, tap, the chicken comes running."

Now the cock: "Tap, tap, tap, the cock picks up the corn."

Now a squirrel which climbs up the tree, going round and round it, or in the same manner climbs down.

Now a miner: "He goes deep down into the shaft."

Or the ball without a string: now the sheep which we must watch; now the horse or colt which springs away; now the dog which comes running, "Bow, wow, wow!" But now, again the ball on the string, on the carriage (or, if it is winter, on the sled or sleigh) which is drawn; and a hundred other things.

The thought now impresses itself upon us as an important one, that by one and the same object, and that, moreover, an inanimate object (in this case the ball), are perceived, and as it were made, many kinds of objects, and above all live ones; from which follows another thought that objects are brought before the child by words here (as also indeed in life) which it has not yet even once seen; which are not to be found at all in its neighborhood.

Yet this might appear inadmissible to many a one who has not yet deeply and universally enough entered into the course of development of the child's life and its conditions, although we have already pointed out its existence in the nature and life of the child. We will therefore briefly justify this procedure, without, however, penetrating deeply into human nature, in which it could be very easily demonstrated as necessary and as required; but this is not the place for it. At some time the anticipation and thus the inner recognition of the special and the general, will be unfolded to the child. But this takes place when, as already remarked, the opposites, having yet some similarity, are compared with one another. Then also the fewer special similarities and qualities that the means of perception or the object used to play with has with the presented object (which, of course, must be connected by preceding connecting links), the more skilled the child becomes thereby; he now considers the actual object in order to obtain a clear impression of it and of its special qualities, so as to rise from the perception of the object to that of its kind, and from the perception of the kind to that of its species, etc.

The second remark is, that objects are here brought before the child which indeed the playing adult has seen, but which as yet the playing child has not seen at all. Though this is not to be scrupulously avoided, as little is it to be thoughtlessly carried too far; kept within right limits it justifies itself to any simple and straightforward mind. The life and the course of development of the human being and the laws of this development make this repeat itself with the most developed man, for, as man is a being destined to attain increasing consciousness, so he is also to become and be a reasoning and judging being. Besides, man has a peculiar presaging power of imagination, as indeed also—what must never be forgotten, but always kept in view as important and guiding—the newborn child is not merely to become a man, *but the man already appears and indeed is in the child with all his talents and the unity of his nature.*

Objects not yet seen in life by the child may therefore be introduced to him through word and playthings that represent these objects, but with the following restriction: this introduction (as, for example, in the preceding pages, of the squirrel) ought not to take place before the child—who is through frequent repetition quite familiar with the object, near, already often seen, and always possible to be seen again (for example, the kitten)—in the qualities of the personifying object (here of the ball), has recognized the qualities of the personified object (here of the kitten), and likewise has seen in and through the first (the ball) the second (the kitten); has learned to represent it, for example, by the jumping. Now the child has also noticed the climbing of the cat, and when it is said, as above, "The squirrel climbs," etc., the child quickly comes to the conclusion that the squirrel is a living thing that climbs. This is enough to excite its attention, so that when he some day sees a squirrel, and the squirrel is named to him as such, he fixes his eyes upon it sharply, and perhaps, indeed, even without hearing its name, recognizes it as such from this quality and other connections. This is a sufficient hint for the justification of this childlike, motherly, and (in the nursery) domestic procedure.

We now go back to the contemplation of the ball as the first plaything, and bring into prominence as essential the fact that it (being, as it were, the representative and means of perception of all that is contained in and rests in itself) offers to be perceived, produced, and handled only the fundamental form, as it were the rough sketch of all which can present itself as a whole and can act spontaneously as such; so that several of the phenomena of the ball—such as presence, departure, return, seeking, finding, getting, catching, grasping, holding, rolling, sliding, turning, etc.—can be represented by each of the said objects as well as by the ball, which is, just on that account, such an excellent and attractive plaything for the child. But though, as just stated, several of the phenomena of the ball can be represented by each of the said objects, this is not the case with all the phenomena—for instance, the multifariousness of movement. For this reason, in order to increase the powers and advance the development of the child, the plays carried through with the ball are, as the opportunity or the demand is made, given in part with other objects—for example, an apple, a handkerchief, a ball of thread, a key, a nut, a flower, etc.—and these objects are thus brought before the child in various kinds of activity. But the ball always remains as the uniting and explaining object, and thus the true means of connection and understanding, and the very plaything to connect the child with his mother and his surroundings.

If the child is now old enough to sit alone and likes to do so, and also to creep or drag himself from one place to another, the play with the ball can be essentially and efficiently extended. Thus a quilt is spread in the room, the child seated on it, and a ball, now with, now without a string, given to him for his own spontaneous handling. Also, if it can be easily accomplished, a ball of suitable size can be fastened by a sufficiently strong cord to the ceiling of the room, so that the child can at times employ himself with swinging himself with the ball, and at times can raise himself up, and so can stand by means of it. He will thus learn to hold himself more surely in equilibrium, and to stand more easily than if he raises himself up by a body which stands firmly—a chair, or a bench—which does away with the necessity for him to maintain his own center of gravity; and if he falls, the fall is less painful, with a good quilt to fall on. Yet more suitable is it, in reference to the child's learning to stand, that the ball, proportionately increased in size and fastened to a strong and sufficiently long string, be given into the hand of the child seated on a sufficiently thick quilt, with the directions to hold it firmly. Now the attempt is made to raise the child higher and higher by means of the cord which is fastened to the ball. The raising and lowering will please the child, as well as strengthen the muscles of the whole body, hips and thighs especially. If he is thus raised by means of the ball and string to a standing position, he can soon easily stand independently.

Here is now the point, as beautiful as it is important, where the life and activity of the father also can exert a fostering and developing influence on the life of the child; and the ball here again appears as a connecting link between child and father, as it was at an earlier period between child and mother. The child in the father's company is to grow up, as it were, climb up to him, and by his aid is to steady itself; all this is now offered in manifold shapes by the above given play with the ball, by which, in order to render it again prominent, the father comes into his right relation to the child, calling out his strength, etc. (consideration, reflection), but also using and thus developing strength, etc. By means of the earlier play, especially of that connected with speech, the mother, with all her mildness, enters into the life of the child. . . .

It is evident to the child that all the various plays proceed from the single ball, and that all in their phenomena refer again to the uniting ball; they make known the manifoldness resting in the ball, which is itself single; they proceed from unity and again lead back to unity. In the second and also opposite view, the play is considered from the child outward; all activity, although connected with the ball, proceeds definitely from the child (who is in himself a unit), and, although using the ball as a means, refers to the child, who is in himself a unit. The child is in himself unity and manifoldness, and destined to develop this unity and manifoldness by the surrounding outer world; and for this, also, the ball serves through the play with it, but especially by its individuality and its properties; for the ball itself, being the representative of all objects, is the unity and union of the essential properties of all objects. Thus the ball shows contents, mass, matter, space, form, size, and figure; it bears within itself an independent power (elasticity), and hence it has rest and movement, and consequently stability and spontaneity; it offers even color, and at least calls forth sound; it is indeed heavy—that is, it is attracted—and thus shares in the general property of all bodies. Therefore the ball, by its fall, by its quicker movement on a shorter and its slower movement on a longer string, leads to the consideration of the most important phenomena and laws of earth-life and the life of Nature, of attraction in general, and first of all of the attraction of the earth, especially of its laws and limitations, in which and through which only, the child himself lives and has his being as a human dweller on the earth, since he lives and exists only through the breathing in of the air. Therefore the ball as a connecting plaything between parent and child, places man in the midst of all, on his entrance into the world and with the activity of his limbs and senses, in the midst of all phenomena and perceptions of Nature, as of all limitations of Nature, and of all life; for what is more attractive than life? But to place man through a skillful education in the understanding of and in harmony with Nature and life, and to maintain him in it with consciousness and circumspection, can not be done too early.

Hence the ball, as we have already seen in many ways, is a bond of connection between mother and child, between parent and child—it is a connection between the child and his nearest surroundings—and thus is it in general a bond of connection between the child and Nature; and the ball connects the child with Nature as much as the universe connects man with God.

As now the ball, by its individuality and by means of the play with it, places man, even in childhood, in the midst of the life of Nature and of all life, and makes itself perceived and felt in it, so in like manner it makes the child early to feel and find himself in the midst of his own life, in the midst of his perceptive (feeling), his operative and creative, and his comparing (thinking) activity. The ball and the play with the ball lay hold of the whole man as a child, in respect to his body as well as in respect to his mind and soul. Thus, in order to bring forward with precision one phemonenon, only one, and here the nearest to us, which has been mentioned, the ball (even in its first swinging movement, if this movement is several times and often repeated, and by the words "tic tac, tic tac," the child is made to notice the movement through space and its regular intervals and remember it) has an exciting effect on the body of the child, which effect is expressed by hopping, also a measured movement. But is not even this single play, developed in harmony with the whole human being, important for his whole life? Is it not even the dim, how much more yet the developed, feeling of the correct time, that is, the feeling of tact or the right instant at which to exert an influence on another by his activity, which later often preserves man from so many disagreeable experiences? And does not this depend on the earlier development of man which always remembers what was opportune, and which is least retarded when it finds itself in harmony with the occasion.

The movement, on the contrary, predominantly full of life and expression, which is comprised in and represented by "bim, bom," etc., acts on the heart; this fact is made known in the course of the development of the child by his laughter as an expression of the arousing of emotions and of the use of his eyes. Do we not already see by this how beneficial, melodious, and therefore harmonious, training is for man at an early stage of his being? But the movement, more suggestive of comparison, comprehended in and represented by the words "there, here," acts predominantly on the intellect, and makes itself known in the course of the child's development by the imperfect speech connected with it as the spontaneous expression of the child's awakening power of thought; and do we not find indicated in this already the peculiarity and requirement of the human mind to render itself intelligible, to clarify itself by communication with others?

As now each of the single plays severally considered lay hold upon the child early in the trinity of his nature as creating, feeling, and thinking, so do yet more the playful employments considered as a whole. The attentive observer can easily perceive that one whole series of the plays belong preeminently to the actual, external, and creative life, or at least refer to it; these may be even described as useful in a certain point of view. With another series of plays, each, without reference to anything extraneous, suffices for itself, because an inner unity, a life which is in itself single, appears in an outward manifoldness which harmonizes with it. The representation of these plays, through which inner unity (existence) appears in and by means of harmonious variety, and shines forth from it, as it were, can not receive a more significant designation than beautiful. So in the third series of plays each single play is likewise only attractive to the child in, by and through its various relations, properties, and connections, each of which has been already suggested—indeed, indicated inwardly—before it appeared outwardly, and therefore before it was recognized. One can not but say of these plays that they early enchain the child's attention on account of their truth, though unconsciously to the little one himself, and perhaps unrecognized by him through his whole life.

Thus, without bringing out from the mentioned plays authentic proofs for the stated series, which is very possible to a thoughtful consideration, we here show only how directly the course of childish employments, to which the path is broken by the first child-plays (which, beginning from the ball, advancing constantly according to inner laws, is now to be pursued uninterruptedly in the production of means for the child's employment), early leads the child to a harmonious training for usefulness, beauty, and truth; and how means are early given to the parents to attain the harmonious cultivation of their child; we are to consider to which side of the cultivation he predominantly inclines; since one excludes the other no more than life, art, and science do, so man, and still more the child, ought not to be educated and cultivated one-sidedly and exclusively for the one or the other.

The cultivation of the mental power of the child in different directions is also attained by the use of the ball as the first plaything. The child learns by the use of it to keep an object in view not only in a state of rest, but also in the changes of its phenomena. The plays carried on with the ball awaken and exercise the power of the child's intellect to place again before him an object not present to his bodily eyes, to perceive it inwardly even when the outward appearance has vanished. These plays awaken and exercise the power of representing, of remembering, of retaining in remembrance an object seen formerly, of again thinking of it—that is, they foster the memory.

The awakening and fostering of the powers of the mind to compare, to conclude, to judge, to think, have been already discussed, and every observer can easily see how by these plays the powers are further awakened and exercised in the child, how they continue to develop and are more and more formed within. Only, we must remark, what is capable of demonstration, that this most delicate growth of the mind is germinated and fostered quietly and gradually by means of the actions, feelings, and thoughts of the mother, and by means of her love, faith, and hope with respect to the child, although yet so imperceptibly in the child's life thus connected with the mother's—by means of the ball and the play with the ball . . .

But one thing remains for us to bring forward in the consideration and contemplation of the plays with the ball: this is the definite, clear, and legitimate development of the child's capacity for speech in the progressive course of the play. As the child, as has been demonstrated in many ways, is placed by this playing in the midst of Nature and of life, or rather finds itself buoyant with life, so it is also by this playing placed in the midst of its capacity for speech, of the legitimate development of that capacity, or rather finds and quietly unfolds itself therein.

A few hints from the many which could be given and clearly presented on the subject must here and now suffice; this subject will be later taken up again and treated of by itself. Here on that subject we will give as hints only the following: The language which accompanies the first child-play seems to be clear, precise, full, significant, simple, and yet completely satisfying. Even the first words of it, to which the play gave rise and which the child discovered, and ever anew discovers, contain the whole material of words—that is, in these words are immediately given vowel sounds, open and closed sounds. Each appears clear and distinct, each comes forth pure in its nature in the childish words, bim, bom (boum). So in au (aou) are defined and given the three fundamental voice sounds, a, o, u, and in i their relating, middle, or conclusion; and thus through them is given the complete compass of vowel sounds in language. Also, the compass of language brought into employment by the play, slight as it appears, embraces the whole province of language proceeding from the perception and comprehension of the object in space. The words used are mostly word stems or roots, and from them develops speech full of life, regular and all-sided, as an image of the two great worlds, the inner and the outer world.

The ball gives to the child all this, and many another thing, which is not at all retained by word as an outside phenomenon in its individualities, and joins itself to all as the first childish plaything; through it the little one develops himself; by it is strengthened in the unity of his nature and life, proportionally in body and in spirit. It is enough that in the first plays with the ball the life of the child makes itself known, and the outer world makes itself known to the child in unity.

The Rules of the Game[1]

JEAN PIAGET

(1932)

How do children play with one another and elaborate
rules for dealing with right and wrong? In his book
The Moral Judgment of the Child, Jean Piaget, the
Swiss child psychologist who has made an intensive study
of the basis of children's knowledge, shows that the society of children develops a distinctive code. These rules
and children's reactions to them are analogous to the
later conditions of adult society. The rules come, first,
from the individual child's pleasure in regularity; the social, or obligatory, element is added to them when he
enters a group. In other words, personal rituals spring
up and are later ramified into "rules" by a group. In
this selection Piaget analyzes the progressively complicated rules children develop in playing the age-old game
of marbles.

Children's games constitute the most admirable social institutions. The game of marbles, for instance, as played by boys,
contains an extremely complex system of rules, that is to say,
a code of laws, a jurisprudence of its own. Only the psychologist, whose profession obliges him to become familiar with
this instance of common law, and to get at the implicit morality underlying it, is in a position to estimate the extraordinary
wealth of these rules by the difficulty he experiences in mastering their details.

If we wish to gain any understanding of child morality, it
is obviously with the analysis of such facts as these that we
must begin. All morality consists in a system of rules, and the
essence of all morality is to be sought for in the respect which
the individual acquires for these rules. The reflective analysis
of Kant, the sociology of Durkheim, or the individualistic
psychology of Bovet all meet on this point. The doctrines be-

[1] With the collaboration of Mme. V. J. Piaget, Messrs. M. Lambercier
and L. Martinez.

gin to diverge only from the moment that it has to be explained how the mind comes to respect these rules. For our part, it will be in the domain of child psychology that we shall undertake the analysis of this "how."

Now, most of the moral rules which the child learns to respect he receives from adults, which means that he receives them after they have been fully elaborated, and often elaborated, not in relation to him and as they are needed, but once and for all and through an uninterrupted succession of earlier adult generations.

In the case of the very simplest social games, on the contrary, we are in the presence of rules which have been elaborated by the children alone. It is of no moment whether these games strike us as "moral" or not in their contents. As psychologists we must ourselves adopt the point of view, not of the adult conscience, but of child morality. Now, the rules of the game of marbles are handed down, just like so-called moral realities, from one generation to another, and are preserved solely by the respect that is felt for them by individuals. The sole difference is that the relations in this case are only those that exist between children. The little boys who are beginning to play are gradually trained by the older ones in respect for the law; and in any case they aspire from their hearts to the virtue, supremely characteristic of human dignity, which consists in making a correct use of the customary practices of a game. As to the older ones, it is in their power to alter the rules. If this is not "morality," then where does morality begin? At least, it is respect for rules, and it appertains to an inquiry like ours to begin with the study of facts of this order. Of course the phenomena relating to the game of marbles are not among the most primitive. Before playing with his equals, the child is influenced by his parents. He is subjected from his cradle to a multiplicity of regulations, and even before language he becomes conscious of certain obligations. These circumstances even exercise, as we shall see, an undeniable influence upon the way in which the rules of games are elaborated. But in the case of play institutions, adult intervention is at any rate reduced to the minimum. We are therefore in the presence here of realities which, if not among the most elementary, should be classed nevertheless among the most spontaneous and the most instructive.

With regard to game rules there are two phenomena which it is particularly easy to study: first the *practice* of rules, *i.e.*, the way in which children of different ages effectively apply rules: second the *consciousness* of rules, *i.e.,* the idea which children of different ages form of the character of these game rules, whether of something obligatory and sacred or of something subject to their own choice, whether of heteronomy or autonomy. . . .

From the point of view of the practice or application of rules four successive stages can be distinguished.

A first stage of a purely *motor* and *individual* character, during which the child handles the marbles at the dictation of his desires and motor habits. This leads to the formation of more or less ritualized schemas, but since play is still purely individual, one can only talk of motor rules and not of truly collective rules.

The second may be called *egocentric* for the following reasons. This stage begins at the moment when the child receives from outside the example of codified rules, that is to say, some time between the ages of two and five. But though the child imitates this example, he continues to play either by himself without bothering to find play-fellows, or with others, but without trying to win, and therefore without attempting to unify the different ways of playing. In other words, children of this stage, even when they are playing together, play each one "on his own" (everyone can win at once) and without regard for any codification of rules. This dual character, combining imitation of others with a purely individual use of the examples received, we have designated by the term Egocentrism.

A third stage appears between seven and eight, which we shall call the stage of incipient *cooperation.* Each player now tries to win, and all, therefore, begin to concern themselves with the question of mutual control and of unification of the rules. But while a certain agreement may be reached in the course of one game, ideas about the rules in general are still rather vague. In other words, children of seven to eight, who belong to the same class at school and are therefore constantly playing with each other, give, when they are questioned separately, disparate and often entirely contradictory accounts of the rules observed in playing marbles.

Finally, between the years of eleven and twelve, appears a fourth stage, which is that of the *codification of rules.* Not only is every detail of procedure in the game fixed, but the actual code of rules to be observed is known to the whole society. There is remarkable concordance in the information given by children of ten to twelve belonging to the same class

at school, when they are questioned on the rules of the game
and their possible variations.

These stages must of course be taken only for what they
are worth. It is convenient for the purposes of exposition to
divide the children up in age-classes or stages, but the facts
present themselves as a continuum which cannot be cut up
into sections. This continuum, moreover, is not linear in
character, and its general direction can only be observed by
schematizing the material and ignoring the minor oscillations
which render it infinitely complicated in detail. So that ten
children chosen at random will perhaps not give the impression
of a steady advance which gradually emerges from the interrogatory put to the hundred odd subjects examined by us at
Geneva and Neuchâtel.

If, now, we turn to the consciousness of rules we shall find
a progression that is even more elusive in detail, but no less
clearly marked if taken on a big scale. We may express this
by saying that the progression runs through three stages, of
which the second begins during the egocentric stage and ends
toward the middle of the stage of cooperation (nine to ten),
and of which the third covers the remainder of this cooperating stage and the whole of the stage marked by the codification
of rules.

During the first stage rules are not yet coercive in character, either because they are purely motor, or else (at the beginning of the egocentric stage) because they are received, as
it were, unconsciously, and as interesting examples rather than
as obligatory realities.

During the second stage (apogee of egocentric and first half
of cooperating stage) rules are regarded as sacred and un-
touchable, emanating from adults and lasting forever. Every
suggested alteration strikes the child as a transgression.

Finally, during the third stage, a rule is looked upon as a
law due to mutual consent, which you must respect if you
want to be loyal but which it is permissible to alter on the condition of enlisting general opinion on your side.

The correlation between the three stages in the development
of the consciousness of rules and the four stages relating to
their practical observance is of course only a statistical correlation and therefore very crude. But broadly speaking the
relation seems to us indisputable. The collective rule is at first
something external to the individual and consequently sacred
to him; then, as he gradually makes it his own, it comes to
that extent to be felt as the free product of mutual agreement

and an autonomous conscience. And with regard to practical use, it is only natural that a mystical respect for laws should be accompanied by a rudimentary knowledge and application of their contents, while a rational and well-founded respect is accompanied by an effective application of each rule in detail.

There would therefore seem to be two types of respect for rules corresponding to two types of social behavior. This conclusion deserves to be closely examined, for if it holds good, it should be of the greatest value to the analysis of child morality. One can see at once all that it suggests in regard to the relation between child and adult. Take the insubordination of the child toward its parents and teachers, joined to its sincere respect for the commands it receives and its extraordinary mental docility. Could not this be due to that complex of attitudes which we can observe during the egocentric stage and which combines so paradoxically an unstable practice of the law with a mystical attitude toward it? And will not cooperation between adult and child, insofar as it can be realized and insofar as it is facilitated by cooperation among children themselves, supply the key to the interiorization of commands and to the autonomy of the moral consciousness? Let us therefore not be afraid of devoting a certain amount of time to the patient analysis of the rules of a game, for we are here in possession of a method infinitely more supple, and consequently more sure, than that of merely questioning children about little stories, a method which we shall be obliged to adopt in the latter part of this book.

The Practice of Rules. I. The First Two Stages

We need not dwell at any length upon the first stage, as it is not directly connected with our subject. At the same time, it is important that we should know whether the rules which come into being previous to any collaboration between children are of the same type as collective rules.

Let us give a handful of ten marbles to a child of three years and four months and take note of its reactions:

Jacqueline has the marbles in her hands and looks at them with curiosity (it is the first time she has seen any); then she lets them drop onto the carpet. After this she puts them in the hollow of an armchair. *"Aren't they animals?—Oh, no.—Are* *they balls?*—Yes." She puts them back on the carpet and lets them drop from a certain height. She sits on the carpet with her legs apart and throws the marbles a few inches in front of her. She then picks them up and puts them on the armchair and in the same hole as before. (The armchair is studded with buttons which create depressions in the material.) Then she collects the lot and lets them drop, first all together, then one by one. After this she replaces them in the armchair, first in the same place and then in the other holes. Then she piles them up in a pyramid: *"What are marbles?*—What do you think?—. . ."* She puts them on the floor, then back onto the armchair, in the same holes.—We both go out onto the balcony: she lets the marbles drop from a height to make them bounce.

The following days, Jacqueline again places the marbles on the chairs and armchairs, or puts them into her little saucepan to cook dinner. Or else she simply repeats the behavior described above.

Three points should be noted with regard to facts such as these. In the first place, the lack of continuity and direction in the sequence of behavior. The child is undoubtedly trying first and foremost to understand the nature of marbles and to adapt its motor schemas to this novel reality. This is why it tries one experiment after another: throwing them, heaping them into pyramids or nests, letting them drop, making them bounce, etc. But once it has got over the first moments of astonishment, the game still remains incoherent, or rather still subject to the whim of the moment. On days when the child plays at cooking dinner, the marbles serve as food to be stewed in a pot. On days when it is interested in classifying and arranging, the marbles are put in heaps in the holes of armchairs, and so on. In the general manner in which the game is carried on there are therefore no rules.

The second thing to note is that there are certain regularities of detail, for it is remarkable how quickly certain particular acts in the child's behavior become schematized and even ritualized. The act of collecting the marbles in the hollow of an armchair is at first simply an experiment, but it immediately becomes a motor schema bound up with the perception of the marbles. After a few days it is merely a rite, still performed with interest, but without any fresh effort of adaptation.

In the third place, it is important to note the symbolism[2] that immediately becomes grafted upon the child's motor schemas. These symbols are undoubtedly enacted in play rather than thought out, but they imply a certain amount of imagination: the marbles are food to be cooked, eggs in a nest, etc.

This being so, the rules of games might be thought to derive either from rites analogous to those we have just examined or from a symbolism that has become collective. Let us briefly examine the genesis and ultimate destiny of these modes of behavior.

Genetically speaking, the explanation both of rites and of symbols would seem to lie in the conditions of preverbal motor intelligence. When it is presented with any new thing, a baby of five to eight months will respond with a dual reaction; it will accommodate itself to the new object and it will assimilate the object to earlier motor schemas. Give the baby a marble, and it will explore its surface and consistency, but will at the same time use it as something to grasp, to suck, to rub against the sides of its cradle, and so on. This assimilation of every fresh object to already existing motor schemas may be conceived of as the starting point of ritual acts and symbols, at any rate from the moment that assimilation becomes stronger than actual accommodation itself. With regard to ritual acts, indeed, one is struck by the fact that from the age of about eight to ten months all the child's motor schemas, apart from moments of adaptation in the real sense, gives rise to a sort of functioning in the void, in which the child takes pleasure as in a game. Thus, after having contracted the habit of pressing her face against her parents' cheeks, crumpling up her nose and breathing deeply the while, Jacqueline began to perform this rite as a joke, crumpling up her nose and breathing deeply in advance, merely suggesting contact with another person's face, but without, as before, expressing any particular affection by the act. Thus from being actual, and incorporated in an effective adaptation this schema has become ritualized and serves only as a game.[3] Or again, Jacqueline in her bath is engaged in rubbing her hair; she lets

---

[2] We use the term "symbol" in the sense given to it in the linguistic school of Saussure, as the contrary of sign. A sign is arbitrary, a symbol is motivated. It is in this sense, too, that Freud speaks of symbolic thought.

[3] Age: ten months.

go of it to splash the water. Immediately, she repeats the movement, touching her hair and the water alternately, and during the next few days the schema has become ritualized to such an extent that she cannot strike the surface of the water without first outlining the movement of smoothing her hair.[4] In no way automatic, this rite is a game that amuses her by its very regularity. Anyone observing a baby of ten to twelve months will notice a number of these rites which undoubtedly anticipate the rules of future games.

As for symbols, they appear toward the end of the first year and in consequence of the ritual acts. For the habit of repeating a given gesture ritually, gradually leads to the consciousness of "pretending." The ritual of going to bed, for instance (laying down one's head and arranging the corner of the pillow with the hundred and one complications which every baby invents), is sooner or later utilized "in the void," and the smile of the child as it shuts its eyes in carrying out this rite is enough to show that it is perfectly conscious of "pretending" to go to sleep. Here already we have a symbol, but a "played" symbol. Finally, when language and imagery come to be added to motor intelligence, the symbol becomes an object of thought. The child who pushes a box along saying "tuff-tuff" is assimilating in imagination the box's movement to that of a motor-car: the play symbol has definitely come into being.

This being so, can one seek among rites and symbols for the origin of the actual rules of games? Can the game of marbles, with its infinite complexity both with regard to the actual rules and to all that relates to the verbo-motor system of signs in use—can the game of marbles, then, be conceived simply as the result of an accumulation of individual rites and symbols? We do not think that it can. We believe that the individual rite and the individual symbol constitute the sub-structure for the development of rules and collective signs, its necessary, but not its sufficient condition. There is something more in the collective rule than in the motor rule or the individual ritual, just as there is something more in the sign than in the symbol.

With regard to motor or ritualistic rules, there can be no doubt that they have something in common with rules in the ordinary sense, namely the consciousness of regularity. When

[4] Age: twelve months.

we see the delight taken by a baby of ten to twelve months or a child of two to three in reproducing a given behavior in all its details, and the scrupulous attention with which it observes the right order in these operations, we cannot help recognizing the *Regelbewusstsein* of which Bühler speaks. But we must distinguish carefully between the behavior into which there enters only the pleasure of regularity, and that into which there enters an element of obligation. It is this consciousness of obligation which seems to us, as to Durkheim[5] and Bovet,[6] to distinguish a rule in the true sense from mere regularity.

Now this element of obligation, or, to confine ourselves to the question of the practice of rules, this element of obedience intervenes as soon as there is a society, *i.e.*, a relation between at least two individuals. As soon as a ritual is imposed upon a child by adults or seniors for whom he has respect (Bovet), or as soon, we would add, as a ritual comes into being as the result of the collaboration of two children, it acquires in the subject's mind a new character which is precisely that of a rule. This character may vary according to the type of respect which predominates (respect for the senior or mutual respect) but in all cases there enters an element of submission which was not contained in the rite pure and simple.

In actual fact, of course, there is every degree of variety between the simple regularity discovered by the individual and the rule to which a whole social group submits itself. Thus during the egocentric stage we can observe a whole series of cases in which the child will use a rule as a mere rite, to be bent and modified at will, while at the same time he already tries to submit to the common laws. Just as the child very soon acquires the use of language and of the abstract and general concepts while retaining in his attitude to these much that still belongs to egocentric modes of thought and even to the methods peculiar to symbolic and play thought, so, under the rules that are imposed upon him, he will for a long time contrive (in all good faith, needless to say) to maintain his own fantasy in the matter of personal decisions. But this factual continuity between ritual and rule does not exclude a qualitative difference between the two types of behavior.

Let us not, however, anticipate what will be said in our analysis of the consciousness of rules, but return to the matter

[5] *L'Education Morale.*

[6] "Les Conditions de l'Obligation de la Conscience," *Année Psychol.*, 1912.

of ritual. The individual rite develops quite naturally, as we have just shown, into a more or less complex symbolism. Can this symbolism be regarded as the starting point of that system of obligatory verbo-motor signs which are connected with the rules of every collective game? As with the previous problem, we believe that the symbol is a necessary, but not a sufficient condition of the appearance of signs. The sign is general and abstract (arbitrary), the symbol is individual and motivated. If the sign is to follow upon the symbol, a group must therefore strip the individual's imagination of all its personal fantasy and then elaborate a common and obligatory imagery which will go hand in hand with the code of rules itself.

Here is an observation showing how far removed are individual rites and symbols from rules and signs, though moving toward these realities insofar as collaboration between children becomes established.

Jacqueline (after the observations given above) is playing with Jacques (two years, eleven months and fifteen days), who sees marbles for the first time. I. Jacques takes the marbles and lets them drop from a height one after another. After which he picks them up and goes away. II. Jacques arranges them on the ground, in a hollow and says, *"I'm making a little nest."* Jacqueline takes one and sticks it in the ground in imitation. III. Jacques also takes one, buries it and makes a mud-pie above it. He digs it up and begins over again. Then he takes two at a time which he buries. Then three, four, five and up to six at a time, increasing the number of marbles systematically each time by one. Jacqueline imitates him: she first puts one marble down and makes a mud-pie over it, then two or three at random and without adopting a fixed system of progression. IV. Jacques puts all the marbles on a pile, then he places an india-rubber ball beside them and says: *"That's the Mummy ball and the baby balls."* V. He piles them together again and covers them up with earth which he levels down. Jacqueline imitates him but with only one marble which she covers up without leveling the earth. She adds: *"It's lost,"* then digs it up and begins over again.

This example shows very clearly how all the elements of individual fantasy or symbolism remain uncommunicated; as soon as the game takes on an imaginative turn each child evokes its favorite images without paying any attention to anyone else's. It will also be observed how totally devoid of any general direction are the ritualized schemas successively tried. But as soon as there is reciprocal imitation (end of II and whole of III) we have the beginnings of a rule: each child tries to bury the marbles in the same way as the other, in a common order only more or less successfully adhered to. In bringing out this aspect, the observation leads us to the stage of egocentrism during which the child learns other peoples' rules but practices them in accordance with his own fantasy.

We shall conclude this analysis of the first stage by repeating that before games are played in common, no rules in the proper sense can come into existence. Regularities and ritualized schemas are already there, but these rites, being the work of the individual, cannot call forth that submission to something superior to the self which characterizes the appearance of any rule.

The second stage is the stage of *egocentrism*. In studying the practice of rules we shall make use of a notion which has served on earlier occasions in the descriptions we have given of the child's intellectual behavior; and, in both cases, indeed, the phenomenon is of exactly the same order. Egocentrism appears to us as a form of behavior intermediate between purely individual and socialized behavior. Through imitation and language, as also through the whole content of adult thought which exercises pressure on the child's mind as soon as verbal intercourse has become possible, the child begins, in a sense, to be socialized from the end of its first year. But the very nature of the relations which the child sustains with the adults around him prevents this socialization for the moment from reaching that state of equilibrium which is propitious to the development of reason. We mean, of course, the state of cooperation, in which the individuals, regarding each other as equals, can exercise a mutual control and thus attain to objectivity. In other words, the very nature of the relation between child and adult places the child apart, so that his thought is isolated, and while he believes himself to be sharing the point of view of the world at large he is really still shut up in his own point of view. The social bond itself, by which the child is held, close as it may seem when viewed from outside, thus implies an unconscious intellectual egocentrism which is further promoted by the spontaneous egocentrism peculiar to all primitive mentality.

Similarly, with regard to the rules of games, it is easy to

see, and greater authorities than ourselves[7] have already
pointed out that the beginnings of children's games are characterized by long periods of egocentrism. The child is dominated on the one hand by a whole set of rules and examples
that are imposed upon him from outside. But unable as he is,
on the other hand, to place himself on a level of equality with
regard to his seniors, he utilizes for his own ends, unaware
even of his own isolation, all that he has succeeded in grasping
of the social realities that surround him.

To confine ourselves to the game of marbles, the child of
three to five years old will discover, according to what other
children he may happen to come across, that in order to play
this game one must trace a square, put the marbles inside it,
try to expel the marbles from the square by hitting them with
another marble, start from a line that has been drawn before-
hand, and so on. But though he imitates what he observes, and
believes in perfect good faith that he is playing like the others,
the child thinks of nothing at first but of utilizing these new
acquisitions for himself. He plays in an individualistic manner
with material that is social. Such as egocentrism.

Let us analyze the facts of the case.

MAR (6)[8] seizes hold of the marbles we offer him, and
without bothering to make a square he heaps them up together and begins to hit the pile. He removes the marbles
he has displaced and puts them aside or replaces them immediately without any method. "Do you always play like that?—
In the street you make a square.—Well, you do the same as
they do in the street.—*I'm making a square, I am.*" (He draws
the square, places the marbles inside it and begins to play
again.) I play with him, imitating each of his movements.
"Who has won?—*We've both won.*—But who has won most?
. . ."—(Mar does not understand.)

BAUM (6½) begins by making a square and puts down
three marbles, adding: "*Sometimes you put four, or three, or
two.*—Or five?—*No, not five, but sometimes six or eight.*—Who

---

[7] Stern in his *Psychology of Early Childhood* notes the identity of the
stages we have established in children's conversations with those he has
himself established with regard to play, pp. 177 and 332.

[8] The numbers in parentheses give the child's age. The words of the
child are in italics, those of the examiner in Roman lettering. Quotation marks indicate the beginning and end of a conversation reported
verbatim. All the subjects are boys unless the letter G is added, indicating that the subject is a girl.

begins when you play with the boys?—*Sometimes me, sometimes the other one.*—Isn't there a dodge for knowing who is to begin?—*No.*—Do you know what a coche is?—*Rather!*" But the sequel shows that he knows nothing about the coche and thinks of this word as designating another game. "And which of us will begin?—*You.*—Why?—*I want to see how you do it.*" We play for a while and I ask who has won: "*The one who has hit a mib,*[9] *well, he has won.*—Well! who has won?—*I have, and then you.*" I then arrange things so as to take four while he takes two: "Who has won?—*I have, and then you.*" We begin again. He takes two, I none. "Who has won?—*I have.* —And I?—*You've lost.*"

LOEFF (6) often pretends to be playing with Mae, of whom we shall speak later. He knows neither how to make a square nor to draw a coche. He immediately begins to "fire" at the marbles assembled in a heap and plays without either stopping or paying any attention to us. "Have you won?—*I don't know. I think I have.*—Why?—*Yes, because I threw the mibs.*—And I?—*Yes, because you threw the mibs.*"

DESARZ (6): "Do you play often?—*Yes, rather!*—With whom?—*All by myself.*—Do you like playing alone best?—*You don't need two. You can play only one.*" He gathers the marbles together without a square and "fires" into the heap.

Let us now see how two children, who have grown accustomed to playing together, set about it when they are left alone. They are two boys of whom one (Mae) is a very representative example of the present stage, while the other (Wid) stands at the border line between the present stage and the next. The analyses of these cases will be all the more conclusive as the children in question are no mere beginners at the game.

MAE (6) and WID (7) declare that they are always playing together. Mae tells us that they both "*played again, yesterday.*" I first examine Mae by himself. He piles his marbles in a corner without counting them and throws his shooter into the pile. He then places four marbles close together and puts a fifth on top (in a pyramid). Mae denies that a square is ever drawn. Then he corrects himself and affirms that he always does so: "How do you and Wid know which is to begin?— *One of the two throws his shooter and the other tries to hit it. If he hits it, he begins.*" Mae then shows us what the game

⁹ English equivalent for "marbre." [Trans.]

consists in: he throws his shooter without taking into account the distances or the manner of playing ("piquette"), and when he succeeds in driving a marble out of the square he immediately puts it back. Thus the game has no end. "Does it go on like that all the time?—*You take one away to make a change* (he takes a marble out of the square, but not the one that he has touched). *It'll only be finished when there's only one left* (he "fires" again twice). *One more shot, and then you take one away*." Then he affirms: *"Every third shot you take one away."* He does so. Mae removes a marble every third shot independently of whether he has hit or missed, which is completely irregular and corresponds to nothing in the game as habitually played, or as we have seen it played in Neuchâtel or Geneva. It is therefore a rule which he has invented then and there but which he has the impression of remembering because it presents a vague analogy with what really happens when the player removes the marble he has just "hit" (touched). This game of Mae's is therefore a characteristic game of the second stage, an egocentric game in which "to win" does not mean getting the better of the others, but simply playing on one's own.

Wid, whom I now prepare to question and who has not assisted at Mae's interrogatory, begins by making a square. He places four marbles at the four corners and one in the middle (the same disposition as Mae's, which was probably a deformation of it). Wid does not know what to do to decide which is to begin, and declares that he understands nothing of the method which Mae had shown me as being familiar to both of them (trying to hit one's partner's shooter). Wid then throws his shooter in the direction of the square, knocking out one marble which he puts in his pocket. Then I take my turn, but fail to touch anything. He plays again and wins all the marbles, one after the other, keeping them each time. He also declares that when you have knocked a marble out, you have the right to play another shot straight away. After having taken everything he says: *"I've won."* Wid therefore belongs to the third stage if this explanation is taken as a whole, but the sequel will show that he takes no notice of Mae's doings when they are playing together. Wid stands therefore at the boundary line which separates the stage of egocentrism from the stage of cooperation.

I then tell Mae to come into the room and the two children begin to play with each other. Mae draws a square and Wid disposes the marbles in accordance with his habitual schema. Mae begins (he plays "roulette" whereas Wid most of the time plays "piquette") and dislodges four marbles. *I can play four times, now,"* adds Mae. This is contrary to all the rules, but Wid finds the statement quite natural. So one game succeeds another. But the marbles are placed in the square by one child or the other as the spirit moves them (according to the rules each must put his "pose") and the dislodged marbles are sometimes put straight back into the square, sometimes retained by the boy who has won them. Each plays from whatever place he chooses, unchecked by his partner, and each "fires" as many times as he likes (it thus often happens that Mae and Wid are playing at the same time).

I now send Wid out of the room and ask Mae to explain the game to us for a last time. Mae places sixteen marbles in the middle of the square. "Why so many as that?—*So as to win.* —How many do you put down at home with Wid?—*I put five, but when I'm alone, I put lots."* Mae then begins to play and dislodges a marble which he puts on one side. I do the same. The game continues in this way, each playing one shot at a time without taking the dislodged marbles into account (which is contrary to what Mae was doing a moment ago). Mae then places five marbles in the square, like Wid. This time I arrange the five marbles as Mae himself had done at the beginning of the interrogatory (four close together and one on top) but Mae seems to have forgotten this way of doing things. In the end Mae plays by taking away a marble every three shots, as before, and says to us: *"It's so that it should stop."*

We have quoted the whole of this example in order to show how little two children from the same class at school, living in the same house, and accustomed to playing with each other, are able to understand each other at this age. Not only do they tell us of totally different rules (this still occurs throughout the third stage), but when they play together they do not watch each other and do not unify their respective rules even for the duration of one game. The fact of the matter is that neither is trying to get the better of the other: each is merely having a game on his own, trying to hit the marbles in the square, *i.e.,* trying to "win" from his point of view.

This shows the characteristics of the stage. The child plays for himself. His interest does not in any way consist in competing with his companions and in binding himself by common rules so as to see who will get the better of the others. His aims are different. They are indeed dual, and it is this mixed behavior that really defines egocentrism. On the one hand, the child feels very strongly the desire to play like the other boys, and especially like those older than himself; he longs, that is to say, to feel himself a member of the very honorable fraternity of those who know how to play marbles correctly. But quickly persuading himself, on the other hand, that his playing is "right" (he can convince himself as easily on this point as in all his attempts to imitate adult behavior) the child thinks only of utilizing these acquisitions for himself: his pleasure still consists in the mere development of skill, in carrying out the strokes he sets himself to play. It is, as in the previous stage, essentially a motor pleasure, not a social one. The true "socius" of the player who has reached this stage is not the flesh and blood partner but the ideal and abstract elder whom one inwardly strives to imitate and who sums up all the examples one has ever received.

It little matters, therefore, what one's companion is doing, since one is not trying to contend against him. It little matters what the details of the rules may be, since there is no real contact between the players. This is why the child, as soon as he can schematically copy the big boys' game, believes himself to be in possession of the whole truth. Each for himself, and all in communion with the "Elder": such might be the formula of egocentric play.

It is striking to note the affinity between this attitude of children of four to six in the game of marbles and the attitude of those same children in their conversations with each other. For alongside of the rare cases of true conversation where there is a genuine interchange of opinions or commands, one can observe in children between two and six a characteristic type of pseudo-conversation or "collective monologue," during which the children speak only for themselves, although they wish to be in the presence of interlocutors who will serve as a stimulus. Now here again, each feels himself to be in communion with the group because he is inwardly addressing the Adult who knows and understands everything, but here again, each is only concerned with himself, for lack of having disassociated the "ego" from the "socius."

These features of the egocentric stage will not, however, appear in their full light until we come to analyze the consciousness of rules which accompanies this type of conduct.

The Practice of Rules.   II. Third and Fourth Stages

Toward the age of seven to eight appears the desire for mutual understanding in the sphere of play (as also, indeed, in the conversations between children). This felt need for understanding is what defines the third stage. As a criterion of the appearance of this stage we shall take the moment when by "winning" the child refers to the fact of getting the better of the others, therefore of gaining more marbles than the others, and when he no longer says he has won when he has done no more than to knock a marble out of the square, regardless of what his partners have done. As a matter of fact, no child, even from among the older ones, ever attributes very great importance to the fact of knocking out a few more marbles than his opponents. Mere competition is therefore not what constitutes the affective motive-power of the game. In seeking to win the child is trying above all to contend with his partners *while observing common rules*. The specific pleasure of the game thus ceases to be muscular and egocentric, and becomes social. Henceforth, a game of marbles constitutes the equivalent in action of what takes place in discussion in words: a mutual evaluation of the competing powers which leads, thanks to the observation of common rules, to a conclusion that is accepted by all.

As to the difference between the third and fourth stages, it is only one of degree. The children of about seven to ten (third stage) do not yet know the rules in detail. They try to learn them owing to their increasing interest in the game played in common, but when different children of the same class at school are questioned on the subject the discrepancies are still considerable in the information obtained. It is only when they are at play that these same children succeed in understanding each other, either by copying the boy who seems to know most about it, or, more frequently, by omitting any usage that might be disputed. In this way they play a sort of simplified game. Children of the fourth stage, on the contrary, have thoroughly mastered their code and even take pleasure in juridical discussions, whether of principle or merely of procedure, which may at times arise out of the points in dispute.

Let us examine some examples of the third stage, and, in order to point more clearly to the differentiating characters of

this stage, let us begin by setting side by side the answers of
two little boys attending the same class at school and accustomed to playing together. (The children were naturally questioned separately in order to avoid any suggestion between
them, but we afterward compared their answers with one another.)

BEN (10) and NUS (11, backward, one year below the
school standard) are both in the fourth year of the lower
school and both play marbles a great deal. They agree in regarding the square as necessary. Nus declares that you always
place four marbles in the square, either at the corners or else
three in the center with one on top (in a pyramid). Ben, however, tells us that you place two to ten marbles in the enclosure (not less than two, not more than ten).

To know who is to begin you draw, according to Nus, a line
called the "coche" and everyone tries to get near it: whoever
gets nearest plays first, and whoever goes beyond it plays last.
Ben, however, knows nothing about the coche: you begin *as
you like.—*Isn't there a dodge for knowing who is to play first?
*—No.—*Don't you try with the coche?*—Yes, sometimes.—*What
is the coche?*— . . .* (he cannot explain)." On the other hand,
Ben affirms that you "fire" the first shot at a distance of two to
three steps from the square. A single step is not enough, and
"four isn't any good either." Nus is ignorant of this law and
considers the distance to be a matter of convention.

With regard to the manner of "firing," Nus is equally tolerant. According to him you can play "piquette" or "roulette,"
but *"when you play piquette everyone must play the same.
When one boy says that you must play roulette, everyone plays
that way."* Nus prefers roulette because *"that is the best way"*:
piquette is more difficult. Ben, however, regards piquette as
obligatory in all cases. He is ignorant, moreover, of the term
roulette and when we show him what it is he says: *"That is
bowled piquette!* (Fr. piquette roulée) *That's cheating!"*

According to Nus everyone must play from the coche, and
all through the game. When, after having shot at the square
you land anywhere, you must therefore come back to the
coche to "fire" the next shot. Ben, on the contrary, who on
this point represents the more general usage, is of opinion that
only the first shot should be fired from the coche: after that
"you must play from where you are."

Nus and Ben thus agree in stating that the marbles that have gone out of the square remain in the possession of the boy who dislodged them. This is the only point, this and the actual drawing of the square, on which the children give us results that are in agreement.

When we begin to play, I arrange to stay in the square (to leave my shooter inside the enclosure). *"You are dished* (Fr. cuit), cries Ben, delighted, *you can't play again until I get you out!"* Nus knows nothing of this rule. Again, when I play carelessly and let the shooter drop out of my hand, Ben exclaims *"Fan-coup"* to prevent me from saying "coup-passé" and having another shot. Nus is ignorant of this rule.

At one point Ben succeeds in hitting my shooter. He concludes from this that he can have another shot, just as though he had hit one of the marbles placed in the square. Nus, in the same circumstances does not draw the same conclusions (each must play in turn according to him) but deduces that he will be able to play the first shot in the next game.

In the same way, Ben thinks that everyone plays from the place the last shot has led him to and knows the rule that authorizes the player to change places, saying *"du mien"* or *"un empan,"* whereas Nus, who has certainly heard those words, does not know what they mean.

These two cases, chosen at random out of a class of ten-year-old pupils, show straight away what are the two differential features of the second stage. 1) There is a general will to discover the rules that are fixed and common to all players (*cf.* the way Nus explains to us that if one of the partners plays piquette *"everyone must play the same"*). 2) In spite of this there is considerable discrepancy in the children's information. Lest the reader should think the above examples exceptional here are, on the same point, the answers of another child from the same class:

Ross (11;I): *"First, every one puts two marbles on the square. You can make the square bigger when there are more playing."* Ross knows the method of the coche for knowing who is to begin. Like Nus, he allows both roulette and piquette. He also allows what is not only contrary to all established usages but also to the sense of the words, a way of playing which he calls "femme-poussette" which consists in carrying one's hand along with the marble as one throws it (push stroke in billiards). Now this is always forbidden, and the very word that Ross has deformed says so—"fan-poussette." According to Ross, you play from the place you have reached with the last shot, and when you have won a marble you have the right to another shot straight away. To change your place you must say "du mien." *"If a stone gets in our way, you say 'coup-passé' and have another shot. If it slips* [if the marble slips out of your hand] *you say 'laché'* (Engl. 'gone'). *If you don't say that, you can't have another turn. It's the rules!"* Ross here stands midway between Nus and Ben. Finally, Ross knows of a rather peculiar custom which is unknown to Nus and Ben. *"If you stay in the square you can be hit and then he picks up the marbles* [= If your shooter stays inside the square and is touched by your opponent's shooter, he is entitled to all the marbles in the square]. *He* (the opponent) *can have two shots* [to try and hit the shooter in question] *and if he misses the first he can take* [at the second shot] *the shooter from anywhere* [though of course only from the outside of the square] *and make the marbles go out* [=take them]." This rule has generally only been described to us by children of the fourth stage, but the rest of Ross' interrogatory is typically third stage.

Such then is the third stage. The child's chief interest is no longer psycho-motor, it is social. In other words, to dislodge a marble from a square by manual dexterity is no longer an aim in itself. The thing now is not only to fight the other boys but also and primarily to regulate the game with a whole set of systematic rules which will ensure the most complete reciprocity in the methods used. The game has therefore become social. We say "become" because it is only after this stage that any real cooperation exists between the players. Before this, each played for himself. Each sought, it is true, to imitate the play of older boys and of the initiated, but more for the satisfaction, still purely personal, of feeling himself to be a member of a mystical community whose sacred institutions are handed down by the elders out of the remote past, than from any real desire to cooperate with his playmates or with anyone else. If cooperation be regarded as more social than this mixture of egocentrism and respect for one's seniors which characterizes the beginnings of collective life among children, then we may say that it is from the third stage onward that the game of marbles begins to be a truly social game.

As yet, however, this cooperation exists to a great extent

only in intention. Being an honest man is not enough to make one to know the law. It is not even enough to enable us to solve all the problems that may arise in our concrete "moral experience." The child fares in the same way during the present stage, and succeeds, at best, in creating for himself a "provisional morality," putting off till a later date the task of setting up a code of laws and a system of jurisprudence. Nor do boys of seven to ten ever succeed in agreeing among themselves for longer than the duration of one and the same game; they are still incapable of legislating on all possible cases that may arise, for each still has a purely personal opinion about the rules of the game.

To use an apter comparison, we may say that the child of seven to ten plays as he reasons. We have already[10] tried to establish the fact that about the age of seven to eight, precisely, that is to say, at the moment when our third stage appears, in the very poor districts where we conducted our work,[11] discussion and reflection gain an increasing ascendency over unproved affirmation and intellectual egocentrism. Now, these new habits of thought lead to genuine deductions (as opposed to primitive "transductions") and to deductions in which the child grapples with a given fact of experience, either present or past. But something is still lacking if deduction is to be generalized and made completely rational: the child must be able to reason formally, *i.e.*, he must have a conscious realization of the rules of reasoning which will enable him to apply them to any case whatsoever, including purely hypothetical cases (mere assumptions). In the same way, a child who, with regard to the rules of games, has reached the third stage, will achieve momentary coordinations of a collective order (a well ordered game may be compared on this point to a good discussion), but feels no interest as yet in the actual legislation of the game, in the discussions of principle which alone will give him complete mastery of the game in all its strictness. (From this point of view the juridico-moral discussions of the fourth stage may be compared to formal reasoning in general.)

It is, on an average, toward the age of eleven or twelve

[10] Piaget, *Judgement & Reasoning in the Child*, chap. IV.

[11] We take this opportunity of reminding the reader of what has not been sufficiently emphasized in our earlier books, viz. that most of our research has been carried out on children from the poorer parts of Geneva. In different surroundings the age averages would certainly have been different.

that these interests develop. In order to understand what is the practice of rules among children of this fourth stage let us question separately several children from the same class at school, and we shall see how subtle are their answers, and how well they agree with one another.

Rit (12), Gros (13) and Vua (13) often play marbles. We questioned them each separately and took steps to prevent them from communicating to each other during our absence the contents of our interrogatory.

With regard to the square, the "pose," the manner of throwing, and generally speaking all the rules we have already examined, these three children are naturally in full agreement with each other. To know who is to play first, Rit, who has lived in two neighboring villages before coming to town, tells us that various customs are in usage. You draw a line, the coche, and whoever gets nearest to it plays first. If you go beyond the line, either, according to some, it does not matter, or else *"there is another game: when you go beyond the line, you play last."* Gros and Vua know only of this custom, the only one that is really put into practice by the boys of the neighborhood.

But there are complications about which the younger boys left us in the dark. *"Whoever,* according to Gros, *says 'queue' plays second. It's easier because he doesn't get 'Hit'* [=if a player's shooter lands near the square, it is exposed to hits from the other players]." In the same way, Vua tells us that *"whoever says 'queue de deux' plays last."* And he adds the following rule, also recognized by Gros: *"When you are all at the same distance from the coche whoever cries 'egaux-queque' plays second"* (the problem is therefore to play sufficiently soon still to find marbles in the square, but not first, for fear of being hit).

On the other hand, Gros tells us: *"Whoever takes out two* [two of the marbles placed inside the square, *i.e.,* the equivalent of the player's 'pose'] *can say 'queue-de-pose.' In that way he can play second from the coche in the next game."* And Vua: *"When there are two outside* [when two marbles have been knocked out of the square] *you can dare to say 'queue-de-pose,' and you can play second from the coche again in the second game."* Rit gives us the same information.

This is not all. According to Rit, *"if you say 'deux-coups-de-coche' you can have two shots from the line. If you say 'deux-coups-d'empan' you play the second shot from where you are. You can only say that when the other* [=the opponent] *has made up his pose* [=has won back as many marbles as he had originally deposited in the square]." This rule is observed in the same way by the other two children.

In addition, there is a whole set of rules, unknown to the younger boys, which bear upon the position of the marbles in the square. According to Gros *"the first boy who says 'place-pour-moi'* [Engl. place-for-me] *does not have to place himself at one of the corners of the square,"* and *"the one who has said 'places-des-marbres'* (Engl. place for the marbles) *can put them down as he likes, in a 'troyat'* (all in a heap) *or at the four corners."* Vua is of the same opinion and adds: *"If you say 'place-pour-toi-pour-tout-le-jeu'* (Engl. your-place-for-the-whole-game) *the other chap* [=the opponent] *must stay at the same place."* Rit, who knows both these rules, adds the further detail that *"you can't say 'place-pour-moi' if you have already said 'place-pour-toi.'* " This gives some idea of the complications of procedure!

Our three legal experts also point the measures of clemency in use for the protection of the weak. According to Vua *"if you knock out three at one shot and there's only one left* [one marble in the square] *the other chap* [the opponent] *has the right to play from halfway* [halfway between the coche and the square] *because the first boy has made more than his 'pose.'* " Also: *"the boy who has been beaten is allowed to begin."* According to Gros, *"if there is one marble left at the end, the boy who has won, instead of taking it, can give it to the other chap."* And again, *"When there's one boy who has won too much, the others say 'coujac,' and he is bound to play another game."*

The number of shots at the disposal of each player also gives rise to a whole series of regulations on which the three boys lay stress, as before, in full agreement with each other. For the sake of brevity we refer the reader on this point to the general rules outlined in Section I.

There is only one point on which we saw our subjects differ. Rit who, it will be remembered, has known the game in three different districts, tells us that the boy whose shooter stays inside the square may generally come out of it. He added, it is true, that in some games the player in such a plight is "dished" (Fr. *brulé*), but this rule does not seem to him obligatory. Vua and Gros, on the contrary, are of opinion that in all cases *"when you stay inside the square you are dished."* We think we may confuse Vua by saying: "Rit didn't say that!—*The fact is,* answers Vua, *that sometimes people play differently. Then you ask each other what you want to do.*—And if you can't agree?—*We scrap for a bit and then we fix things up."*

These answers show what the fourth stage is. Interest seems to have shifted its ground since the last stage. Not only do these children seek to cooperate, to "fix things up," as Vua puts it, rather than to play for themselves alone, but also—and this undoubtedly is something new—they seem to take a peculiar pleasure in anticipating all possible cases and in codifying them. Considering that the square game is only one of the five or ten varieties of the game of marbles, it is almost alarming in face of the complexity of rules and procedure in the square game, to think of what a child of twelve has to store away in his memory. These rules, with their overlapping and their exceptions, are at least as complex as the current rules of spelling. It is somewhat humiliating, in this connection, to see how heavily traditional education sets about the task of making spelling enter into brains that assimilate with such ease the mnemonic contents of the game of marbles. But then, memory is dependent upon activity, and a real activity presupposes interest.

Throughout this fourth stage, then, the dominating interest seems to be interest in the rules themselves. For mere cooperation would not require such subtleties as those attending the disposition of the marbles in the square ("place-pour-moi," "place-des-marbres," "place-pour-toi-pour-tout-le-jeu," etc.). The fact that the child enjoys complicating things at will proves that what he is after is rules for their own sake. We have described elsewhere[12] the extraordinary behavior of eight boys of ten to eleven who, in order to throw snowballs at each other, began by wasting a good quarter of an hour in electing a president, fixing the rules of voting, then in dividing themselves into two camps, in deciding upon the distances of the shots, and finally in foreseeing what would be the sanctions to be applied in cases of infringement of these laws. Many other facts analogous to this could be culled from studies that have been made on children's societies.

In conclusion, the acquisition and practice of the rules of a

[12] Piaget, *Judgement & Reasoning in the Child,* p. 96.

game follow very simple and very natural laws, the stages of which may be defined as follows: 1) Simple individual regularity. 2) Imitation of seniors with egocentrism. 3) Cooperation. 4) Interest in rules for their own sake. Let us now see whether the consciousness of rules describes in its evolution an equally uncomplicated curve.

Property and Possessiveness[1]

SUSAN ISAACS

(1949)

Susan Isaacs, the English child analyst, examines here
the motives and manifestations of possessiveness in children, and how concepts of "mine" and "the biggest"
develop into adult attitudes toward wealth. She points
out that the possession of objects never satisfies in itself,
but is an instrument which implies victory or dominance
over other persons. Ownership, she stresses, often symbolizes more abstract rivalries—motives of power, love
and guilt.

1. *Introduction*

I was invited to take part in this symposium on the assumption that some knowledge of the possessive attitudes of young
children, and their behavior with regard to property, would
be likely to throw light upon the psychological problem in
adult society. I believe this view to be a correct one, and that
it is only on the basis of a *genetic* study of feelings and attitudes in the development of children's behavior that we can
come to understand the mental processes which become crystallized into adult sentiments, the institutions of property and
the warfare of classes. That young children show a strong desire to possess material objects cannot be doubted; but a closer
study of their actual behavior, from infancy up to the time
when the so-called "collecting instinct" appears in the middle
years of childhood, will show that all behavior relating to property is in fact a complex manifestation of many diverse psychological trends, including love, hate and rivalry with *people*.
I do not believe that the relation between a person and a
physical object, whether it be a toy, a utensil, a weapon, a
dwelling place, an ornament or a conventional unit of cur-

[1] A Contribution to a Symposium at the Medical Section of the British Psychological Society, 1934.

rency, is ever a simple affair between a person and a thing; it is always a triangular relation between at least *two* people and the thing in question. The object is a pawn in the game, an instrument for controlling and defining the relation between two or more persons. It may be a symbol of a significant bodily part of one or both of them.

This view of the complexity of the motives which enter into the overt attitudes of adults regarding material wealth is greatly strengthened by psychoanalytic experience. In the analysis of both adults and children, we find that their attitudes to material possessions frequently change a great deal during the course of the analysis. This change is often in the direction of a lessening of the strength of the wish to own, and a growth of the wish and the ability to love, to give and to create. Whatever the direction of the change, however, the fact that marked alterations occur under analysis, as the life history of feelings, fantasies and experiences is disentangled, makes it impossible to support the view that we are ever dealing with a simple "instinct of acquisitiveness" as such, let alone with "rational self-interest."

I propose to develop this broad conclusion by considering direct evidence, first, from the observed behavior of young children in a group; and secondly, from the psychoanalysis of a boy in whom the craving for property and the wish for gifts was inordinately strong.

2. *Evidence from the Behavior of Young Children*[2]

A group of young children (between two and six years) playing together in a free environment, which includes a variety of material for common use as well as a certain number of privately owned objects, will furnish countless examples of behavior bearing witness to the strength and urgency of the naïve wish to own, the desire to have exclusive possession, or at least the biggest share or main use, of whatever properties happen to be the center of interest. To a little child, the satisfaction of having things that are all one's own is deep, the chagrin if others have more than one's self very bitter.

The possessive impulse takes various forms. One is the direct wish to own an actual object, or to have exclusive use

[2] This topic is also dealt with in *The Social Development of Young Children*, 1933.

of it (which makes it "mine" for all intents and purposes). Any situation in which there is only one thing of a kind, an insufficient number of things for the group, or an assortment of things of varying sizes, will give rise to immediate tension as to who shall have "it" or "the biggest." With very young children it is often the mere size of the thing that counts, rather than its appropriateness; it is always the smallest children who insist on having the largest-sized tools, although they cannot manage them, and would get on much better with a medium-sized; the older and more experienced child will more commonly choose the more appropriate tool, and defend his right to that with equal tenacity.

A certain amount of teasing play will occur among children, in which they take away the property of others, not because they want to have that object itself, but because they want to rob the other child of it. This is a playful revenge, rather than a direct wish for actual possession. It has in it less of love of the object and more of hate of the other person.

Ownership is felt in things other than actual objects. Some children show a keen sense of property in the nursery rhymes and songs, or in phonograph records of a kind they have heard at home. No one else has the right to sing or hear these things without their permission. Again, children feel that anything is "theirs" if they have used it first, or have made it, even with material that belonged to the community. Sometimes they feel a thing is "theirs" if they have "thought" of it, or "mentioned it first"; and so on.

Some children will take it upon themselves now and then to act as dispensers of the public property and materials— the plasticine, the phonograph, etc. They may be quite well aware that the property in question is not "theirs," but they get a sense of power from deciding who shall use it and who not, or how much they shall have, trying to favor friends and exclude enemies. And if argument arises, the child who has constituted himself the master of ceremonies will often assert that the plasticine, etc., *does* belong to him, on the ground that *he* is "using it."

One of the commonest situations in which the possessive impulse is aroused occurs when a number of children want to use one of the larger pieces of school apparatus at the same time—the swing, the seesaw, a tricycle, the sandbox. "Taking turns" is one of the hardest lessons for children under five years to learn. The young child cannot without much experience believe that "his turn" really will come in due time.

All that he knows is that the others "have got it" and he hasn't. A few minutes is an eternity when one is eagerly waiting for a prized pleasure such as riding on a tricycle or a seesaw. Nor does one believe in the good-will of the others who are enjoying their turns first—one knows only too well how readily one would exclude *them* if one were allowed! Only the proved evenness of justice of a controlling adult will make a transition possible from the impetuous assertion of "I want it *now*" to that trust in the future which makes "taking turns" possible.

A particular incident occurring between two little girls of four illustrates the complicated processes that go to the development of a sense of justice in the use of property. One child was using the tricycle and the other wanted it. The latter complained to me that "A wants to have the tricycle all the morning, and won't give it to me." I suggested that B should ask A to let her have it after A had gone, say, four times more round the garden with it. B agreed, and I then added: "And perhaps when you've had it for four times round the garden, you would let A have it again for four times, and take turns in that way." B replied instantly: "Oh no! I shall have it more than four times—as many times as she has had it altogether—not just four—that wouldn't be *fair*, would it?" When the child argues thus she feels that if her enjoyment has to suffer limitations for someone's else's pleasure, then she must have at the least as much as that other one. The logic runs: "If I cannot be supreme, we must all be equal. My wish for exclusive possession is tamed by my fear of the other's encroachments and the hope that if I admit him to equal rights he will take no more. But I cannot concede more." Equality is the least common multiple to these conflicting wishes and fears. If all are equal, no one has any advantage. And so "justice" is born.

Even in the simpler instances of the direct wish to own, it is plain that the relation to another *person* is a very important element. Neither the pleasure of ownership nor the chagrin of envy bears much relation to the intrinsic value of the things owned or coveted. Few objects, other than food when hungry, have an absolute and intrinsic value to little children, independent of what other children are having and wanting. What is so desperately desired may be wanted simply because someone else has it or desires it. A thing that has long been treated with indifference or contempt by the owner may suddenly assume great value in his eyes, if another person begins to take an interest in it; an ordinary object in the common environment, which has had no attention from the children, may suddenly become the center of an intense struggle for ownership, if one of the children (especially the older ones), or an adult, shows that it now has value for him.

Turning to the situations which give rise to friendly cooperative play rather than to quarrels between children, one of the commonest and naïvest grounds for feeling friendly to other children (or adults) is gratitude for gifts received. In the frank and open-hearted attitudes of little children, both giving and gift are love itself. Much more is involved, however, than the simple desire for a material gift, than the wish to receive a gift as a sign of love. The child to whom a gift is offered shows by his response that he then feels *loveworthy;* and he who is denied, shows that he feels he has been denied *because* he is bad, because he is or has been hostile to the giver. It is this which brings poignancy to the child's gratitude for gifts, and bitterness to his sense of loss when he is left out of the giving. The gift is not only a sign that the giver loves and does not hate; it is also a sign that the *recipient* is believed to be loving, not hating and hateful. It thus brings him reassurance against his own sense of guilt and the pressure of his super-ego. The giver becomes *a good helper* (parent or ally) against the bad inside the child who receives. Whereas when he withholds, he abandons the child not only to his need, but to the rages and jealousies which that need and the sight of others' satisfactions arouse in him.

The obverse of all this is seen from the side of the child who makes gifts to those whom he loves. The wish to be *potent in giving* is very clear in much of the behavior of little children. For if one has the wherewithal to give, one is indeed both safe and good. One is no longer the helpless ruling infant, dependent upon the gifts of others, and driven by helpless anxieties to rage and jealousy. One is now the omnipotent parent, full of good things, safe from unsatisfied desire, and all-powerful to help others (viz. one's children). It is more blessed to give than to receive, because to be able to give is *not to need.* It is (in unconscious meaning) to be omnipotently safe and good.

Even in the least complicated situation, where the value of the thing owned is intrinsic, the means of satisfying some (primary or derived) personal need, the actual wish to *own* it can best be understood in terms of power—or rather of *powerlessness.* "I want to own it because if I do not it may not be there when I need it, and my need will go unsatisfied. If another has it, he might keep it for ever. If I am at the mercy of another's will for the satisfaction of my need, I am helpless before it. Only if the means of satisfaction of my need is *mine,* mine to have and to hold, can I feel safe." Even here, there is a reference to other people, as potential frustrators, challengers or rivals. But, as we have seen, a great part of the value of those things which little children want to own is far from intrinsic. It arises directly from the fact that others have or want the object. And thus we enter the open field of *rivalry.* Not to have what others have, or to have less than they, is to feel small and weak and helpless. Not to be given what others have been given, or as much as they, is to feel shut out from the love and regard of the person giving. It is to be treated as not loveworthy. We can go further and say that the child who is not given what others receive (whether from playmate or adult) feels this exclusion to be not merely a denial of gifts and of love, but a judgment upon him. That is its chief bitterness, and the main source of the intensity of desire.

The ultimate situation from which the wish to own arises is that of the infant at the breast, whose satisfactions are indeed at the mercy of another's will. It is to the infant's sense of helplessness before the urgency of his need for love and nourishment, and the equally helpless rage stirred by the denial of immediate satisfaction, that we have to look for an understanding of the child's imperious wish to own.

To think of the motive of possession as a simple irreducible instinct is thus to miss its most significant aspect, viz. its intimate relation with the motives of power, of rivalry, of guilt and of love. It is essentially a *social* response, not a simple direct reaction to the physical objects which may serve individual purposes.

3. *Evidence from the Analysis of a Seven-Year-Old Boy*

Further light is thrown upon these overt group phenomena by the evidence gained from the psyschoanalysis of a boy of seven and a half. This boy came to me for analysis because of an inability to learn, an inordinate craving for gifts and material objects, and a mildly asocial general attitude. His relations to people consisted almost entirely in asking: "Can I have that?" and "Will you give me this?" He was restless and inattentive, incurious and unable to learn at school, and generally unloving and unlovable. An incomplete analysis of two years changed this picture considerably. The excessive craving for gifts and objects was greatly lessened, he became more affectionate and more generally liked, able to learn more freely, to show more of the adventuriousness normal to a boy of nine, and at the same time a greater capacity for penitence if his adventurousness gave rise to difficulties. During the course of the analysis, he constantly took away the toys from the drawer in the analytic room, and a certain amount of stealing occurred in his real life. A great deal of the play in the analysis was concerned with attack and robbery in one form or another. At one period we played out the Dick Turpin drama at great length and in detail. Sometimes I myself had to play the part of a thief, *e.g.* a black thief, an African, with black fingers, made black by black deeds of robbery. Briefly, the various *unconscious* meanings of material possessions and of his craving to get them, whether by asking or stealing, can be summarized as follows:

(1) The earliest bodily source of satisfaction, namely, his mother's breast. Unsatisfied oral cravings played a large part in his wish for objects. The boy had in fact suffered a good deal of oral deprivation in his early life.

(2) It was, however, not only the original primary satisfaction of both love and hunger, which he sought from the suckling; there was also a secondary need to find the "good" breast, as a reassurance against his fear of the "bad" mother who had been spoiled by his own attacks of frustrated rage. These attacks had been made partly in fantasy, partly in real behavior, by the means which every infant has at his disposal, biting, screaming, grasping, wetting and dirtying. The objects which he continually got or stole for himself, in later childhood, ceased each in turn to be satisfactory, as soon as he got it, because it then became the damaged breast which he had attacked. This was the deepest level of experience represented in the boy's craving for objects.

(3) His early disappointment at the breast, and fear of it as a result of his attacks, had led him after infancy to transfer his love wishes to his father and his father's penis. He then wished to attack and rob his mother of his father's penis, which she enjoyed in intercourse. This fantasy, and the wishes and anxieties associated with it, was played out in the analysis in, for example, the Dick Turpin play already referred to, but in many other forms as well.

The anxieties about the ruined mother led to a greater intensification of the need to get good from her, as a proof that she
was not yet altogether destroyed and dead. The constant
taking of the toys away from the analytic room mainly arose
from the absolute necessity to have proof that I still had
good to give him.

(4) Furthermore, these violent wishes to separate the parents, and to gain the father for himself, led thereafter to the
urgent need to *restore* to his mother the things which had been
taken from her, whether the contents of her breast, milk and
food, or of her body, the father's penis, her feces and her
children.

This wish to restore was very strong in the boy, and was
played out in many ways in the analysis; *e.g.* by covering
the walls of my room with drawings of telephones (some of
them remarkably phallic in style). But since the boy's own
penis had so often been the instrument of urinary attack
upon his mother, it was felt to be incapable of itself giving
good, of restoring, or creating. Hence the necessity to get good
from some other source, to do good with. A "good" father
had to be found to give the boy a "good" penis, as a means for
restoring the mother. The boy felt he could not himself bear
the guilt and responsibility, or endure the enormous burden of
putting his mother right. If he tried to do this, he would
himself be reduced to helpless penury and starvation, would
be castrated, turned out and ruined. For a long period in his
analysis he had much more faith in the possibility of finding
a good father than a good mother. He made friends with men
in the street, with bus conductors and truck drivers, and openly
wished to have a man analyst.

The anxiety to which the *good* impulses, the wish to restore
and to create, led in this boy was enormous. It was strikingly
shown in one particular analytic hour. There was a cupboard
in the room where I kept my outdoor garments and my purse,
and which was always locked. The boy knew that my purse
and garments were in the cupboard, and had often begged
to be allowed to open the cupboard and to have money given
to him. One day he so managed circumstances with regard
to his fare for traveling home from the analysis (a fairly considerable distance on the subway), that he was left with too
little. He begged me to lend him a penny, to save a very long
walk. I, of course, agreed, and opened the cupboard to get
out my purse. The boy looked inside the cupboard; then at

once said, "Good-by—I'm going," and went straight out of the room and away without waiting for the penny. I did not at once understand what in the cupboard could have frightened him so much that he could not stay with me a moment longer, but had to leave immediately. I knew that he had had fantasies about marvelous things inside the cupboard, but it did not seem that the disappointment of these fantasies was enough to make the boy so terrified as to drive him instantly away. The next day he came twenty minutes late. After a good deal of play in which the theme was of my being an old woman with starving children; and having to beg or to play the piano in the street to earn my living, he spoke of a particular newspaper placard actually seen on the previous day, which ran: "Duke's son begs in street." He then suddenly asked me: "Haven't you *got* a coat?" This was the key to the overwhelming anxiety of the previous day. It was winter, but the day had been a mild one and I had come a very short distance to my consulting room and had not bothered to wear my coat. When I opened the cupboard the boy saw only a hat, and his instant belief was that I *had* no coat. And here was he borrowing (*i.e.* stealing, since he had no intention of returning the penny) from a poor woman who had no winter coat! Since he had been in analysis now with me for a year, had experienced the real benefits of understanding and felt he owed me a real debt, this notion stirred up an enormous terror that *he* would have to be responsible for providing me with a coat. As he was now in fact learning to play the piano, he would thus have to play it in the street, as he often saw a man doing in Wimpole Street, in order to pay for a coat for me. With many other threads which I cannot quote here, this led back to his despair as a small child, faced with the need to make good the damage he has done to his parents. His intense morbid craving to have things given to him was not only for the purpose of doing good with them, but even more to deny his guilt and responsibility, to prove to himself that he was still only a helpless baby who had never done anything wrong and who deserved only to receive.

In all these fantasies there were actual links with his real experience. The boy's father was a professional man with limited income and financial problems were of real urgency. From early childhood he had heard bickerings and mutual recriminations between the parents about financial difficulties. In his fantasy, it was his own early attacks upon his mother and his intense desire to obtain his father's love for himself which had led to these quarrels; and his own early greed and oral necessities which had made his parents poor.

Finally, the inhibition with regard to learning in this boy, whilst naturally very complex, had the following connection with his craving for material possessions. Learning is seeing and knowing, and to see and know about a thing is to want it; to want it is to damage it. So it is better not to learn. At the age of two years the boy had in fact been taken to sleep in his parents' bedroom, although occupying a room alone up to that time. He had undoubtedly been present at parental intercourse. He had not seen, but he had heard. He had wanted to see and to understand; and this wish had necessarily interfered with and separated his parents. Moreover, to see and know and learn is to accept responsibility, and since responsibility leads to the overwhelming task of restoring the poor quarreling parents, it is better not to grow up, not to learn, not to know, but to deny responsibility altogether by being a child too little to learn, fit only to accept gifts from others. For him, the only alternative to this demand for material gifts was actual suicide, and the analysis uncovered definite suicidal tendencies, which were relieved by the later work of the analysis.

It will be remarked that in these notes I have said very little about the phenomenon of *anal fixation* in the love of property, whether in this boy or the children of the group described. That is not because I do not accept the fact of anal fixations operating in inordinate love of material possessions, but because I believe that, through the work of Melanie Klein, we understand a good deal more about the way in which these fixations arise.

It is possible to suggest that the desire for property, and in especial miserly cravings, owe their origin in large part to a shifting of desire *from* the living, human body to removable objects and lifeless material things, mainly because of anxiety about damaging the living bodies of persons. Sweets are craved instead of the breast because the person who gives them remains undamaged by the loss. Feces, money and mechanical toys are feverishly sought instead of the penis, because these, if broken or ruined, can be thrown away and easily replaced. They can be taken without real bodily harm to the person from whom they come. The anal fixations represented in love of material possessions are thus strongly reinforced by displacement from the breast and the penis. The material objects embody and substitute relations with people. They are in the main a substitute for love, and counter the fear of loss of love.

In conclusion, I admit that I have not made any attempt to forge direct links between these deepest most personal and primitive feelings in the individual child, on the one hand, and adult social phenomena on the other. What I wanted to do was to challenge the crude psychological theory which uses a simple "instinct of acquisitiveness" as an explanatory notion for adult behavior; and to plead for a closer cooperation between those most qualified to speak about the real psychological significance of material possessions to the individual, and the sociologists, who are concerned with the conscious sentiments of the adult, with large-scale behavior and social institutions.

Children's Humor: Sex, Names, and Double Meanings

MARTHA WOLFENSTEIN

(1954)

Being able to joke is a uniquely human resource which the young child seizes upon in order to transform his painful feelings into pleasure and thus gain the gratification denied him at every turn by parents and environment. His problems are the substance of his humor: being little and powerless, dealing with arbitrary moral standards and capricious parental love, confused and embarrassed by his sexuality. The following paper on word-play, one of the earliest forms of children's humor, shows that children use ambiguity and the magic power of words they feel to change their own identities, even to drop for a moment the burden of being a child.

I

Play on the ambiguity of words draws upon two basic ambiguities, those of sex and of emotion. Every individual has bisexual tendencies, and children especially feel that sex is indeterminate, that a boy could be changed into a girl or a girl into a boy. As far as emotion is concerned, every relationship partakes of some ambiguity: there is an admixture of hate in every love, and conversely love tends to infuse hostilities. These two major ambiguities of life are involved in the verbal ambiguities which are played upon in joking. It will be objected that playing on double meanings of words is a trivial amusement, incommensurate with the fateful ambiguities of sex and of emotion. This is true for adults. But this triviality is arrived at by a reduction of feelings which are originally serious and disturbing. It is the same kind of reduction as that by which the names of gods become for the unbelieving almost meaningless swear words; awesome and taboo syllables with which the supernatural was once invoked are reduced to exclamations of mild annoyance.

Everything in life at first seems invested with mysterious, wonderful, and dangerous powers. Words are weighted with magical force. The child feels that in learning the names of persons and things he gains a marvelous power over them. When he calls the name of a person, does not that person come to him? When he calls the name of a thing, is it not supplied? To exchange names or to shift their meanings has at first an eerie and disturbing effect, as if in this way the things designated would themselves be transformed. Words must be divested of their magical significance before playing with them can become a joke. Then the formerly fearful, which we have found has really no terrible effect, becomes the comic.

If we trace the prehistory of word-play to the early playing with ambiguity which we can observe in children, we can see how it derives from the two basic ambiguities, of sex and of emotion. Both these ambiguities invest in a high degree the proper name. One's name is the mark of sexual as well as individual identity. Children's wishes to change their names often express a wish to be of the opposite sex or to have better sexual equipment. The child also learns that his name can be used lovingly or angrily: the same name seems to have exactly opposite meanings as it is used in a tender or an accusing tone of voice. It is these ambiguities of the proper name which provide the material for children's early word-play.

The focus of children's word-play is to begin with the proper name, which is used jokingly long before play on common names is mastered. I was struck by how often the ambiguous word in the jokes of school-age children was presented as a proper name. These proper names (in jokes which I shall analyze presently) were words of sexual or aggressive significance, turned for the purpose of the joke into names of persons, such as "Heinie," "Tits," "Free-show," "Fuckerfaster," "Pinch-me," "Shut-up," and "None-of-your-business." In younger children, I observed how they tended to seize on a new name and to wrest from it a meaning by which they attacked the person whose name it was. In still younger children I found a simpler form of name play; they made a joke of reassigning names, calling Johnny "Mary," and so on. When such a game was played, there was usually some child who protested at its unsettling effect, refusing to accept the changed name of himself or another. Thus one could see how taking it as a joke represented a mastery of disturbing emotions. On the youngest level to which I was able to trace word-play, the joke consisted in calling a girl a boy, or a boy a girl.

I should like to trace first the line of development from the playful changing of sex and names to word-play, and later to take up the kinds of jokes which derive from the ambivalent connotations of the proper name (as a love name and a bad name).

II

The joke about the change of sex was initiated in a group of three-year-old children in this way. A boy who had a new baby sister frequently asserted: "I'm a boy." No doubt he had a strong need to reassure himself on this point. The other children would sometimes retort in a teasing way: "You're a bad boy." One day the boy said to one of the little girls: "You're a boy." The girl repudiated this, saying: "Why, I don't even look like a boy." Apparently she was still too pre-occupied with stabilizing her feminine identity to be able to take this proposed reversal lightly. However, from here on the idea of a sex change was taken up by the other children as a joke. According to the teacher's observation, it was the favorite joke of the group throughout the course of the year. At first the joke was apt to be enjoyed more by the initiator than by the child whose sex was allegedly changed, but in time it came to be accepted as a joke by the second child as well. Saying to a girl, "You're a boy," and to a boy, "You're a girl," represented the height of wit for these three-year-olds. It was a particularly good joke when the boy who had started it one day said to the teacher: "You're a boy."

Behind this joke lay the fantasy, the wish and the fear that one's sex could be changed. Might not the assignment of the opposite sex name work a real transformation? The initial reaction was one of uneasiness. The boy who first called a girl a boy was struggling against his fear of losing his masculinity, and tried to ward it off by denying the existence of any but male creatures. The child who first laughed at the alleged sex reversal was probably the one who had achieved the most certainty about his or her sexual identity. As the playful sex switch became a generally accepted joke it meant for each child a mastery of doubts about his own sex.

One's name is a peculiarly valuable possession, the mark of one's sexual and personal identity. Before a child is born, speculations on whether it will be a boy or a girl are closely linked with the choice of a name. In the unconscious one's name may be equated with one's sexual parts. In primitive cultures the speaking of one's own name is often taboo. To utter one's name involves shameful feelings, or sometimes has a provocative effect, as if one had exposed one's genital.

The significance of the name as a promise of sexual power is found in the Bible. When God foretells to Abraham the number and greatness of his progeny, he gives him in the same breath a new name. "Behold, my covenant is with thee, and thou shalt be the father of a multitude of nations. Neither shall thy name any more be called Abram, but thy name shall be Abraham; for the father of a multitude have I made thee. And I will make thee exceedingly fruitful, and I will make nations of thee, and kings shall come out of thee." And the hundred-year-old Abraham, though he laughs at what he considers an improbability, having been given a new name, becomes a father.

The loss of a name appears as a portent of castration in a humorous epic (castration, as is often the case, being here equated with total fatality). In Lewis Carroll's "Hunting of the Snark" the unfortunate hero is haunted by the prediction that he will "softly and suddenly vanish away" in an encounter with a nightmarish beast. This disaster, which eventually occurs, is anticipated by the hero's loss of his name. Having embarked on his fateful voyage, he finds that all his belongings have been left behind,

> . . . . but the worst of it was
> He had wholly forgotten his name.
> He would answer to "Hi!" or to any loud cry,
>   Such as "Fry me!" or "Fritter my wig!"
> To "What-you-may-call-um!" or "What-was-his-name!"
>   But especially "Thing-um-a-jig!"
> While, for those who preferred a more forcible word,
>   He had different names from these:
> His intimate friends called him "Candle ends,"
>   And his enemies "Toasted cheese."

The new names acquired by this luckless character suggest that he is destined to be consumed (fried, toasted, turned to a fritter) or that he has already undergone a diminution of his masculinity (the candle end representing a dwindled phallus). Thus names gained or lost can be heroically or comically prophetic of sexual triumph or catastrophe.

The equation of name and sex underlies the joking exchange of names which young children are so fond of. Exchanging names is substituted for calling a boy a girl and vice versa. Four-year-olds find exchanging names endlessly amusing. In a group of four-year-old children, a boy starts the game by switching the names of two of the children. He says to Billy, "You're Carol," and to Carol, "You're Billy." He continues, "Herbert is David," and the other children join in. The teacher's name is assigned to a girl named Susan, whereupon the teacher obligingly says, "I'm Susan," which is hailed by particularly loud laughter from the children. As often happens with these joking transformations of identity, one of the children feels threatened and affirms his own name. Having been called "Carol," he protests, "No, I'm Billy." The leader of the game assures him again that he is "Carol."

These name exchanges do not, however, necessarily coincide with sex reversals; the names of two girls or of two boys may be interchanged. The discovery of sex difference is the starting point for many explorations of similarity in difference and difference in similarity. A little boy and girl of four may take great interest in comparing the parts of their bodies which are alike; two little girls may discuss differences in the length of their hair, in their dresses or the color of their socks. In this way the sex difference is glossed over; boys and girls are alike, and children of the same sex are different. While overtones of the sex difference pervade the recognition of other likenesses and differences, a sense of individual identity is also reinforced. To the question "Am I a boy or a girl?" is added: "Who am I?" The joking reassignment of names plays on both these uncertainties. To be able to laugh the child must have mastered his uneasiness about both his sexual and his individual identity.

A name is a means of gaining power over its owner. In primitive cultures the real name of a baby is often concealed lest any ill-disposed person use it to do the child injury. Odysseus demonstrated in his encounter with the Cyclops how the concealment of a name could be life-preservative. He told the Cyclops that his name was "No-man." When the blinded giant cried out against him, he could only say that he had been injured by No-man, so that the other Cyclops were prevented from pursuing his attacker. The disguise of "No-man," may also be taken as a protective denial of masculinity, which made it possible for the hero to escape retribution for the blinding (castration) which he inflicted on the giant. In a bit of American folklore doggerel, a child, being questioned, refuses to give his right name:

> What's your name?—
> Pudden tame!
> Ask me again and I'll tell you the same.

Children's playful changing of their names is sometimes motivated by this wish for concealment. Instead of transforming others, the child here veils an important part of himself from the curiosity of a stranger. I was visiting a group of four-year-old children for the first time, and wanted to see if I had got their names right. When I came to Mary, she denied that was her name: "My name isn't Mary. I changed it to Pokey Joe." A little boy, Freddy, assured me: "And my name is Pokey Peter."

The danger of revealing one's name is played upon in a form of joking interchange used by older children. An eight-year-old girl gives me the formula: "You say to someone, 'Can you keep a secret?' And they say, 'Yes.' Then you say, 'What's your name?' And they tell you, and then you say, 'You can't keep a secret because you told me your name.'" The reproach against the one who has been seduced into revealing his name involves the equation of the name with the sexual parts. The child who perpetrates the joke seems to offer mutual sexual activity (secrets), but cheats the other into exposing himself and getting nothing in return.

III

Children often associate name changes with body transformations in joking play and humorous stories. In a group of four-year-old girls, Jean says with an amused expression: "I'll pull out my nose." She and two other little girls proceed laughingly to pull out their noses, eyelids, and lips, and then their blouses. Bonnie says: "I'm pulling out my stomach." Ella then pulls up her skirt and stretches the elastic of her underpants. She and Bonnie pull at their genitals and giggle at each other. Bonnie says: "I wouldn't like to be cut in half. No one could cut us in half, we're too hard." As the girls become noisy, the teacher warns them to quiet down. Jean says mockingly: "Children are teachers and teachers are children." Bonnie and Ella play a game of pretending to mistake the location of various body parts. One points to the side of her head and says "Here's my eyes." The other points to her buttocks and says: "Here's my nose." Jean then proposes: "Let's change names. I'll be the changing names one. You're Mr. Goosh, and you're Mr. Sloosh, and my name is Mr. Foosh." She laughs over this and repeats it several times. Here the children have produced a series of joking fantasies about transforming themselves, which ends in the changing of names. They play at extending various body parts, expressing ideas of pregnancy and of having male organs. Pulling out the genitals may have been associated with the wish to obtain a male organ by cutting it off, since this is followed by the speculation whether the little girls themselves might (in retaliation) be cut in two. There is a joking reversal of adult and child roles (children are teachers and vice versa) which, while following the trend of the transformation fantasies, also serves to ward off adult interference with the game. Having changed themselves about so much, the little girls pretend to be confused about their body images, mistaking the location of various parts. Finally they assume strange and comical names. These are men's names, expressing their wish for a sex reversal. But as the names have a dirty slobbering sound they have the effect of mocking the envied male role. . . .

Name-calling is another form of name change, which can be carried out in a seriously attacking or a joking way. In name-calling the victim is degraded often by stressing his lower body functions (as calling people "dog," "pig," or some other dirty animal) or connecting him with improper sexual activities of his parents ("bastard"). A favored form of name-calling in young children equates the person attacked with body-products. This is a favorite dirty joke of four-year-olds. One says to another: "You're a doody" ("duty," frequently pronounced "doody," meaning bowel movement in the bathroom language of this generation). With an admixture of mocking politeness, a child may hail someone with, "Hello, Mr. Doody." In the game of a group of four-year-old children thing-words were first substituted for proper names; after a certain stage of hilarity was reached, the thing-words were replaced by words for body parts. As I entered the room, one of the boys hailed me with: "Hello, Glue!" I replied, "Hello, Paste!" This evoked laughter from the children and was followed by an extended series of similar mutual greetings using thing-terms for names. The children then proceeded to eyes, nose, etc., culminating in "Hello, Penis! Hello, Booboo!"

In a more complicated form of name play there is an attempt to discover a meaning in the name, usually as a joking attack against the person whose name it is. When the teacher introduced me to one five-year-old group, the children began to shout: "Wolf, ugh! she's a wolf!" They thus expressed in a joking way their fears of the strange adult as well as feelings or repugnance. In another group of children, some five and some six, where I was asked my name, the last syllable was played on: "Stains!" "Everything you put on you stains!" "Stains a stinkin' duty on your face!" The girl who initiated the idea of the stain, and who pictured the stain on my face, had previously noticed a mole on my forehead and expressed distress at its ugliness. She had then shown me two moles on her own neck which she evidently regarded as blemishes. Thus she found in my name (-stein, stain, stain on the face) an exposure of the physical defect which she had observed. In a six-year-old group, the teacher introduced a Mr. Rock. There were immediate cries of "What? Rot?" "Rock candy!" "Rock on your head!" Children even up to adolescence seem to play with proper names with greater avidity than they show in word-play on common names. There is a strong tendency to distort proper names in order to find a meaning by which their owners may be attacked or mockingly exposed. For eleven-year-olds, for instance, a teacher named Bernheimer becomes "Mr. Burpheimer." That such a play on names is considered extremely impolite among adults in our society contributes to the children's pleasure. Besides making fun of a particular victim, they are, with the impunity insured by their banding together, overstepping a general prohibition.

In contrast to cultures with stringent name taboos, ours provides little elaboration for the feeling that names are fraught with danger. The adult attitude that playing on people's names is impolite represents a weak vestige of feelings which in many primitive cultures make certain names (one's own or those of various relatives) unspeakable. Where such name taboos prevail the underlying feeling seems to be that uttering a name is equivalent to a forbidden (sexual or aggressive) contact with the person. The idea that changing or playing on a name has the effect of changing or exposing the person also occurs in children in our own culture. But since there is no elaborate superstructure of taboo about this, they are able to play with names in a joking way. The incipient fear of the hazards of tampering with names is quickly dissipated. Instead of magical transformation, there are, one recognizes, only certain harmless emotional effects. It has been observed that a similar abatement of magical associations conditions the development of caricature. Where tampering with an image was believed to work a magical transformation of the original, caricature was lacking. Comic deformation of images becomes possible when it is recognized that this only affects the feelings of the onlookers.

Where taboos attach to proper names, common names are subject to frequent changes. In many primitive cultures, the names of persons coincide with the words for common objects. If the proper name is taboo, the object called by the same name must be dealt with by a circumlocution. The tie which binds a common name to a thing yields to the superior claim of personal associations. In our culture, on the other hand, proper names are mainly dissociated from thing-names. When children discover a thing-name in the name of a person, it strikes them as something surprising and funny. The person is playfully transformed into the thing rather than the thing assuming the aura of the person. For us the bond between a common name and the thing it designates is firmly fixed, and not ordinarily subject to dissolution through personal associations. The unsettling of the connection between a common name and its object arouses uneasiness. Piaget has observed how children resist the suggestion of shifting or exchanging common names. They feel that the word is inseparable from the thing it denotes. A child of nine, for instance, while admitting that his brother could have been calling something else, balks at the idea of calling the sun the moon and vice versa. He says that this would be wrong "because the sun can't change, it can't become smaller . . . the sun is always bigger, it always stays like it is and so does the moon." Here there seems to be the underlying thought that to change the names would mean to change the things. The sun and moon, if called by each other's names, would change their identities. We may suspect that the boy's disturbance at the proposed name change derives from a concern about sexual identity: how could the sun (father) be smaller than the moon (mother)? It would mean that a man could be turned into a woman and vice versa. The same feeling, however, extends to words of less obvious symbolic significance than "sun" and "moon." Thus it would seem that we have invested the re-

lation between common names and their objects with a trace
of the taboo feeling which applies in other cultures to tampering with proper names. Conversely the fact that the magical
associations of proper names are given little cultural sanction,
but tend to remain a matter of private fantasy, contributes to
the ease with which children can turn name play into a joke.

IV

Play on the ambiguity of common words begins with twisting the sense of what someone else has said. You say something and, by discovering an ambiguity in it, I transform its
meaning to something you did not intend. This device gains its
effect from the close involvement of the speaker with his
words. In terms of underlying feelings, a person is what he
says; to transform his meaning is to transform him. Thus play
on words takes its place in the series which began with calling
a boy a girl or vice versa: I change your sex; I change your
name; I change your meaning. For young children the latter
transformation has a similar impact to the preceding ones.

Let us observe how a word-play joke originates in a four-
year-old child and how it is received by an age-mate. Several
children are seated around a table with pencils and paper trying to make letters. Leonard, who is one of the most expert,
keeps looking over at Bernice's letters and finding fault with
them: "You made an 'E' backwards." Bernice feels quite unsettled by Leonard's criticisms (which are in fact well founded)
and retorts defensively: "*You* made an 'E' backwards!"
(which is not true). A moment later Bernice announces
proudly: "I made a 'U,' " Leonard, smiling, points at her and
exclaims: "You, you, you!" Bernice reacts with intense distress: "Don't do that!" Almost in tears she appeals to the
teacher: "I made a 'U' and Leonard says it's me," pointing
to herself, "and it's a letter!"

In his word-play the boy has transformed the girl's image
of herself, saying in effect: You're not as good as you think
you are. The joking attack has arisen out of his immediately
preceding criticisms of the little girl and her attempts to turn
them back against him (especially with her emphatic
"you"). A feeling of the boy's superiority and the girl's inadequacy has been evoked in both of them. When he then
deprives what she says of its intended meaning, it carries the
impact of a massive devaluation of her ambitions: she does

not mean what she thinks she means; she is not what she would like to be. Just as children at first react with distress to the playful change of sex and names, so here the shift of meaning has a disturbing effect. By the change of her meaning the little girl feels deprived of something of hers that she values. In time such a playful transformation of one's meaning becomes less of a threat. One realizes that one has not really lost anything through the verbal shift, and one is able to laugh. But even with adults, if their vanity is intense or they feel very strongly about what they are saying at the moment, making a pun on what they have said may rouse annoyance rather than amusement. What Freud called "harmless wit," a play on words whose meaning is neither sexual nor hostile, is thus initially not so harmless or simply pleasant. Word-play, associated in its beginnings with sex- and name-changes, has originally the force of a sexual and hostile attack, regardless of the meaning of the words involved. To accept it as harmless, we must overcome the tendency to react to it as dangerous. We are then able to laugh through an economy of emotion, as the threat of the transformed meaning ceases to affect us with its original force. The one who initiates the shift of meaning with joking intent feels that his attack is not really dangerous. He realizes that in mutilating another's meaning he is not doing any actual damage. By expressing his aggression in a joking way he reduces his anxiety about the dangerousness of his impulses. . . .

In their play children change meanings and identities in a friendly and collaborative way which contrasts with the more forcible procedure of joking. For purposes of play the meaning to be assigned to an object or the role to be assumed by an individual is decided by common agreement. One child says to another: "This block will be the engine, OK?" or "We're going to play house—will you be the daddy?" And the child waits for the other to agree so that they can proceed on the basis of mutually accepted conventions. Joking, as we have seen, follows a different line: a pretended transformation is imposed on the other person without his consent. Joking resembles playful scaring in which one child surprises another with an unforeseen transformation of role, pretending to be a dangerous attacker, and where the victim (though partial mastery of fear, enjoyment of scary feelings in moderate doses, and identification with the aggressor) becomes able to react with laughter.

Children's first word-play consists in playing on someone else's words. Later the joker himself presents both sides of the double meaning. The listener is induced to think of the first meaning and is then subjected to a reversal of it. The joker in this way makes himself independent of the variable opportunities provided by the other person's utterances. He does not have to wait for the other to say something the meaning of which he can turn around. With the double meaning joke he makes the other assume a meaning which he then unexpectedly transforms. We have seen that the change of another person's meaning has the underlying implication: You are not what you think you are. Similarly the transformation of one's own meaning suggests: I am not what you think I am. This also has initially an unsettling effect. In children's joking changes of names, those who found them disturbing often reacted with distress when a playmate maintained he was someone else. The safe and familiar person was transformed into a stranger.

The self-transformation involved in comic acting may also serve as an attack against others. Mocking impersonations convey a critique of their models. Charlie Chaplin, in assuming the role of the little tramp, expressed hostile feelings in another way. By showing himself as helpless, tattered, and derelict, he directed a bitter reproach to the parents who had abandoned him in his childhood: Look what you have made of me! In word-play jokes the drama of self-transformation is enacted in a very small compass. But the theme is the same: I change myself (change my meaning) as an attack against someone else. In the shift of meaning, however, something enjoyable may be revealed which compensates the hearer. Also in the content of the joke the attack may be diverted to a third person against whom the joker and listener are allied. Finally the joking aggression may be directed against the joker himself. We shall have occasion to examine these alternatives in more detail later on.

V

We have seen how children's interest in playing with names proceeds from the joking reversal of sex and leads to more general word-play. Thus we reconstructed the series of joking transformations: I change your sex; I change your name; I change your meaning. The proper name constitutes the link between the ambiguity of sex and the wide range of verbal ambiguities. But the joking play on names, which children find so fascinating, has another major derivation. The child learns from experience that his own name can be used in two opposite ways, lovingly and angrily. The proper name itself thus possesses a double meaning.

The child first learns his own name in the course of loving interchange between himself and his mother. The mother asks: "Where's Johnny?" and points to the child, informing him: "There he is!" After a sufficient number of repetitions, the child succeeds in responding to the question, "Where's Johnny?" by pointing to himself. The mother is delighted with his achievement, hugs and kisses him, and repeats, "Yes, there he is!" Thus the child feels that he acquires a separate identity (symbolized by his name), only as a prelude to a complete and loving reunion with the mother, in which he hopes to recapture with intensified pleasure his earlier sense of fusion with her. This expectation is inevitably disappointed. The mother fails to gratify the child's longings for physical love, and indeed prohibits to a large extent his strivings in this direction. His name, originally a love name, assumes an aura of mingled feelings, regret and frustration as well as love and pride. Then he also learns that his name can be used in a sharply negative way: "Johnny Jones! What have you been doing!" His name now underscores a reprimand. The tone of voice in which it is uttered turns it into a bad name. "Johnny Jones!" called out in that angry and reproachful way clearly means: You're a bad boy. The child thus has two names: the love name and the bad name. His name is ambiguous, its meaning depending on the mother's tone of voice.

Both the love name and the bad name provide themes for jokes. The name of a child-figure may be turned into a means of retaliation against the adult. The love name serves to obtain sexual gratification from the withholding mother or to expose her against her will. The child wrests from the mother in a forcible and mocking way the satisfactions which the love name first seemed to promise. There is a series of jokes, very popular with children of about nine, which deal with a mother and her child named "Heinie" (behind). The following is typical: Heinie gets lost and the mother asks a policeman: "Have you seen my Heinie?" The policeman replies: "No, but I'd sure like to." There are endless variations. The mother buys Heinie some ice cream, which he gets smeared over his face. The mother then asks the man behind the counter: "Can

I have a tissue for my Heinie?" The mother goes to a shoe store and says: "I want a pair of shoes for my Heinie." Through some farfetched mishap, Heinie at a fiesta gets suspended by a lasso from a balcony and the mother cries: "Oh, my Heinie is hanging over the banisters!"

By setting up a situation in which the mother calls the child "my Heinie," the loving union of child and mother is achieved in a mocking way: the child becomes again a part of the mother's body. The mother in the joke does not know what she is saying, just as in actuality she did not acknowledge the wishes she evoked by the love name. While the mocking love name accomplishes a symbolic fusion of mother and child, the action of the joke consists in the mother's unwitting self-exposure. Her concern for her child keeps impelling her to reveal an intimate part of her body. This is just what the child would have wished, but the mother in actuality was not so compliant. The joke places her in a predicament where she exposes herself without realizing what she is doing. Involuntary self-exposure regularly has a comic effect; the person appears to have made a foolish mistake in letting down his guard. Such a person becomes not only a source of unexpectedly easy gratification for the onlooker, but also an object of disparagement. Thus the mother in the joke is exposed as both sexually accessible and foolish. She is punished for having been so withholding. Her image is degraded; from having been ideally desirable she becomes ridiculous. In the joke it is usually to a man that the mother offers herself, as when she asks the policeman: "Have you seen my Heinie?" This conveys the further reproach against the mother for yielding to the father what she denies to the child. The child wonders how the forbidding mother can indulge in sexual activity. The joke represents her as not knowing what she is doing.

In another joke, a woman has a dog named "Tits." The dog's ball rolls away, and the woman hands the dog to a man, saying: "Will you hold my Tits while I go and get the ball?" (I should guess that there was originally a double word-play in this joke, implying that the woman also holds the man's balls, but the nine-year-old boy who told it to me apparently had not caught this.) Here the child, represented by the dog, is again identified through his name with a part of the mother's body, this time merging with the breast. The mother unwittingly exposes herself by using the child's name and offers herself to a man under the guise of solicitude for her child. There is an irony in this, since the child feels that if the mother loved him as much as she pretends she would not give herself to the father.

In a similar joke, the child's name is a signal for the mother's total body exposure. A woman has a little dog named "Free-show." While the woman is taking a bath, the dog runs out of the house. The woman jumps up and runs out after the dog calling, "Free-show! Free-show!" And, as a nine-year-old girl explained, "All the people thought she meant it was a free show." Here the child (dog) evidently resents the mother's excluding him from the bathroom. He withdraws from her in turn, runs away, and thus induces the wished-for exhibition of the mother, again by the use of his name.

When the mother calls the child's name in the following joke she directly incites him to sexual activity. As told by an eleven-year-old boy: "There was this guy named Johnny Fuckerfaster. In school one day he did something wrong and the teacher told him to stay after school. Everyone was dismissed and he said to the teacher, 'Take off your socks.' It was a French teacher. And he said, 'Take off your girdle, take off your underwear.' Finally she was all undressed. And his mother came looking for him and she called him: 'Johnny Fuckerfaster! Johnny Fuckerfaster! And he was over by the teacher, and he thought she meant 'fuck her faster.' And his mother called him again and he said: 'Mom, I'm fucking her as fast as I can.'" Here the child's name resumes its early associations as an inducement to love, though the mother does not mean to use it in this sense. The mother is given a double representation; she unwittingly stimulates amorous impulses in the child by calling his name, and, as the teacher, she gratifies these impulses. The teacher's being French accounts for her sexual freedom, and also affirms her remoteness from the incestuous object. By means of these two complementary figures, the forbidding mother is transformed into one who makes excessive sexual demands on the child. It is not the child who wants too much from the mother, but she who requires more than a little boy can perform. As in the Heinie jokes, the withholding mother is mockingly exposed as too easy and eager.

The exaction of love from a presumably unwilling object, combined with hostility toward the object, is expressed in the following joke which works with changes of identity rather than with names. A ten-year-old girl instructs me: "Whatever kind of lock I say I am, you say you're that kind of a key. I'm a gold lock." "I'm a gold key." "I'm a silver lock." "I'm a silver key." . . . "I'm a don lock." "I'm a don key." The child here transforms herself into a female sex symbol and asks the other person to become the corresponding male symbol. Through a series of transformations (gold, silver, etc.) they remain inseparable partners. This is a love fantasy. But it is not the real thing, and in the end the resentment for present and past frustrations asserts itself. The partner is tricked into confessing he is a donkey. In effect: You don't really love me—what a fool you are! The withholding person is punished by being devalued.

The bad name also provides a theme for jokes. The hostile associations which the child's name has acquired in reprimands are turned back against the adult. The name which has been used scoldingly against the child is transformed into a hostile retort. Here is a joke of this kind which I heard repeatedly from children between the ages of seven and nine. As an eight-year-old boy tells it: "Once upon a time there were two boys, one named Shut-up and the other named Trouble. And they were walking out one day and Shut-up got lost. And he went to the police station and the policeman asked him his name so he said 'Shut-up.' So the policeman thought—you see he said 'Shut-up' because his name was Shut-up. So the policeman said: 'Are you looking for trouble?' You see Trouble was the other boy's name. And he said 'Yes.' Get the trick?" In other versions the first boy's name is "None-of-your-business" or "Mind-your-own-business." The narration may be prolonged by having the policeman question the boy repeatedly, bring him before the judge for further questioning and so on, so that the boy can say "Shut-up" or "Mind-your-own-business" many more times.

When the grown-ups scold the child, he feels that they are cutting him off from contact with them. His name, called out angrily, seems equivalent to "Shut up!" or "Mind your own business!" The child's name in the joke is thus transformed into its bad meaning. A situation is contrived in which this bad name can be turned back against the adults. When they ask his name, as grown-ups so often ask a child, he retorts with the bad name. It becomes a means of retaliation; the adults' aggression boomerangs. There is also mocking compliance in the child's response. In saying "Shut up" to the policeman, the representative of punishing authorities, the child is only answering his question; implicitly he is only repeating the bad name that has been given him. The rebellious and critical child feels that the adults indulge their hostility against him while demanding that he inhibit the corresponding feelings in himself. The joke gives him an opportunity to reply in kind, with the justification that they have asked for it. The two children, "Shut-up" and "Trouble," are sometimes made explicitly two brothers or a brother and a sister. One boy who told me the joke remarked immediately afterward that his little sister is a lot of trouble. When the two children in the joke wonder off and one loses the other, the child has got rid of the troublesome sibling. This is the naughtiness for which the authorities are reproaching him. The child replies in effect that it is all their fault for having had another child, and that he is not his brother's keeper.

Starting with his painful awareness of his parents' ambivalence toward him, as they are sometimes loving and sometimes angry, the child is quick to observe the inconsistency of their behavior toward other people as well. He overhears what the parents say between themselves about the guests whom they have invited with such demonstrations of friendliness, and he sometimes discomfits his parents by repeating their strictures to the company. In the following joke children parody the grown-ups' politeness which they understand often conceals hostility. A child pretends to introduce himself, saying: "My name is Cliff. Why don't you drop over some time?" Or, "My name is East River. Why don't you drop in some time?" (I heard these from six-year-olds.) The children have understood that underneath the courteous interchanges of grown-ups there may be the suppressed wish to say: Go jump in the lake! This ambivalence is again conveyed through the medium of the name, with its potentiality for expressing positive and negative feelings.

VI

We have seen how the ambiguity of words, the major resource of verbal joking, derives its effect from two basic ambiguities: those of sex and of emotion. For the child the two crucial questions, "Am I a boy or a girl?" and "Am I loved or hated?" give an aura of ambiguity to his name. His name is the mark of his sexual identity, but might it not be changed? After playing quite simply at calling a boy a girl and vice versa, children turn to the game of changing names. As the unsettling loss of identity ceases to be frightening, it becomes a joke. The child's name also has the ambiguity of being a

love name or a bad name depending on whether the parents
are affectionate or scolding. In jokes revolving around the
love name, the intimacy withheld by the mother is mockingly
extorted. The bad name is used in a similar way to retaliate
against the parents; the aggression which they have expressed
against the child boomerangs. Again we see, as in the preceding chapter, how joking provides a rectification of painful
experiences. In so far as the child has been disappointed in
connection with the love name which he has been called and
has found the bad name unbearable, his twisting of others'
meanings implies: I will get from what you say something I
like better than what you intend. A gratifying sexual meaning
is read in, or a way is found to turn the words into an attack
against the speaker. These devices, which for children so often
remain bound to the original context of the proper name, are
capable of extension to every utterance. It is only as a result
of long development that we can take some verbal communi-
cations impersonally. To begin with, every word that is addressed to us is felt as either gratifying or painful. For the
child every word that he receives from the adults has to some
degree the same emotional significance as that which attaches
to his own name: it can be a promise of gratification or a
rebuke. From this we may derive the impulse to play on words,
to extract a forbidden (withheld) sexual meaning or to bring
out and redirect against others the hostility which was felt to
be implicit in their words.

The ambiguities which attach to the proper name are extended to common words also by virtue of the feeling of
identity of the person with what he says. To transform the
meaning of what a person says has for children originally the
impact of transforming the other person's sex or identity
against his will. What a person is and what he means are
taken as the same thing; hence such word-play signifies: You
are not what you think you are. We have seen how young
children initially regard the playful change of their sex, or
identity, or meaning as an attack. In the course of development, it gets to be understood on both sides that no real transformation is worked by these verbal shifts. The willful change,
divested of magical force, becomes a joke.

Word-play has for children originally an aggressive and sexual significance. To distort another's meaning is to transform
him radically since what he means and what he is are the
same. It is only as particular utterances become to some extent
isolated from the total personality, so that one does not cease

to be oneself if one's meaning is inverted, that play on words becomes harmless. The original impact of word-play is then restored by the infusion of a sexual or aggressive content. For adults the "U—you" joke of the four-year-old could not have such a devastating impact. To recapture the earlier effect of word-play we must find more overt aggression or sex in the words themselves.

As early feelings about word-play become attenuated, it assumes the harmless quality which suits it to be a façade for sexual or hostile joking. There is a concurrence of two lines of development in the production of the complex joke form which uses word-play as a façade. There is the progressive and drastic reduction of the original disturbance about shifts of meaning, which we have discussed in this chapter. Concurrently increasing inhibitions against sexual and aggressive impulses are instituted which require their masking by the joke façade. Word-play, having become harmless, is then utilized for this purpose.

The Lore and Language of School Children

PETER AND IONA OPIE

(1959)

Children have a worldwide underground through which
they escape the humdrum verbal barrage of adults and
transmit their cherished, traditional oral lore. It is a lore
of rich language, bursting with mischief and fear, ad-
hering to its own rigid code, which venerates custom and
respects superstition. With wit, guile, impropriety and
often cruelty, children express themselves in parody, riddle, refrain, epithet, jeer, dare, tongue-twister and prank
—all of which are surprisingly similar whether one is
in Scotland or New York. The Opies' *Lore and Language
of School Children* was produced by a ten-year study of
some 5000 British children. It bears out Douglas Newton's observation that "The worldwide fraternity of children is the greatest of savage tribes, and the only one
which shows no sign of dying out."

The scraps of lore which children learn from each other are
at once more real, more immediately serviceable, and more
vastly entertaining to them than anything which they learn
from grown-ups. To a child it can be a "known fact" that
the Lord's Prayer said backward raises the devil, that a small
knife-wound between the thumb and forefinger gives a person
lockjaw, that a hair from the head placed on the palm will
split the master's cane. It can be a useful piece of knowledge
that the reply to "A pinch and a punch for the first of the
month" is "A pinch and a kick for being so quick." And a
verse a child hears the others saying,

> Mister Fatty Belly, how is your wife?
> Very ill, very ill, up all night,
> Can't eat a bit of fish
> Nor a bit of liquorice.
> o-u-t spells out and out you must go
> With a jolly good clout upon your ear hole spout,

may seem the most exciting piece of poetry in the language.

Such a verse, recited by eight-year-olds in Birmingham, can be as traditional and as well-known to children as a nursery rhyme; yet no one would mistake it for one of Mother Goose's compositions. It is not merely that there is a difference in cadence and subject matter, the manner of its transmission is different. While a nursery rhyme passes from a mother or other adult to the small child on her knee, the school rhyme circulates simply from child to child, usually outside the home, and beyond the influence of the family circle. By its nature a nursery rhyme is a jingle preserved and propagated not by children but by adults, and in this sense it is an "adult" rhyme. It is a rhyme which is adult approved. The schoolchild's verses are not intended for adult ears. In fact part of their fun is the thought, usually correct, that adults know nothing about them. Grown-ups have outgrown the schoolchild's lore. If made aware of it they tend to deride it; and they actively seek to suppress its livelier manifestations. Certainly they do nothing to encourage it. And the folklorist and anthropologist can, without traveling a mile from his door, examine a thriving unselfconscious culture (the word "culture" is used here deliberately) which is as unnoticed by the sophisticated world, and quite as little affected by it, as is the culture of some dwindling aboriginal tribe living out its helpless existence in the hinterland of a native reserve. Perhaps, indeed, the subject is worthy of a more formidable study than is accorded it here. As Douglas Newton has pointed out: "The worldwide fraternity of children is the greatest of savage tribes, and the only one which shows no sign of dying out."

Continuity

No matter how uncouth schoolchildren may outwardly appear, they remain tradition's warmest friends. Like the savage, they are respecters, even venerators, of custom; and in their self-contained community their basic lore and language seems scarcely to alter from generation to generation. Boys continue to crack jokes that Swift collected from his friends in Queen Anne's time; they play tricks which lads used to play on each other in the heyday of Beau Brummel; they ask riddles which were posed when Henry VIII was a boy. Young girls continue to perform a magic feat (levitation) of which Pepys heard

tell ("One of the strangest things I ever heard"); they hoard
bus tickets and milk-bottle tops in distant memory of a love-
lorn girl held to ransom by a tyrannical father; they learn to
cure warts (and are successful in curing them) after the manner which Francis Bacon learnt when he was young. They
call after the tearful the same jeer Charles Lamb recollected;
they cry "Halves!" for something found as Stuart children
were accustomed to do; and they rebuke one of their number
who seeks back a gift with a couplet used in Shakespeare's
day. They attempt, too, to learn their fortune from snails, nuts,
and apple-parings—divinations which the poet Gay described
nearly two and a half centuries ago; they span wrists to know
if someone loves them in the way that Southey used at school
to tell if a boy was a bastard; and when they confide to each
other that the Lord's Prayer said backward will make Lucifer
appear, they are perpetuating a story which was gossip in
Elizabethan times.[1]

The same continuity obtains in their games and play songs.
When the Birmingham eight-year-olds chant about "Mister
Fatty Belly" they are perpetuating a verse with a lineage going
back to schooldays under the Regency, for P. H. Gosse (the
father of Sir Edmund) recorded that when he was at school,
1818–23: "One boy meeting another would address him with
these queries; the other giving the replies:

> Doctor! Doctor! how's your wife?
> Very bad, upon my life.
> Can she eat a bit of pie?
> Yes, she can, as well as I."[2]

Today, sets of these responses, usually repeated for counting-
out or skipping, have been collected from schoolchildren in
Aberdeen, Bath, Manchester, Market Rasen, Scarborough,

[1] Witches were supposed to say their prayers backward, with awful
effect, as is noted in Robert Greene's *A Quip for an Upstart Courtier*,
1592, sig. D3, and this method of raising the devil is also mentioned
by Defoe in his *System of Magick*, 1727, pp. 259–60. References to
schoolboys' possession of the secret occur in *Notes and Queries*, 1st
ser., vol. iv, 1851, p. 53, and 3rd ser., vol. iv, 1863, p. 492; and we
knew it ourselves in our schooldays, but never dared test it. For accounts
of boys who did, see William Henderson, *Folk Lore of the Northern
Counties*, 1866, p. 19, and *The Listener*, 3 January 1957, p. 10. A 13-
year-old Tredegar, Monmouthshire, girl tells us it is believed there that
if one runs round the church three times the devil will appear.

[2] "A Country Day-School Seventy Years Ago," *Longman's Magazine*,
vol. xiii, 1889, p. 518.

Spennymoor, Tunstall, and York City; and some of the versions are all but identical with the rhyme as it was known more than 130 years ago. Thus a twelve-year-old Spennymoor girl reports:

"When I get home from school there is usually some little girls out of the infants school playing in the street, and their special little rhyme is:

> Little fatty doctor, how's your wife?
> Very well, thank you, she's alright.
> Can she eat a twopenny pie?
> Yes sir, yes sir, and so can I.

The older girls think that rhyme is silly for them, so they play faster games."

Apparent Uniformity of the Lore

The fact that schoolchild lore continues to thrive in a natural manner among unselfconscious adherents, and that we have been able to watch it functioning in a number of widely separated communities, has allowed us to carry our study a step further than we thought possible at the outset; it has enabled us to obtain a picture of the state of traditional lore over the country as a whole. Thus it has shown that traditional lore exists everywhere; that as many, if not more, traditional games are known to city children as to country children; and that children with homes and backgrounds as different from each other as mining community and garden suburb share jokes, rhymes, and songs, which are basically identical.[3] Conscious as we were of the economy of human invention, and the tenacity of oral tradition (the two elements without which there would be no folklore), we were not prepared for quite the identity of ritual and phraseology which has been revealed throughout the land in children's everyday witticisms, and in the newer of their self-organized amusements.

[3] The city child usually knows more games than the country child, for he has more time to play them. The real country child, living in a village or on a smallholding, is generally expected to do jobs around the home when he returns from school, and once he has passed the singing-game stage, his play tends to be limited to whatever free time there is at school. However, his knowledge of traditional wisdom—proverbs, dark sayings, and seasonal customs—is correspondingly greater.

The faithfulness with which one child after another sticks to the same formulas even of the most trivial nature is remarkable. A meaningless counting-out phrase such as "Pig snout, walk out," sometimes adapted to "Boy Scout, walk out," or a tag for two-balls like "Shirley Temple is a star, S-T-A-R," is apparently in use throughout England, Scotland, and Wales. If, in the vicinity of Westminster, a visitor hears for the first time children skipping to the simple chant,

> Big Ben strikes one,
> Big Ben strikes two,
> Big Ben strikes three,

he may well suppose that the words are the just-for-the-minute invention of a particularly unimaginative local child. Yet this formula is repeated all over London, down side streets behind the Victorian mansions of Kensington, in the bustle of Hackney, in Manor Park, and outside London in Croydon, Enfield, and Welwyn. Traveling farther afield it will be found in use at Scunthorpe in Lincolnshire, at Cwmbran in Monmouthshire, in Edinburgh, in Glasgow, and, in fact, apparently everywhere. Nor is it a passing fad of the juvenile fancy, for it will be found that Norman Douglas quotes it in *London Street Games* (p. 49); and the fact has to be faced that since 1916 some 30,000,000 children have dashed through the nation's playgrounds, respecters neither of persons nor property, yet preserving the silly chant as carefully as if it was a magic incantation. Similarly "Pig snout, walk out" is known to have been current in the Island of Bute in 1911.[4] And although "Shirley Temple is a star" cannot be so old, children have carried it to Australia and Canada and have planted it in those countries, or, perhaps, have brought it here from across the sea.

Even when it seems certain that a rhyme must be purely local, such as the song little girls skip to in Manchester,

> Manchester Guardian, Evening News,
> I sell Evening News,

it may be no more than a variation on an established theme. In Radcliffe, Lancashire, one girl skips while two others turn the rope chanting,

> Manchester, Bolton Evening News,
> I sell evening one . . .

[4] *Miscellanea of the Rymour Club*, vol. ii, pt. ii, 1913, p. 69.

In Wellington, Shropshire, the girls skip to,

> Wellington Journal, Evening News,
> Ever see a cat in a pair of shoes?

In Shrewsbury,

> London, Liverpool, Weekly Post,
> I say number one, two, three.

In Swansea, among several variants,

> South Wales Evening Post,
> Un, dau, tri [*one, two, three*].

And our own correspondents, and correspondents to the *Manchester Guardian* (April 23 and 28, 1955), recall skipping to versions of this chant in northwest England as far back as the nineties.[5]

Speed of Oral Transmission

Since, through our collaborators, it has been possible to keep an eye on several widely separated places simultaneously, we have, on occasion, been afforded glimpses of oral transmission in actual operation. The speed with which a newly made-up rhyme can travel the length and breadth of the country by the schoolchild grapevine seems to be little short of miraculous. Some idea of the efficiency of oral transmission can be obtained by following verses which are topical, or which are parodies of newly published songs, and can consequently be dated, although for test purposes it is, unfortunately, best to study specimens which are of a scurrilous or indelicate nature for with these there is, in general, less likelihood of dissemination by means other than word-of-mouth.

---

[5] Children, it seems, are no more inventive than the ridiculed old countryfolk with their ancient multiadaptable weather proverbs, e.g.:

> When Roseberry Topping puts on a hat,
> Let Cleveland then beware of that.
> > *North Riding of Yorkshire.*

> When Traprain puts on his hat,
> The Lothian lads may look at that.
> > *East Lothian.*

> When Bredon Hill puts on his hat,
> Ye men of the vale, beware of that.
> > *Worcestershire.*

A notorious instance of the transmission of scurrilous verses occurred in 1936 at the time of the Abdication. The word-of-mouth rhymes which then gained currency were of a kind which could not possibly, at that time, have been printed, broadcast, or even repeated in the music halls. One verse, in particular, made up one can only wonder by whom,

> Hark the Herald Angels sing,
> Mrs. Simpson's pinched our king,

was on juvenile lips not only in London, but as far away as Chichester in the south, and Liverpool and Oldham in the north. News that there was a constitutional crisis did not become public property until around November 25 of that year, and the king abdicated on December 10. Yet at a school Christmas party in Swansea given before the end of term, Christmas 1936, when the tune played happened to be "Hark the Herald Angels Sing," a mistress found herself having to restrain her small children from singing this lyric, known to all of them, which cannot have been composed much more than three weeks previously. Many an advertising executive with a six-figure budget at his disposal might envy such crowd penetration. Similarly, the ultra juvenile verse,

> Temptation, temptation, temptation,
> Dick Barton went down to the station,
> Blondie was there
> All naked and bare,
> Temptation, temptation, temptation,

wherever it may have originated, was reported to us in quick succession as rife among children in Kirkcaldy in January 1952, as known to children in Swansea in January 1952, and it reached children in Alton in February 1952. These three places are up to 400 miles apart; yet an instance of even more distant transmission can be cited. At the beginning of 1956 "The Ballad of Davy Crockett" was launched on the radio. It was especially intended to appeal to children, and quickly reached the top of the adult hit parade. But the official words of the ballad, beginning,

> Born on a mountain top in Tennessee,
> Greenest state in the Land of the Free,

were very small beer compared with the word-of-mouth stanzas which rapidly won approval in juvenile society. One composition, beginning "The Yellow Rose of Texas," was collected in

Perth in April 1956, in Alton, Battersea, Great Bookham, Reading, and Scarborough in July 1956, in Kent in August 1956, and in Swansea in September 1956. Another parody sung by schoolgirls in Swansea in September 1956, appeared to have local associations:

> Born on a table top in Joe's Café,
> Dirtiest place in the U.S.A.
> Polished off his father when he was only three,
> Polished off his mother with D.D.T.
> > Davy, Davy Crockett,
> > King of the Wild Frontier.

The teacher who sent this verse remarked that Joe's Café was a popular Swansea establishment near the beach. Subsequently, however, we had news of the verse being current in Brentwood, Hornchurch, Reading, Upminster, and Woolwich, all naming "Joe's Café." But unknown to any of our home observers, and before the official Davy Crockett song had reached Britain, an Australian correspondent, writing January 3, 1956, had reported that the following ditty was "sweeping the schools" in Sydney:

> Reared on a paddle-pop in Joe's café,
> The dirtiest dump in the U.S.A.,
> Poisoned his mother with D.D.T.
> And shot his father with a .303.
> > Davy, Davy Crockett,
> > The man who is no good.

It seems that the schoolchild underground also employs transworld couriers.

Wear and Repair During Transmission

The previous section has shown how quickly a rhyme passes from one schoolchild to the next, and illustrates a further difference between school lore and nursery lore. In nursery lore a verse or tradition, learned in early childhood, is not usually passed on again until the little listener has grown up, and has children of his own, or even grandchildren. The period between learning a nursery rhyme and transmitting it may be anything from twenty to seventy years. With the playground lore, however, a rhyme may be excitedly passed on within the very hour it is learned; and, in general, it passes between children who are the same age, or nearly so, since it is uncommon for the difference in age between playmates to be more than five years. If, therefore, a playground rhyme can be shown to have been current for a hundred years, or even just for fifty, it follows that it has been retransmitted over and over again; very possibly it has passed along a chain of two or three hundred young hearers and tellers, and the wonder is that it remains alive after so much handling, let alone that it bears resemblance to the original wording.

In most schools there is a wholly new generation of children every six years; and when a rhyme such as "Little fatty doctor, how's your wife?" can be shown to be more than 130 years old it may be seen that it has passed through the keeping of not less than twenty successive generations of schoolchildren, and been exposed to the same stresses that nursery lore would meet only after 500 years of oral conveyance. This, in itself, makes schoolchild lore of peculiar value to the student of oral communication, for the behavior and defects of oral transmission can be seen in operation during a relatively short period, much as if the phenomenon had been placed in a mechanical stresser to speed up the wear and tear.

Thus we find that variations, even apparently creative ones, occur more often by accident than by design. Usually they come about through mishearing or misunderstanding, as in the well-known hymnal misapprehension:

> Can a woman's tender care
> Cease towards the child she-bear?

A line in the song "I'm a knock-kneed sparrow" quickly becomes "I'm a cockney sparrow." "Calico breeches," no longer familiar to youth today, become "comical breeches." "Elecampane" becomes "elegant pain." "Green gravel, green gravel" becomes by association "Greengages, greengages." And the unmeaning "Alligoshee, alligoshee," in the marching game, is rationalized to "Adam and Eve went out to tea." At one school the pledges "Die on oath," "Dianothe," and "Diamond oath" were all found to be current at the same time. The common tendency to speed up a ritual or abridge a formula also produces surprising results. At a Surrey school the pledge "Cub's honor" became, by jest, "Cub's-on-a-car," which was presently abridged, so that the standard pledge became "Car." Indeed the corruptive influence of the pun on language and custom is more considerable than might be supposed. When a child, as a sign of derision, expels air through his compressed lips, the stock retort is "We have them with custard." The chain here is that breaking wind was, at one time, by the process of rhyming slang, known as a "raspberry tart," hence "raspberry." Subsequently this became the name for the imitative noise made with the mouth; and this term is still retained, although it has disappeared as a name for the original exhalation.

Again, a fool is very generally called a "blockhead," his head being likened to the denseness of wood. Consequently, as a joke, when somebody says "touch wood" he is liable on occasion to touch the head of a notorious dunce, or of a child whom he wishes to make out to be a dunce, or, in self-deprecation, his own head. This joke has in fact become so commonplace that many children are already forgetting that touching the head is a joke, and state seriously: "If you say that something nice is going to happen you must either touch wood or your head," or, without qualification, "To avert ill-luck it is the custom to touch your head." So it is that the time is upon us when, in a prefabricated classroom with desks and fittings manufactured entirely out of plastic and chromium, it will not be possible for children to touch wood, only their heads; and when these children grow up it may become normal with the adult population, too, to put a finger to their brow as a superstitious act of self-protection.

Thus, it may be seen, oral lore is subject to a continual process of wear and repair, for folklore, like everything else in nature, must adapt itself to new conditions if it is to survive. An old rustic prognostication about magpies, for instance, is now commonly repeated by city children (who probably would not recognize a magpie even if they saw one) when telling fortunes with bus tickets. The lyrics of certain obsolescent singing games have obtained a new lease on life by being speeded up and sung while skipping. Cigarette cards, which have become scarce, are being replaced in flicking games by milk-bottle tops, known as "flying saucers." The bonfires of Halloween have been postponed five days to become part of the effigy burning on Guy Fawkes Night. And a ribald rhyme of sixty years ago such as "Lottie Collins has no drawers" is now chanted in honor of a modern idol, Miss Diana Dors.

To illustrate this mutation it may be interesting to set out some recordings of a playground rhyme at different stages in its history to show how, over the course of 200 years, it has been remolded and brought up to date. In 1725 a song about a cup-shot grenadier, probably dating from the previous century, had already, according to Henry Carey, become proverbial as a children's play-rhyme. Grenadiers, however, are no longer objects of popular derision, and, although the grenadier still survives as the disgraceful hero of the rhyme in nursery lore where change is slower,[6] in the playground the rhyme has developed along more contemporary lines.

Development of a Playground Rhyme

1725

Now he acts the *Grenadier,*
Calling for *a Pot of Beer:*
Where's his Money? He's for-
  got:
Get him gone, a Drunken
  Sot.

  Lines from Henry Carey's bal-
  lad "Namby Pamby" (1726
  ed., E3–4).

1774

Whoes there
  A Granidier
What dye want
  A Pint of Beer.
Whoes there
  A Granidier
What dye want
  A Pint of Beer.

  "Catch, The Soldier and the
  Ale House Man" as noted
  down, with tune, by Samuel
  Wesley when 8 years old
  (British Museum, MS. Adds.
  34998, f. 34).

1780

Who comes here?
  A Grenadier.
What do you want?
  A Pot of Beer.
Where is your Money?
  I've forgot.
Get you gone
  You drunken Sot.

  "Mother Goose's Melody"
  (1795 ed., p. 42).

1916

Rat a tat tat, who is that?
Only grandma's pussy-cat.
What do you want?
A pint of milk.
Where's your money?
In my pocket.
Where is your pocket?
I forgot it.
O you silly pussy-cat.

  Used for skipping, "Lon-
  don Street Games," 1916, p.
  64.

c. 1907

Eenty, teenty, tuppenny bun,
Pitching tatties doon the lum;
Who's there? John Blair.
What does he want? A bottle
  of beer.

1939

A frog walked into a public
  house
And asked for a pint of beer.
Where's your money?
In my pocket.

[6] See the *Oxford Dictionary of Nursery Rhymes,* 1951, p. 195.

Where's your money? I forgot.
Go downstairs, you drunken
sot.

*Collected from schoolchildren
in Edinburgh. Used for counting-out. Rymour Club, "Miscellanea," vol. i, 1911, p. 104.*

c. 1910

Far are ye gaein'?
Across the gutter.
Fat for?
A pund o' butter.
Far's yer money?
In my pocket.
Far's yer pocket?
Clean forgot it!

*Current among children in
Forfar, c. 1910. Jean C. Rod-
ger, "Lang Strang," 1948.*

1950

Mickey Mouse
In a public house
Drinking pints of beer.
Where's your money?
In my pocket.
Where's your pocket?
I forgot it.
Please walk out.

*Used for counting-out in
Alton.*

1952

A pig walked into a public
house
And asked for a drink of
beer.
Where's your money, sir?
In my pocket, sir.
Where's your pocket, sir?
In my jacket, sir.
Where's your jacket, sir?
I forgot it, sir.
Please walk out.

*Used for counting-out. Girl,
12, Cleethorpes.*

Where's your pocket?
I forgot it.
Well, please walk out.

*Used for counting-out in
Swansea.*

1943

Rat tat tat, who is that?
Only Mrs. Pussy Cat.
What do you want?
A pint of milk.
Where's your penny?
In my pocket.
Where's your pocket?
I forgot it.
Please walk out.

*Used for skipping at Castle
Eden, Co. Durham.*

1952

A monkey came to my shop
I asked him what he wanted.
A loaf, sir. A loaf, sir.
Where's your money?
In my pocket.
Where's your pocket?
I ain't got it.
Well, out you bunk.

*"Skipping for two." Girl, 12,
Market Rasen.*

1954

I had a little beer shop
A man walked in.
I asked him what he wanted.
A bottle of gin.
Where's your money?
In my pocket.
Where's your pocket?
I forgot it.
Please walk out.

*Used for skipping in York
City.*

In illustrating the variations which have occurred in this rhyme over the years (most of them due to contact with newer verses), we should repeat that to us the remarkable feature of schoolchild lore is how comparatively little it alters considering the usage it receives.

Sources of the Rhymes

The children themselves often have a touching faith in the novelty of their oral acquisitions. Of the rhyme,

> House to let, apply within,
> Lady turned out for drinking gin,

which we have collected from twenty-four places in the British Isles, also from South Africa, Australia, and the United States, and which was recorded as traditional in 1892 (G. F. Northall, *English Folk-Rhymes*, p. 306) an Alton girl remarked: "Here's one you won't know because it's only just made up." Of the couplet,

> Mrs. Mason broke a basin
> How much did it cost?

lines which are the recollection of a counting-out formula recorded in 1883 (G. F. Jackson, *Shropshire Folklore*, p. 573), a Birmingham child vouched the newness because it was "named after a teacher's wife." Children are, in fact, prone to claim the authorship of a verse when they have done no more than alter a word in it, for instance substitute a familiar name for a name unknown to them; and they tend to be passionately loyal to the presumed genius of a classmate, or of a child who has just left their school, who is credited with the invention of each newly heard composition. The unromantic truth, however, is that children do not "go on inventing games out of their heads all the time," as Norman Douglas believed; for the type of person who is a preserver is rarely also creative, and the street child is every bit as conservative as was George VI with his life-long preference for the hymns he sang in the choir at Dartmouth. The nearest the normal child gets to creativeness is when he stumbles on a rhyme, as we have overheard: an eight-year-old, playing in some mud, suddenly chanted "Stuck in the muck, stuck in the muck," whereupon his playmates took up the refrain, "Stuck in the muck, stuck in the muck." A ten-year-old added:

> It's a duck, it's a duck,
> Stuck in the muck, stuck in the muck,

and the group echoed this too, and went on chanting it, spasmodically, with apparent satisfaction, for over an hour, so that it seemed certain that we were in at the birth of a new oral rhyme. But when we asked them about it a week later they did not know what we were talking about. The fact is that even a nonsense verse must have some art and rhythm in it if it is to obtain a hold on a child's mind, although exactly what the quality is which gives some verses immortality is difficult to discover.

Where, then, do the rhymes come from? The origins of only a few can be traced, but these few may be indicative. The popular verse,

> Sam, Sam, the dirty man,
> Washed his face in a frying pan;
> He combed his hair with a donkey's tail,
> And scratched his belly with a big toe nail,

known throughout Britain in a multitude of versions (this one is from a thirteen-year-old boy in Pontefract) is a relic of a once famous song "Old Dan Tucker" composed by the black-faced minstrel Daniel Decatur Emmett, of "Dixie" fame, and printed in 1843. Similarly Nellie Bligh who "shuts her eye" ("because she cannot shut her ears"), or who catches a fly and ties it to a pin, was the heroine of a mid-nineteenth-century Negro minstrel song by Stephen Foster; while a further "Ethiopian" legacy is the little tongue-tripping verse,

> I saw Esau sawing wood,
> And Esau saw I saw him;
> Though Esau saw I saw him saw
> Still Esau went on sawing,

sometimes sung by children when skipping (this version from an eight-year-old Alton girl), which is descended from the lyric "I saw Esau kissing Kate" written by Harry Hunter for the Mohawk Minstrels sometime about 1875.[7] Again, the child rhyme,

[7] The song was revived as a comedy item in 1956, though not before we had collected versions from children who had received it from the nineteenth century, apparently by oral conveyance.

> Johnny Morgan played the organ,
> Jimmy played the drum,
> His sister played the tambourine
> Till Father smacked her bum,

is a perverted recollection of the chorus of John Read's music-hall song "Johnny Morgan" published in 1877; and the little *jeu d'esprit,* known to children from one end of Britain to the other,

> Tiddly Wink the barber
> Went to shave his father,
> The razor slip
> And cut his lip,
> Tiddly Wink the Barber,

is further living testimony to Read's genius. In 1878 the original chorus of "Tiddle-a-Wink the Barber, The Popular Comic Song, Written, Composed & Sung with Immense Success by John Read," went:

> Tiddle-a-Wink, Tiddle-a-Wink, Tiddle-a-Wink the Barber,
> Tiddle-a-Wink, Tiddle-a-Wink, went to shave his father
> But he made a slip and cut his lip,
> Which made his father roar,
> The father knock'd poor Tiddle-a-Wink
> Bang upon the floor.

This process of children adopting or adapting popular songs for use in their games continues, of course, in the present day. Songs such as "The more we are together," "Show me the way to go home," "Horsie, horsie, don't you stop," and "The Lambeth Walk" (now sometimes "Lambert's Walk") have a playground existence today far removed from their dance-band origins. More recently, the American song "Music! Music! Music!" ("Put another nickel in") written by Stephan Weiss and Bernie Baum, and published in 1950, seems assured of immortality, for both the original lyric, and juvenile extemporizations of it extolling film stars or denigrating teachers, can still frequently be heard in the playground, seven years and a whole school generation after its original publication. It is, perhaps, only to be expected that the most memorable verses should turn out to be the work of professional humorists and songwriters.

Regional Variation

If the uniformity of schoolchild lore, to which we have so far been witness, was the whole story it would of course only be necessary to study one locality to know what goes on in every locality; and no matter how comprehensive and virile the lore was found to be, if it was the same everywhere, it would confirm the apprehensions of those who suppose that standardized education, mass entertainment, and national periodical literature have already subverted local traditions and characteristics. Happily our tale is not yet complete. Two distinct streams of oral lore flow into the unending river of schoolchild chant and chatter, and these two streams are as different from each other as slang and dialect. The slangy superficial lore of comic songs, jokes, catch phrases, fashionable adjectives, slick nicknames, and crazes, in short that noise which is usually the first that is encountered in playground and street, spreads everywhere but, generally speaking, is transitory. The dialectal lore flows more quietly but deeper; it is the language of the children's darker doings: playing truant, giving warning, sneaking, swearing, sniveling, tormenting, and fighting. It belongs to all time, but is limited in locality. It is so timeworn indeed that it cannot be dated, and words of which Shakespeare would have known the meaning, as "cog," "lag," and "miching," are, in their particular districts, still common parlance; while the language which children use to regulate their relationships with each other, such as their terms for claiming, securing precedence, and making a truce, vary from one part of the country to another, and can in some instances be shown to have belonged to their present localities not merely for the past two or three generations, but for centuries.

Conflicting as are the characteristics of these two types of lore, the one rapidly spreading from place to place and having a brief existence, the other having a prolonged existence but rarely spreading, it is not impossible to see how they subsist together. When a child newly arrives in a district any slang expression he knows, any jokes or tricks, or any new skipping or "dipping" rhymes he brings with him, are eagerly listened to, and if found amusing, are added to the local repertoire, and may eventually supplant similar pieces of lore already known. But the local children, while willing to enlarge their store of jokes and rhymes, will not consciously brook any alteration to what they already know. The new child must learn, and very quickly does so, the "legislative" language of his new playmates. He must learn the local names for the playground games, and the expressions used while playing them. Unless he does this, he will not merely be thought peculiar, he will not be understood. A child who moves from Lincoln and cries "Screams" for mercy in Leicester will find that he receives no sympathy, since the accepted truce term in Leicester is "Croggies." Similarly a twelve-year-old Spennymoor girl who says,

> "When the rope is turning away from the nobby-ender it is lupey-dyke. When the nobby-ender is out he takes the laggy-ender's place and the laggy-ender takes the foggy-ender's place so that the foggy-ender becomes the nobby-ender,"

will be thought out of her mind if she says this in the hearing of a Spitalfields girl, although both children in fact adhere to this practice while skipping, and both may skip to the same rhymes.

This regional variation in the children's dialectal lore has been as unexpected as the slavish uniformity of their slang lore; and when the children's customs and superstitious practices are examined, in particular their calendar customs, the regional differences are remarkable. While some children roll eggs at Easter, or nettle the legs of classmates on the twenty-ninth of May, or leave little gifts on people's doorsteps on St. Valentine's Day, or act under the delusion that they are above the law on the night of November 4, other children, sometimes living only on the other side of a hill, will have no knowledge of these activities. It is not perhaps of much consequence that in different parts of England children have different ritual ways of disposing of their milk teeth, that there are more than sixty names for the illegal pursuit of knocking at doors and running away, that in some places walking under a ladder can be lucky and seeing a black cat can be unlucky, and that some children make fools on the first of May with more zeal than on the first of April; but the children's loyalty to local customs and forms of speech is at least evidence that the young in Britain do not take as their authority only what they hear and see on the radio and television and at the cinema.

Continuities and Discontinuities
in Cultural Conditioning

RUTH BENEDICT

(1938)

As all parents inevitably shape their child's emotional
life, so all cultures are responsible for molding the individual and impressing upon him the community's ideals
and ideologies. In the following famous paper, the American anthropologist Ruth Fulton Benedict shows how conventional childrearing in our culture creates a severe
disparity between childhood and adulthood that first
creates the peculiar turbulence of adolescence and may
later contribute to maladjustment and personality up-
heaval.

All cultures must deal in one way or another with the cycle of
growth from infancy to adulthood. Nature has posed the situation dramatically: on the one hand, the newborn baby,
physiologically vulnerable, unable to fend for itself, or to par-
ticipate of its own initiative in the life of the group, and, on
the other, the adult man or woman. Every man who rounds
out his human potentialities must have been a son first and a
father later and the two roles are physiologically in great contrast; he must first have been dependent upon others for his
very existence and later he must provide such security for
others. This discontinuity in the life cycle is a fact of nature
and is inescapable. Facts of nature, however, in any discussion
of human problems, are ordinarily read off not at their bare
minimal but surrounded by all the local accretions of behavior
to which the student of human affairs has become accustomed
in his own culture. For that reason it is illuminating to examine comparative material from other societies in order to
get a wider perspective on our own special accretions. The
anthropologist's role is not to question the facts of nature, but
to insist upon the interposition of a middle term between
"nature" and "human behavior"; his role is to analyze that
term, to document local man-made doctorings of nature and
to insist that these doctorings should not be read off in any one

culture as nature itself. Although it is a fact of nature that the child becomes a man, the way in which this transition is effected varies from one society to another, and no one of these particular cultural bridges should be regarded as the "natural" path to maturity.

From a comparative point of view our culture goes to great extremes in emphasizing contrasts between the child and the adult. The child is sexless, the adult estimates his virility by his sexual activities; the child must be protected from the ugly facts of life, the adult must meet them without psychic catastrophe; the child must obey, the adult must command this obedience. These are all dogmas of our culture, dogmas which in spite of the facts of nature, other cultures commonly do not share. In spite of the physiological contrasts between child and adult these are cultural accretions.

It will make the point clearer if we consider one habit in our own culture in regard to which there is not this discontinuity of conditioning. With the greatest clarity of purpose and economy of training, we achieve our goal of conditioning everyone to eat three meals a day. The baby's training in regular food periods begin at birth and no crying of the child and no inconvenience to the mother is allowed to interfere. We gauge the child's physiological make-up and at first allow it food oftener than adults, but, because our goal is firmly set and our training consistent, before the child is two years old it has achieved the adult schedule. From the point of view of other cultures this is as startling as the fact of three-year-old babies perfectly at home in deep water is to us. Modesty is another sphere in which our child training is consistent and economical; we waste no time in clothing the baby and in contrast to many societies where the child runs naked till it is ceremonially given its skirt or its pubic sheath at adolescence, the child's training fits it precisely for adult conventions.

In neither of these aspects of behavior is there need for an individual in our culture to embark before puberty, at puberty or at some later date upon a course of action which all his previous training has tabued. He is spared the unsureness inevitable in such a transition.

The illustration I have chosen may appear trivial, but in larger and more important aspects of behavior, our methods are obviously different. Because of the great variety of child training in different families in our society, I might illustrate continuity of conditioning from individual life histories in our culture, but even these, from a comparatve point of view, stop

far short of consistency and I shall therefore confine myself
to describing arrangements in other cultures in which training
which with us is idiosyncratic, is accepted and traditional and
does not therefore involve the same possibility of conflict. I
shall choose childhood rather than infant and nursing situations
not because the latter do not vary strikingly in different cultures but because they are nevertheless more circumscribed
by the baby's physiological needs than is its later training.
Childhood situations provide an excellent field in which to
illustrate the range of cultural adjustments which are possible
within a universally given, but not so drastic, set of physiological facts.

The major discontinuity in the life cycle is of course that
the child who is at one point a son must later be a father.
These roles in our society are strongly differentiated; a good
son is tractable, and does not assume adult responsibilities; a
good father provides for his children and should not allow his
authority to be flouted. In addition the child must be sexless
so far as his family is concerned, whereas the father's sexual
role is primary in the family. The individual in one role must
revise his behavior from almost all points of view when he
assumes the second role.

I shall select for discussion three such contrasts that occur
in our culture between the individual's role as child and as
father: 1. responsible—non-responsible status role, 2. dominance—submission, 3. contrasted sexual role. It is largely upon
our cultural commitments to these three contrasts that the discontinuity in the life cycle of an individual in our culture depends.

1. *Responsible—Non-Responsible Status Role*

The techniques adopted by societies which achieve continuity during the life cycle in this sphere in no way differ from
those we employ in our uniform conditioning to three meals
a day. They are merely applied to other areas of life. We think
of the child as wanting to play and the adult as having to work,
but in many societies the mother takes the baby daily in her
shawl or carrying net to the garden or to gather roots, and
adult labor is seen even in infancy from the pleasant security
of its position in close contact with its mother. When the child
can run about it accompanies its parents still, doing tasks
which are essential and yet suited to its powers, and its dichot-

omy between work and play is not different from that its parents recognize, namely the distinction between the busy day and the free evening. The tasks it is asked to perform are graded to its powers and its elders wait quietly by, not offering to do the task in the child's place. Everyone who is familiar with such societies has been struck by the contrast with our child training. Dr. Ruth Underhill tells me of sitting with a group of Papago elders in Arizona when the man of the house turned to his little three-year-old granddaughter and asked her to close the door. The door was heavy and hard to shut. The child tried, but it did not move. Several times the grandfather repeated, "Yes, close the door." No one jumped to the child's assistance. No one took the responsibility away from her. On the other hand there was no impatience, for after all the child was small. They sat gravely waiting till the child succeeded and her grandfather gravely thanked her. It was assumed that the task would not be asked of her unless she could perform it, and having been asked the responsibility was hers alone just as if she were a grown woman.

The essential point of such child training is that the child is from infancy continuously conditioned to responsible social participation while at the same time the tasks that are expected of it are adapted to its capacity. The contrast with our society is very great. A child does not make any labor contribution to our industrial society except as it competes with an adult; its work is not measured against its own strength and skill but against high-geared industrial requirements. Even when we praise a child's achievement in the home we are outraged if such praise is interpreted as being of the same order as praise of adults. The child is praised because the parent feels well disposed, regardless of whether the task is well done by adult standards, and the child acquires no sensible standard by which to measure its achievement. The gravity of a Cheyenne Indian family ceremoniously making a feast out of the little boy's first snowbird is at the furthest remove from our behavior. At birth the little boy was presented with a toy bow, and from the time he could run about serviceable bows suited to his stature were specially made for him by the man of the family. Animals and birds were taught him in a graded series beginning with those most easily taken, and as he brought in his first of each species his family duly made a feast of it, accepting his contribution as gravely as the buffalo his father brought. When he finally killed a buffalo, it was only the final step of his childhood conditioning, not a new adult role with which his childhood experience had been at variance.

The Canadian Ojibwa show clearly what results can be achieved. This tribe gains its livelihood by winter trapping and the small family of father, mother and children live during the long winter alone on their great frozen hunting grounds. The boy accompanies his father and brings in his catch to his sister as his father does to his mother; the girl prepares the meat and skins for him just as his mother does for her husband. By the time the boy is 12, he may have set his own line of traps on a hunting territory of his own and return to his parents' house only once in several months—still bringing the meat and skins to his sister. The young child is taught consistently that it has only itself to rely upon in life, and this is as true in the dealings it will have with the supernatural as in the business of getting a livelihood. This attitude he will accept as a successful adult just as he accepted it as a child.[1]

2. Dominance—Submission

Dominance—submission is the most striking of those categories of behavior where like does not respond to like but where one type of behavior stimulates the opposite response. It is one of the most prominent ways in which behavior is patterned in our culture. When it obtains between classes, it may be nourished by continuous experience; the difficulty in its use between children and adults lies in the fact that an individual conditioned to one set of behavior in childhood must adopt the opposite as an adult. Its opposite is a pattern of approximately identical reciprocal behavior, and societies which rely upon continuous conditioning characteristically invoke this pattern. In some primitive cultures the very terminology of address between father and son, and more commonly, between grandchild and grandson or uncle and nephew, reflects this attitude. In such kinship terminologies one reciprocal expresses each of these relationships so that son and father, for instance, exchange the same term with one another, just as we exchange the same term with a cousin. The child later will exchange it with his son. "Father—son," therefore, is a continuous relationship he enjoys throughout life. The same con-

[1] Ruth Landes, *The Ojibwa Woman*, Part 1, Youth—Columbia University Contributions to Anthropology, Volume XXXI.

tinuity, backed up by verbal reciprocity, occurs far oftener in the grandchild-grandson relationship or that of mother's brother-sister's son. When these are "joking" relationships, as they often are, travelers report wonderingly upon the liberties and pretensions of tiny toddlers in their dealings with these family elders. In place of our dogma of respect to elders such societies employ in these cases a reciprocity as nearly identical as may be. The teasing and practical joking the grandfather visits upon his grandchild, the grandchild returns in like coin; he would be led to believe that he failed in propriety if he did not give like for like. If the sister's son has right of access without leave to his mother's brother's possessions, the mother's brother has such rights also to the child's possessions. They share reciprocal privileges and obligations which in our society can develop only between age mates.

From the point of view of our present discussion, such kinship conventions allow the child to put in practice from infancy the same forms of behavior which it will rely upon as an adult; behavior is not polarized into a general requirement of submission for the child and dominance for the adult.

It is clear from the techniques described above by which the child is conditioned to a responsible status role that these depend chiefly upon arousing in the child the desire to share responsibility in adult life. To achieve this little stress is laid upon obedience but much stress upon approval and praise. Punishment is very commonly regarded as quite outside the realm of possibility, and natives in many parts of the world have drawn the conclusion from our usual disciplinary methods that white parents do not love their children. If the child is not required to be submissive however, many occasions for punishment melt away; a variety of situations which call for it do not occur. Many American Indian tribes are especially explicit in rejecting the ideal of a child's submissive or obedient behavior. Prince Maximilian von Wied who visited the Crow Indians over a hundred years ago describes a father's boasting about his young son's intractability even when it was the father himself who was flouted; "He will be a man," his father said. He would have been baffled at the idea that his child should show behavior which would obviously make him appear a poor creature in the eyes of his fellows if he used it as an adult. Dr. George Devereaux tells me of a special case of such an attitude among the Mohave at the present time. The child's mother was white and protested to its father that he must take action when the child disobeyed and struck him.

"But why?" the father said, "he is little. He cannot possibly injure me." He did not know of any dichotomy according to which an adult expects obedience and a child must accord it. If his child had been docile he would simply have judged that it would become a docile adult—an eventuality of which he would not have approved.

Child training which brings about the same result is common also in other areas of life than that of reciprocal kinship obligations between child and adult. There is a tendency in our culture to regard every situation as having in it the seeds of a dominance-submission relationship. Even where dominance-submission is patently irrelevant we read in the dichotomy, assuming that in every situation there must be one person dominating another. On the other hand some cultures, even when the situation calls for leadership do not see it in terms of dominance-submission. To do justice to this attitude it would be necessary to describe their political and especially their economic arrangements, for such an attitude to persist must certainly be supported by economic mechanisms that are congruent with it. But it must also be supported by—or what comes to the same thing, express itself in—child training and familial situations.

3. *Contrasted Sexual Role*

Continuity of conditioning in training the child to assume responsibility and to behave no more submissively than adults is quite possible in terms of the child's physiological endowment if his participation is suited to his strength. Because of the late development of the child's reproductive organs continuity of conditioning in sex experience presents a difficult problem. So far as their belief that the child is anything but a sexless being is concerned, they are probably more nearly right than we are with an opposite dogma. But the great break is presented by the universally sterile unions before puberty and the presumably fertile ones after maturation. This physiological fact no amount of cultural manipulation can minimize or alter, and societies therefore which stress continuous conditioning most strongly sometimes do not expect children to be interested in sex experience until they have matured physically. This is striking among American Indian tribes like the Dakota; adults observe great privacy in sex acts and in no way stimulate children's sexual activity. There need be no discontinuity, in the sense in which I have used the term, in such a program if the child is taught nothing it does not have to unlearn later. In such cultures adults view children's experimentation as in no way wicked or dangerous but merely as innocuous play which can have no serious consequences. In some societies such play is minimal and the children manifest little interest in it. But the same attitude may be taken by adults in societies where such play is encouraged and forms a major activity among small children. This is true among most of the Melanesian cultures of Southeast New Guinea; adults go as far as to laugh off sexual affairs within the prohibited class if the children are not mature, saying that since they cannot marry there can be no harm done.

It is this physiological fact of the difference between children's sterile unions and adults' presumably fertile sex relations which must be kept in mind in order to understand the different mores which almost always govern sex expression in children and in adults in the same culture. A great many cultures with preadolescent sexual license require marital fidelity and a great many which value pre-marital virginity in either male or female arrange their marital life with great license. Continuity in sex experience is complicated by factors which it was unnecessary to consider in the problems previously discussed. The essential problem is not whether or not the child's sexuality is consistently exploited—for even where such exploitation is favored in the majority of cases the child must seriously modify his behavior at puberty or at marriage. Continuity in sex expression means rather that the child is taught nothing it must unlearn later. If the cultural emphasis is upon sexual pleasure the child who is continuously conditioned will be encouraged to experiment freely and pleasurably, as among the Marquesans[2]; if emphasis is upon reproduction, as among the Zuni of New Mexico, childish sex proclivities will not be exploited for the only important use which sex is thought to serve in his culture is not yet possible to him. The important contrast with our child training is that although a Zuni child is impressed with the wickedness of premature sex experimentation he does not run the risk as in our culture of associating this wickedness with sex itself rather than with sex at his age. The adult in our culture has often failed to unlearn the wickedness or the dangerousness of sex, a lesson which was impressed upon him strongly in his most formative years.

[2] Ralph Linton, class notes on the Marquesans.

Discontinuity in Conditioning

Even from this very summary statement of continuous conditioning the economy of such mores is evident. In spite of the obvious advantages, however, there are difficulties in its way. Many primitive societies expect as different behavior from an individual as child and as adult as we do, and such discontinuity involves a presumption of strain.

Many societies of this type however minimize strain by the techniques they employ, and some techniques are more successful than others in ensuring the individual's functioning without conflict. It is from this point of view that age-grade societies reveal their fundamental significance. Age-graded cultures characteristically demand different behavior of the individual at different times of his life and persons of a like age-grade are grouped into a society whose activities are all oriented toward the behavior desired at that age. Individuals "graduate" publicly and with honor from one of these groups to another. Where age society members are enjoined to loyalty and mutual support, and are drawn not only from the local group but from the whole tribe as among the Arapaho, or even from other tribes as among the Wagawaga of Southeast New Guinea, such an institution has many advantages in eliminating conflicts among local groups and fostering intra-tribal peace. This seems to be also a factor in the tribal military solidarity of the similarly organized Masai of East Africa. The point that is of chief interest for our present discussion however is that by this means an individual who at any time takes on a new set of duties and virtues is supported not only by a solid phalanx of age mates but by the traditional prestige of the organized "secret" society into which he has now graduated. Fortified in this way, individuals in such cultures often swing between remarkable extremes of opposite behavior without apparent psychic threat. For example, the great majority exhibit prideful and nonconflicted behavior at each stage in the life cycle even when a prime of life devoted to passionate and aggressive head hunting must be followed by a later life dedicated to ritual and to mild and peaceable civic virtues.[3]

Our chief interest here, however, is in discontinuity which

[3] Henry Elkin, manuscript on the Arapaho.

primarily affects the child. In many primitive societies such discontinuity has been fostered not because of economic or political necessity or because such discontinuity provides for a socially valuable division of labor, but because of some conceptual dogma. The most striking of these are the Australian and Papuan cultures where the ceremony of the "Making of Man" flourishes. In such societies it is believed that men and women have opposite and conflicting powers, and male children, who are of undefined status, must be initiated into the male role. In Central Australia the boy child is of the woman's side and women are tabu in the final adult stages of tribal ritual. The elaborate and protracted initiation ceremonies of the Arunta therefore snatch the boy from the mother, dramatize his gradual repudiation of her. In a final ceremony he is reborn as a man out of the men's ceremonial "baby pouch." The men's ceremonies are ritual statements of a masculine solidarity, carried out by fondling one another's *churingas,* the material symbol of each man's life, and by letting out over one another blood drawn from their veins. After this warm bond among men has been established through the ceremonies, the boy joins the men in the men's house and participates in tribal rites.[4] The enjoined discontinuity has been tribally bridged.

West of the Fly River in southern New Guinea there is a striking development of this Making of Men cult which involves a childhood period of passive homosexuality. Among the Keraki[5] it is thought that no boy can grow to full stature without playing the role for some years. Men slightly older take the active role, and the older man is a jealous partner. The life cycle of the Keraki Indians includes, therefore, in succession, passive homosexuality, active homosexuality and heterosexuality. The Keraki believe that pregnancy will result from post-pubertal passive homosexuality and see evidences of such practices in any fat man whom even as an old man, they may kill or drive out of the tribe because of their fear. The ceremony that is of interest in connection with the present discussion takes place at the end of the period of passive homosexuality. This ceremony consists in burning out the possibility of pregnancy from the boy by pouring lye down

[4] B. Spencer and F. J. Gillen, *The Arunta;* N.Y., Macmillan, 1927 (2 vols.). Géza Róheim, Psycho-Analysis of Primitive Cultural Types. *Internat. J. Psychoanal.* (1932) 13: 1–224—in particular, Chapter III, on the Aranda, The Children of the Desert.

[5] Francis E. Williams, *Papuans of the Trans-Fly;* Oxford, 1936.

his throat, after which he has no further protection if he gives way to the practice. There is no technique for ending active homosexuality, but this is not explicitly tabu for older men; heterosexuality and children however are highly valued. Unlike the neighboring Marindanim who share their homosexual practices, Keraki husband and wife share the same house and work together in the gardens.

I have chosen illustrations of discontinuous conditioning where it is not too much to say that the cultural institutions furnish adequate support to the individual as he progresses from role to role or interdicts the previous behavior in a summary fashion. The contrast with arrangements in our culture is very striking, and against this background of social arrangements in other cultures the adolescent period of *Sturm und Drang* with which we are so familiar becomes intelligible in terms of our discontinuous cultural institutions and dogmas rather than in terms of physiological necessity. It is even more pertinent to consider these comparative facts in relation to maladjusted persons in our culture who are said to be fixated at one or another pre-adult level. It is clear that if we were to look at our social arrangements as an outsider, we should infer directly from our family institutions and habits of child training that many individuals would not "put off childish things"; we should have to say that our adult activity demands traits that are interdicted in children, and that far from redoubling efforts to help children bridge this gap, adults in our culture put all the blame on the child when he fails to manifest spontaneously the new behavior or, overstepping the mark, manifests it with untoward belligerence. It is not surprising that in such a society many individuals fear to use behavior which has up to that time been under a ban and trust instead, though at great psychic cost, to attitudes that have been exercised with approval during their formative years. In so far as we invoke a physiological scheme to account for these neurotic adjustments we are led to overlook the possibility of developing social institutions which would lessen the social cost we now pay; instead we elaborate a set of dogmas which prove inapplicable under other social conditions.

IV

THE CHILD REACTS TO PAINFUL EVENTS

The Child's Idea of Death

SYLVIA ANTHONY

(1965)

Death, extremely upsetting to adults who witness it, does
not seem initially to cause great anxiety in children. In
this paper Sylvia Anthony, the English analyst, follows
the child's developing concept of death. Since children at
first attribute all events to personal causes, death in their
eyes is inevitably a kind of "killing," and thus it is often
associated with their aggressive impulses. Similarly, death
is associated with birth in a child's mind because it is the
second great, irrevocable experience of separation. In
fairy tales death incidents often correspond to the early
reactions of children to death. The fact that children do
not realize the generality and impersonality of death until ages seven to twelve must be borne in mind by adults
as they attempt to explain death to young children.

Parents today are mostly well prepared to answer their children's questions about birth and sex, but may be troubled
when they have to deal with questions about death. The facts
and the thought may be distressing to themselves. They may
repress thought on the subject. Freud's biographer, Dr. Ernest
Jones, suggests that Freud himself did so. Maybe it is a general, normal tendency, taking forms which we only recognize
when they are different from those we have elaborated ourselves. Certainly the adult is often ready to suppose that his
own distress at thoughts of death will be shared by the child
who inquires about its meaning. Observation shows that, in the
beginning at any rate, this is seldom the case. Knowledge,
gained by controlled observation and record, of the way the
idea of death and the emotion arising from it develops in
childhood may help the adult to guide the child along a path
which later has some hard going for every human being.

In the world of the young child, even after he can walk
and talk, there is at first no conception of death, or of the
meaning of the adjective *dead*. (In most European languages

the two words have the same root and obvious phonetic similarity; in Hungarian they have not, as appears from a study of
children's ideas of death reported by Nagy[1] from Budapest.
The development of the idea is then somewhat different from
that among children in whose language the words are similar.)
Some adults can remember the time when to them everything
had, in those very early days, a quality of permanence. Two
writers, Traherne[2] and Proust,[3] describe the immense
value—in psychoanalytic terminology, the strong cathexis—of
all the objects perceived around them at that time:—"Boys and
girls playing were moving jewels; I knew not that they were
born or should die; but all things abided eternally in their
proper places." The child at this stage often shows a powerful aversion to any change in his own environment.

I must break off here to say that I shall try to make no
general statement about children without reference to actual
observations which, in ways I cannot here specify, bear the
stamp of reliability. Some of these statements I shall be able
to illustrate with reports of individual children's behavior; for
others the examples are to be found in the literature listed for
reference, or listed within those references.

The first step in what I have called elsewhere the child's
discovery of death is not generally undertaken with strong
emotional accompaniment. It is simply an incident in the normal day-to-day process by which the child explores his environment. Here is a record by S. Isaacs[4] of such an incident: Ur-
sula, aged 3:iv, and her mother found a dead moth in the
garden and discovered that it could not move. *U:* "Like the
crab (on the beach) . . . and a boy took the pail and got
water and put it in to see if it would move and it didn't move.
Why didn't it move, Mummie?" These first questions differ,
of course, as regards their objective reference, which may be
to animals, plants, pictures or actuality, human beings known
or historical. One thing the queries will have in common. The
inquiring child has reached the stage of asking Why? or What-
for (Pour-quoi?). He is no longer mainly concerned to know
the names of things. He seeks a further kind of knowledge and
understanding.

[1] M. Nagy, The Child's Theories Concerning Death, *Journal of
Genetic Psychology*, 73, 1948.
[2] T. Traherne, *Centuries of Childhood.*
[3] M. Proust. See G. Poulet, *Studies in Human Time*, 1936.
[4] S. Isaacs, *Intellectual Growth in Young Children*, 1931.

A mother of two little boys aged four and two years found that the elder was puzzled by the dead birds in poultry shops, asking if they were asleep, whereas the younger was not concerned with them. There are, however, reports of children as young as two years who do show concern about a dead animal. Sully noted how a boy of this age seemed surprised and disturbed after killing a fly, and after awaiting an explanation, gave it himself: "Mr. F'y dom to by-by" (gone to sleep). Even at this early age the state of death seemed to puzzle, and to cause some anxiety. Often no such puzzlement occurs until the fifth or sixth year; death may come very close to the child of two or three years old without arousing anxiety.

Often there is a definite interval between the child's first questions about dead objects and the arousal of emotion in connection with the idea. It seems that in that interval the meaning given to the observation and the word has developed, and it is through these associations that the emotion creeps or floods in, rather than through the circumstances of the original perception, such as of dead birds in a shop or dead flowers in the garden. The earliest associations may be very limited, and different for different individuals. To one child death may be signified by immobility, to another, sleep; to another, being put in the ground; to another, going up in the sky; to another, by going to the hospital, or going on a journey, or by disappearance.

Sometimes with his first conception of death, often only later, the child is faced with the thought of the loss of someone upon whom he depends for company and comfort. This may cause great distress, as in the case of Jane which I shall quote below. More usual are the signs of an anxiety relatively mild, or coupled with active search for the means of its own alleviation. Thus Sonia (4:vii), daughter of the Norwegian psychologist Rasmussen, said, "Supposing I hadn't any Mummy and supposing I hadn't any Daddy, I daresay there'd be some lady or other who would give me sixpence." Nor is the child's feeling for his parents one of simple love and dependence, to arouse simple grief or distress at the anticipation of parting. More complex sentiments may arise.

The record which I shall now quote is peculiar in one respect only, namely, that the sequence of development is so rapid. For this reason it is apt to our present purpose. A process which in most cases takes place gradually over months or years has here been telescoped and brought within the compass of a single observer and report. The account was given me in a letter from a mother whom I did not know and have never met. It is abbreviated but otherwise unchanged except for the name of the child.

Jane (3:IX) is a first and only child; healthy; started to speak at one year . . . very affectionate . . . physically a little clumsy . . . She has received no religious instruction of any kind on my orders, and has so far never met death in connection with any human being of her acquaintance, nor its description in any books . . . A few days ago she began asking me questions about death. She had two hours previously asked me how babies were born and she had seemed quite satisfied with my explanation and the analogy with our cat having had kittens. The death conversation . . . began by Jane asking if people came back again in the spring like flowers. (A week or so before she had been very upset by her favorite flowers dying down and we had consoled her by saying they would return in the spring.) As I have no orthodox religious beliefs I said, I now realize foolishly, that they did not return the same, but different, possibly as babies. This answer obviously worried her—she hates change and people getting old—for she said "I don't want Nan (her nursemaid) to be different, I don't want her to change and grow old." Then, "Will Nan die? Shall I die too, does everyone die?" On my saying yes, she broke into really heartbreaking tears and kept on saying, "But *I* don't want to die, I don't want to die." This rather upset me and I stupidly tried to console her by hedging . . . I tried to make things better by saying every one and everything died, when they were old and tired and therefore glad to do so. She then asked how people died (as if it hurt), whether when they were dead they opened their eyes again (she has seen a dead bird once), whether they spoke, ate and wore clothes. Suddenly in the middle of all these questions and tears she said, "Now I will go on with my tea," and the matter was temporarily forgotten.

Not for long. The next day she heard a nurse out of doors say a child she knew had nearly died. Shortly after she came and told me with an anxious look. It upset the little I had told her about only old people dying, I feared (not that she has an idea of age—as far as she is concerned she may be "old" by next birthday). I replied he was quite well now (which he is) and said when people were ill you put them to bed and the doctors came and they got well. She seemed really pleased. The following day November 11th the matter cropped up again over the armistice poppies. She came in to me flourishing her purchase, saying cheerfully, "You see, *it* won't die!" Since then no more.

No one child can adequately exemplify the course of development of this or any other idea among children in general. Variations in personality and in the immediate and the cultural environment produce variations in individual behavior and in the speed at which successive stages occur. Jane's reactions occurred, as we have noted, at an extraordinarily rapid rate, but otherwise they were not abnormal. It is common for an intelligent three-year-old to be puzzled over a dead bird or dead flowers, though such behavior seems to be more common at about five years of age. The transition to the thought of death as applicable to a loved human being is a usual next stage, though it does not generally happen immediately. The further transition which brings the realization that the self is also mortal is usually still further delayed. This is the stage which may involve the child in deep anxiety.

That it does not usually do so seems to be due to the operation of the same psychological processes which have protected the normal adult from neurosis arising from this source, and have shaped the collective manifestations of human culture in respect of death through the ages. The relation between individual neurosis and cultural participation is too large a question to be discussed here. To illustrate the way the child responds to his anxiety by methods developed in cultures with which he is unacquainted, let me quote a record of Jeremy, aged 5:x. Devoted to his nursemaid, he had begged her to stay with him always, to which she replied that surely he would not want her when she was ninety and very old. At this his elder sister broke in, "Why, Mummie will be dead then; you won't live to be older than that, will you, Mummie?" Four days later when going to bed, alone with the maid, Jeremy said that he was going to die, but he wouldn't die without Booby (his toy rabbit, which he always took to bed with him). Thus also the ancient Egyptians, and many other peoples, have taken with them into their tombs those objects they deeply valued.

The famous Swiss psychoanalyst C. G. Jung[5] suggested that on such matters the state of infantile thinking "is nothing but a re-echo of the prehistoric and the ancient. We may draw a parallel," he wrote, "between the fantastical, mythological thinking of antiquity and the similar thinking of children, between the lower human races and dreams. This train of thought is familiar through our knowledge of comparative

[5] C. G. Jung, *Collected Works*, 1953.

anatomy . . . which shows us how the structure and function of the human body are the results of a series of embryonic changes which correspond to similar changes in the history of the race. Therefore the supposition is justified that ontogenesis (the development of the individual) corresponds in psychology to phylogenesis (the development of the species)." This theory of psychological recapitulation was developed by a number of eminent psychologists some fifty years ago, but is now discredited, both in embryology and psychology. As regards similarities between the thought of children and of what Jung described as the lower human races, the theory has been rejected by anthropologists. Not only does Dr. Margaret Mead,[6] for instance, deny the reality of *the primitive* or *the child* as a synthetic personality, but she holds that the behavior of individuals in primitive society may resemble that of the child not yet fully trained, in respect of any aspect of behavior which has not been given importance in the social pattern of the particular culture, but that a fully acculturated member of a living culture differs entirely and systematically from members of any other culture. The argument applies equally to the apparent echoes by children of the thought of ancient peoples. Similar environmental pressures lead individuals to similar conceptual solutions of problems. Any one concept or solution worked out by an individual may have been elaborated in the cultural pattern of a society different from his own. It is not, however, a mystical echo, but a recrudescence of similar form due to the similar pressures. In the culture in which the child grows up, therefore, solutions tried out by different individual children are necessarily abandoned as they accept the cultural norms. Those problems for which there may be no wholly acceptable solution, however, may present the adult with special difficulty in his contact with children, and lead him to improvise a solution in a sense regressive (like the suggestion of Jane's mother that the dead return as babies), being a solution elaborated in other cultures than their own, and sometimes (as I shall show) suggested spontaneously by children in our own culture.

Most children are looked after by their mothers, not by nursemaids. I have quoted the behavior of Jeremy and Jane partly in order to show that the fear of separation aroused by the early conception of death is as readily applied by the

[6] Margaret Mead, "Research on Primitive Children," *Manual of Child Psychology*, editor, L. Carmichael, 1954.

child to the mother-substitute as to the mother herself, and this even when the mother is also present and affectionate.

Nevertheless the actual genetic relationships of parent and child have special importance in the development of the death concept in childhood. Separation of mother from child often seems to be the first concept and concern of the child in his thinking about death. He may then assure himself, half in fantasy, that there will be no such separation. Rasmussen reported Sonia (6:viii) saying to her mother, "You must stay with me every day, and when I die you must be in the coffin with me." In our records is one of a boy of 7:xi who said to his mother that he would like to die so as to be in the same grave as her. Such ideas are recorded also by adults, and may be traced in many funerary customs. The earth of the country where a man is born represents in his fantasy (as often in language) a loved parent. Greeks repatriated from Albania in 1963 lay down and kissed the soil as they landed. Burial in earth is, in unconscious thought, a return to the body of the mother.

In other ways also, the mother-child relationship enters into the conception of death. Jane's mother, who, as she wrote, had no orthodox religious beliefs, suggested to her distressed child that the dead might come back as babies. A mother who had made no such suggestion to her children, but taught them orthodox Christian beliefs, recorded that one of them, aged 5:i, after seeing a coffin carried into a house, said "Of course the person who went away (in the coffin) will become a baby," and on being asked why he thought so, added "When John (his baby brother) was born, somone must have died." The spontaneous association of birth and death in a child's thought also appears in the following (abbreviated) report:—

> When Philip was three years old his father had to go to the hospital, and said seriously to the child, "Philip, you must be a good boy." This obviously impressed the child, who would afterward become more amenable if reminded, "Papa said Philip should be a good boy," though he was seldom difficult or bad-tempered. For some months his father was ill, most of the time at home, and when the child was 3:viii the father died, in the hospital. This brought no questions about death from the child. When he was 5:ii, he and his mother were being seen off at a railway station by his grandmother, who said, "Philip, remember papa said you should be a good boy." Some quarter-hour later, as they sat waiting for the train, Philip said, "Mama, is papa borned yet?"

It might be supposed that Philip had forgotten his father, but this was not so; he constantly saw and recognized his photograph, and often spoke of him and of past events in which they had participated. But he knew of the existence of babies not yet born, so that the reference to someone not visible induced him to identify the dead with the unborn. So much we may suggest, perhaps rationalizing the particular incident. At the same time one must recognize the wide ramifications of this identification, with its implications of reincarnation, fundamental and elaborated in the religious code of many cultures both primitive and sophisticated.

The young child's concept of death may be primarily associated with sorrowful ideas of separation from things or people loved. On the other hand, the primary association may be with violence, aggressive desires, destruction or victimization. In the folk-lore of European peoples which we call fairy stories, death-incidents are frequently of a kind corresponding to a very early stage of children's emotional maturation, when the center of interest and activity is the mouth and the digestive system. In the stories of *Little Red Riding-Hood* and *Jack and the Beanstalk*, for instance, death comes by eating. It may not be final. The victim may return to life, extracted from the aggressor's body. Aggressor and victim communicate with each other with alternate friendliness (or eating together) and hostility. The wolf takes the place of the grandmother. At the level of thinking at which death is oral, it is an incorporation idea, and killing-dying is also a communication of life. This thought finds a place, as does that of reincarnation, in religious systems primitive and civilized.

At this level of thinking, killing-dying requires no special motivation, or not more than eating and drinking. It appears as part of the unquestioned, instinctive process of living. It belongs before the stage of *Why* questions. At the beginning of the *Why* stage, according to the Swiss psychologist, Piaget,[7] children attribute all events and existences to personal motivations. Causality is the will or intention of human or divine beings.

The dead birds in the shops which puzzled the four-year-old had indeed been intentionally killed in order to be eaten. We are told by psychoanalysts who study the evidence for unconscious modes of thought that the frustrated child wants

[7] Jean Piaget, *The Language and Thought of the Child*, 3rd ed. 1959; *The Child's Conception of Causality*, 1930.

to kill, or has a death-wish against, the parent, even at an age when he can have no conception of death. Certainly as the idea of death acquires meaning it enters the complex of result-of-aggression. It is scarcely necessary to recapitulate here the Oedipus legend, or the way it has been applied to explain the emotional and ideational development of the child, except to repeat that in that story the planned death of the infant by the parents led to the unwitting killing of father by son. Many children of primary-school age will define the word *dead* by reference to violent action, as *killed* or even *murdered*. Such definitions are also sometimes given by adolescents of very low mental age. Crime and Western pictures on television and cinema films tend to encourage this association of ideas.

In the Oedipus legend the innocent-incorporation and the guilty-aggressive concepts of death are linked through the theme of incest. The two themes are not kept apart as the idea of death develops in individual thinking, though the incest motive is unlikely to become conscious except by psychoanalytic techniques. In the aggressive theme the typical victim is often pictured as an animal, since animals are killed and eaten without conscious sense of guilt. Children's stories, new and old, are full of animal identifications. Animals act and often dress as human beings; they may turn into human beings, as did the Frog Prince, who mated with the Princess. In games, parent and small child will alternately act as lion, bear, tiger, pretending to eat each other. The child jealous of younger siblings may imagine them as small animals, and after learning to restrain his hostility toward the younger child, may be peculiarly distressed at the killing of small living things. In ancient cultures the animal is scapegoat and Paschal lamb; the Olympian gods took animal form for sexual adventures. The animal gods of the Egyptians seem to have been more sedate and inscrutable. They were very much concerned with death and resurrection.

A French psychologist, Wallon,[8] has stated that to the child death is not at first felt as a threat to his instinct for life but seems like another state altogether. This may be observed in the behavior of many children who do not telescope experience so rapidly as Jane did. The dead are seen as a separate category of individuals. Often this category is that of the old. The ideas of death and age are often associated in an

[8] H. Wallon, *Les Origines de la Pensée chez l'Enfant.*

early explanation given to the child of the death of an animal or human being. Schilder and Wechsler,[9] in an investigation of the attitudes of children toward death, found that some of the boys they examined in clinics believed that children do not die, and from this generalized that they themselves would not die. Other children have been found to believe that only the enemies of their country die. Whatever the category imagined immune from mortality, the realization later dawns upon the child that he will not be exempt (though "dawns" is in many cases an incorrect description of the intellectual process, which may be a conscious logical activity). Rasmussen[10] records a conversation with his daughter Ruth aged 4:vii. R: Will you die, Father? F: Yes, but not before I grow old. R: Will you grow old? F: Yes. R: Shall I grow old, too? F: Yes. He adds that both Ruth and her younger sister at this age were extremely afraid of death, and Ruth is reported as saying, three months after the above conversation, "Every day I'm afraid of dying . . . I wish I might never grow old, for then I'd never die, would I?"

As we have seen in the case of Jane and her mother, it is the anxiety which arises for the child when he realizes that he himself will die which tends to cause the parent the greatest difficulty and even distress. A practicing psychiatrist, Dr. C. E. Wahl,[11] suggests that even if the parent turns to the psychoanalyst or to psychoanalytic literature for help, he is unlikely to find it. "The phenomenon of the fear of death or anxiety about it (thanatophobia as it is called) while certainly no clinical rarity, has almost no description in the psychiatric or psychoanalytic literature," he writes. "When it is noted . . . it is usually described solely as a derivative and secondary phenomenon, often as a more easily endurable form of 'castration fear.' There is a good clinical evidence that this kind of displacement occurs. But it is also important to discover if this formulation also subserves in part a defensive need on the part of the psychiatrists themselves. Freud expected (fear of death) to appear, if at all, subsequently to the oedipal period, and as a symbolic product of fear of castration attendant upon the improper resolution of the Oedipus complex. Present day

[9] P. Schilder and D. Wechsler, "The Attitudes of Children Toward Death." Journal of Abnormal Social Psychology, 45, 1934.

[10] V. Rasmussen, Diary of a Child's Life, 1919; Child Psychology, 1921.

[11] C. E. Wahl, "The Fear of Death," The Meaning of Death, ed. H. Feifel, 1959.

experience does not altogether support these views. Thanatophobia is frequently encountered in children. . . . Its appearance seems to be contiguous to the development of concept
formation and the formation of guilt, both of which greatly
antedate the Oedipus complex."

Many children are taught that there is an after-life in
heaven. This offers a defense against death-anxiety. Many parents cannot sincerely teach resurrection or reincarnation, or
they may be unable to make the lesson comprehensible or
acceptable to the child. Children, however, may develop their
own "mechanisms of defense." There are rare unhappy cases,
such as one described by E. H. Erikson,[12] in which the idea
of death may act as "psychic stimulus to a latent potentiality"
for psychotic (in that case epileptic) attacks. In such cases
psychiatric advice and assistance is called for. Whether the
development is preventible we do not know. Normally, however, there may occur death-anxiety in childhood which, with
immediate sympathetic handling, and appreciation of the depth
of the problem, may be successfully surmounted. One such
incident is recorded by the Katz parents. The mother, on this
occasion, told the child that he himself need not die, but could
live forever. In two out of three such cases of which I have
record, this reaction by the mother, made with some reluctance
was accepted as comfort by the child at the time and was
followed by no neurosis. In the third case a similar assurance
was delayed for several days, and an adolescent neurosis was
associated with this incident by the psychoanalyst treating the
neurosis.

It seems at first sight strange that such a denial should have
the desired effect, for the child thus suffering is also realizing
that he cannot be an exception to what he has now recognized
as a general law. The child's behavior becomes comprehensible, however, as an instance of a psychological process described by Freud. An unpleasant theme may be initially admitted to consciousness by its negation. The child who says,
"I shall never die" is by this very statement refusing to repress the knowledge that he himself is mortal, though he cannot yet consciously assent to it.

In dreams, Freud wrote, death as most hated thing may be
represented by a most loved person, and its necessity by the
opposite of compulsion, namely, free choice. In later childhood death is denied by mockery and defiance, which is an

[12] Erik Erikson, *Childhood and Society*, 1953.

acting out of this assertion of free choice. The age to which Freud assigned sexual latency is the great period of "daring" and accepting "dares." "The thing I most hated (was) death," says Arturo in Morante's imaginative autobiography of an Italian boy. "In my own natural happiness, I chased all my thoughts away from death . . . But at the same time, the more I hated death the more I exaltedly enjoyed giving proofs of my own temerity: no game was enough fun if it lacked the fascination of risk."

This stage of daring comes usually rather later than the seventh year, in which Piaget noted a boy's preoccupation with death. Piaget considered this of great importance in the development of mature concepts of causality, from the early thinking in which motivation is the source of all explanation of the existence of things. Everything seems well regulated, he suggests, until the child becomes aware of the difference between life and death. "From this moment, the idea of death sets the child's curiosity in motion, precisely because, if every cause is coupled with a motive, then death calls for a special explanation." Clearly death cannot be explained in terms of motive of the being that dies, for in the case of animals the question of suicide does not arise, nor does it occur to the child in the case of human beings. If death is attributed to the activity of other persons, a causal explanation may still be given. Obviously such cases occur, as when animals are killed for food, or when animals harmful to man are killed in order to safeguard human life. There are also occasions when men are killed by men, and, as we have seen, some children will define *dead* as *killed* or *murdered*. Wallon[13] has reported a response from a child who had found a logical solution to the problem of causality, death and personal motivation in accordance with what he had been taught of the laws of God and man:

M (aged 7) said of the storm that it was due to a ball of fire. Q: Who made this ball of fire? M: The devil . . . Q: Where is he? M: In heaven (*Au ciel*) . . . Q: What else does the devil do? M: He makes people die (*Il fait mourir du monde*) . . . Q: If there were no devil, would old people not die? M: That is so (*Si*).

Lacking some such mythology, human mortality, unlike that of animals, cannot be explained by the child in terms of motivation consistently with any rule of social law and pro-

[13] H. Wallon, *Les Origines de la Pensée chez l'Enfant*, 1945.

priety, the maintenance of that due organization of life in society which the young child generally shows himself so well aware of, and so much concerned to have surrounding him, even if only that he may sometimes break out of it. The law that permits death must be a law of nature; a law uniform and impersonal.

The steps by which children come intellectually to the conception of laws of nature, and of causality operating in accordance with such laws, may be said to start from those reactions which lead them to the thought, traditionally opening the study of classical logic, that all men are mortal. This intellectual ascent may be painful. But like the storied Pilgrim's Progress, there is an early stage at which a former burden is cast off. This burden is a sense of guilt for sins which the child earlier wished but was in fact powerless to commit. The infant cannot clearly distinguish between those events which happen as he desires *because* he desires them, and those which happen thus independently of his wishing. If he is fed when he wants to be, is it not because he wants to be? So if he wishes ill and it occurs, he is not certain his wish was not the cause of the event. He has a sense of magical power by which every mischance to members of his family piles on him a load of guilt. Maturity brings humility; he finds that he, like all other living beings, is impotent against death. If love cannot save, neither can hate of itself destroy. His "death-wishes" were powerless.

It may happen that a child who has scarcely grown out of the stage of doubt about the efficacy of his own desires may suffer the sudden loss of a member of his family, or learn later that such a loss had occurred when he was younger, and attribute the death to his own antagonisms. He may then suffer from a fear of punishment or a state of depression which will appear irrational. I have described some actual cases of this nature in *The Child's Discovery of Death*[14]; the children in question were not noted as neurotic, though obviously sad. These, however, are unusual cases, calling for special understanding. In many children not suffering in this way, an unconscious sense of guilt may persist as a burden until the generality and impersonality of death is realized. This process is normally achieved between the seventh and twelfth years of age.

The art of comedy developed from the jesters who, in ancient Greece, followed the mourners at funerals, mocking

[14] Sylvia Anthony, *The Child's Discovery of Death*, 1940.

death itself with obscenities. At the period of childhood when rationality is beginning to triumph, the school child by tradition learns to make a mock of death. "When they are about ten years old," write the Opies about English children, they "enter a period in which the outward material facts about death seem extraordinarily funny. They ask each other: 'You going to be burnt or buried?' They have mock laments:

> Little Willie's dead,
> Jam him in the coffin,
> For you don't get the chance
> Of a funeral of'en.

They inscribe their names on the flyleaf of their schoolbooks, 'When I am dead and in my grave and all my bones are rotten, This little book will tell my name when I am quite forgotten,' a version of which is found on a sampler of 1736. Certain songs like Whyte-Melville's *Wrap me up in my tarpaulin jacket,* Montrose's *Clementine,* and the popular song, 'When I die, don't bury me at all, Just pickle my bones in alcohol' become an obsession, chorused over and over again . . . Death, which when they were younger, they may have regarded as a frightening and private subject, has now come out into the open. They have found that it is still a long way off, and these songs are a sign of their emancipation."[15]

The behavior of these children is in the group. Their emancipation from anxiety is acted out in the fellowship which they have found outside the emotional circle of the parental family. The defiance of death develops out of the earlier anxiety, the mockery out of the new companionship. Its obsessional character marks its origin. Later it is more soberly and more happily expressed in the old student song

"Gaudeamus igitur/juvenes dum sumus,"

with its overtones recognizing the transience of youth and life. The ten-year-old's mockery is a halfway house to the defense available to the adult through sex and reproduction. Not that that, of course, is a complete safeguard; it is but a biological contribution to the total defensive strategy by which the idea of death is contained and employed in the life process. It is not a part available in childhood; the defenses to be worked out during the long human infancy are distinctively human.

[15] Peter and Iona Opie, *The Lore and Language of School Children,* 1959.

War and Children

ANNA FREUD AND DOROTHY BURLINGHAM

(1943)

Anna Freud has applied psychoanalysis to clinical work
with children. During World War II Miss Freud and Mrs.
Burlingham directed three wartime nurseries in England
for the Foster Parents' Plan for War Children, an organization that had been working with children since
1936, when Spain's children were victims of bombard-
ment. Later they worked in France with French, Polish,
Dutch and Belgian children. More than 20,000 children
were studied through daily contact on the home front
and in actual bombed areas; *War and Children* emerged
from that study. With Alice Balint, Anna Freud holds
that children are born devoid of a super-ego, which is
created by regular and rigorous training. In socially dis-
ruptive catastrophes like war, the healthy development of
personality is endangered. A child's aggressive infantilism,
which wishes unpleasant persons "killed," is confirmed by
the destruction he sees around him, and the separation
from his parents that often occurs in war arouses his
resentment and guilt (did he offend them?). Therefore
the care and education of young children cannot be
neglected in wartime without severe psychic damage to
the next generation.

It is a common misunderstanding of the child's nature which
leads people to suppose that children will be saddened by the
sight of destruction and aggression. Children between the ages
of one and two years, when put together in a playpen will
bite each other, pull each other's hair and steal each other's
toys without regard for the other child's unhappiness. They
are passing through a stage of development where destruction
and aggression play one of the leading parts. If we observe
young children at play, we notice that they will destroy their
toys, pull off the arms and legs of their dolls or soldiers, punc-
ture their balls, smash whatever is breakable, and will only
mind the result because complete destruction of the toy blocks

further play. The more their strength and independence are growing the more they will have to be watched so as not to create too much damage, not to hurt each other or those weaker than themselves. We often say, half jokingly, that there is continual war raging in a nursery. We mean by this, that at this time of life destructive and aggressive impulses are still at work in children in a manner in which they only recur in grown-up life when they are let loose for the purposes of war.

It is one of the recognized aims of education to deal with the aggressiveness of the child's nature, i.e. in the course of the first four or five years to change the child's own attitude toward these impulses in himself. The wish to hurt people, and later the wish to destroy objects, undergo all sorts of changes. They are usually first restricted, then suppressed by commands and prohibitions; a little later they are repressed, which means that they disappear from the child's consciousness. The child does not dare any more to have knowledge of these wishes. There is always the danger that they might return from the unconscious; therefore, all sorts of protections are built up against them—the cruel child develops pity, the destructive child will become hesitant and overcareful. If education is handled intelligently the main part of these aggressive impulses will be directed away from their primitive aim of doing harm to somebody or something, and will be used to fight the difficulties of the outer world—to accomplish tasks of all kinds, to measure one's strength in competition and to use it generally to "do good" instead of "being bad" as the original impulse demanded.

In the light of these considerations it is easier to determine what the present war conditions, with their incidents of wholesale destruction may do to a child. Instead of turning away from them in instinctive horror, as people seem to expect, the child may turn toward them with primitive excitement. The real danger is not that the child, caught up all innocently in the whirlpool of the war, will be shocked into illness. The danger lies in the fact that the destruction raging in the outer world may meet the very real aggressiveness which rages in the inside of the child. At the age when education should start to deal with these impulses, confirmation should not be given from the outside world that the same impulses are uppermost in other people. Children will play joyfully on bombed sites and around bomb craters, they will play with blasted bits of furniture and throw bricks from crumbled walls at each other. But it becomes impossible to educate them toward a repression of, a reaction against destruction while they are doing so. After their first years of life they fight against their own wishes to do away with people of whom they are jealous, who disturb or disappoint them, or who offend their childish feelings in some other way. It must be very difficult for them to accomplish this task of fighting their own death wishes when, at the same time, people are killed and hurt every day around them. Children have to be safeguarded against the primitive horrors of the war, not because horrors and atrocities are so strange to them, but because we want them at this decisive stage of their development to overcome and estrange themselves from the primitive and atrocious wishes of their own infantile nature.

Development of the Mother Relationship and the Effect of Separation from the Mother at the Various Stages

In the relationship of the small child to its mother there are definite main phases to be distinguished from each other.

The first phases which comprise the first few months of life are characteristically selfish and material. The young baby's life is governed by sensations of need and satisfaction, pleasure and discomfort. The mother plays a part in it in so far as she brings satisfaction and removes discomfort. When the baby is fed, warm and comfortable, it withdraws its interest from the outer world and falls asleep. When it is hungry, cold and wet or disturbed by sensations in its own intestines it cries for attention. It is certain that the care and attention given by the mother, i.e. in a special atmosphere of affection which only the mother can supply, is more satisfactory to the baby than more indifferent and mechanical ministrations to its needs.

But the fact is that a baby, who at this time of life is separated from its mother, will accept food and care from a mother substitute. Its needs are overwhelming, its helplessness is extreme, and its distinction between one person and another is still in the beginning stage. Babies of this age who are left with us by mothers will usually have a short time of upset, may cry a while, have more difficulty in falling asleep and show some irregularity in their digestion for a day or two.

We still have to learn exactly how much of this upset is due to the disturbance of routine and how much to the change away from the individual handling and from the particular atmosphere of intimacy created by the mother. The upset caused, is of course, of a more serious nature and of far longer duration in cases where the mother has been breast-feeding the baby and weaning has to occur simultaneously with the separation. Weaning in itself acts on the child as a loss of satisfaction and a separation from the mother in an important sense. When the mother, who has left, reappears after a few days, the baby at this stage will probably not show signs of recognition.

The second phase starts roughly, in the second half of the first year of life. The material relationship to the mother still exists. The mother remains, as she will remain for several years, the instrument of satisfaction for the child. But out of this ignoble beginning of a human relationship something different begins to grow.

The baby begins to pay attention to the mother also at times when there is no urgent necessity for it to be attended to. It likes its mother's company, enjoys her fondling, and dislikes to be left alone. So far the absence of the mother has only been a potential danger; some inner need might arise and there might be nobody outside to fulfill it. Now, in this later phase, the mother is already appreciated or missed for her own sake. The child is conscious of her presence, follows her around with its eyes, can answer her smile and is, as described above, moved by her moods. Its need for her affection becomes as urgent for its psychological satisfaction as the need to be fed and taken care of is for its bodily comfort. Disturbance after parting from the mother will last somewhat longer at this stage.

Babies of this age are sometimes off their feed when left with us. Many show signs of restlessness during sleep and often seem unfriendly or rather withdrawn from contact with the outer world. Smiles, friendliness, playfulness, will only reappear after the bodily functions have returned to normality. This interruption of psychic contact with the outer world is not simply the consequence of the bodily discomfort which the baby experiences; when once used to us the same baby will not cut off its contact with the nurse who handles it even in times of illness.

But at this period of separation it repeats what it did in the beginning of its mother relationship—it establishes personal contact with the mother substitute only on the basis of the fulfillment and satisfaction provided for its bodily needs.

The personal attachment of the child to its mother, which starts in this manner in the first year of life, comes to its full development in the second one. It was said before that the child is attached to its mother; it can now be safely said that it loves her. The feelings for her which it is able to experience acquire the strength and variety of adult human love. This love makes demands and is possessive. All the child's instinctive wishes are now centered on the mother. While she is breast-feeding it, it wants to "eat" her; later on it will bite her, handle her, and whatever impulse starts up in it will try to find satisfaction on her person.

This relationship between small child and mother might be a happy one except for two reasons. The child's demands are too great; it is virtually insatiable. However long the mother may have fed it at the breast, it will express by its resentment at weaning time that it was not long enough; however much time she spends near it, it will still bitterly resent being left alone at other times. Also, the child soon becomes aware of the fact that there are other people in the world besides itself and its mother. It realizes the presence of brothers and sisters who claim equal rights and become its rivals. It becomes aware, sometimes at a very early age, of the presence of the father, and includes him in its world. It recognizes him as a dangerous rival where family life is normal. It loves him at the same time. With this conflict of feelings it enters into the whole complicated entanglement of feelings which characterize the emotional life of human beings.

Reactions to parting at this time of life are particularly violent. The child feels suddenly deserted by all the known persons in its world to whom it has learned to attach importance. Its new ability to love finds itself deprived of the accustomed objects, and its greed for affection remains unsatisfied. Its longing for its mother becomes intolerable and throws it into states of despair which are very similar to the despair and distress shown by babies who are hungry and whose food does not appear at the accustomed time. For several hours, or even for a day or two this psychological craving of the child, the "hunger" for its mother, may override all bodily sensations.

There are some children of this age who will refuse to eat or to sleep. Very many of them will refuse to be handled or comforted by strangers. The children cling to some object or to some form of expression which means to them, at that moment, memory of the material presence of the mother.

Some will cling to a toy which the mother has put into their hands at the moment of parting; others to some item of bedding or clothing which they have brought from home.

Some will monotonously repeat the word by which they are used to call their mothers, as for instance, Christine, seventeen months old, who said: "Mum, mum, mum, mum, mum . . ."

She repeated it continually in a deep voice for at least three days.

Observers seldom appreciate the depth and seriousness of this grief of a small child. Their judgment of it is misled for one main reason. This childish grief is short-lived. Mourning of equal intensity in an adult person would have to run its course throughout a year; the same process in the child between one and two years will normally be over in thirty-six to forty-eight hours. It is a psychological error to conclude from this short duration that the reaction is only a superficial one and can be treated lightly. The difference in duration is due to certain psychological differences between the state of childhood and adulthood. The child's life is still entirely governed by the principle which demands that it should seek pleasure and avoid pain and discomfort. It cannot wait for the arrival of pleasure and bear discomfort in the idea that in this way ultimate pleasure may again be reached.

An adult person may find himself in the same situation of being suddenly cut off from all the people he loves, and will also experience intense longing. But his memories of the past and his outlook into the future will help him maintain an inner relationship to the loved objects and thus to bridge the period until reunion is possible.

The psychological situation of the child is completely different. A love object who does not give it immediate satisfaction is no good to it. Its memories of the past are spoiled by the disappointment which it feels at the present moment. It has no outlook into the future and it would be of no help to it if it had. Its needs are so urgent that they need immediate gratification; promises of pleasure are no help.

The little child will therefore, after a short while, turn away from the mother image in its mind and, though at first unwillingly, will accept the comfort which is offered. In some cases acceptance may come in slow stages. Christine, for instance, would at first only let herself be fondled or held by an unseen person. She would sit on somebody's lap, turn her head away, enjoy the familiar sensation of being held, and probably add to it in her own mind the imaginary picture of her own mother. Whenever she looked at the face of the person who held her she began to cry.

There are other children who are spared these violent reactions. They seem placid, dazed, and more or less indifferent. It takes a few days or even a week before this placidity is disturbed by a realization of the fact that they are among strangers; all sorts of slighter depressive reactions and problems of behavior will then result. All children of this age, those with the violent reactions as well as those where reaction is delayed, will show a tendency to fall ill under the new conditions; they will develop colds, sore throats, or slight intestinal troubles.

That the shock of parting at this stage is really serious is further proven by the observation that a number of these children fail to recognize their mothers when they are visited after they have "settled down" in their new surroundings. The mothers themselves realize that this lack of recognition is not due to any limitations of the faculty of memory as such. The same child who looks at its mother's face with stony indifference as if she were a complete stranger, will have no difficulty in recognizing lifeless objects which have belonged to its past. When taken home again it will recognize the rooms, the position of the beds and will remember the contents of cupboards, etc.

Fathers also are treated better in this respect. The children were always more or less used to their coming and going and not dependent on them for their primitive gratifications. Consequently, parting from them is no real shock and their memory remains more undisturbed. Failure to recognize the mother occurs when something has happened to the image of the mother in the child's mind, i.e., to its inner relationship to her. The mother has disappointed the child and left its longing for her unsatisfied; so it turns against her with resentment and rejects the memory of her person from its consciousness.

Mother and Child Relationship in the Early Stages

What is true about the small child remains true with certain modifications for the next two or three years of life. Changes are brought about slowly by development in various directions. Intelligence grows and enables the child to get some understanding of real situations, for instance, of the real reasons for being sent away; toward the age of five this mental understanding already acts as a real help in lessening the shock. More comfort can be derived from memories, and hopes for the future begin to play a part.

On the other hand the relations between children and their parents are less simple and harmonious at this time of life. All sorts of complicating factors have been added to the home situation and confuse the picture when the family has to break up. The child of this age has ceased to live in partnership with its mother only; it has become a member of a larger family group, and this factor has a bearing on its emotions and affections.

So far the emotional development of boys and girls has appeared rather similar; at this age they begin to develop definitely along different lines. The boy begins to identify himself with his father and to imitate him in various ways. This changes his position toward the mother; he ceases to be a dependent baby, and turns into a small demanding male who claims her attention, desires her admiration, and longs to possess her in more grown-up ways. The little girl, on the other hand, has grown away from her complete absorption in the mother. She begins to imitate her in turn, she tries to play mother herself with dolls or with her younger brothers and sisters. She turns her affection and interest more toward the father, and would like him to appreciate her in the mother's place.

Both sexes in this manner have their first experience in being in love. As a result of circumstances it is inevitable that this first love is disappointing. In comparison with the rival parent the child feels itself to be small, ineffective and inferior. It experiences feelings of anger toward one parent, jealousy toward the other, and feels generally discontented that its fantastic wishes to be big can find no real fulfillment.

It acts as a second disturbing factor that the parents use the love which children feel for them to educate the children. The early upbringing of children is not at all an easy undertaking.

Children are born as little savages; when they enter school at the age of five they are expected to be more or less civilized human beings. This means that the first years of life are completely filled with the struggle between the demands of the parents and the instinctive wishes of the child. Already in the first two years weaning has been carried out against the desire of the child and habit training has been enforced. The child's hunger and greed have had to adapt themselves to regular meal times. In this new period the parents criticize and restrict the child's aggression and its wishes to destroy things. They not only train it to cleanliness, they want it to dislike dirt as much as they do. When it is naturally cruel, they want it to feel pity. Its first sexual impulses are interfered with when it tries to satisfy itself on its own body; it certainly finds no satisfaction when it turns toward its parents. The curiosity of the child is left largely unsatisfied, and its natural desire to be admired is criticized as a wish to "show off." In this first education of the child, the parents do not usually apply compulsion; they simply make use of the dependence of the child and of its love for father and mother. The child is quite helpless in the hands of the parents; therefore, even a slight punishment will frighten it into obedience. The parents' love is all-important to the child; therefore it is used as a reward when the child is "good" and its withdrawal is threatened when the child is "naughty." In this unequal battle nothing is left to the child in the end but to give in and become civilized.

These two factors, disappointment in early love and the pressure of education, threaten to spoil the pleasantness of the relations between child and parent. Whenever the child is denied some pleasure it becomes resentful, when it is too much restricted it turns obstinate. When it is punished it hates the parents; but it can never stand hating father or mother without feeling the strongest guilt about it.

Children are quick in their anger and know only one main punishment for anybody who offends them, i.e. that this person should go away and not return, which in childish language means that he should die. In everyday life at home these emotions are natural and necessary; they create small outbursts and settle down again. The father or mother who have been wished dead at one moment are reinstated in the child's affections in the next. On the other hand, it is probably these violent negative feelings of the child which determine its reaction to separation at this period. The negative feelings toward the parents are meant to be only transitory. Under the influence of daily contact they are held in check and neutralized by the affection for the parents which is constantly produced in answer to all the satisfactions which the child receives.

It does not seem so very dangerous to kill a parent in fantasy if at the same time outward evidence shows that this same parent is alive and well. But separation seems to be an intolerable confirmation of all these negative feelings. Father and mother are now really gone. The child is frightened by their absence and suspects that their desertion may be another punishment or even the consequence of its own bad wishes. To overcome this guilt it overstresses all the love which it has ever felt for its parents. This turns the natural pain of separation into an intense longing which is hard to bear. In these moods of homesickness children are usually particularly good. Commands and prohibitions which they formerly opposed at home are now religiously observed in the absence of the parents. Whatever might be interpreted as implied criticism of the parents is violently resented. They search their thoughts for past wrongs about which they might feel guilty.

Patrick, three and one half years old, when he heard that his mother had gone to the hospital with a bad leg began to remember a time when he had kicked her, and began to wonder whether her illness was his fault.

Visits or lack of them is understood as rewards and punishments. We had several little girls of three and four who would "hang around" the doors for hours when their mothers were expected to come. But the visits at these times never brought the desired satisfaction. When the mothers were present the children would be gloomy, shy, and hang onto them without talking; when the mothers left again the affection broke through and violent scenes were produced. The children acted as if they could only feel love toward the absent mother; toward the present mother, resentment was uppermost.

Again, the reactions toward the father do not develop on quite the same lines. There are two main attitudes which we were able to observe. The first is that many children will adopt every father who enters the nursery as if he were their own. They will demand to sit on his lap or wish to be carried around by him. A visiting mother will never be claimed in this manner by strange children. The second is that some little girls, two to four years old, will suddenly develop acute anxiety at the sight of any man, will turn their face away, cover their eyes with their hands, shriek with fear and run to the nurses for protection. The first reaction may easily be due to the general scarcity of the male element in nursery life. The second is probably based on the inner rejection of the father due to the child's disappointment caused by separation.

Prejudice and the Young Child

GORDON W. ALLPORT

(1954)

In the following chapter from Gordon W. Allport's comprehensive study *The Nature of Prejudice,* prejudice is
considered from the time of childhood training, when
the child contracts bigotry, like an infection, through
exposure to the established prejudices of his parents. Firm
prejudices, according to Allport, grow in an atmosphere
that encourages children to place order, not trust, at the
center of their values by creating in them an anxious
veneration for power and authority. He reduces much
prejudice to the literally black-and-white thinking emphasized in early cleanliness learning, and discusses the
power of linguistic tags—children's rhymes and phrases—
to foster bigotry.

How is prejudice learned? We have opened our discussion of
this pivotal problem by pointing out that the home influence
has priority, and that the child has excellent reasons for adopting his ethnic attitudes ready-made from his parents. We likewise called attention to the central role of identification in the
course of early learning. In the present chapter we shall consider additional factors operating in preschool years. The first
six years of life are important for the development of all social
attitudes, though it is a mistake to regard early childhood as
alone responsible for them. A bigoted personality may be well
under way by the age of six, but by no means fully fashioned.

Our analysis will be clearer if at the outset we make a
distinction between *adopting* prejudice and *developing* prejudice. A child who adopts prejudice is taking over attitudes
and stereotypes from his family or cultural environment. Most
of the cases cited in the previous chapter are instances in
point.

But there is also a type of training that does not transfer
ideas and attitudes directly to the child, but rather creates an
atmosphere in which he *develops* prejudice as his style of

life. In this case the parents may or may not express their own prejudices (usually they do). What is crucial, however, is that their mode of handling the child (disciplining, loving, threatening) is such that the child cannot help acquire suspicions, fears, hatreds that sooner or later may fix on minority groups.

In reality, of course, these forms of learning are not distinct. Parents who *teach* the child specific prejudices are also likely to *train* the child to develop a prejudiced nature. Still it is well to keep the distinction in mind, for the psychology of learning is so intricate a subject that it requires analytical aids of this type.

Child Training

We consider now the style of child training that is known to be conducive to the *development* of prejudice.

One line of proof that a child's prejudice is related to the manner of his upbringing comes from a study of Harris, Gough, and Martin.[1] These investigators first determined the extent to which 240 fourth-, fifth-, and sixth-grade children expressed prejudiced attitudes toward minority groups. They then sent questionnaires to the mothers of these children, asking their views on certain practices in child training. Most of these were returned with the mothers' replies. The results are highly instructive. Mothers of prejudiced children, *far more often* than the mothers of unprejudiced children, held that:

> Obedience is the most important thing a child can learn.
> A child should never be permitted to set his will against that of his parents.
> A child should never keep a secret from his parents.
> "I prefer a quiet child to one who is noisy."
> (In the case of temper tantrums) "Teach the child that two can play that game, by getting angry yourself."

In the case of sex-play (masturbation) the mother of the prejudiced child is much more likely to believe she should punish the child; the mother of the unprejudiced child is much more likely to ignore the practice.

All in all, the results indicate that pervasive family atmospheres do definitely slant the child. Specifically, a home that

---

[1] D. B. Harris, H. G. Gough, and W. E. Martin, Children's ethnic attitudes: II, Relationship to parental beliefs concerning child training. *Child Development*, 1950, *21*, 169–181.

is suppressive, harsh, or critical—where the parents' word is law—is more likely to prepare the groundwork for group prejudice.

It seems a safe assumption that the mothers who expressed their philosophies of child training in this questionnaire actually carried out their ideas in practice. If so, then we have strong evidence that children are more likely to be prejudiced if they have been brought up by mothers who insist on obedience, who are suppressive of the child's impulses, and who are sharp disciplinarians.

What does such a style of child training do to a child? For one thing it puts him on guard. He has to watch his impulses carefully. Not only is he punished for them when they counter the parents' convenience and rules, as they frequently do, but he feels at such times that love is withdrawn from him. When love is withdrawn he is alone, exposed, desolate. Thus he comes to watch alertly for signs of parental approval or disapproval. It is they who have power, and they who give or withhold their conditional love. Their power and their will are the decisive agents in the child's life.

What is the result? First of all, the child learns that power and authority dominate human relationships—not trust and tolerance. The stage is thus set for a hierarchical view of society. Equality does not really prevail. The effect goes even deeper. The child mistrusts his impulses: he must not have temper tantrums, he must not disobey, he must not play with his sex organs. He must fight such evil in himself. Through a simple act of projection the child comes to fear evil impulses in others. They have dark designs; their impulses threaten the child; they are not to be trusted.

If this style of training prepares the ground for prejudice, the opposite style seems to predispose toward tolerance. The child who feels secure and loved whatever he does, and who is treated not with a display of parental power (being punished usually through shaming rather than spanking), develops basic ideas of equality and trust. Not required to repress his own impulses, he is less likely to project them upon others, and less likely to develop suspicion, fear, and a hierarchical view of human relationships.[2]

While no child is always treated according to one and only

[2] These two contrasting styles of child training are described more fully by D. P. Ausubel in *Ego Development and the Personality Disorders*, New York: Grune & Stratton, 1952.

one pattern of discipline or affection, we might venture to classify prevailing home atmospheres according to the following scheme:

Permissive treatment by parents
Rejective treatment
    suppressive and cruel (harsh, fear-inspiring)
    domineering and critical (overambitious parents nagging
      and dissatisfied with the child as he is)
Neglectful
Overindulgent
Inconsistent (sometimes permissive, sometimes rejective, some-
    times overindulgent)

Although we cannot yet be dogmatic about the matter, it seems very likely that rejective, neglectful, and inconsistent styles of training tend to lead to the development of prejudice.[3] Investigators have reported how impressed they are by the frequency with which quarrelsome or broken homes have occurred in the childhood of prejudiced people.

> Ackerman and Jahoda made a study of anti-Semitic patients who were undergoing psychoanalysis. Most of them had had an unhealthy home life as children, marked by quarreling, violence, or divorce. There was little or no affection or sympathy between the parents. The rejection of the child by one or both parents was the rule rather than the exception.[4]

These investigators could not find that specific parental indoctrination in anti-Semitic attitudes was a necessary element. It is true that the parents, like the children, were anti-Semitic, but the authors explain the connection as follows:

> In those cases where parents and children are anti-Semitic, it is more reasonable to assume that the emotional predispositions of the parents created a psychological atmosphere conducive to the development of similar emotional dispositions in the child, than to maintain the simple imitation hypothesis.[5]

[3] The most extensive evidence is contained in researches conducted at the University of California. See: T. W. Adorno, Else Frenkel-Brunswik, D. J. Levinson, and R. N. Sanford, *The Authoritarian Personality*, New York: Harper, 1950; also, Else Frenkel-Brunswik, Patterns of social and cognitive outlook in children and parents, *American Journal of Orthopsychiatry*, 1951, *21*, 543–558.

[4] N. W. Ackerman and Marie Jahoda, *Anti-Semitism and Emotional Disorder*. New York: Harper, 1950, 45.

[5] *Ibid.*, 85.

In other words, prejudice was not *taught* by the parent but was *caught* by the child from an infected atmosphere.

Without stretching the evidence too far, we may at least make a guess: children who are too harshly treated, severely punished, or continually criticized are more likely to develop personalities wherein group prejudice plays a prominent part. Conversely, children from more relaxed and secure homes, treated permissively and with affection, are more likely to develop tolerance.

Fear of the Strange

Let us return again to the question whether there is an inborn source of prejudice. As soon as infants are able (perhaps at six months of age) to distinguish between familiar and unfamiliar persons, they sometimes show anxiety when strangers approach. They do so especially if the stranger moves abruptly or makes a "grab" for the child. They may show special fear if the stranger wears eyeglasses, or has skin of an unfamiliar color, or even if his expressive movements are different from what the child is accustomed to. This timidity usually continues through the preschool period—often beyond. Every visitor who has entered a home where there is a young child knows that it takes several minutes, perhaps several hours, for the child to "warm up" to him. But usually the initial fear gradually disappears.

The almost universal anxiety of a child in the presence of strangers is no more striking than his rapid adaptability to their presence.

In a certain household a Negro maid came to work. The young children in the family, aged three and five, showed fear and for a few days were reluctant to accept her. The maid stayed with the family for five or six years and came to be loved by all. Several years later, when the children were young adults, the family was discussing the happy period of Anna's services in the household. She had not been seen for the past ten years, but her memory was affectionately held. In the course of the conversation it came out that she was colored. The children were utterly astonished. They insisted that they had never known this fact, or had completely forgotten it if they ever knew it.

Situations of this type are not uncommon. Their occurrence makes us doubt that instinctive fear of the strange has any necessary bearing upon the organization of permanent attitudes.

Dawn of Racial Awareness

The theory of "home atmosphere" is certainly more convincing than the theory of "instinctive roots." But neither theory tells us just when and how the child's ethnic ideas begin to crystallize. Granted that the child possesses relevant emotional equipment, and that the family supplies a constant undertone of acceptance or rejection, anxiety or security, we still need studies that will show how the child's earliest sense of group differences develops. An excellent setting for such a study is a biracial nursery school.

In investigations conducted in this setting, it appears that the earliest age at which children take any note of race is two and a half.

> One white child of this age, sitting for the first time beside a Negro child, said, "Dirty face." It was an unemotional remark, prompted only by his observing a wholly dark-skinned visage—for the first time in his life.

The purely sensory observation that some skins are white, some colored, seems in many cases to be the first trace of racial awareness. Unless there is the quiver of fear of the strange along with this observation, we may say that race difference at first arouses a sense of curiosity and interest —nothing more. The child's world is full of fascinating distinctions. Facial color is simply one of them. Yet we note that even this first perception of racial difference may arouse associations with "clean" and "dirty."

The situation is more insistent by the age of three and a half or four. The sense of dirt still haunts the children. They have been thoroughly scrubbed at home to eradicate dirt. Why then does it exist so darkly on other children? One colored boy, confused concerning his membership, said to his mother, "Wash my face clean; some of the children don't wash well, especially colored children."

Dr. Goodman's nursery school study shows one particularly revealing result. Negro children are, by and large, "racially aware" earlier than are white children.[6] They tend to be confused, disturbed, and sometimes excited by the problem. Few of them seem to know that they are Negroes. (Even at the age of seven one little Negro girl said to a white playmate, "I'd hate to be colored, wouldn't you?")

The interest and disturbance take many forms. Negro children ask more questions about racial differences; they may fondle the blond hair of a white child; they are often rejective toward Negro dolls. When given a white and Negro doll to play with, they almost uniformly prefer the white doll; many slap the Negro doll and call it dirty or ugly. As a rule, they are more rejective of Negro dolls than are white children. They tend to behave self-consciously when tested for racial awareness.

Especially interesting is Dr. Goodman's observation that Negro children tend to be fully as active as white children at the nursery school age. They are on the whole more sociable —particularly those who are rated as high on "racial awareness." A larger proportion of the Negro children are rated as "leaders" in the group. Although we cannot be certain of the meaning of this finding, it may well come from the fact that Negro children are more highly stimulated by the dawning awareness of race. They may be excited by a challenge they do not fully understand, and may seek reassurance through activity and social contacts for the vague threat that hangs over them. The threat comes not from nursery school, where they are secure enough, but from their first contacts with the world outside and from discussions at home, where their Negro parents cannot fail to talk about the matter.

What is so interesting about this full-scale activity at the nursery school age is its contrast to the adult demeanor of many Negroes who are noted for their poise, passivity, apathy, laziness—or whatever the withdrawing reaction may be called. Earlier we noted that the Negro's conflicts sometimes engender a quietism, a passivity. Many people hold that this "laziness" is a biological trait of Negroes—but in the nursery school we find flatly contradictory evidence.

Why is there, even in the dawning race-awareness of four-year-olds, a nebulous sense of inferiority associated with dark

[6] Mary E. Goodman, *Race Awareness in Young Children.* Cambridge, Massachusetts: Addison-Wesley, 1952. Other studies have confirmed the fact that Negro children are race-aware before white children: e.g., Ruth Horowitz, Racial aspects of self-indentification in nursery school children, *Journal of Psychology,* 1939, 7, 91–99.

skin? A significant part of the answer lies in the similarity between dark pigmentation and dirt. A third of Dr. Goodman's children (both Negro and white) spoke of this matter. Many others no doubt had it in their minds, but did not happen to mention it to the investigators. An additional part of the answer may lie in those subtle forms of learning—not yet fully understood—whereby value-judgments are conveyed to the child. Some parents of white children may, by word or act, have conveyed to their children a vague sense of their rejection of Negroes. If so, the rejection is still only nascent in the four-year-old, for in virtually no case could the investigators find anything they were willing to label "prejudice" at this age level. Some of the Negro parents, too, may have conveyed to their children a sense of the handicaps of people with black skin, even before the children themselves knew their own skin was black.

To sum up: four-year-olds are normally interested, curious, and appreciative of differences in racial groups. A slight sense of white superiority seems to be growing, largely because of the association of white with cleanness—cleanliness being a value learned very early in life. But contrary associations can be, and sometimes are, easily built up.

> One four-year-old boy was taken by train from Boston to San Francisco. He was enchanted by the friendly Negro porter. For fully two years thereafter he fantasied that he was a porter, and complained bitterly that he was not colored so that he could qualify for the position.

Linguistic Tags: Symbols of Power and Rejection

We have discussed the immensely important role of language in building fences for our mental categories and our emotional responses. This factor is so crucial that we return to it again—as it bears on childhood learning.

In Goodman's study it turned out that fully half the nursery school children knew the word "nigger." Few of them understood what the epithet culturally implies. But they knew that the word was potent. It was forbidden, taboo, and always fetched some type of strong response from the teachers. It was therefore a "power word." Not infrequently in a temper tantrum a child would call his teacher (whether white or colored) a "nigger" or a "dirty nigger." The term expressed an emotion—nothing more. Nor did it always express anger—sometimes merely excitement. Children wildly racing around, shrieking at play might, in order to enhance their orgies, yell "nigger, nigger, nigger." As a strong word it seemed fit to vocalize the violent expenditure of energy under way.

One observer gives an interesting example of aggressive verbalization during wartime play:

> Recently, in a waiting room, I watched three youngsters who sat at a table looking at magazines. Suddenly the smaller boy said: "Here's a soldier and an airplane. He's a Jap." The girl said: "No, he's an American." The little fellow said: "Get him, soldier. Get the Jap." The older boy added, "And Hitler too." "And Mussolini," said the girl. "And the Jews," said the big boy. Then the little fellow started a chant, the others joining in: "The Japs, Hitler, Mussolini, and the Jews! The Japs, Hitler, Mussolini, and the Jews!"[7] It is certain that these children had very little understanding of their bellicose chant. The names of their enemies had an expressive but not a denotative significance.

One little boy was agreeing with his mother, who was warning him never to play with "niggers." He said, "No, Mother, I never play with niggers. I only play with white and black children." This child was developing aversion to the term "nigger," without having the slightest idea what the term meant. In other words, the aversion is being set up prior to acquiring a referent.

Other examples could be given of instances where words appear strong and emotionally laden to the child (goy, kike, dago). Only later does he attach the word to a group of people upon whom he can visit the emotions suggested by the word.

We call this process "linguistic precedence in learning." The emotional word has an effect prior to the learning of the referent. Later, the emotional effect becomes attached to the referent.

Before a firm sense of the referent is acquired, the child may go through stages of puzzlement and confusion. This is particularly true because emotional epithets are most likely to be learned when some exciting or traumatic experience is under way.

[7] Mildred M. Eakin, *Getting Acquainted with Jewish Neighbors.* New York: Macmillan, 1944.

Children sometimes confess their perplexity concerning emotional tags. They seem to be groping for proper referents. Trager and Radke, from their work with kindergarten, first- and second-grade children, give several examples:[8]

Johnny (helping Louis pull off his leggings): A man called my father a goy.
Louis: What's a goy?
Johnny: I think everybody around here is a goy. But not me. I'm Jewish.

On being called a "white cracker" by a Negro boy in the class, the teacher said to her class, "I am puzzled by the meaning of two words. Do you know what 'white cracker' means?"
A number of vague answers were received from the children, one being "You're supposed to say it when you're mad."

Even while the child is having difficulty with words, they have a great power over him. To him they are often a type of magic, of verbal realism.

A little boy in the South was playing with the child of the washerwoman. Everything was going smoothly until a neighbor white child called over the fence, "Look out, you'll catch it."
"Catch what?" asked the first white child.
"Catch the black. You'll get colored too."
Just this assertion (reminding the child, no doubt, of expressions such as "catch the measles") frightened him. He deserted his colored companion then and there, and never played with him again.

Children often cry if they are called names. Their self-esteem is wounded by any epithet: naughty, dirty, harum-scarum, nigger, dago, Jap, or what not. To escape this verbal realism of early childhood, they often reassure themselves, when they are a little older, with the self-restorative jingle: Sticks and stones may break my bones, but names can never hurt me. But it takes a few years for them to learn that a name is not a thing-in-itself. Verbal realism may never be fully shaken off. The rigidity of linguistic categories may continue in adult thinking. To some adults "communist" or "Jew" is a dirty word—and a dirty thing—an indissoluble unity, as it may be to a child.

[8] Helen G. Trager and Marian Radke, Early childhood airs its views. *Educational Leadership*, 1947, *5*, 16–23.

The First Stage in Learning Prejudice

Janet, six years of age, was trying hard to integrate her obedience to her mother with her daily social contacts. One day she came running home and asked, "Mother, what is the name of the children I am supposed to hate?"

Janet's wistful question leads us into a theoretical summary of the present chapter.

Janet is stumbling at the threshold of some abstraction. She wishes to form the right category. She intends to oblige her mother by hating the right people when she can find out who they are.

In this situation we suspect the preceding stages in Janet's developmental history:

1. She identifies with the mother, or at least she strongly craves the mother's affection and approval. We may imagine that the home is not "permissive" in atmosphere, but somewhat stern and critical. Janet may have found that she must be on her toes to please her parent. Otherwise she will suffer rejection or punishment. In any event, she has developed a habit of obedience.

2. While she has apparently no strong fear of strangers at the present time, she has learned to be circumspect. Experiences of insecurity with people outside the family circle may be a factor in her present effort to define her circle of loyalties.

3. She undoubtedly has gone through the initial period of curiosity and interest in racial and ethnic differences. She knows now that human beings are clustered into groups—that there are important distinctions if only she can identify them. In the case of Negro and white the visibility factor has helped her. But then she discovered that subtler differences were also important; Jews somehow differed from gentiles; wops from Americans; doctors from salesmen. She is now aware of group differences, though not yet clear concerning all the relevant cues.

4. She has encountered the stage of linguistic precedence in learning. In fact, she is now in this stage. She knows that group X (she knows neither its name nor its identity) is somehow hate-worthy. She already has the emotional meaning but lacks the referential meaning. She seeks now to integrate the proper content with the emotion. She wishes to define her category so as to make her future behavior conform to her

mother's desires. As soon as she has the linguistic tag at her command, she will be like the little Italian boy for whom "Polish" and "bad" were synonymous terms.

Up to the present, Janet's development marks what we might call the first stage of ethnocentric learning. Let us christen it the period of *pregeneralized* learning. This label is not altogether satisfactory, but none better describes the potpourri of factors listed above. The term draws attention primarily to the fact that the child has not yet generalized after the fashion of adults. He does not quite understand what a Jew is, what a Negro is, or what his own attitude toward them should be. He does not know even what *he* is—in any consistent sense. He may think he is an American only when he is playing with his toy soldiers (this type of categorizing was not uncommon in wartime). It is not only in ethnic matters that thoughts are prelogical from an adult point of view. A little girl may not think that her mother is her mother when the latter is working at the office; and may not regard her mother as an officeworker when she is at home tending the family.[9]

The child seems to live his mental life in specific contexts. What exists here and now makes up the only reality. The strange-man-who-knocks-at-the-door is something to be feared. It does not matter if he is a delivery man. The Negro boy at school is dirty. He is not a member of a race.

Now the place of linguistic tags in the course of mental development is crucial. They stand for adult abstractions, for logical generalizations of the sort that mature adults accept. The child learns the tags before he is fully ready to apply them to the adult categories. They prepare him for prejudice. But the process takes time. Only after much fumbling—in the manner of Janet and other children described in this chapter —will the proper categorizing take place.

The Second Stage in Learning Prejudice

As soon as Janet's mother gives a clear answer to Janet, she will in all probability enter a second period of prejudice —one that we may call the period of *total rejection*. Suppose the mother answers, "I told you not to play with Negro children. They are dirty; they have diseases; and they will hurt

---

[9] E. L. Hartley, M. Rosenbaum, and S. Schwartz, Children's perceptions of ethnic group membership. *Journal of Psychology*, 1948, *26*, 387–398.

you. Now don't let me catch you at it." If Janet by now has learned to distinguish Negroes from other groups, even from the dark-skinned Mexican children, or Italians—in other words, if she now has the adult category in mind—she will undoubtedly reject all Negroes, in all circumstances, and with considerable feeling.

Research by Blake and Dennis well illustrates the point.[10] It will be recalled that these investigators studied Southern white children in the fourth and fifth grades (ten- and eleven-year-olds). They asked such questions as, "Which are more musical—Negroes or white people?" "Which are more clean?" —and many questions of a similar type. These children had, by the age of ten, learned to reject the Negro category *totally*. No favorable quality was ascribed to Negroes more often than to whites. In effect, whites had all the virtues; Negroes, none.

While this totalized rejection certainly starts earlier (in many children it will be found by the age of seven or eight), it seems to reach its ethnocentric peak in early puberty. First- and second-grade children often elect to play with, or sit beside, a child of different race or ethnic membership. This friendliness usually disappears in the fifth grade. At that time children choose their own group almost exclusively. Negroes select Negroes, Italians select Italians, and so on.[11]

As children grow older, they normally lose this tendency to total rejection and overgeneralization. Blake and Dennis found that in the 12th grade the white youth ascribed several favorable stereotypes to Negroes. They considered them more musical, more easygoing, better dancers.

Thus, after a period of *total rejection*, a stage of *differentiation* sets in. The prejudices grow less totalized. Escape clauses are written into the attitude in order to make it more rational and more acceptable to the individual. One says, "Some of my best friends are Jews." Or, "I am not prejudiced against Negroes—I always loved my black Mammy." The child who is first learning adult categories of rejection is not able to make such gracious exceptions. It takes him the first six to eight years of his life to learn total rejection, and another six years or so to modify it. The actual adult creed

[10] R. Blake and W. Dennis, The development of stereotypes concerning the Negro. *Journal of Abnormal and Social Psychology*, 1943, *38*, 525–531.

[11] J. H. Criswell, A sociometric study of race cleavage in the classroom. *Archives of Psychology*, 1939, No. 235.

in his culture is complex indeed. It allows for (and in many ways encourages) ethnocentrism. At the same time, one must give lip service to democracy and equality, or at least ascribe some good qualities to the minority group and somehow plausibly justify the remaining disapproval that one expresses. It takes the child well into adolescence to learn the peculiar double-talk appropriate to prejudice in a democracy.

V

The Training and Education of a Child

Emile

JEAN-JACQUES ROUSSEAU

(1762)

Jean-Jacques Rousseau held that man, neither good nor
bad by nature, was corrupted by civilization. He called
for a "charter of childhood," a declaration of children's
rights and a *rapprochement* of child-rearing with nature.
His pedagogical novel *Emile* pictures the newborn child
as unspoiled and education as the provision of latitude
for the child to develop his natural gifts, unhampered by
the corruptive influence of culture. Rousseau's child can
learn from a kind of self-realization which Rousseau set
against the rote learning prevalent in his day. *Emile* has
influenced child-rearing since, from breast-feeding to educational method. In the following passage, Rousseau raises
the greatest pedagogical problem resulting from his own
theory, one that continues to worry modern educators:
How much freedom?

There is only one man who gets his own way—he who can get
it single-handed; therefore freedom, not power, is the greatest
good. That man is truly free who desires what he is able to
perform, and does what he desires. This is my fundamental
maxim. Apply it to childhood, and all the rules of education
spring from it.

Society has enfeebled man, not merely by robbing him
of the right to his own strength, but still more by making his
strength insufficient for his needs. This is why his desires
increase in proportion to his weakness; and this is why the
child is weaker than the man. If a man is strong and a child
is weak it is not because the strength of the one is absolutely
greater than the strength of the other, but because the one
can naturally provide for himself and the other cannot. Thus
the man will have more desires and the child more caprices,
a word which means, I take it, desires which are not true
needs, desires which can only be satisfied with the help of
others.

I have already given the reason for this state of weakness. Parental affection is nature's provision against it; but parental affection may be carried to excess, it may be wanting, or it may be ill applied. Parents who live under our ordinary social conditions bring their child into these conditions too soon. By increasing his needs they do not relieve his weakness; they rather increase it. They further increase it by demanding of him what nature does not demand, by subjecting to their will what little strength he has to further his own wishes, by making slaves of themselves or of him instead of recognizing that mutual dependence which should result from his weakness or their affection.

The wise man can keep his own place; but the child, who does not know what his place is, is unable to keep it. There are a thousand ways out of it, and it is the business of those who have charge of the child to keep him in his place, and this is no easy task. He should be neither beast nor man, but a child. He must feel his weakness, but not suffer through it; he must be dependent, but he must not obey; he must ask, not command. He is only subject to others because of his needs, and because they see better than he what he really needs, what may help or hinder his existence. No one, not even his father, has the right to bid the child do what is of no use to him.

When our natural tendencies have not been interfered with by human prejudice and human institutions, the happiness alike of children and of men consists in the enjoyment of their liberty. But the child's liberty is restricted by his lack of strength. He who does as he likes is happy provided he is self-sufficing; it is so with the man who is living in a state of nature. He who does what he likes is not happy if his desires exceed his strength; it is so with a child in like conditions. Even in a state of nature children only enjoy an imperfect liberty, like that enjoyed by men in social life. Each of us, unable to dispense with the help of others, becomes so far weak and wretched. We were meant to be men, laws and customs thrust us back into infancy. The rich and great, the very kings themselves are but children; they see that we are ready to relieve their misery; this makes them childishly vain, and they are quite proud of the care bestowed on them, a care which they would never get if they were grown men.

These are weighty considerations, and they provide a solution for all the conflicting problems of our social system. There are two kinds of dependence: dependence on things, which is the work of nature; and dependence on men, which is the work of society. Dependence on things, being non-moral, does no injury to liberty and begets no vices; dependence on men, being out of order,[1] gives rise to every kind of vice, and through this master and slave become mutually depraved. If there is any cure for this social evil, it is to be found in the substitution of law for the individual; in arming the general will with a real strength beyond the power of any individual will. If the laws of nations, like the laws of nature, could never be broken by any human power, dependence on men would become dependence on things; all the advantages of a state of nature would be combined with all the advantages of social life in the commonwealth. The liberty which preserves a man from vice would be united with the morality which raises him to virtue.

Keep the child dependent on things only. By this course of education you will have followed the order of nature. Let his unreasonable wishes meet with physical obstacles only, or the punishment which results from his own actions, lessons which will be recalled when the same circumstances occur again. It is enough to prevent him from wrong doing without forbidding him to do wrong. Experience or lack of power should take the place of law. Give him, not what he wants, but what he needs. Let there be no question of obedience for him or tyranny for you. Supply the strength he lacks just so far as is required for freedom, not for power, so that he may receive your services with a sort of shame, and look forward to the time when he may dispense with them and may achieve the honor of self-help.

Nature provides for the child's growth in her own fashion, and this should never be thwarted. Do not make him sit still when he wants to run about, nor run when he wants to be quiet. If we did not spoil our children's wills by our blunders their desires would be free from caprice. Let them run, jump, and shout to their heart's content. All their own activities are instincts of the body for its growth in strength; but you should regard with suspicion those wishes which they cannot carry out for themselves, those which others must carry out for them. Then you must distinguish carefully between natural and artificial needs, between the needs of budding caprice and the needs which spring from the overflowing life just described.

[1] In my *Principles of Political Law* it is proved that no private will can be ordered in the social system.

I have already told you what you ought to do when a child cries for this thing or that. I will only add that as soon as he has words to ask for what he wants and accompanies his demands with tears, either to get his own way quicker or to over-ride a refusal, he should never have his way. If his words were prompted by a real need you should recognize it and satisfy it at once; but to yield to his tears is to encourage him to cry, to teach him to doubt your kindness, and to think that you are influenced more by importunity than your own good-will. If he does not think you kind he will soon think you unkind; if he thinks you weak he will soon become obstinate; what you mean to give must be given at once. Be chary of refusing, but, having refused, do not change your mind.

Above all, beware of teaching the child empty phrases of politeness, which serve as spells to subdue those around him to his will, and to get him what he wants at once. The artificial education of the rich never fails to make them politely imperious, by teaching them the words to use so that no one will dare to resist them. Their children have neither the tone nor the manner of suppliants; they are as haughty or even more haughty in their entreaties than in their commands, as though they were more certain to be obeyed. You see at once that "If you please" means "It pleases me," and "I beg" means "I command." What a fine sort of politeness which only succeeds in changing the meaning of words so that every word is a command! For my own part, I would rather Emile were rude than haughty, that he should say "Do this" as a request, rather than "Please" as a command. What concerns me is his meaning, not his words.

There is such a thing as excessive severity as well as excessive indulgence, and both alike should be avoided. If you let children suffer you risk their health and life; you make them miserable now; if you take too much pains to spare them every kind of uneasiness you are laying up much misery for them in the future; you are making them delicate and oversensitive; you are taking them out of their place among men, a place to which they must sooner or later return, in spite of all your pains. You will say I am falling into the same mistake as those bad fathers whom I blamed for sacrificing the present happiness of their children to a future which may never be theirs.

Not so; for the liberty I give my pupil makes up for the slight hardships to which he is exposed. I see little fellows playing in the snow, stiff and blue with cold, scarcely able to stir a finger. They could go and warm themselves if they chose, but they do not choose; if you forced them to come in they would feel the harshness of constraint a hundredfold more than the sharpness of the cold. Then what becomes of your grievance? Shall I make your child miserable by exposing him to hardships which he is perfectly ready to endure? I secure his present good by leaving him his freedom, and his future good by arming him against the evils he will have to bear. If he had his choice, would he hesitate for a moment between you and me?

Do you think any man can find true happiness elsewhere than in his natural state; and when you try to spare him all suffering, are you not taking him out of his natural state? Indeed I maintain that to enjoy great happiness he must experience slight ills; such is his nature. Too much bodily prosperity corrupts the morals. A man who knew nothing of suffering would be incapable of tenderness toward his fellow-creatures and ignorant of the joys of pity; he would be hard-hearted, unsocial, a very monster among men.

Do you know the surest way to make your child miserable? Let him have everything he wants; for as his wants increase in proportion to the ease with which they are satisfied, you will be compelled, sooner or later, to refuse his demands, and this unlooked-for refusal will hurt him more than the lack of what he wants. He will want your stick first, then your watch, the bird that flies, or the star that shines above him. He will want all he sets eyes on, and unless you were God himself, how could you satisfy him?

Man naturally considers all that he can get as his own. In this sense Hobbes' theory is true to a certain extent: Multiply both our wishes and the means of satisfying them, and each will be master of all. Thus the child, who has only to ask and have, thinks himself the master of the universe; he considers all men as his slaves; and when you are at last compelled to refuse, he takes your refusal as an act of rebellion, for he thinks he has only to command. All the reasons you give him, while he is still too young to reason, are so many pretenses in his eyes; they seem to him only unkindness; the sense of injustice embitters his disposition; he hates every one. Though he has never felt grateful for kindness, he resents all opposition.

How should I suppose that such a child can ever be happy? He is the slave of anger, a prey to the fiercest passions.

Happy! He is a tyrant, at once the basest of slaves and the most wretched of creatures. I have known children brought up like this who expected you to knock the house down, to give them the weather-cock on the steeple, to stop a regiment on the march so that they might listen to the band; when they could not get their way they screamed and cried and would pay no attention to any one. In vain everybody strove to please them; as their desires were stimulated by the ease with which they got their own way, they set their hearts on impossibilities, and found themselves face to face with opposition and difficulty, pain and grief. Scolding, sulking, or in a rage, they wept and cried all day. Were they really so greatly favored? Weakness, combined with love of power, produces nothing but folly and suffering. One spoiled child beats the table; another whips the sea. They may beat and whip long enough before they find contentment.

If their childhood is made wretched by these notions of power and tyranny, what of their manhood, when their relations with their fellow-men begin to grow and multiply? They are used to find everything give way to them; what a painful surprise to enter society and meet with opposition on every side, to be crushed beneath the weight of a universe which they expected to move at will. Their insolent manners, their childish vanity, only draw down upon them mortification, scorn, and mockery; they swallow insults like water; sharp experience soon teaches them that they have realized neither their position nor their strength. As they cannot do everything, they think they can do nothing. They are daunted by unexpected obstacles, degraded by the scorn of men; they become base, cowardly, and deceitful, and fall as far below their true level as they formerly soared above it.

Let us come back to the primitive law. Nature has made children helpless and in need of affection; did she make them to be obeyed and feared? Has she given them an imposing manner, a stern eye, a loud and threatening voice with which to make themselves feared? I understand how the roaring of the lion strikes terror into the other beasts, so that they tremble when they behold his terrible mane, but of all unseemly, hateful, and ridiculous sights, was there ever anything like a body of statesmen in their robes of office with their chief at their head bowing down before a swaddled babe, addressing him in pompous phrases, while he cries and slavers in reply?

If we consider childhood itself, is there anything so weak and wretched as a child, anything so utterly at the mercy of those about it, so dependent on their pity, their care, and their affection? Does it not seem as if his gentle face and touching appearance were intended to interest every one on behalf of his weakness and to make them eager to help him? And what is there more offensive, more unsuitable, than the sight of a sulky or imperious child, who commands those about him, and impudently assumes the tones of a master toward those without whom he would perish?

On the other hand, do you not see how children are fettered by the weakness of infancy? Do you not see how cruel it is to increase this servitude by obedience to our caprices, by depriving them of such liberty as they have? a liberty which they can scarcely abuse, a liberty the loss of which will do so little good to them or us. If there is nothing more ridiculous than a haughty child, there is nothing that claims our pity like a timid child. With the age of reason the child becomes the slave of the community; then why forestall this by slavery in the home? Let this brief hour of life be free from a yoke which nature has not laid upon it; leave the child the use of his natural liberty, which, for a time at least, secures him from the vices of the slave. Bring me those harsh masters, and those fathers who are the slaves of their children, bring them both with their frivolous objections, and before they boast of their own methods let them for once learn the method of nature.

A Treatise on Parents and Children

GEORGE BERNARD SHAW

(1914)

G. B. Shaw was active in the theater and literature for almost sixty years, during which he delivered himself of opinions on all subjects with frankness and facility. Much of Shaw's nearly legendary acerbity was poured out in the prefaces to his plays. "A Treatise on Parents and Children," the preface to *Misalliance,* maintains that education is thrust upon children in order to curb them for the peace, comfort and self-satisfaction of their parents. With Whitehead, he believed that "learning is a passion in children" and that the best teachers are those who can exploit that passion for fact and accumulation, turning it toward knowledge rather than possessions. Like Buber, Shaw was convinced that the best education is in effect religious, since secular education teaches that the only reason for doing well is to avoid punishment. A good education, like religion, imparts a code of honor and a conscience which is, throughout one's life, again and again confirmed and revised.

The Child Is Father to the Man

Is he? Then in the name of common sense why do we always treat children on the assumption that the man is father to the child? Oh, these fathers! And we are not content with fathers: we must have godfathers, forgetting that the child is godfather to the man. Has it ever struck you as curious that in a country where the first article of belief is that every child is born with a godfather whom we all call "our father which art in heaven," two very limited individual mortals should be allowed to appear at its baptism and explain that they are its godparents, and that they will look after its salvation until it is no longer a child. I had a godmother who made herself responsible in this way for me. She presented me with a Bible with a gilt clasp and edges, larger than the Bibles similarly presented to my sisters, because my sex entitled me to a heavier article. I must have seen that lady at least four times in the twenty years following. She never alluded to my salvation in any way. People occasionally ask me to act as godfather to their children with a levity which convinces me that they have not the faintest notion that it involves anything more than calling the helpless child George Bernard without regard to the possibility that it may grow up in the liveliest abhorrence of my notions.

A person with a turn for logic might argue that if God is the Father of all men, and if the child is father to the man, it follows that the true representative of God at the christening is the child itself. But such posers are unpopular, because they imply that our little customs, or, as we often call them, our religion, mean something, or must originally have meant something, and that we understand and believe that something.

However, my business is not to make confusion worse confounded, but to clear it up. Only, it is as well to begin by a sample of current thought and practice which shows that on the subject of children we are very deeply confused. On the whole, whatever our theory or no theory may be, our practice is to treat the child as the property of its immediate physical parents, and to allow them to do what they like with it as far as it will let them. It has no rights and no liberties: in short, its condition is that which adults recognize as the most miserable and dangerous politically possible for themselves: namely, the condition of slavery. For its alleviation we trust to the natural affection of the parties, and to public opinion. A father cannot for his own credit let his son go in rags. Also, in a very large section of the population, parents finally become dependent on their children. Thus there are checks on child slavery which do not exist, or are less powerful, in the case of manual and industrial slavery. Sensationally bad cases fall into two classes, which are really the same class: namely, the children whose parents are excessively addicted to the sensual luxury of petting children, and the children whose parents are excessively addicted to the sensual luxury of physically torturing them. There is a Society for the Prevention of Cruelty to Children which has effectually made an end of our belief that mothers are any more to be trusted than stepmothers, or fathers than slave-drivers. And there is a growing body of law designed to prevent parents from using their children ruthlessly to make money for the household. Such legislation has always been furiously resisted by the parents, even when the horrors of factory slavery were at their worst; and the extension of such legislation at present would be impossible if it were not that the parents affected by it cannot control a majority of votes in Parliament. In domestic life a great deal of service is done by children, the girls acting as nursemaids and general servants, and the lads as errand boys. In the country both boys and girls do a substantial share of farm labor. This is why it is necessary to coerce poor parents to send their children to school, though in the relatively small class which keeps plenty of servants it is impossible to induce parents to keep their children at home instead of paying schoolmasters to take them off their hands.

It appears then that the bond of affection between parents and children does not save children from the slavery that denial of rights involves in adult political relations. It sometimes intensifies it, sometimes mitigates it; but on the whole children and parents confront one another as two classes in which all the political power is on one side; and the results are not at all unlike what they would be if there were no immediate consanguinity between them, and one were white and the other black, or one enfranchised and the other disenfranchised, or one ranked as gentle and the other simple. Not that Nature counts for nothing in the case and political rights for everything. But a denial of political rights, and the resultant delivery of one class into the mastery of another, affects their relations so extensively and profoundly that it is impossible to ascertain what the real natural relations of the two classes are until this political relation is abolished.

What Is a Child?

An experiment. A fresh attempt to produce the just man made perfect: that is, to make humanity divine. And you will vitiate the experiment if you make the slightest attempt to abort it into some fancy figure of your own: for example, your notion of a good man or a womanly woman. If you treat it as a little wild beast to be tamed, or as a pet to be played with, or even as a means to save you trouble and to make money for you (and these are our commonest ways), it may fight its way through in spite of you and save its soul alive; for all its instincts will resist you, and possibly be strengthened in the resistance; but if you begin with its own holiest aspirations, and suborn them for your own purposes, then there is hardly any limit to the mischief you may do. Swear at a child, throw your boots at it, send it flying from the room with a cuff or a kick; and the experience will be as instructive to the child as a difficulty with a short-tempered dog or a bull. Francis Place tells us that his father always struck his children when he found one within his reach. The effect on the young Places seems to have been simply to make them keep out of their father's way, which was no doubt what he desired, as far as he desired anything at all. Francis records the habit without bitterness, having reason to thank his stars that his father respected the inside of his head whilst cuffing the outside of it; and this made it easy for Francis to do yeoman's service to his country as that rare and admirable thing, a Freethinker: the only sort of thinker, I may remark, whose thoughts, and consequently whose religious convictions, command any respect.

Now Mr. Place, senior, would be described by many as a bad father; and I do not contend that he was a conspicuously good one. But as compared with the conventional good father who deliberately imposes himself on his son as a god; who takes advantage of childish credulity and parent worship to persuade his son that what he approves of is right and what he disapproves of is wrong; who imposes a corresponding conduct on the child by a system of prohibitions and penalties, rewards and eulogies, for which he claims divine sanction: compared to this sort of abortionist and monster maker, I say, Place appears almost as a Providence. Not that it is possible to live with children any more than with grown-up people without imposing rules of conduct on them. There is a point at which every person with human nerves has to say to a child "Stop that noise." But suppose the child asks why! There are various answers in use. The simplest: "Because it irritates me," may fail; for it may strike the child as being rather amusing to irritate you; also the child, having comparatively no nerves, may be unable to conceive your meaning vividly enough. In any case it may want to make a noise more than to spare your feelings. You may therefore have to explain that the effect of the irritation will be that you will do something unpleasant if the noise continues. The something unpleasant may be only a look of suffering to rouse the child's affectionate sympathy (if it has any), or it may run to forcible expulsion from the room with plenty of unneces-

sary violence; but the principle is the same: there are no
false pretenses involved: the child learns in a straightforward
way that it does not pay to be inconsiderate. Also, perhaps,
that Mamma, who made the child learn the Sermon on the
Mount, is not really a Christian. . . .

The Manufacture of Monsters

This industry is by no means peculiar to China. The Chinese
(they say) make physical monsters. We revile them for it and
proceed to make moral monsters of our own children. The
most excusable parents are those who try to correct their own
faults in their offspring. The parent who says to his child:
"I am one of the successes of the Almighty: therefore imitate
me in every particular or I will have the skin off your back"
(a quite common attitude) is a much more absurd figure
than the man who, with a pipe in his mouth, thrashes his boy
for smoking. If you must hold yourself up to your children
as an object lesson (which is not at all necessary), hold
yourself up as a warning and not as an example. But you
had much better let the child's character alone. If you once
allow yourself to regard a child as so much material for you
to manufacture into any shape that happens to suit your fancy
you are defeating the experiment of the Life Force. You are
assuming that the child does not know its own business, and
that you do. In this you are sure to be wrong: the child feels
the drive of the Life Force (often called the Will of God);
and you cannot feel it for him. Handel's parents no doubt
thought they knew better than their child when they tried to
prevent his becoming a musician. They would have been
equally wrong and equally unsuccessful if they had tried to
prevent the child becoming a great rascal had its genius lain
in that direction. Handel would have been Handel, and Napo-
leon and Peter of Russia *them*selves in spite of all the parents in creation, because, as often happens, they were stronger
than their parents. But this does not happen always. Most
children can be, and many are, hopelessly warped and wasted
by parents who are ignorant and silly enough to suppose that
they know what a human being ought to be, and who stick
at nothing in their determination to force their children into
their molds. Every child has a right to its own bent. It has a
right to be a Plymouth Brother though its parents be con-

vinced atheists. It has a right to dislike its mother or father or sister or brother or uncle or aunt if they are antipathetic to it. It has a right to find its own way and go its own way, whether that way seems wise or foolish to others, exactly as an adult has. It has a right to privacy as to its own doings and its own affairs as much as if it were its own father. . . .

Childhood as a State of Sin

Unfortunately all this nonsense tends to accumulate as we become more sympathetic. In many families it is still the custom to treat childhood frankly as a state of sin, and impudently proclaim the monstrous principle that little children should be seen and not heard, and to enforce a set of prison rules designed solely to make cohabitation with children as convenient as possible for adults without the smallest regard for the interests, either remote or immediate, of the children. This system tends to produce a tough, rather brutal, stupid, unscrupulous class, with a fixed idea that all enjoyment consists in undetected sinning; and in certain phases of civilization people of this kind are apt to get the upper hand of more amiable and conscientious races and classes. They have the ferocity of a chained dog, and are proud of it. But the end of it is that they are always in chains, even at the height of their military or political success: they win everything on condition that they are afraid to enjoy it. Their civilizations rest on intimidation, which is so necessary to them that when they cannot find anybody brave enough to intimidate them they intimidate themselves and live in a continual moral and political panic. In the end they get found out and bullied. But that is not the point that concerns us here, which is, that they are in some respects better brought up than the children of sentimental people who are always anxious and miserable about their duty to their children, and who end by neither making their children happy nor having a tolerable life for themselves. A selfish tyrant you know where you stand, and he (or she) at least does not confuse your affections; but a conscientious and kindly meddler may literally worry you out of your senses. It is fortunate that only very few parents are capable of doing what they conceive their duty continuously or even at all, and that still fewer are tough enough to ride roughshod over their children at home. . . .

What We Do Not Teach, and Why

To my mind, a glance at the subjects now taught in schools ought to convince any reasonable person that the object of the lessons is to keep children out of mischief, and not to qualify them for their part in life as responsible citizens of a free State. It is not possible to maintain freedom in any State, no matter how perfect its original constitution, unless its publicly active citizens know a good deal of constitutional history, law, and political science, with its basis of economics. If as much pains had been taken a century ago to make us all understand Ricardo's law of rent as to learn our catechisms, the face of the world would have been changed for the better. But for that very reason the greatest care is taken to keep such beneficially subversive knowledge from us, with the result that in public life we are either place-hunters, anarchists, or sheep shepherded by wolves.

But it will be observed that these are highly controversial subjects. Now no controversial subject can be taught dogmatically. He who knows only the official side of a controversy knows less than nothing of its nature. The abler a schoolmaster is, the more dangerous he is to his pupils unless they have the fullest opportunity of hearing another equally able person do his utmost to shake his authority and convict him of error.

At present such teaching is very unpopular. It does not exist in schools; but every adult who derives his knowledge of public affairs from the newspapers can take in, at the cost of an extra half-penny, two papers of opposite politics. Yet the ordinary man so dislikes having his mind unsettled, as he calls it, that he angrily refuses to allow a paper which dissents from his views to be brought into his house. Even at his club he resents seeing it, and excludes it if it happens to run counter to the opinions of all the members. The result is that his opinions are not worth considering. A churchman who never reads The Freethinker very soon has no more real religion than the atheist who never reads The Church Times. The attitude is the same in both cases: they want to hear nothing good of their enemies; consequently they remain enemies and suffer from bad blood all their lives; whereas men who know their opponents and understand their case, quite commonly respect and like them, and always learn something from them.

Here, again, as at so many points, we come up against the abuse of schools to keep people in ignorance and error, so that they may be incapable of successful revolt against their industrial slavery. The most important simple fundamental economic truth to impress on a child in complicated civilizations like ours is the truth that whoever consumes goods or services without producing by personal effort the equivalent of what he or she consumes, inflicts on the community precisely the same injury that a thief produces, and would, in any honest State, be treated as a thief, however full his or her pockets might be of money made by other people. The nation that first teaches its children that truth, instead of flogging them if they discover it for themselves, may have to fight all the slaves of all the other nations to begin with; but it will beat them as easily as an unburdened man with his hands free and with all his energies in full play can beat an invalid who has to carry another invalid on his back.

This, however, is not an evil produced by the denial of children's rights, nor is it inherent in the nature of schools. I mention it only because it would be folly to call for a reform of our schools without taking account of the corrupt resistance which awaits the reformer.

A word must also be said about the opposition to reform of the vested interest of the classical and coercive schoolmaster. He, poor wretch, has no other means of livelihood; and reform would leave him as a workman is now left when he is superseded by a machine. He had therefore better do what he can to get the workman compensated, so as to make the public familiar with the idea of compensation before his own turn comes. . . .

Children's Rights and Duties

Now let us ask what are a child's rights, and what are the rights of society over the child. Its rights, being clearly those of any other human being, are summed up in the right to live: that is, to have all the conclusive arguments that prove that it would be better dead, that it is a child of wrath, that the population is already excessive, that the pains of life are greater than its pleasures, that its sacrifice in a hospital or laboratory experiment might save millions of lives, etc., etc., etc., put out of the question, and its existence accepted as necessary and sacred, all theories to the contrary notwithstanding, whether by Calvin or Schopenhauer or Pasteur or the nearest person with a taste for infanticide. And this right to live includes, and in fact is, the right to be what the child likes and can, to do what it likes and can, to make what it likes and can, to think what it likes and can, to smash what it dislikes and can, and generally to behave in an altogether unaccountable manner within the limits imposed by the similar rights of its neighbors. And the rights of society over it clearly extend to requiring it to qualify itself to live in society without wasting other people's time: that is, it must know the rules of the road, be able to read placards and proclamations, fill voting papers, compose and send letters and telegrams, purchase food and clothing and railway tickets for itself, count money and give and take change, and, generally, know how many beans make five. It must know some law, were it only a simple set of command-ments, some political economy, agriculture enough to shut the gates of fields with cattle in them and not to trample on grow-ing crops, sanitation enough not to defile its haunts, and reli-gion enough to have some idea of why it is allowed its rights and why it must respect the rights of others. And the rest of its education must consist of anything else it can pick up; for beyond this society cannot go with any certainty, and indeed can only go this far rather apologetically and provisionally, as doing the best it can on very uncertain ground. . . .

The New Laziness

The child of the future, then, if there is to be any future but one of decay, will work more or less for its living from an early age; and in doing so it will not shock anyone, pro-vided there be no longer any reason to associate the concep-tion of children working for their living with infants toiling in a factory for ten hours a day or boys drudging from nine to six under gas lamps in underground city offices. Lads and lasses in their teens will probably be able to produce as much as the most expensive person now costs in his own person (it is retinue that eats up the big income) without working too hard or too long for quite as much happiness as they can enjoy. The question to be balanced then will be, not how soon people should be put to work, but how soon they should be released from any obligation of the kind. A life's work is like a day's work: it can begin early and leave off early or begin late and leave off late, or, as with us, begin too early and never leave off at all, obviously the worst of all possible plans. In any event we must finally reckon work, not as the curse our schools and prisons and capitalist profit factories make it seem today, but as a prime necessity of a tolerable existence. And if we cannot devise fresh wants as fast as we develop the means of supplying them, there will come a scarcity of the needed, cut-and-dried, appointed work that is always ready to everybody's hand. It may have to be shared out among people all of whom want more of it. And then a new sort of laziness will become the bugbear of society: the laziness that refuses to face the mental toil and adventure of making work by inventing new ideas or extending the domain of knowledge, and insists on a readymade routine. It may come to forcing people to retire before they are willing to make way for younger ones: that is, to driving all persons of a certain age out of industry, leaving them to find something experimental to occupy them on pain of perpetual holiday. Men will then try to spend twenty thousand a year for the sake of having to earn it. Instead of being what we are now, the cheapest and nastiest of the animals, we shall be the costliest, most fastidious, and best bred. In short, there is no end to the astonishing things that may happen when the curse of Adam becomes first a blessing and then an incurable habit. And in that day we must not grudge children their share of it. . . .

The Rewards and Risks of Knowledge

In a word, we have no right to insist on educating a child; for its education can end only with its life and will not even then be complete. Compulsory completion of education is the last folly of a rotten and desperate civilization. It is the rattle in its throat before dissolution. All we can fairly do is to prescribe certain definite acquirements and accomplishments as qualifications for certain employments; and to secure them, not by the ridiculous method of inflicting injuries on the persons who have not yet mastered them, but by attaching certain privileges (not pecuniary) to the employments.

Most acquirements carry their own privileges with them. Thus a baby has to be pretty closely guarded and imprisoned because it cannot take care of itself. It has even to be carried about (the most complete conceivable infringement of its liberty) until it can walk. But nobody goes on carrying children after they can walk lest they should walk into mischief, though Arab boys make their sisters carry them, as our own spoiled children sometimes make their nurses, out of mere laziness, because sisters in the East and nurses in the West are kept in servitude. But in a society of equals (the only reasonable and permanently possible sort of society) children are in much greater danger of acquiring bandy legs through being left to walk before they are strong enough than of being carried when they are well able to walk. Anyhow, freedom of movement in a nursery is the reward of learning to walk; and in precisely the same way freedom of movement in a city is the reward of learning how to read public notices, and to count and use money. The consequences are of course much larger than the mere ability to read the name of a street or the number of a railway platform and the destination of a train. When you enable a child to read these, you also enable it to read this preface, to the utter destruction, you may quite possibly think, of its morals and docility. You also expose it to the danger of being run over by taxicabs and trains. The moral and physical risks of education are enormous: every new power a child acquires, from speaking, walking, and coordinating its vision, to conquering continents and founding religions, opens up immense new possibilities of mischief. Teach a child to write and you teach it how to forge: teach it to speak and you teach it how to lie: teach it to walk and you teach it how to kick its mother to death.

The great problem of slavery for those whose aim is to maintain it is the problem of reconciling the efficiency of the slave with the helplessness that keeps him in servitude; and this problem is fortunately not completely soluble; for it is not in fact found possible for a duke to treat his solicitor or his doctor as he treats his laborers, though they are all equally his slaves: the laborer being in fact less dependent on his favor than the professional man. Hence it is that men come to resent, of all things, protection, because it so often means restriction of their liberty lest they should make a bad use of it. If there are dangerous precipices about, it is much easier and cheaper to forbid people to walk near the edge than to put up an effective fence: that is why both legislators and parents and the paid deputies of parents are always inhibiting and prohibiting and punishing and scolding and laming and cramping and delaying progress and growth instead of making the dangerous places as safe as possible and then boldly taking and allowing others to take the irreducible minimum of risk.

English Physical Hardihood and Spiritual Cowardice

It is easier to convert most people to the need for allowing their children to run physical risks than moral ones. I can remember a relative of mine who, when I was a small child, unused to horses and very much afraid of them, insisted on putting me on a rather rambunctious pony with little spurs on my heels (knowing that in my agitation I would use them unconsciously), and being enormously amused at my terrors. Yet when that same lady discovered that I had found a copy of The Arabian Nights and was devouring it with avidity, she was horrified, and hid it away from me lest it should break my soul as the pony might have broken my neck. This way of producing hardy bodies and timid souls is so common in country houses that you may spend hours in them listening to stories of broken collar bones, broken backs, and broken necks without coming upon a single spiritual adventure or daring thought.

But whether the risks to which liberty exposes us are moral or physical our right to liberty involves the right to run them. A man who is not free to risk his neck as an aviator or his soul as a heretic is not free at all; and the right to liberty begins, not at the age of 21 years but of 21 seconds. . . .

The Experiment Experimenting

And now all the modern schoolmaster abortionists will rise up beaming, and say, "We quite agree. We regard every child in our school as a subject for experiment. We are always experimenting with them. We challenge the experimental test for our system. We are continually guided by our experience in our great work of molding the character of our future citizens, etc., etc., etc." I am sorry to seem irreconcilable; but it is the Life Force that has to make the experiment and not the schoolmaster; and the Life Force for the child's purpose is in the child and not in the schoolmaster. The schoolmaster is another experiment; and a laboratory in which all the experiments begin experimenting on one another would not produce intelligible results. I admit, however, that if my schoolmasters had treated me as an experiment of the Life Force: that is, if they had set me free to do as I liked subject only to my political rights and theirs, they could not have watched the experiment very long, because the first result would have been a rapid movement on my part in the direction of the door, and my disappearance therethrough.

It may be worth inquiring where I should have gone to. I should say that practically every time I should have gone to a much more educational place. I should have gone into the country, or into the sea, or into the National Gallery, or to hear a band if there was one, or to any library where there were no schoolbooks. I should have read very dry and difficult books: for example, though nothing would have induced me to read the budget of stupid party lies that served as a textbook of history in school, I remember reading Robertson's Charles V. and his history of Scotland from end to end most laboriously. Once, stung by the airs of a schoolfellow who alleged that he had read Locke On The Human Understanding, I attempted to read the Bible straight through, and actually got to the Pauline Epistles before I broke down in disgust at what seemed to me their inveterate crookedness of mind. If there had been a school where children were really free, I should have had to be driven out of it for the sake of my health by the teachers; for the children to whom a literary education can be of any use are insatiable: they will read and study far more than is good for them. In fact the real difficulty is to prevent them from wasting their time by reading for the sake of reading and studying for the sake of studying, instead of taking some trouble to find out what they really like and are capable of doing some good at. Some silly person will probably interrupt me here with the remark that many children have no appetite for a literary education at all, and would never open a book if they were not forced to. I have known many such persons who have been forced to the point of obtaining University degrees. And for all the effect their literary exercises has left on them they might just as well have been put on the treadmill. In fact they are actually less literate than the treadmill would have left them; for they might by chance have picked up and dipped into a volume of Shakespeare or a translation of Homer if they had not been driven to loathe every famous name in literature. I should probably

know as much Latin as French, if Latin had not been made
the excuse for my school imprisonment and degradation.

Why We Loathe Learning and Love Sport

If we are to discuss the importance of art, learning, and
intellectual culture, the first thing we have to recognize is
that we have very little of them at present; and that this little
has not been produced by compulsory education: nay, that
the scarcity is unnatural and has been produced by the violent
exclusion of art and artists from schools. On the other hand
we have quite a considerable degree of bodily culture: indeed
there is a continual outcry against the sacrifice of mental accomplishments to athletics. In other words a sacrifice of the
professed object of compulsory education to the real object
of voluntary education. It is assumed that this means that
people prefer bodily to mental culture; but may it not mean
that they prefer liberty and satisfaction to coercion and priva-
tion? Why is it that people who have been taught Shakespeare
as a school subject loathe his plays and cannot by any means
be persuaded ever to open his works after they escape from
school, whereas there is still, 300 years after his death, a wide
and steady sale for his works to people who read his plays as
plays, and not as task work? If Shakespeare, or for that matter, Newton and Leibnitz, are allowed to find their readers and
students they will find them. If their works are annotated
and paraphrased by dullards, and the annotations and para-
phrases forced on all young people by imprisonment and
flogging and scolding, there will not be a single man of letters
or higher mathematician the more in the country: on the contrary there will be less, as so many potential lovers of literature and mathematics will have been incurably prejudiced
against them. Everyone who is conversant with the class in
which child imprisonment and compulsory schooling is carried out to the final extremity of the university degree knows
that its scholastic culture is a sham; that it knows little about
literature or art and a great deal about point-to-point races;
and that the village cobbler, who has never read a page of
Plato, and is admittedly a dangerously ignorant man politically,
is nevertheless a Socrates compared to the classically educated
gentlemen who discuss politics in country houses at election
time (and at no other time) after their day's earnest and skill-

ful shooting. Think of the years and years of weary torment the women of the piano-possessing class have been forced to spend over the keyboard, fingering scales. How many of them could be bribed to attend a pianoforte recital by a great player, though they will rise from sick beds rather than miss Ascot or Goodwood?

Another familiar fact that teaches the same lesson is that many women who have voluntarily attained a high degree of culture cannot add up their own housekeeping books, though their education in simple arithmetic was compulsory, whereas their higher education has been wholly voluntary. Everywhere we find the same result. The imprisonment, the beating, the taming and laming, the breaking of young spirits, the arrest of development, the atrophy of all inhibitive power except the power of fear, are real: the education is sham. Those who have been taught most know least.

Wanted: a Child's Magna Charta

Whether we shall presently be discussing a Juvenile Magna Charta or Declaration of Rights by way of including children in the Constitution is a question on which I leave others to speculate. But if it could once be established that a child has an adult's Right of Egress from uncomfortable places and unpleasant company, and there were children's lawyers to sue pedagogues and others for assault and imprisonment, there would be an amazing change in the behavior of schoolmasters, the quality of school books, and the amenities of school life. That Consciousness of Consent which, even in its present delusive form, has enabled Democracy to oust tyrannical systems in spite of all its vulgarities and stupidities and rancors and ineptitudes and ignorances, would operate as powerfully among children as it does now among grown-ups. No doubt the pedagogue would promptly turn demogogue, and woo his scholars by all the arts of demagogy; but none of these arts can easily be so dishonorable or mischievous as the art of caning. And, after all, if larger liberties are attached to the acquisition of knowledge, and the child finds that it can no more go to the seaside without a knowledge of the multiplication and pence tables than it can be an astronomer without mathematics, it will learn the multiplication table, which is more than it always does at present, in spite of all the canings and keepings in.

The Pursuit of Learning

When the Pursuit of Learning comes to mean the pursuit of learning by the child instead of the pursuit of the child by Learning, cane in hand, the danger will be precocity of the intellect, which is just as undesirable as precocity of the emotions. We still have a silly habit of talking and thinking as if intellect were a mechanical process and not a passion; and in spite of the German tutors who confess openly that three out of every five of the young men they coach for examinations are lamed for life thereby; in spite of Dickens and his picture of little Paul Dombey dying of lessons, we persist in heaping on growing children and adolescent youths and maidens tasks Pythagoras would have declined out of common regard for his own health and common modesty as to his own capacity. And this overwork is not all the effect of compulsion; for the average schoolmaster does not compel his scholars to learn: he only scolds and punishes them if they do not, which is quite a different thing, the net effect being that the school prisoners need not learn unless they like. Nay, it is sometimes remarked that the school dunce—meaning the one who does not like—often turns out well afterward, as if idleness were a sign of ability and character. A much more sensible explanation is that the so-called dunces are not exhausted before they begin the serious business of life. It is said that boys will be boys; and one can only add one wishes they would. Boys really want to be manly, and are unfortunately encouraged thoughtlessly in this very dangerous and overstraining aspiration. All the people who have really worked (Herbert Spencer for instance) warn us against work as earnestly as some people warn us against drink. When learning is placed on the voluntary footing of sport, the teacher will find himself saying every day "Run away and play: you have worked as much as is good for you." Trying to make children leave school will be like trying to make them go to bed; and it will be necessary to surprise them with the idea that teaching is work, and that the teacher is tired and must go play or rest or eat: possibilities always concealed by that infamous humbug the current schoolmaster, who achieves a spurious divinity and a witch doctor's authority by persuading children that he is not human, just as ladies persuade them that they have no legs.

Children's Rights and Parents' Wrongs

A very distinguished man once assured a mother of my acquaintance that she would never know what it meant to be hurt until she was hurt through her children. Children are extremely cruel without intending it; and in ninety-nine cases out of a hundred the reason is that they do not conceive their elders as having any human feelings. Serve the elders right, perhaps, for posing as superhuman! The penalty of the impostor is not that he is found out (he very seldom is) but that he is taken for what he pretends to be, and treated as such. And to be treated as anything but what you really are may seem pleasant to the imagination when the treatment is above your merits; but in actual experience it is often quite the reverse. When I was a very small boy, my romantic imagination, stimulated by early doses of fiction, led me to brag to a still smaller boy so outrageously that he, being a simple soul, really believed me to be an invincible hero. I cannot remember whether this pleased me much; but I do remember very distinctly that one day this admirer of mine, who had a pet goat, found the animal in the hands of a larger boy than either of us, who mocked him and refused to restore the animal to his rightful owner. Whereupon, naturally, he came weeping to me, and demanded that I should rescue the goat and annihilate the aggressor. My terror was beyond description: fortunately for me, it imparted such a ghastliness to my voice and aspect as I, under the eye of my poor little dupe, advanced on the enemy with that hideous extremity of cowardice which is called the courage of despair, and said "You let go that goat," that he abandoned his prey and fled, to my unforgettable, unspeakable relief. I have never since exaggerated my prowess in bodily combat.

Now what happened to me in the adventure of the goat happens very often to parents, and would happen to schoolmasters if the prison door of the school did not shut out the trials of life. I remember once, at school, the resident head master was brought down to earth by the sudden illness of his wife. In the confusion that ensued it became necessary to leave one of the schoolrooms without a master. I was in the class that occupied that schoolroom. To have sent us home would have been to break the fundamental bargain with our parents by which the school was bound to keep us out of their way for half the day at all hazards. Therefore an appeal had to be made to our better feelings: that is, to our common humanity, not to make a noise. But the head master had never admitted any common humanity with us. We had been carefully broken in to regard him as a being quite aloof from and above us: one not subject to error or suffering or death or illness or mortality. Consequently sympathy was impossible; and if the unfortunate lady did not perish, it was because, as I now comfort myself with guessing, she was too much pre-occupied with her own pains, and possibly making too much noise herself, to be conscious of the pandemonium downstairs.

A great deal of the fiendishness of schoolboys and the cruelty of children to their elders is produced just in this way. Elders cannot be superhuman beings and suffering fellow-creatures at the same time. If you pose as a little god, you must pose for better or worse.

How Little We Know about Our Parents

The relation between parent and child has cruel moments for the parent even when money is no object, and the material worries are delegated to servants and school teachers. The child and the parent are strangers to one another necessarily, because their ages must differ widely. Read Goethe's autobiography; and note that though he was happy in his parents and had exceptional powers of observation, divination, and story-telling, he knew less about his father and mother than about most of the other people he mentions. I myself was never on bad terms with my mother: we lived together until I was forty-two years old, absolutely without the smallest friction of any kind; yet when her death set me thinking curiously about our relations, I realized that I knew very little about her. Introduce me to a strange woman who was a child when I was a child, a girl when I was a boy, an adolescent when I was an adolescent; and if we take naturally to one another I will know more of her and she of me at the end of forty days (I had almost said of forty minutes) than I knew of my mother at the end of forty years. A contemporary stranger is a novelty and an enigma, also a possibility; but a mother is like a broomstick or like the sun in the heavens, it does not matter which as far as one's knowledge of her is concerned: the broomstick

is there and the sun is there; and whether the child is beaten by
it or warmed and enlightened by it, it accepts it as a fact in
nature, and does not conceive it as having had youth, passions, and weaknesses, or as still growing, yearning, suffering,
and learning. If I meet a widow I may ask her all about her
marriage; but what son ever dreams of asking his mother
about her marriage, or could endure to hear of it without
violently breaking off the old sacred relationship between
them, and ceasing to be her child or anything more to her than
the first man in the street might be?

Yet though in this sense the child cannot realize its parent's
humanity, the parent can realize the child's; for the parents
with their experience of life have none of the illusions about
the child that the child has about the parents; and the consequence is that the child can hurt its parents' feelings much
more than its parents can hurt the child's, because the child,
even when there has been none of the deliberate hypocrisy
by which children are taken advantage of by their elders, cannot conceive the parent as a fellow-creature, whilst the parents
know very well that the children are only themselves over
again. The child cannot conceive that its blame or contempt
or want of interest could possibly hurt its parent, and therefore expresses them all with an indifference which has given
rise to the term *enfant terrible* (a tragic term in spite of the
jests connected with it); whilst the parent can suffer from
such slights and reproaches more from a child than from anyone else, even when the child is not beloved, because the child
is so unmistakably sincere in them. . . .

Art Teaching

By art teaching I hasten to say that I do not mean giving
children lessons in freehand drawing and perspective. I am
simply calling attention to the fact that fine art is the only
teacher except torture. I have already pointed out that nobody,
except under threat of torture, can read a school book. The
reason is that a school book is not a work of art. Similarly,
you cannot listen to a lesson or a sermon unless the teacher
or the preacher is an artist. You cannot read the Bible if
you have no sense of literary art. The reason why the continental European is, to the Englishman or American, so surprisingly ignorant of the Bible, is that the authorized English

version is a great work of literary art, and the continental versions are comparatively artless. To read a dull book; to listen to a tedious play or prosy sermon or lecture; to stare at uninteresting pictures or ugly buildings: nothing, short of disease, is more dreadful than this. The violence done to our souls by it leaves injuries and produces subtle maladies which have never been properly studied by psychopathologists. Yet we are so inured to it in school, where practically all the teachers are bores trying to do the work of artists, and all the books artless, that we acquire a truly frightful power of enduring boredom. We even acquire the notion that fine art is lascivious and destructive to the character. In church, in the House of Commons, at public meetings, we sit solemnly listening to bores and twaddlers because from the time we could walk or speak we have been snubbed, scolded, bullied, beaten and imprisoned whenever we dared to resent being bored or twaddled at, or to express our natural impatience and derision of bores and twaddlers. And when a man arises with a soul of sufficient native strength to break the bonds of this inculcated reverence and to expose and deride and tweak the noses of our humbugs and panjandrums, like Voltaire or Dickens, we are shocked and scandalized, even when we cannot help laughing. Worse, we dread and persecute those who can see and declare the truth, because their sincerity and insight reflects on our delusion and blindness. We are all like Nell Gwynne's footman, who defended Nell's reputation with his fists, not because he believed her to be what he called an honest woman, but because he objected to be scorned as the footman of one who was no better than she should be.

This wretched power of allowing ourselves to be bored may seem to give the fine arts a chance sometimes. People will sit through a performance of Beethoven's ninth symphony or of Wagner's Ring just as they will sit through a dull sermon or a front bench politician saying nothing for two hours whilst his unfortunate country is perishing through the delay of its business in Parliament. But their endurance is very bad for the ninth symphony, because they never hiss when it is murdered. I have heard an Italian conductor (no longer living) take the *adagio* of that symphony at a lively *allegretto*, slowing down for the warmer major sections into the speed and manner of the heroine's death song in a Verdi opera; and the listeners, far from relieving my excruciation by rising with yells of fury and hurling their programs and opera glasses at

the miscreant, behaved just as they do when Richter con-
ducts it. The mass of imposture that thrives on this combination of ignorance with despairing endurance is incalculable.
Given a public trained from childhood to stand anything tedious, and so saturated with school discipline that even with
the doors open and no schoolmasters to stop them they will
sit there helplessly until the end of the concert or opera gives
them leave to go home; and you will have in great capitals
hundreds of thousands of pounds spent every night in the
season on professedly artistic entertainments which have no
other effect on fine art than to exacerbate the hatred in which
it is already secretly held in England.

Fortunately, there are arts that cannot be cut off from
the people by bad performances. We can read books for ourselves; and we can play a good deal of fine music for ourselves with the help of a pianola. Nothing stands between us
and the actual handwork of the great masters of painting except distance; and modern photographic methods of reproduction are in some cases quite and in many nearly as effective in
conveying the artist's message as a modern edition of Shakespeare's plays is in conveying the message that first existed in
his handwriting. The reproduction of great feats of musical
execution is already on the way: the phonograph, for all its
wheezing and snarling and braying, is steadily improving in its
manners; and what with this improvement on the one hand,
and on the other that blessed selective faculty which enables us
to ignore a good deal of disagreeable noise if there is a thread
of music in the middle of it (few critics of the phonograph
seem to be conscious of the very considerable mechanical
noise set up by choirs and orchestras) we have at last reached
a point at which, for example, a person living in an English
village where the church music is the only music, and that
music is made by a few well-intentioned ladies with the help
of a harmonium, can hear masses by Palestrina very passably
executed, and can thereby be led to the discovery that Jackson
in F and Hymns Ancient and Modern are not perhaps the last
word of beauty and propriety in the praise of God.

In short, there is a vast body of art now within the reach of
everybody. The difficulty is that this art, which alone can educate us in grace of body and soul, and which alone can make
the history of the past live for us or the hope of the future
shine for us, which alone can give delicacy and nobility to our
crude lusts, which is the appointed vehicle of inspiration and

the method of the communion of saints, is actually branded as sinful among us because, wherever it arises, there is resistance to tyranny, breaking of fetters, and the breath of freedom. The attempt to suppress art is not wholly successful: we might as well try to suppress oxygen. But it is carried far enough to inflict on huge numbers of people a most injurious art starvation, and to corrupt a great deal of the art that is tolerated. You will find in England plenty of rich families with little more culture than their dogs and horses. And you will find poor families, cut off by poverty and town life from the contemplation of the beauty of the earth, with its dresses of leaves, its scarves of cloud, and its contours of hill and valley, who would positively be happier as hogs, so little have they cultivated their humanity by the only effective instrument of culture: art. The dearth is artificially maintained even when there are the means of satisfying it. Story books are forbidden, picture post cards are forbidden, theaters are forbidden, operas are forbidden, circuses are forbidden, sweetmeats are forbidden, pretty colors are forbidden, all exactly as vice is forbidden. The Creator is explicitly prayed to, and implicitly convicted of indecency every day. An association of vice and sin with everything that is delightful and of goodness with everything that is wretched and detestable is set up. All the most perilous (and glorious) appetites and propensities are at once inflamed by starvation and uneducated by art. All the wholesome conditions which art imposes on appetite are waived: instead of cultivated men and women restrained by a thousand delicacies, repelled by ugliness, chilled by vulgarity, horrified by coarseness, deeply and sweetly moved by the graces that art has revealed to them and nursed in them, we get indiscriminate rapacity in pursuit of pleasure and a parade of the grossest stimulations in catering for it. We have a continual clamor for goodness, beauty, virtue, and sanctity, with such an appalling inability to recognize it or love it when it arrives that it is more dangerous to be a great prophet or poet than to promote twenty companies for swindling simple folk out of their savings. Do not for a moment suppose that uncultivated people are merely indifferent to high and noble qualities. They hate them malignantly. At best, such qualities are like rare and beautiful birds: when they appear the whole country takes down its guns; but the birds receive the statuary tribute of having their corpses stuffed.

And it really all comes from the habit of preventing children from being troublesome. You are so careful of your boy's morals, knowing how troublesome they may be, that you keep him away from the Venus de Milo only to find him in the arms of the scullery maid or someone much worse. You decide that the Hermes of Praxiteles and Wagner's Tristan are not suited for young girls; and your daughter marries somebody appallingly unlike either Hermes or Tristan solely to escape from your parental protection. You have not stifled a single passion nor averted a single danger: you have depraved the passions by starving them, and broken down all the defenses which so effectively protect children brought up in freedom. You have men who imagine themselves to be ministers of religion openly declaring that when they pass through the streets they have to keep out in the wheeled traffic to avoid the temptations of the pavement. You have them organizing hunts of the women who tempt them—poor creatures whom no artist would touch without a shudder—and wildly clamoring for more clothes to disguise and conceal the body, and for the abolition of pictures, statues, theaters, and pretty colors. . . .

The Impossibility of Secular Education

Now children must be taught some sort of religion. Secular education is an impossibility. Secular education comes to this: that the only reason for ceasing to do evil and learning to do well is that if you do not you will be caned. This is worse than being taught in a church school that if you become a dissenter you will go to hell; for hell is presented as the instrument of something eternal, divine, and inevitable: you cannot evade it the moment the schoolmaster's back is turned. What confuses this issue and leads even highly intelligent religious persons to advocate secular education as a means of rescuing children from the strife of rival proselytizers is the failure to distinguish between the child's personal subjective need for a religion and its right to an impartially communicated historical objective knowledge of all the creeds and Churches. Just as a child, no matter what its race and color may be, should know that there are black men and brown men and yellow men, and, no matter what its political convictions may be, that there are Monarchists and Republicans and Positivists, Socialists and Unsocialists, so it should know that there are Christians and Mahometans and Buddhists and Shintoists and so forth, and that they are on the average just as honest and well-behaved as its own father. For example, it should not be told that Allah is a false god set up by the Turks and Arabs, who will all be damned for taking that liberty; but it should be told that many English people think so, and that many Turks and Arabs think the converse about English people. It should be taught that Allah is simply the name by which God is known to Turks and Arabs, who are just as eligible for salvation as any Christian. Further, that the practical reason why a Turkish child should pray in a mosque and an English child in a church is that as worship is organized in Turkey in mosques in the name of Mahomet and in England in churches in the name of Christ, a Turkish child joining the Church of England or an English child following Mahomet will find that it has no place for its worship and no organization of its religion within its reach. Any other teaching of the history and present facts of religion is false teaching, and is politically extremely dangerous in an empire in which a huge majority of the fellow subjects of the governing island do not profess the religion of that island.

But this objectivity, though intellectually honest, tells the child only what other people believe. What it should itself believe is quite another matter. The sort of Rationalism which says to a child "You must suspend your judgment until you are old enough to choose your religion" is Rationalism gone mad. The child must have a conscience and a code of honor (which is the essence of religion) even if it be only a provisional one, to be revised at its confirmation. For confirmation is meant to signalize a spiritual coming of age, and may be a repudiation. Really active souls have many confirmations and repudiations as their life deepens and their knowledge widens. But what is to guide the child before its first confirmation? Not mere orders, because orders must have a sanction of some sort or why should the child obey them? If, as a Secularist, you refuse to teach any sanction, you must say "You will be punished if you disobey." "Yes," says the child to itself, "if I am found out; but wait until your back is turned and I will do as I like, and lie about it." There can be no objective punishment for successful fraud; and as no espionage can cover the whole range of a child's conduct, the upshot is that the child becomes a liar and schemer with an atrophied conscience. And a good many of the orders given to it are not obeyed after all. Thus the Secularist who is not a fool is forced to appeal to the child's vital impulse toward perfection, to the divine spark; and no resolution not to call this impulse an impulse of loyalty to the Fellowship of the Holy Ghost, or obedience to the Will of God, or any other standard theological term, can alter the fact that the Secularist has stepped outside Secularism and is educating the child religiously, even if he insists on repudiating that pious adverb and substituting the word metaphysically. . . .

My Pedagogic Creed

JOHN DEWEY

(1897)

In education as in ethics, the American philosopher John Dewey thought the democratic principle was fundamental. He urged that educators reject authoritarian discipline and the rote communication of information to favor learning by doing and discipline proceeding from the life of the group—in this case, the school. Many of Dewey's suggestions, radical in his own day, have become standard operating procedure in American education: the extensive use of psychology in education, standardized testing, "expressive activities" such as physical education and home economics classes. Perhaps his major influence continues to be exerted on curriculum: from his view that academic studies should be correlated through a study of present-day society has developed the "core curriculum" for social studies. Dewey's *Pedagogic Creed,* written in 1897, is a passionate manifesto of his conviction that education should reflect in embryo the life of the world beyond the classroom.

Article I—What Education Is

I believe that all education proceeds by the participation of the individual in the social consciousness of the race. This process begins unconsciously almost at birth, and is continually shaping the individual's powers, saturating his consciousness, forming his habits, training his ideas, and arousing his feelings and emotions. Through this unconscious education the individual gradually comes to share in the intellectual and moral resources which humanity has succeeded in getting together. He becomes an inheritor of the funded capital of civilization. The most formal and technical education in the world cannot safely depart from this general process. It can only organize it or differentiate it in some particular direction.

I believe that the only true education comes through the stimulation of the child's powers by the demands of the social situations in which he finds himself. Through these demands he is stimulated to act as a member of a unity, to emerge from his original narrowness of action and feeling, and to conceive of himself from the standpoint of the welfare of the group to which he belongs. Through the responses which others make to his own activities he comes to know what these mean in social terms. The value which they have is reflected back into them. For instance, through the response which is made to the child's instinctive babblings the child comes to know what those babblings mean; they are transformed into articulate language and thus the child is introduced into the consolidated wealth of ideas and emotions which are now summed up in language.

I believe that this educational process has two sides—one psychological and one sociological; and that neither can be subordinated to the other or neglected without evil results following. Of these two sides, the psychological is the basis. The child's own instincts and powers furnish the material and give the starting point for all education. Save as the efforts of the educator connect with some activity which the child is carrying on of his own initiative independent of the educator, education becomes reduced to a pressure from without. It may, indeed, give certain external results, but cannot truly be called educative. Without insight into the psychological structure and activities of the individual, the educative process will, therefore, be haphazard and arbitrary. If it chances to coincide with the child's activity it will get a leverage; if it does not, it will result in friction, or disintegration, or arrest of the child nature.

I believe that knowledge of social conditions, of the present state of civilization, is necessary in order properly to interpret the child's powers. The child has his own instincts and tendencies, but we do not know what these mean until we can translate them into their social equivalents. We must be able to carry them back into a social past and see them as the inheritance of previous race activities. We must also be able to project them into the future to see what their outcome and end will be. In the illustration just used, it is the ability to see in the child's babblings the promise and potency of a future social intercourse and conversation which enables one to deal in the proper way with that instinct.

I believe that the psychological and social sides are organically related and that education cannot be regarded as a compromise between the two, or a superimposition of one upon the other. We are told that the psychological definition of education is barren and formal—that it gives us only the idea of a development of all the mental powers without giving us any idea of the use to which these powers are put. On the other hand, it is urged that the social definition of education, as getting adjusted to civilization, makes of it a forced and external process, and results in subordinating the freedom of the individual to a preconceived social and political status.

I believe that each of these objections is true when urged against one side isolated from the other. In order to know what a power really is we must know what its end, use, or function is; and this we cannot know save as we conceive of the individual as active in social relationships. But, on the other hand, the only possible adjustment which we can give to the child under existing conditions, is that which arises through putting him in complete possession of all his powers. With the advent of democracy and modern industrial conditions, it is impossible to foretell definitely just what civilization will be twenty years from now. Hence it is impossible to prepare the child for any precise set of conditions. To prepare him for the future life means to give him command of himself; it means so to train him that he will have the full and ready use of all his capacities; that his eye and ear and hand may be tools ready to command, that his judgment may be capable of grasping the conditions under which it has to work, and the executive forces be trained to act economically and efficiently. It is impossible to reach this sort of adjustment save as constant regard is had to the individual's own powers, tastes, and interests—say, that is, as education is continually converted into psychological terms.

In sum, I believe that the individual who is to be educated is a social individual and that society is an organic union of individuals. If we eliminate the social factor from the child we are left only with an abstraction; if we eliminate the individual factor from society, we are left only with an inert and lifeless mass. Education, therefore, must begin with a psychological insight into the child's capacities, interests, and habits. It must be controlled at every point by reference to these same considerations. These powers, interests, and habits must be continually interpreted—we must know what they mean.

They must be translated into terms of their social equivalents —into terms of what they are capable of in the way of social service.

Article II—What the School Is

I believe that the school is primarily a social institution. Education being a social process, the school is simply that form of community life in which all those agencies are concentrated that will be most effective in bringing the child to share in the inherited resources of the race, and to use his own powers for social ends.

I believe that education, therefore, is a process of living and not a preparation for future living.

I believe that the school must represent present life—life as real and vital to the child as that which he carries on in the home, in the neighborhood, or on the playground.

I believe that education which does not occur through forms of life, or that are worth living for their own sake, is always a poor substitute for the genuine reality and tends to cramp and to deaden.

I believe that the school, as an institution, should simplify existing social life; should reduce it, as it were, to an embryonic form. Existing life is so complex that the child cannot be brought into contact with it without either confusion or distraction; he is either overwhelmed by the multiplicity of activities which are going on, so that he loses his own power of orderly reaction, or he is so stimulated by these various activities that his powers are prematurely called into play and he becomes either unduly specialized or else disintegrated.

I believe that as such simplified social life, the school life should grow gradually out of the home life; that it should take up and continue the activities with which the child is already familiar in the home.

I believe that it should exhibit these activities to the child, and reproduce them in such ways that the child will gradually learn the meaning of them, and be capable of playing his own part in relation to them.

I believe that this is a psychological necessity, because it is the only way of securing continuity in the child's growth, the only way of giving a background of past experience to the new ideas given in school.

I believe that it is also a social necessity because the home is the form of social life in which the child has been nurtured and in connection with which he has had his moral training. It is the business of the school to deepen and extend his sense of the values bound up in his home life.

I believe that much of present education fails because it neglects this fundamental principle of the school as a form of community life. It conceives the school as a place where certain information is to be given, where certain lessons are to be learned, or where certain habits are to be formed. The value of these is conceived as lying largely in the remote future; the child must do these things for the sake of something else he is to do; they are mere preparation. As a result they do not become a part of the life experience of the child and so are not truly educative.

I believe that the moral education centers upon this conception of the school as a mode of social life, that the best and deepest moral training is precisely that which one gets through having to enter into proper relations with others in a unity of work and thought. The present educational systems, so far as they destroy or neglect this unity, render it difficult or impossible to get any genuine, regular moral training.

I believe that the child should be stimulated and controlled in his work through the life of the community.

I believe that under existing conditions far too much of the stimulus and control proceeds from the teacher, because of neglect of the idea of the school as a form of social life.

I believe that the teacher's place and work in the school is to be interpreted from this same basis. The teacher is not in the school to impose certain ideas or to form certain habits in the child, but is there as a member of the community to select the influences which shall affect the child and to assist him in properly responding to these influences.

I believe that the discipline of the school should proceed from the life of the school as a whole and not directly from the teacher.

I believe that the teacher's business is simply to determine on the basis of larger experience and riper wisdom, how the discipline of life shall come to the child.

I believe that all questions of the grading of the child and his promotion should be determined by reference to the same standard. Examinations are of use only so far as they test the child's fitness for social life and reveal the place in which he can be of the most service and where he can receive the most help.

Article III—The Subject Matter of Education

I believe that the social life of the child is the basis of concentration, or correlation, in all his training or growth. The social life gives the unconscious unity and the background of all his efforts and of all his attainments.

I believe that the subject matter of the school curriculum should mark a gradual differentiation out of the primitive unconscious unity of social life.

I believe that we violate the child's nature and render difficult the best ethical results, by introducing the child too abruptly to a number of special studies, of reading, writing, geography, etc., out of relation to this social life.

I believe, therefore, that the true center of correlation on the school subjects is not science, nor literature, nor history, nor geography, but the child's own social activities.

I believe that education cannot be unified in the study of science, or so-called nature study, because apart from human activity, nature itself is not a unity; nature in itself is a number of diverse objects in space and time, and to attempt to make it the center of work by itself, is to introduce a principle of radiation rather than one of concentration.

I believe that literature is the reflex expression and interpretation of social experience; that hence it must follow upon and not precede such experience. It, therefore, cannot be made the basis, although it may be made the summary of unification.

I believe once more that history is of educative value in so far as it presents phases of social life and growth. It must be controlled by reference to social life. When taken simply as history it is thrown into the distant past and becomes dead and inert. Taken as the record of man's social life and progress it becomes full of meaning. I believe, however, that it cannot be so taken excepting as the child is also introduced directly into social life.

I believe accordingly that the primary basis of education is in the child's powers at work along the same general constructive lines as those which have brought civilization into being.

I believe that the only way to make the child conscious of his social heritage is to enable him to perform those fundamental types of activity which make civilization what it is.

I believe, therefore, in the so-called expressive or constructive activities as the center of correlation.

I believe that this gives the standard for the place of cooking, sewing, manual training, etc., in the school.

I believe that they are not special studies which are to be introduced over and above a lot of others in the way of relaxation or relief, or as additional accomplishments. I believe rather that they represent, as types, fundamental forms of social activity; and that it is possible and desirable that the child's introduction into the more formal subjects of the curriculum be through the medium of these activities.

I believe that the study of science is educational in so far as it brings out the materials and processes which make social life what it is.

I believe that one of the greatest difficulties in the present teaching of science is that the material is presented in purely objective form, or is treated as a new peculiar kind of experience which the child can add to that which he has already had. In reality, science is of value because it gives the ability to interpret and control the experience already had. It should be introduced, not as so much new subject matter, but as showing the factors already involved in previous experience and as furnishing tools by which that experience can be more easily and effectively regulated.

I believe that at present we lose much of the value of literature and language studies because of our elimination of the social element. Language is almost always treated in the books of pedagogy simply as the expression of thought. It is true that language is a logical instrument, but it is fundamentally and primarily a social instrument. Language is the device for communication; it is the tool through which one individual comes to share the ideas and feelings of others. When treated simply as a way of getting individual information, or as a means of showing off what one has learned, it loses its social motive and end.

I believe that there is, therefore, no succession of studies in the ideal school curriculum. If education is life, all life has, from the outset, a scientific aspect, an aspect of art and culture, and an aspect of communication. It cannot, therefore, be true that the proper studies for one grade are mere reading and writing, and that at a later grade, reading, or literature, or science, may be introduced. The progress is not in the succession of studies but in the development of new attitudes toward, and new interests in, experience.

I believe finally, that education must be conceived as a

continuing reconstruction of experience; that the process and the goal of education are one and the same thing.

I believe that to set up any end outside of education, as furnishing its goal and standard, is to deprive the educational process of much of its meaning and tends to make us rely upon false and external stimuli in dealing with the child.

Article IV—The Nature of Method

I believe that the question of method is ultimately reducible to the question of the order of development of the child's powers and interests. The law for presenting and treating material is the law implicit within the child's own nature. Because this is so I believe the following statements are of supreme importance as determining the spirit in which education is carried on:

1. I believe that the active side precedes the passive in the development of the child nature; that expression comes before conscious impression; that the muscular development precedes the sensory; that movements come before conscious sensations; I believe that consciousness is essentially motor or impulsive; that conscious states tend to project themselves in action.

I believe that the neglect of this principle is the cause of a large part of the waste of time and strength in school work. The child is thrown into a passive, receptive, or absorbing attitude. The conditions are such that he is not permitted to follow the law of his nature; the result is friction and waste.

I believe that ideas (intellectual and rational processes) also result from action and devolve for the sake of the better control of action. What we term reason is primarily the law of orderly or effective action. To attempt to develop the reasoning powers, the powers of judgment, without reference to the selection and arrangement of means in action, is the fundamental fallacy in our present methods of dealing with this matter. As a result we present the child with arbitrary symbols. Symbols are a necessity in mental development, but they have their place as tools for economizing effort; presented by themselves they are a mass of meaningless and arbitrary ideas imposed from without.

2. I believe that the image is the great instrument of instruction. What a child gets out of any subject presented to him is simply the images which he himself forms with regard to it.

I believe that if nine tenths of the energy at present directed toward making the child learn certain things, were spent in seeing to it that the child was forming proper images, the work of instruction would be indefinitely facilitated.

I believe that much of the time and attention now given to the preparation and presentation of lessons might be more wisely and profitably expended in training the child's power of imagery and in seeing to it that he was continually forming definite, vivid, and growing images of the various subjects with which he comes in contact in his experience.

3. I believe that interests are the signs and symptoms of growing power. I believe that they represent dawning capacities. Accordingly the constant and careful observation of interests is of the utmost importance for the educator.

I believe that these interests are to be observed as showing the state of development which the child has reached.

I believe that they prophesy the stage upon which he is about to enter.

I believe that only through the continual and sympathetic observation of childhood's interests can the adult enter into the child's life and see what it is ready for, and upon what material it could work most readily and fruitfully.

I believe that these interests are neither to be humored nor repressed. To repress interest is to substitute the adult for the child, and so to weaken intellectual curiosity and alertness, to suppress initiative, and to deaden interest. To humor the interests is to substitute the transient for the permanent. The interest is always the sign of some power below; the important thing is to discover this power. To humor the interest is to fail to penetrate below the surface and its sure result is to substitute caprice and whim for genuine interest.

4. I believe that the emotions are the reflex of actions.

I believe that to endeavor to stimulate or arouse the emotions apart from their corresponding activities, is to introduce an unhealthy and morbid state of mind.

I believe that if we can only secure right habits of action and thought, with reference to the good, the true, and the beautiful, the emotions will for the most part take care of themselves.

I believe that next to deadness and dullness, formalism and routine, our education is threatened with no greater evil than sentimentalism.

I believe that this sentimentalism is the necessary result of the attempt to divorce feeling from action.

Article V—The School and Social Progress

I believe that education is the fundamental method of social progress and reform.

I believe that all reforms which rest simply upon the enactment of law, or the threatening of certain penalties, or upon changes in mechanical or outward arrangements, are transitory and futile.

I believe that education is a regulation of the process of coming to share in the social consciousness; and that the adjustment of individual activity on the basis of this social consciousness is the only sure method of social reconstruction.

I believe that this conception has due regard for both the individualistic and socialistic ideals. It is duly individual because it recognizes the formation of a certain character as the only genuine basis of right living. It is socialistic because it recognizes that this right character is not to be formed by merely individual precept, example, or exhortation, but rather by the influence of a certain form of institutional or community life upon the individual, and that the social organism through the school, as its organ, may determine ethical results.

I believe that in the ideal school we have the reconciliation of the individualistic and the institutional ideals.

I believe that the community's duty to education is, therefore, its paramount moral duty. By law and punishment, by social agitation and discussion, society can regulate and form itself in a more or less haphazard and chance way. But through education society can formulate its own purposes, can organize its own means and resources, and thus shape itself with definiteness, and economy in the direction in which it wishes to move.

I believe that when society once recognizes the possibilities in this direction, and the obligations which these possibilities impose, it is impossible to conceive of the resources of time, attention, and money which will be put at the disposal of the educator.

I believe that it is the business of every one interested in education to insist upon the school as the primary and most effective interest of social progress and reform in order that society may be awakened to realize what the school stands for, and aroused to the necessity of endowing the educator with sufficient equipment properly to perform his task.

I believe that education thus conceived marks the most perfect and intimate union of science and art conceivable in human experience.

I believe that the art of thus giving shape to human powers and adapting them to social service, is the supreme art; one calling into its service the best of artists; that no insight, sympathy, tact, executive power, is too great for such service.

I believe that with the growth of psychological service, giving added insight into individual structure and laws of growth; and with growth of social science, adding to our knowledge of the right organization of individuals, all scientific resources can be utilized for the purposes of education.

I believe that when science and art thus join hands the most commanding motive for human action will be reached; the most genuine springs of human conduct aroused and the best service that human nature is capable of guaranteed.

I believe, finally, that the teacher is engaged, not simply in the training of individuals, but in the formation of the proper social life.

I believe that every teacher should realize the dignity of his calling; that he is a social servant set apart for the maintenance of proper social order and the securing of the right social growth.

I believe that in this way the teacher always is the prophet of the true God and the usherer in of the true kingdom of God.

The Rhythm of Education

ALFRED NORTH WHITEHEAD

(1922)

Alfred North Whitehead, the British mathematician and
philosopher, viewed nature as organic and the world's
progress as the adjustment of interrelated organisms to
an environment which in turn is itself altered by these
adjustments. Learning, in Whitehead's opinion, is a similar
periodic process occurring between the child and the
facts he encounters. First, the child is excited by facts
and realizes that there may be important relations among
them. Next, he must learn to handle facts precisely
through the grammars of various disciplines: science,
art, and literature. Finally, excitement and definition bear
fruit in generalizations which become, for some men,
guides to action and, for a few, significant advances in
human knowledge. In the following essay, Whitehead
holds that education consists of a continual repetition of
this process at ever higher levels of sophistication. In
structural terms, he believes that lower schooling should
be devoted mostly to amassing useful facts and techniques, while "the function of a university is to enable
you to shed details in favor of principles."

By the Rhythm of Education I denote a certain principle
which in its practical application is well known to everyone
with educational experience. Accordingly, when I remember
that I am speaking to an audience of some of the leading educationists in England, I have no expectation that I shall be
saying anything that is new to you. I do think, however, that
the principle has not been subjected to an adequate discussion
taking account of all the factors which should guide its application.

I first seek for the baldest statement of what I mean by the
Rhythm of Education, a statement so bald as to exhibit the
point of this address in its utter obviousness. The principle
is merely this—that different subjects and modes of study

should be undertaken by pupils at fitting times when they have reached the proper stage of mutual development. You will agree with me that this is a truism, never doubted and known to all. I am really anxious to emphasize the obvious character of the foundational idea of my address; for one reason, because this audience will certainly find it out for itself. But the other reason, the reason why I choose this subject for discourse, is that I do not think that this obvious truth has been handled in educational practice with due attention to the psychology of the pupils.

The Tasks of Infancy

I commence by challenging the adequacy of some principles by which the subjects for study are often classified in order. By this I mean that these principles can only be accepted as correct if they are so explained as to be explained away. Consider first the criterion of difficulty. It is not true that the easier subjects should precede the harder. On the contrary, some of the hardest must come first because nature so dictates, and because they are essential to life. The first intellectual task which confronts an infant is the acquirement of spoken language. What an appalling task, the correlation of meanings with sounds! It requires an analysis of ideas and an analysis of sounds. We all know that the infant does it, and that the miracle of his achievement is explicable. But so are all miracles, and yet to the wise they remain miracles. All I ask is that with this example staring us in the face we should cease talking nonsense about postponing the harder subjects.

What is the next subject in the education of the infant minds? The acquirement of written language; that is to say, the correlation of sounds with shapes. Great heavens! Have our educationists gone mad? They are setting babbling mites of six years old to tasks which might daunt a sage after lifelong toil. Again, the hardest task in mathematics is the study of the elements of algebra, and yet this stage must precede the comparative simplicity of the differential calculus.

I will not elaborate my point further; I merely restate it in the form, that the postponement of difficulty is no safe clue for the maze of educational practice.

The alternative principle of order among subjects is that of necessary antecedence. There we are obviously on firmer ground. It is impossible to read *Hamlet* until you can read;

and the study of integers must precede the study of fractions. And yet even this firm principle dissolves under scrutiny. It is certainly true, but it is only true if you give an artificial limitation to the concept of a subject for study. The danger of the principle is that it is accepted in one sense, for which it is almost a necessary truth, and it is applied in another sense for which it is false. You cannot read Homer before you can read; but many a child, and in ages past many a man, has sailed with Odysseus over the seas of Romance by the help of the spoken word of a mother, or of some wandering bard. The uncritical application of the principle of the necessary antecedence of some subjects to others has, in the hands of dull people with a turn for organization, produced in education the dryness of the Sahara.

Stages of Mental Growth

The reason for the title which I have chosen for this address, the Rhythm of Education, is derived from yet another criticism of current ideas. The pupil's progress is often conceived as a uniform steady advance undifferentiated by change of type or alteration in pace; for example, a boy may be conceived as starting Latin at ten years of age and by a uniform progression steadily developing into a classical scholar at the age of eighteen or twenty. I hold that this conception of education is based upon a false psychology of the process of mental development which has gravely hindered the effectiveness of our methods. Life is essentially periodic. It comprises daily periods, with their alternations of work and play, of activity and of sleep, and seasonal periods, which dictate our terms and our holidays; and also it is composed of well-marked yearly periods. These are the gross obvious periods which no one can overlook. There are also subtler periods of mental growth, with their cyclic recurrences, yet always different as we pass from cycle to cycle, though the subordinate stages are reproduced in each cycle. That is why I have chosen the term "rhythmic," as meaning essentially the conveyance of difference within a framework of repetition. Lack of attention to the rhythm and character of mental growth is a main source of wooden futility in education. I think that Hegel was right when he analyzed progress into three stages, which he called Thesis, Antithesis, and Synthesis; though for the purpose of the application of his idea to educational theory I do not think that the names he gave are very happily suggestive. In relation to intellectual progress I would term them, the stage of romance, the stage of precision, and the stage of generalization.

The Stage of Romance

The stage of romance is the stage of first apprehension. The subject matter has the vividness of novelty; it holds within itself unexplored connections with possibilities half-disclosed by glimpses and half-concealed by the wealth of material. In this stage knowledge is not dominated by systematic procedure. Such system as there must be is created piecemeal *ad hoc*. We are in the presence of immediate cognizance of fact, only intermittently subjecting fact to systematic dissection. Romantic emotion is essentially the excitement consequent on the transition from the bare facts to the first realizations of the import of their unexplored relationships. For example, Crusoe was a mere man, the sand was mere sand, the footprint was a mere footprint, and the island a mere island, and Europe was the busy world of men. But the sudden perception of the half-disclosed and half-hidden possibilities relating Crusoe and the sand and the footprint and the lonely island secluded from Europe constitutes romance. I have had to take an extreme case for illustration in order to make my meaning perfectly plain. But construe it as an allegory representing the first stage in a cycle of progress. Education must essentially be a setting in order of a ferment already stirring in the mind: you cannot educate mind *in vacuo*. In our conception of education we tend to confine it to the second stage of the cycle; namely, to the stage of precision. But we cannot so limit our task without misconceiving the whole problem. We are concerned alike with the ferment, with the acquirement of precision, and with the subsequent fruition.

The Stage of Precision

The stage of precision also represents an addition to knowledge. In this stage, width of relationship is subordinated to exactness of formulation. It is the stage of grammar, the grammar of language and the grammar of science. It proceeds by forcing on the student's acceptance a given way of analyzing the facts, bit by bit. New facts are added, but they are the facts which fit into the analysis.

It is evident that a stage of precision is barren without a previous stage of romance: unless there are facts which have already been vaguely apprehended in their broad generality, the previous analysis is an analysis of nothing. It is simply a series of meaningless statements about bare facts, produced artificially and without any further relevance. I repeat that in this stage we do not merely remain within the circle of the facts elicited in the romantic epoch. The facts of romance have disclosed ideas with possibilities of wide significance, and in the stage of precise progress we acquire other facts in a systematic order, which thereby form both a disclosure and an analysis of the general subject matter of the romance.

The Stage of Generalization

The final stage of generalization is Hegel's synthesis. It is a return to romanticism with added advantage of classified ideas and relevant technique. It is the fruition which has been the goal of the precise training. It is the final success. I am afraid that I have had to give a dry analysis of somewhat obvious ideas. It has been necessary to do so because my subsequent remarks presuppose that we have clearly in our minds the essential character of this threefold cycle.

The Cyclic Processes

Education should consist in a continual repetition of such cycles. Each lesson in its minor way should form an eddy cycle issuing in its own subordinate process. Longer periods should issue in definite attainments, which then form the starting grounds for fresh cycles. We should banish the idea of a mythical, far-off end of education. The pupils must be continually enjoying some fruition and starting afresh—if the teacher is stimulating in exact proportion to his success in satisfying the rhythmic cravings of his pupils.

An infant's first romance is its awakening to the apprehension of objects and to the appreciation of their connections. Its growth in mentality takes the exterior form of occupying itself in the coordination of its perceptions with its bodily activities. Its first stage of precision is mastering spoken language as an instrument for classifying its contemplation of objects and for strengthening its apprehension of emotional relations with other beings. Its first stage of generalization is the use of language for a classified and enlarged enjoyment of objects.

This first cycle of intellectual progress from the achievement of perception to the acquirement of language, and from the acquirement of language to classified thought and keener perception, will bear more careful study. It is the only cycle of progress which we can observe in its purely natural state. The later cycles are necessarily tinged by the procedure of the current mode of education. There is a characteristic of it which is often sadly lacking in subsequent education; I mean, that it achieves complete success. At the end of it the child *can* speak, its ideas *are* classified, and its perceptions *are* sharpened. The cycle achieves its object. This is a great deal more than can be said for most systems of education as applied to most pupils. But why should this be so? Certainly, a new-born baby looks a most unpromising subject for intellectual progress when we remember the difficulty of the task before it. I suppose it is because nature, in the form of surrounding circumstances, sets it a task for which the normal development of its brain is exactly fitted. I do not think that there is any particular mystery about the fact of a child learning to speak and in consequence thinking all the better; but it does offer food for reflection.

In the subsequent education we have not sought for cyclic processes which in a finite time run their course and within their own limited sphere achieve a complete success. This completion is one outstanding character in the natural cycle for infants. Later on we start a child on some subject, say Latin, at the age of ten, and hope by a uniform system of formal training to achieve success at the age of twenty. The natural result is failure, both in interest and in acquirement. When I speak of failure, I am comparing our results with the brilliant success of the first natural cycle. I do not think that it is because our tasks are intrinsically too hard, when I remember that the infant's cycle is the hardest of all. It is because our tasks are set in an unnatural way, without rhythm and without the stimulus of intermediate successes and without concentration.

I have not yet spoken of this character of concentration which so conspicuously attaches to the infant's progress. The whole being of the infant is absorbed in the practice of its cycle. It has nothing else to divert its mental development. In this respect there is a striking difference between this natural cycle and the subsequent history of the student's development. It is perfectly obvious that life is very various and that the mind and brain naturally develop so as to adapt themselves to the many-hued world in which their lot is cast. Still, after making allowance for this consideration, we will be wise to preserve some measure of concentration for each of the subsequent cycles. In particular, we should avoid a competition of diverse subjects in the same stage of their cycles. The fault of the older education was unrhythmic concentration on a single undifferentiated subject. Our modern system, with its insistence on a preliminary general education, and with its easy toleration of the analysis of knowledge into distinct subjects, is an equally unrhythmic collection of distracting scraps. I am pleading that we shall endeavor to weave in the learner's mind a harmony of patterns, by coordinating the various elements of instruction into subordinate cycles each of intrinsic worth for the immediate apprehension of the pupil. We must garner our crops each in its due season.

The Romance of Adolescence

We will now pass to some concrete applications of the ideas which have been developed in the former part of my address.

The first cycle of infancy is succeeded by the cycle of adolescence, which opens with by far the greatest stage of romance which we ever experience. It is in this stage that the lines of character are graven. How the child emerges from the romantic stage of adolescence is how the subsequent life will be molded by ideals and colored by imagination. It rapidly follows on the generalization of capacity produced by the acquirements of spoken language and of reading. The stage of generalization belonging to the infantile cycle is comparatively short because the romantic material of infancy is so scanty. The initial knowledge of the world in any developed sense of the word "knowledge" really commences after the achievement of the first cycle, and thus issues in the tremendous age of romance. Ideas, facts, relationships, stories, histories, possibilities, artistry in words, in sounds, in form and in color, crowd into the child's life, stir his feelings, excite his appreciation, and incite his impulses to kindred activities. It is a saddening thought that on this golden age there falls so often the shadow of the crammer. I am thinking of a period of about four years of the child's life, roughly, in ordinary cases, falling between the ages of eight and twelve or thirteen. It is the first great period of the utilization of the native language, and of developed powers of observation and of manipulation. The infant cannot manipulate, the child can; the infant cannot observe, the child can; the infant cannot retain thoughts by the recollection of words, the child can. The child thus enters upon a new world.

Of course, the stage of precision prolongs itself as recurring in minor cycles which form eddies in the great romance. The perfecting of writing, of spelling, of the elements of arithmetic, and of lists of simple facts, such as the Kings of England, are all elements of precision, very necessary both as training in concentration and as useful acquirements. However, these are essentially fragmentary in character, whereas the great romance is the flood which bears on the child toward the life of the spirit.

The success of the Montessori system is due to its recognition of the dominance of romance at this period of growth. If this be the explanation, it also points to the limitations in the usefulness of that method. It is the system which in some measure is essential for every romantic stage. Its essence is browsing and the encouragement of vivid freshness. But it lacks the restraint which is necessary for the great stages of precision.

The Mastery of Language

Toward the end of the great romance the cyclic course of growth is swinging the child ever toward an aptitude for exact knowledge. Language is now the natural subject matter for concentrated attack. It is the mode of expression with which he is thoroughly familiar. He is acquainted with stories, histories, and poems illustrating the lives of other people and of other civilizations. Accordingly, from that age of eleven onward there is wanted a gradually increasing concentration toward precise knowledge of language. Finally, the three years from twelve to fifteen should be dominated by a mass attack upon language, so planned that a definite result, in itself worth having, is thereby achieved. I should guess that within these limits of time, and given adequate concentration, we might ask that at the end of that period the children should have command of English, should be able to read fluently fairly simple French, and should have completed the elementary stage of Latin; I mean, a precise knowledge of the more straightforward parts of Latin grammar, the knowledge of the construction of Latin sentences, and the reading of some parts of appropriate Latin authors, perhaps simplified and largely supplemented by the aid of the best literary translations so that their reading of the original, plus translation, gives them a grip of the book as a literary whole. I conceive that such a measure of attainment in these three languages is well within the reach of the ordinary child, provided that he has not been distracted by the effort at precision in a multiplicity of other subjects. Also some more gifted children could go further. The Latin would come to them easily, so that it would be possible to start Greek before the end of the period, always provided that their bent is literary and that they mean later to pursue that study at least for some years. Other subjects will occupy a subordinate place in the timetable and will be undertaken in a different spirit. In the first place, it must be remembered that the semi-literary subjects, such as history, will largely have been provided in the study of the languages. It will be hardly possible to read some English, French, and Latin literature without imparting some knowledge of European history. I do not mean that all special history teaching should be abandoned. I do, however, suggest that the subject should be exhibited in what I have termed the romantic spirit, and that the pupils should not be subjected to the test of precise recollection of details on any large systematic scale.

At this period of growth science should be in its stage of romance. The pupils should see for themselves, and experiment for themselves, with only fragmentary precision of thought. The essence of the importance of science, both for interest in theory or for technological purposes, lies in its application to concrete detail, and every such application evokes a novel problem for research. Accordingly, all training in science should begin as well as end in research, and in getting hold of the subject matter as it occurs in nature. The exact form of guidance suitable to this age and the exact limitations of experiment are matters depending on experience. But I plead that this period is the true age for the romance of science.

Concentration on Science

Toward the age of fifteen the age of precision in language and of romance in science draws to its close, to be succeeded by a period of generalization in language and of precision in science. This should be a short period, but one of vital importance. I am thinking of about one year's work, and I suggest that it would be well decisively to alter the balance of the preceding curriculum. There should be a concentration on science and a decided diminution of the linguistic work. A year's work on science, coming on the top of the previous romantic study, should make everyone understand the main principles which govern the development of mechanics, physics, chemistry, algebra and geometry. Understand that they are not beginning these subjects, but they are putting together a previous discursive study by an exact formulation of their main ideas. For example, take algebra and geometry, which I single out as being subjects with which I have some slight familiarity. In the previous three years there has been work on the applications of the simplest algebraic formulae and geometrical propositions to problems of surveying, or of some other scientific work involving calculations. In this way arithmetic has been carefully strengthened by the insistence on definite numerical results, and familiarity with the ideas of literal formulae and of geometrical properties has been gained; also some minor methods of manipulation have been inculcated. There is thus no long time to be wasted in getting used to the ideas of the sciences. The pupils are ready for the small body of algebraic and geometrical truths which they ought to know thoroughly. Furthermore, in the previous period some boys will have shown an aptitude for mathematics and will have pushed on a little more, besides in the final year somewhat emphasizing their mathematics at the expense of some of the other subjects. I am simply taking mathematics as an illustration.

Meanwhile, the cycle of language is in its stage of generalization. In this stage the precise study of grammar and composition is discontinued, and the language study is confined to reading the literature with emphasized attention to its ideas and to the general history in which it is embedded; also the time allotted to history will pass into the precise study of a short definite period, chosen to illustrate exactly what does happen at an important epoch and also to show how to pass the simpler types of judgments on men and policies.

I have now sketched in outline the course of education from babyhood to about sixteen and a half, arranged with some attention to the rhythmic pulses of life. In some such way a general education is possible in which the pupil throughout has the advantage of concentration and of freshness. Thus precision will always illustrate subject matter already apprehended and crying out for drastic treatment. Every pupil will have concentrated in turn on a variety of different subjects, and will know where his strong points lie. Finally—and this of all the objects to be attained is the most dear to my heart—the science students will have obtained both an invaluable literary education and also at the most impressionable age an early initiation into habits of thinking for themselves in the region of science.

After the age of sixteen new problems arise. For literary students science passes into the stage of generalization, largely in the form of lectures on its main results and general ideas. New cycles of linguistic, literary, and historical study commence. But further detail is now unnecessary. For the scientists the preceding stage of precision maintains itself to the close of the school period with an increasing apprehension of wider general ideas.

However, at this period of education the problem is too individual, or at least breaks up into too many cases, to be susceptible of broad general treatment. I do suggest, nevertheless, that all scientists should now keep up their French, and initiate the study of German if they have not already acquired it.

University Education

I should now like, if you will bear with me, to make some remarks respecting the import of these ideas for a University education.

The whole period of growth from infancy to manhood forms one grand cycle. Its stage of romance stretches across the first dozen years of life, its stage of precision comprises the whole school period of secondary education, and its stage of generalization is the period of entrance into manhood. For those whose formal education is prolonged beyond the school age, the University course or its equivalent is the great period of generalization. The spirit of generalization should dominate a University. The lectures should be addressed to those to whom details and procedure are familiar; that is to say, familiar at least in the sense of being so congruous to pre-existing training as to be easily acquirable. During the school period the student has been mentally bending over his desk; at the University he should stand up and look around. For this reason it is fatal if the first year at the University be frittered away in going over the old work in the old spirit. At school the boy painfully rises from the particular toward glimpses at general ideas; at the University he should start from general ideas and study their applications to concrete cases. A well-planned University course is a study of the wide sweep of generality. I do not mean that it should be abstract in the sense of divorce from concrete fact, but that concrete fact should be studied as illustrating the scope of general ideas.

Cultivation of Mental Power

This is the aspect of University training in which theoretical interest and practical utility coincide. Whatever be the detail with which you cram your student, the chance of his meeting in afterlife exactly that detail is almost infinitesimal; and if he does meet it, he will probably have forgotten what you taught him about it. The really useful training yields a comprehension of a few general principles with a thorough grounding in the way they apply to a variety of concrete details. In subsequent practice the men will have forgotten your particular details; but they will remember by an unconscious common sense how to apply principles to immediate circumstances. Your learning is useless to you till you have lost your textbooks, burned your lecture notes, and forgotten the minutiae which you learned by heart for the examination. What, in the way of detail, you continually require will stick in your memory as obvious facts like the sun and moon; and what you casually require can be looked up in any work of reference. The function of a University is to enable you to shed details in favor of principles. When I speak of principles I am hardly even thinking of verbal formulations. A principle which has thoroughly soaked into you is rather a mental habit than a formal statement. It becomes the way the mind reacts to the appropriate stimulus in the form of illustrative circumstances. Nobody goes about with his knowledge clearly and consciously before him.

Mental cultivation is nothing else than the satisfactory way in which the mind will function when it is poked up into activity. Learning is often spoken of as if we are watching the open pages of all the books which we have ever read, and then, when occasion arises, we select the right page to read aloud to the universe.

Luckily, the truth is far otherwise from this crude idea; and for this reason the antagonism between the claims of pure knowledge and professional acquirement should be much less acute than a faulty view of education would lead us to anticipate. I can put my point otherwise by saying that the ideal of a University is not so much knowledge, as power. Its business is to convert the knowledge of a boy into the power of a man.

The Rhythmic Character of Growth

I will conclude with two remarks which I wish to make by way of caution in the interpretation of my meaning. The point of this address is the rhythmic character of growth. The interior spiritual life of man is a web of many strands. They do not all grow together by uniform extension. I have tried to illustrate this truth by considering the normal unfolding of the capacities of a child in somewhat favorable circumstances but otherwise with fair average capacities. Perhaps I have misconstrued the usual phenomena. It is very likely that I have so failed, for the evidence is complex and difficult. But do not let any failure in this respect prejudice the main point which I am here to enforce. It is that the development of mentality exhibits itself as a rhythm involving an interweaving of cycles, the whole process being dominated by a greater cycle of the same general character as its minor eddies. Furthermore, this rhythm exhibits certain ascertainable general laws which are valid for most pupils, and the quality of our teaching should be so adapted as to suit the stage in the rhythm to which our pupils have advanced. The problem of a curriculum is not so much the succession of subjects; for all subjects should in essence be begun with the dawn of mentality. The truly important order is the order of quality which the educational procedure should assume.

My second caution is to ask you not to exaggerate into sharpness the distinction between the three stages of a cycle. I strongly suspect that many of you, when you heard me detail the three stages in each cycle, said to yourselves—How like a mathematician to make such formal divisions! I assure you that it is not mathematics but literary incompetence that may have led me into the error against which I am warning you. Of course, I mean throughout a distinction of emphasis, of pervasive quality—romance, precision, generalization, are all present throughout. But there is an alternation of dominance, and it is this alternation which constitutes the cycles.

Readiness for Learning

JEROME S. BRUNER

(1960)

In 1960, the National Academy of Sciences asked Jerome S. Bruner to direct a conference of scientists and teachers interested in improving science teaching in primary and secondary schools. The following selection, a portion of that epochal conference report, is from his book *The Process of Education*. Like Whitehead, Bruner suggests that our schools may be wasting precious years by postponing the teaching of many important subjects on the ground that they are too difficult for young children. He contends that the elements of any subject may be taught in some form to anyone at any age. The fundamental principles of physical and natural science are often as simple as they are powerful. They may be introduced to the young child intuitively and revisited at levels of greater complexity in later years.

We begin with the hypothesis that any subject can be taught effectively in some intellectually honest form to any child at any stage of development. It is a bold hypothesis and an essential one in thinking about the nature of a curriculum. No evidence exists to contradict it; considerable evidence is being amassed that supports it.

To make clear what is implied, let us examine three general ideas. The first has to do with the process of intellectual development in children, the second with the act of learning, and the third with the notion of the "spiral curriculum" introduced earlier.

Intellectual development. Research on the intellectual development of the child highlights the fact that at each stage of development the child has a characteristic way of viewing the world and explaining it to himself. The task of teaching a subject to a child at any particular age is one of representing the structure of that subject in terms of the child's way of viewing things. The task can be thought of as one of translation. The general hypothesis that has just been stated is premised on the considered judgment that any idea can be represented honestly and usefully in the thought forms of children of school age, and that these first representations can later be made more powerful and precise the more easily by virtue of this early learning. To illustrate and support this view, we present here a somewhat detailed picture of the course of intellectual development, along with some suggestions about teaching at different stages of it.

The work of Piaget and others suggests that, roughly speaking, one may distinguish three stages in the intellectual development of the child. The first stage need not concern us in detail, for it is characteristic principally of the pre-school child. In this stage, which ends (at least for Swiss school children) around the fifth or sixth year, the child's mental work consists principally in establishing relationships between experience and action; his concern is with manipulating the world through action. This stage corresponds roughly to the period from the first development of language to the point at which the child learns to manipulate symbols. In this so-called pre-operational stage, the principal symbolic achievement is that the child learns how to represent the external world through symbols established by simple generalization; things are represented as equivalent in terms of sharing some common property. But the child's symbolic world does not make a clear separation between internal motives and feelings on the one hand and external reality on the other. The sun moves because God pushes it, and the stars, like himself, have to go to bed. The child is little able to separate his own goals from the means for achieving them, and when he has to make corrections in his activity after unsuccessful attempts at manipulating reality, he does so by what are called intuitive regulations rather than by symbolic operations, the former being of a crude trial-and-error nature rather than the result of taking thought.

What is principally lacking at this stage of development is what the Geneva school has called the concept of reversibility. When the shape of an object is changed, as when one changes the shape of a ball of plasticine, the preoperational child cannot grasp the idea that it can be brought back readily to its original state. Because of this fundamental lack the child cannot understand certain fundamental ideas that lie at the basis of mathematics and physics—the mathematical idea that one conserves quantity even when one partitions a set of things into subgroups, or the physical idea that one conserves mass and weight even though one transforms the shape of an object. It goes without saying that teachers are severely limited in transmitting concepts to a child at this stage, even in a highly intuitive manner.

The second stage of development—and now the child is in school—is called the stage of concrete operations. This stage is operational in contrast to the preceding stage, which is merely active. An operation is a type of action: it can be carried out rather directly by the manipulation of objects, or internally, as when one manipulates the symbols that represent things and relations in one's mind. Roughly, an operation is a means of getting data about the real world into the mind and there transforming them so that they can be organized and used selectively in the solution of problems. Assume a child is presented with a pinball machine which bounces a ball off a wall at an angle. Let us find out what he appreciates about the relation between the angle of incidence and the angle of reflection. The young child sees no problem: for him, the ball travels in an arc, touching the wall on the way. The somewhat older child, say age ten, sees the two angles as roughly related—as one changes so does the other. The still older child begins to grasp that there is a fixed relation between the two, and usually says it is a right angle. Finally, the thirteen- or fourteen-year-old, often by pointing the ejector directly at the wall and seeing the ball come back at the ejector, gets the idea that the two angles are equal. Each way of looking at the phenomenon represents the result of an operation in this sense, and the child's thinking is constrained by his way of pulling his observations together.

An operation differs from simple action or goal-directed behavior in that it is internalized and reversible. "Internalized" means that the child does not have to go about his problem-solving any longer by overt trial and error, but can actually carry out trial and error in his head. Reversibility is present because operations are seen as characterized where appropriate by what is called "complete compensation"; that is to say, an operation can be compensated for by an inverse operation. If marbles, for example, are divided into subgroups, the child can grasp intuitively that the original collection of marbles can be restored by being added back together again. The child tips a balance scale too far with a weight and then searches systematically for a lighter weight or for something with which to get the scale rebalanced. He may carry reversibility too far by assuming that a piece of paper, once burned, can also be restored.

With the advent of concrete operations, the child develops an internalized structure with which to operate. In the example of the balance scale, the structure is a serial order of weights that the child has in his mind. Such internal structures are of the essence. They are the internalized symbolic systems by which the child represents the world, as in the example of the pinball machine and the angles of incidence and reflection. It is into the language of these internal structures that one must translate ideas if the child is to grasp them.

But concrete operations, though they are guided by the logic of classes and the logic of relations, are means for structuring only immediately present reality. The child is able to give structure to the things he encounters, but he is not yet readily able to deal with possibilities not directly before him or not already experienced. This is not to say that children operating concretely are not able to anticipate things that are not present. Rather, it is that they do not command the operations for conjuring up systematically the full range of alternative possibilities that could exist at any given time. They cannot go systematically beyond the information given them to a description of what else might occur. Somewhere between ten and fourteen years of age the child passes into a third stage, which is called the stage of "formal operations" by the Geneva school.

Now the child's intellectual activity seems to be based upon an ability to operate on hypothetical propositions rather than being constrained to what he has experienced or what is before him. The child can now think of possible variables and even deduce potential relationships that can later be verified by experiment or observation. Intellectual operations now appear to be predicated upon the same kinds of logical operations that are the stock in trade of the logician, the scientist, or the abstract thinker. It is at this point that the child is able to give formal or axiomatic expression to the concrete ideas that before guided his problem-solving but could not be described or formally understood.

Earlier, while the child is in the stage of concrete operations, he is capable of grasping intuitively and concretely a great many of the basic ideas of mathematics, the sciences, the humanities, and the social sciences. But he can do so only in terms of concrete operations. It can be demonstrated that fifth-grade children can play mathematical games with rules modeled on highly advanced mathematics; indeed, they can arrive at these rules inductively and learn how to work with them. They will flounder, however, if one attempts to force upon them a formal mathematical description of what they have been doing, though they are perfectly capable of guiding their behavior by these rules. At the Woods Hole Conference we were privileged to see a demonstration of teaching in which fifth-grade children very rapidly grasped central ideas from the theory of functions, although had the teacher attempted to explain to them what the theory of functions was, he would have drawn a blank. Later, at the appropriate stage of development and given a certain amount of practice in concrete operations, the time would be ripe for introducing them to the necessary formalism.

What is most important for teaching basic concepts is that the child be helped to pass progressively from concrete thinking to the utilization of more conceptually adequate modes of thought. But it is futile to attempt this by presenting formal explanations based on a logic that is distant from the child's manner of thinking and sterile in its implications for him. Much teaching in mathematics is of this sort. The child learns not to understand mathematical order but rather to apply certain devices or recipes without understanding their significance and connectedness. They are not translated into his way of thinking. Given this inappropriate start, he is easily led to believe that the important thing is for him to be "accurate"— though accuracy has less to do with mathematics than with computation. Perhaps the most striking example of this type of thing is to be found in the manner in which the high school student meets Euclidian geometry for the first time, as a set of axioms and theorems, without having had some experience with simple geometric configurations and the intuitive means whereby one deals with them. If the child were earlier given the concepts and strategies in the form of intuitive geometry at a level that he could easily follow, he might be far better able to grasp deeply the meaning of the theorems and axioms to which he is exposed later.

But the intellectual development of the child is no clockwork sequence of events; it also responds to influences from the environment, notably the school environment. Thus instruction in scientific ideas, even at the elementary level, need not follow slavishly the natural course of cognitive development in the child. It can also lead intellectual development by providing challenging but usable opportunities for the child to forge ahead in his development. Experience has shown that it is worth the effort to provide the growing child with problems that tempt him into next stages of development. As David Page, one of the most experienced teachers of elementary mathematics, has commented: "In teaching from kindergarten to graduate school, I have been amazed at the intellectual similarity of human beings at all ages, although children are perhaps more spontaneous, creative, and energetic than adults. As far as I am concerned young children learn almost anything faster than adults do if it can be given to them in terms they understand. Giving the material to them in terms they understand, interestingly enough, turns out to involve knowing the mathematics oneself, and the better one knows it, the better it can be taught. It is appropriate that we warn ourselves to be careful of assigning an absolute level of difficulty to any particular topic. When I tell mathematicians that fourth-grade students can go a long way into 'set theory' a few of them reply: 'Of course.' Most of them are startled. The latter ones are completely wrong in assuming that 'set theory' is intrinsically difficult. Of course it may be that nothing is intrinsically difficult. We just have to wait until the proper point of view and corresponding language for presenting it are revealed. Given particular subject matter or a particular concept, it is easy to ask trivial questions or to lead the child to ask trivial questions. It is also easy to ask impossibly difficult questions. The trick is to find the medium questions that can be answered and that take you somewhere. This is the big job of teachers and textbooks." One leads the child by the well-wrought "medium questions" to move more rapidly through the stages of intellectual development, to a deeper understanding of mathematical, physical, and historical principles. We must know far more about the ways in which this can be done.

Professor Inhelder of Geneva was asked to suggest ways in which the child could be moved along faster through the various stages of intellectual development in mathematics and physics. What follows is part of a memorandum she prepared for the Conference.

"The most elementary forms of reasoning—whether logical, arithmetical, geometrical, or physical—rest on the principle of the invariance of quantities: that the whole remains, whatever may be the arrangement of its parts, the change of its form, or its displacement in space or time. The principle of invariance is no *a priori* datum of the mind, nor is it the product of purely empirical observation. The child discovers invariance in a manner comparable to scientific discoveries generally. Grasping the idea of invariance is beset with difficulties for the child, often unsuspected by teachers. To the young child, numerical wholes, spatial dimensions, and physical quantities do not seem to remain constant but to dilate or contract as they are operated upon. The total number of beads in a box remains the same whether subdivided into two, three, or ten piles. It is this that is so hard for the child to understand. The young child perceives changes as operating in one direction without being able to grasp the idea that certain fundamental features of things remain constant over change, or that if they change the change is reversible.

"A few examples among many used in studying the child's concept of invariance will illustrate the kinds of materials one could use to help him to learn the concept more easily. The child transfers beads of a known quantity or liquids of a known volume from one receptacle to another, one receptacle being tall and narrow, the other flat and wide. The young child believes there is more in the tall receptacle than the flat one. Now the child can be confronted concretely with the nature of one-to-one correspondence between two versions of the same quantity. For there is an easy technique of checking: the beads can be counted or the liquid measured in some standard way. The same operations work for the conservation of spatial quantity if one uses a set of sticks for length or a set of tiles for surface, or by having the child transform the shape of volumes made up of the same number of blocks. In physics dissolving sugar or transforming the shapes of balls of plasticene while conserving volume provides comparable instruction. If teaching fails to bring the child properly from his perceptual, primitive notions to a proper intuition of the idea of invariance, the result is that he will count without having acquired the idea of the invariance of numerical quantities. Or he will use geometrical measures while remaining ignorant of the operation of transitivity—that if A includes B, and B includes C, then A also includes C. In physics he will apply calculations to imperfectly understood physical notions such as weight, volume, speed, and time. A teaching method that takes into account the natural thought processes will allow the child to discover such principles of invariance by giving him an opportunity to progress beyond his own primitive mode of thinking through confrontation by concrete data—as when he notes that liquid that looks greater in volume in a tall, thin receptacle is in fact the same as that quantity in a flat, low vessel. Concrete activity that becomes increasingly formal is what leads the child to the kind of mental mobility that approaches the naturally reversible operations of mathematics and logic. The child gradually comes to sense that any change may be mentally canceled out by the reverse operation—addition by subtraction—or that a change may be counterbalanced by a reciprocal change.

"A child often focuses on only one aspect of a phenomenon at a time, and this interferes with his understanding. We can set up little teaching experiments in such a way that he is forced to pay attention to other aspects. Thus, children up to about age seven estimate the speed of two automobiles by assuming that the one that gets there first is the faster, or that if one passes the other it is faster. To overcome such errors, one can, by using toy automobiles, show that two objects starting at different distances from a finish line cannot be judged by which one arrives first, or show that one car can pass another by circling it and still not finish first. These are simple exercises, but they speed the child toward attending to several features of a situation at once.

"In view of all this it seems highly arbitrary and very likely incorrect to delay the teaching, for example, of Euclidian or metric geometry until the end of the primary grades, particularly when projective geometry has not been given earlier. So too with the teaching of physics, which has much in it that can be profitably taught at an inductive or intuitive level much earlier. Basic notions in these fields are perfectly accessible to children of seven to ten years of age, *provided that they are divorced from their mathematical expression and studied through materials that the child can handle himself.*

"Another matter relates particularly to the ordering of a mathematics curriculum. Often the sequence of psychological development follows more closely the axiomatic order of a subject matter than it does the historical order of development of concepts within the field. One observes, for instance, that certain topological notions, such as connection, separation, being interior to, and so forth, precede the formation of

Euclidian and projective notions in geometry, though the former ideas are newer in their formalism in the history of mathematics than the latter. If any special justification were needed for teaching the structure of a subject in its proper logical or axiomatic order rather than its order of historical development, this should provide it. This is not to say that there may not be situations where the historical order is important from the point of view of its cultural or pedagogical relevance.

"As for teaching geometrical notions of perspective and projection, again there is much that can be done by the use of experiments and demonstrations that rest on the child's operational capacity to analyze concrete experience. We have watched children work with an apparatus in which rings of different diameter are placed at different positions between a candle and a screen with a fixed distance between them so that the rings cast shadows of varying sizes on the screen. The child learns how the cast shadow changes size as a function of the distance of the ring from the light source. By bringing to the child such concrete experience of light in revealing situations, we teach him maneuvers that in the end permit him to understand the general ideas underlying projective geometry.

"These examples lead us to think that it is possible to draw up methods of teaching the basic ideas in science and mathematics to children considerably younger than the traditional age. It is at this earlier age that systematic instruction can lay a groundwork in the fundamentals that can be used later and with great profit at the secondary level.

"The teaching of probabilistic reasoning, so very common and important a feature of modern science, is hardly developed in our educational system before college. The omission is probably due to the fact that school syllabi in nearly all countries follow scientific progress with a near-disastrous time lag. But it may also be due to the widespread belief that the understanding of random phenomena depends on the learner's grasp of the meaning of the rarity or commonness of events. And admittedly, such ideas are hard to get across to the young. Our research indicates that the understanding of random phenomena requires, rather, the use of certain concrete logical operations well within the grasp of the young child—provided these operations are free of awkward mathematical expression. Principal among these logical operations are disjunction ('either A *or* B is true') and combination.

Games in which lots are drawn, games of roulette, and games involving a Gaussian distribution of outcomes are all ideal for giving the child a basic grasp of the logical operation needed for thinking about probability. In such games, children first discover an entirely qualitative notion of chance defined as an uncertain event, contrasted with deductive certainty. The notion of probability as a fraction of certainty is discovered only later. Each of these discoveries can be made before the child ever learns the techniques of the calculus of probabilities or the formal expressions that normally go with probability theory. Interest in problems of a probabilistic nature could easily be awakened and developed before the introduction of any statistical processes or computation. Statistical manipulation and computation are only tools to be used *after* intuitive understanding has been established. If the array of computational paraphernalia is introduced first, then more likely than not it will inhibit or kill the development of probabilistic reasoning.

"One wonders in the light of all this whether it might not be interesting to devote the first two years of school to a series of exercises in manipulating, classifying, and ordering objects in ways that highlight basic operations of logical addition, multiplication, inclusion, serial ordering, and the like. For surely these logical operations are the basis of more specific operations and concepts of all mathematics and science. It may indeed by the case that such an early science and mathematics 'pre-curriculum' might go a long way toward building up in the child the kind of intuitive and more inductive understanding that could be given embodiment later in formal courses in mathematics and science. The effect of such an approach would be, we think, to put more continuity into science and mathematics and also to give the child a much better and firmer comprehension of the concepts which, unless he has this early foundation, he will mouth later without being able to use them in any effective way."

A comparable approach can surely be taken to the teaching of social studies and literature. There has been little research done on the kinds of concepts that a child brings to these subjects, although there is a wealth of observation and anecdote. Can one teach the structure of literary forms by presenting the child with the first part of a story and then having him complete it in the form of a comedy, a tragedy, or a farce—without ever using such words? When, for example, does the idea of "historical trend" develop, and what are its precursors in the child? How does one make a child aware of literary style? Perhaps the child can discover the idea of style through the presentation of the same content written in drastically different styles, in the manner of Beerbohm's *Christmas Garland*. Again, there is no reason to believe that any subject cannot be taught to any child at virtually any age in some form.

Here one is immediately faced with the question of the economy of teaching. One can argue that it might be better to wait until the child is thirteen or fourteen before beginning geometry so that the projective and intuitive first steps can immediately be followed up by a full formal presentation of the subject. Is it worth while to train the young inductively so that they may discover the basic order of knowledge before they can appreciate its formalism? In Professor Inhelder's memorandum, it was suggested that the first two grades might be given over to training the child in the basic logical operations that underlie instruction in mathematics and science. There is evidence to indicate that such rigorous and relevant early training has the effect of making later learning easier. Indeed the experiments on "learning set" seem to indicate just that—that one not only learns specifics but in so doing learns how to learn. So important is training per se that monkeys who have been given extensive training in problem solving suffer considerably less loss and recover more quickly after induced brain damage than animals who had not been previously thus educated. But the danger of such early training may be that it has the effect of training out original but deviant ideas. There is no evidence available on the subject, and much is needed.

The act of learning. Learning a subject seems to involve three almost simultaneous processes. First there is *acquisition* of new information—often information that runs counter to or is a replacement for what the person has previously known implicitly or explicitly. At the very least it is a refinement of previous knowledge. Thus one teaches a student Newton's laws of motion, which violate the testimony of the senses. Or in teaching a student about wave mechanics, one violates the student's belief in mechanical impact as the sole source of real energy transfer. Or one bucks the language and its built-in way of thinking in terms of "wasting energy" by introducing the student to the conservation theorem in physics which asserts that no energy is lost. More often the situation is less drastic, as when one teaches the details of the circulatory system to a student who already knows vaguely or intuitively that blood circulates.

A second aspect of learning may be called *transformation* —the process of manipulating knowledge to make it fit new tasks. We learn to "unmask" or analyze information, to order it in a way that permits extrapolation or interpolation or conversion into another form. Transformation comprises the ways we deal with information in order to go beyond it.

A third aspect of learning is *evaluation:* checking whether the way we have manipulated information is adequate to the task. Is the generalization fitting, have we extrapolated appropriately, are we operating properly? Often a teacher is crucial in helping with evaluation, but much of it takes place by judgments of plausibility without our actually being able to check rigorously whether we are correct in our efforts.

In the learning of any subject matter, there is usually a series of episodes, each episode involving the three processes. Photosynthesis might reasonably comprise material for a learning episode in biology, fitted into a more comprehensive learning experience such as learning about the conversion of energy generally. At its best a learning episode reflects what has gone before it and permits one to generalize beyond it.

A learning episode can be brief or long, contain many ideas or a few. How sustained an episode a learner is willing to undergo depends upon what the person expects to get from his efforts, in the sense of such external things as grades but also in the sense of a gain in understanding.

We usually tailor material to the capacities and needs of students by manipulating learning episodes in several ways: by shortening or lengthening the episode, by piling on extrinsic rewards in the form of praise and gold stars, or by dramatizing the shock of recognition of what the material means when fully understood. The unit in a curriculum is meant to be a recognition of the importance of learning episodes, though many units drag on with no climax in understanding. There is a surprising lack of research on how one most wisely devises adequate learning episodes for children at different ages and in different subject matters. There are many questions that need answers based on careful research, and to some of these we turn now.

There is, to begin with, the question of the balance between extrinsic rewards and intrinsic ones. There has been much written on the role of reward and punishment in learning, but very little indeed on the role of interest and curiosity and the lure of discovery. If it is our intention as teachers to inure the child to longer and longer episodes of learning, it may well be that intrinsic rewards in the form of quickened awareness and understanding will have to be emphasized far more in the detailed design of curricula. One of the least discussed ways of carrying a student through a hard unit of material is to challenge him with a chance to exercise his full powers, so that he may discover the pleasure of full and effective functioning. Good teachers know the power of this lure. Students should know what it feels like to be completely absorbed in a problem. They seldom experience this feeling in school. Given enough absorption in class, some students may be able to carry over the feeling to work done on their own.

There is a range of problems that have to do with how much emphasis should be placed on acquisition, transformation, and evaluation in a learning episode—getting facts, manipulating them, and checking one's ideas. Is it the case, for example, that it is best to give the young child a minimum set of facts first and then encourage him to draw the fullest set of implications possible from this knowledge? In short, should an episode for a young child contain little new information but emphasize what can be done to go beyond that bit on one's own? One teacher of social studies has had great success with fourth-graders through this approach: he begins, for example, with the fact that civilizations have most often begun in fertile river valleys—the only "fact." The students are encouraged in class discussion to figure out why this is the case and why it would be less likely for civilizations to start in mountainous country. The effect of this approach, essentially the technique of discovery, is that the child generates information on his own, which he can then check or evaluate against the sources, getting more new information in the process. This obviously is one kind of learning episode, and doubtless it has limited applicability. What other kinds are there, and are some more appropriate to certain topics and ages than others? It is not the case that "to learn is to learn is to learn," yet in the research literature there appears to be little recognition of differences in learning episodes.

With respect to the optimum length of a learning episode, there are a few commonsense things one can say about it, and these are perhaps interesting enough to suggest fruitful research possibilities. It seems fairly obvious, for example, that the longer and more packed the episode, the greater the pay-off must be in terms of increased power and understanding if the person is to be encouraged to move to a next episode with zest. Where grades are used as a substitute for the reward of understanding, it may well be that learning will cease as soon as grades are no longer given—at graduation.

It also seems reasonable that the more one has a sense of the structure of a subject, the more densely packed and longer a learning episode one can get through without fatigue. Indeed, the amount of new information in any learning episode is really the amount that we cannot quite fit into place at once. And there is a severe limit, as we have already noted, on how much of such unassimilated information we can keep in mind. The estimate is that adults can handle about seven independent items of information at a time. No norms are available for children—a deplorable lack.

There are many details one can discuss concerning the shaping of learning episodes for children, but the problems that have been mentioned will suffice to give their flavor. Inasmuch as the topic is central to an understanding of how one arranges a curriculum, it seems obvious that here is an area of research that is of the first importance.

The "spiral curriculum." If one respects the ways of thought of the growing child, if one is courteous enough to translate material into his logical forms and challenging enough to tempt him to advance, then it is possible to introduce him at an early age to the ideas and styles that in later life make an educated man. We might ask, as a criterion for any subject taught in primary school, whether, when fully developed, it is worth an adult's knowing, and whether having known it as a child makes a person a better adult. If the answer to both questions is negative or ambiguous, then the material is cluttering the curriculum.

If the hypothesis with which this section was introduced is true—that any subject can be taught to any child in some honest form—then it should follow that a curriculum ought to be built around the great issues, principles, and values that a society deems worthy of the continual concern of its members. Consider two examples—the teaching of literature and of science. If it is granted, for example, that it is desirable to give children an awareness of the meaning of human tragedy and a sense of compassion for it, is it not possible at the earliest appropriate age to teach the literature of tragedy in a manner that illuminates but does not threaten? There are many possible ways to begin: through a retelling of the great myths, through the use of children's classics, through presentation of and commentary on selected films that have proved themselves. Precisely what kinds of materials should be used at what age with what effect is a subject for research—research of several kinds. We may ask first about the child's conception of the tragic, and here one might proceed in much the same way that Piaget and his colleagues have proceeded in studying the child's conception of physical causality, of morality, of number, and the rest. It is only when we are equipped with such knowledge that we will be in a position to know how the child will translate whatever we present to him into his own subjective terms. Nor need we wait for all the research findings to be in before proceeding, for a skillful teacher can also experiment by attempting to teach what seems to be intuitively right for children of different ages, correcting as he goes. In time, one goes beyond to more complex versions of the same kind of literature or simply revisits some of the same books used earlier. What matters is that later teaching build upon earlier reactions to literature, that it seek to create an ever more explicit and mature understanding of the literature of tragedy. Any of the great literary forms can be handled in the same way, or any of the great themes—be it the form of comedy or the theme of identity, personal loyalty, or what not.

So too in science. If the understanding of number, measure, and probability is judged crucial in the pursuit of science, then instruction in these subjects should begin as intellectually honestly and as early as possible in a manner consistent with the child's forms of thought. Let the topics be developed and redeveloped in later grades. Thus, if most children are to take a tenth-grade unit in biology, need they approach the subject cold? Is it not possible, with a minimum of formal laboratory work if necessary, to introduce them to some of the major biological ideas earlier, in a spirit perhaps less exact and more intuitive?

Many curricula are originally planned with a guiding idea much like the one set forth here. But as curricula are actually executed, as they grow and change, they often lose their original form and suffer a relapse into a certain shapelessness. It is not amiss to urge that actual curricula be reexamined with an eye to the issues of continuity and development referred to in the preceding pages. One cannot predict the exact forms that revision might take; indeed, it is plain that there is now available too little research to provide adequate answers. One can only propose that appropriate research be undertaken with the greatest vigor and as soon as possible.

Education

MARTIN BUBER

(1926)

In the following lecture, Martin Buber declares that compulsion in education humiliates the child, creating re-
belliousness and ultimately alienation from a community
of human beings. Still, he cautions against the exaltation
of freedom in itself as a substantial good: "Freedom
is . . . the fruitful zero." The alternative to compulsion
is not freedom but communion—in education, the mutual
enjoyment of "pure dialogue" between teacher and pupil.
Education cultivates the individual's sensitivity to the
collective needs of his kind: to Buber it is thus, in the
best sense of the word, "religious." Noteworthy are his
remarks on the necessary asceticism of the educator, who
must influence but not interfere with his pupils—interference being caused by his desire for power or love.

"The development of the creative powers in the child" is our
present subject. I must not conceal from you for a single moment the fact that of the nine words in which it is expressed
only the last three raise no question for me.

The child, not just the individual child, individual children,
but the child, is certainly a reality. That in this hour, while we
make a beginning with the "development of creative powers,"
across the whole extent of this planet new human beings are
born who are characterized already and yet have still to be
characterized—this is a myriad realities, but also one reality.
In every hour the human race begins. We forget this too
easily in face of the massive fact of past life, of so-called world
history, of the fact that each child is born with a given disposition of "world-historical" origin, that is, inherited from the
riches of the whole human race, and that he is born into a
given situation of "world-historical" origin, that is, produced
from the riches of the world's events. This fact must not obscure the other no less important fact that in spite of everything, in this as in every hour, what has not been invades the

structure of what is, with ten thousand countenances, of which
not one has been seen before, with ten thousand souls still undeveloped but ready to develop—a creative event if ever there
was one, newness rising up, primal potential might. This potentiality, streaming unconquered, however much of it is
squandered, is the reality *child:* this phenomenon of uniqueness, which is more than just begetting and birth, this grace
of beginning again and ever again.

What greater care could we cherish or discuss than that this
grace may not henceforth be squandered as before, that the
might of newness may be preserved for renewal? Future history is not inscribed already by the pen of a causal law on a
roll which merely awaits unrolling; its characters are stamped
by the unforeseeable decisions of future generations. The part
to be played in this by everyone alive today, by every adolescent and child, is immeasurable, and immeasurable is our
part if we are educators. The deeds of the generations now
approaching can illumine the gray face of the human world
or plunge it in darkness. So, then, with education: if it at last
rises up and exists indeed, it will be able to strengthen the light-
spreading force in the hearts of the doers—how much it can
do this cannot be guessed, but only learned in action.

The child is a reality; education must become a reality. But
what does the "development of the creative powers" mean? Is
that the reality of education? Must education become that in
order to become a reality? Obviously those who arranged this
session and gave it its theme think this is so. They obviously
think that education has failed in its task till now because it has
aimed at something different from this development of what
is in the child, or has considered and promoted other powers
in the child than the creative. And probably they are amazed
that I question this objective, since I myself talk of the treasure
of eternal possibility and of the task of unearthing it. So I
must make clear that this treasure cannot be properly designated by the notion of "creative powers," nor its unearthing
by the notion of "development."

Creation originally means only the divine summons to the
life hidden in non-being. When Johann Georg Hamann and his
contemporaries carried over his term metaphorically to the
human capacity to give form, they marked a supreme peak of
mankind, the genius for forming, as that in which man's imag-
ing of God is authenticated in action. The metaphor has since
been broadened; there was a time (not long ago) when "creative" meant almost the same as "of literary ability"; in face

of this lowest condition of the word it is a real promotion for it to be understood, as it is here, quite generally as something dwelling to some extent in all men, in all children of men, and needing only the right cultivation. Art is then only the province in which a faculty of production, which is common to all, reaches completion. Everyone is elementally endowed with the basic powers of the arts, with that of drawing, for instance, or of music; these powers have to be developed, and the education of the whole person is to be built up on them as on the natural activity of the self.

We must not miss the importance of the reference which is the starting-point of this conception. It concerns a significant but hitherto not properly heeded phenomenon, which is certainly not given its right name here. I mean the existence of an autonomous instinct, which cannot be derived from others, whose appropriate name seems to me to be the "originator instinct." Man, the child of man, wants to make things. He does not merely find pleasure in seeing a form arise from material that presented itself as formless. What the child desires is its own share in this becoming of things: it wants to be the subject of this event of production. Nor is the instinct I am speaking of to be confused with the so-called instinct to busyness or activity which for that matter does not seem to me to exist at all (the child wants to set up or destroy, handle or hit, and so on, but never "busy himself"). What is important is that by one's own intensively experienced action something arises that was not there before. A good expression of this instinct is the way children of intellectual passion produce speech, in reality not as something they have taken over but with the headlong powers of utter newness: sound after sound tumbles out of them, rushing from the vibrating throat past the trembling lips into the world's air, and the whole of the little vital body vibrates and trembles, too, shaken by a bursting shower of selfhood. Or watch a boy fashioning some crude unrecognizable instrument for himself. Is he not astonished, terrified, at his own movement like the mighty inventors of prehistoric times? But it is also to be observed how even in the child's apparently "blind" lust for destruction his instinct of origination enters in and becomes dominant. Sometimes he begins to tear something up, for example, a sheet of paper, but soon he takes an interest in the form of the pieces, and it is not long before he tries—still by tearing—to produce definite forms.

It is important to recognize that the instinct of origination is autonomous and not derivatory. Modern psychologists are inclined to derive the multiform human soul from a single primal element—the "libido," the "will to power," and the like. But this is really only the generalization of certain degenerate states in which a single instinct not merely dominates but also spreads parasitically through the others. They begin with the cases (in our time of inner loss of community and oppression the innumerable cases) where such a hypertrophy breeds the appearance of exclusiveness, they abstract rules from them, and apply them with the whole theoretical and practical questionableness of such applications. In opposition to these doctrines and methods, which impoverish the soul, we must continually point out that human inwardness is in origin a polyphony in which no voice can be "reduced" to another, and in which the unity cannot be grasped analytically, but only heard in the present harmony. One of the leading voices is the instinct of origination.

This instinct is therefore bound to be significant for the work of education as well. Here is an instinct which, no matter to what power it is raised, never becomes greed, because it is not directed to "having" but only to doing; which alone among the instincts can grow only to passion, not to lust; which alone among the instincts cannot lead its subject away to invade the realm of other lives. Here is pure gesture which does not snatch the world to itself, but expresses itself to the world. Should not the person's growth into form, so often dreamed of and lost, at last succeed from this starting-point? For here this precious quality may be unfolded and worked out unimpeded. Nor does the new experiment lack demonstration. The finest demonstration I know, that I have just got to know, is this Children's Choir led by the marvelous Bakule of Prague, with which our conference opened. How under his leadership crippled creatures, seemingly condemned to lifelong idleness, have been released to a life of freely moving persons, rejoicing in their achievement, formable and forming, who know how to shape sights and sounds in multiform patterns and also how to sing out their risen souls wildly and gloriously; more, how a community of achievement, proclaimed in glance and response, has been welded together out of dull immured solitary creatures: all this seems to prove irrefutably not merely what fruitfulness but also what power, streaming through the whole constitution of man, the life of origination has.

But this very example, seen more deeply, shows us that the decisive influence is to be ascribed not to the release of an instinct but to the forces which meet the released instinct, namely, the educative forces. It depends on them, on their purity and fervor, their power of love and their discretion, into what connections the freed element enters and what becomes of it.

There are two forms, indispensable for the building of true human life, to which the originative instinct, left to itself, does not lead and cannot lead: to sharing in an undertaking and to entering into mutuality.

An individual achievement and an undertaking are two very different matters. To make a thing is mortal man's pride; but to be conditioned in a common job, with the unconscious humility of being a part, of participation and partaking, is the true food of earthly immortality. As soon as a man enters effectively into an undertaking, where he discovers and practices a community of work with other men, he ceases to follow the originative instinct alone.

Action leading to an individual achievement is a "one-sided" event. There is a force within the person, which goes out, impresses itself on the material, and the achievement arises objectively: the movement is over, it has run in one direction from the heart's dream into the world, and its course is finished. No matter how directly, as being approached and claimed, as perceiving and receiving, the artist experiences his dealings with the idea which he faces and which awaits embodiment, so long as he is engaged in his work spirit goes out from him and does not enter him, he replies to the world but he does not meet it anymore. Nor can he foster mutuality with his work: even in the legend Pygmalion is an ironical figure.

Yes, as an originator man is solitary. He stands wholly without bonds in the echoing hall of his deeds. Nor can it help him to leave his solitariness that his achievement is received enthusiastically by the many. He does not know if it is accepted, if his sacrifice is accepted by the anonymous receiver. Only if someone grasps his hand not as a "creator" but as a fellow creature lost in the world, to be his comrade or friend or lover beyond the arts, does he have an awareness and a share of mutuality. An education based only on the training of the instinct of origination would prepare a new human solitariness which would be the most painful of all.

The child, in putting things together, learns much that he can learn in no other way. In making something he gets to know its possibility, its origin and structure and connections, in a way he cannot learn by observation. But there is something else that is not learned in this way, and that is the viaticum of life. The being of the world as an object is learned from within, but not its being as a subject, its saying of *I* and *Thou*. What teaches us the saying of *Thou* is not the originative instinct but the instinct for communion.

This instinct is something greater than the believers in the "libido" realize: it is the longing for the world to become present to us as a person, which goes out to us as we to it, which chooses and recognizes us as we do it, which is confirmed in us as we in it. The child lying with half-closed eyes, waiting with tense soul for its mother to speak to it—the mystery of its will is not directed toward enjoying (or dominating) a person, or toward doing something of its own accord; but toward experiencing communion in face of the lonely night, which spreads beyond the window and threatens to invade.

But the release of powers should not be any more than a *presupposition* of education. In the end it is not the originative instinct alone which is meant by the "creative powers" that are to be "developed." These powers stand for human spontaneity. Real education is made possible—but is it also established?—by the realization that youthful spontaneity must not be suppressed but must be allowed to give what it can.

Let us take an example from the narrower sphere of the originative instinct—from the drawing class. The teacher of the "compulsory" school of thought began with rules and current patterns. Now you knew what beauty was, and you had to copy it; and it was copied either in apathy or in despair. The teacher of the "free" school places on the table a twig of broom, say, in an earthenware jug, and makes the pupils draw it. Or he places it on the table, tells the pupils to look at it, removes it, and then makes them draw it. If the pupils are quite unsophisticated soon not a single drawing will look like another. Now the delicate, almost imperceptible and yet important influence begins—that of criticism and instruction. The children encounter a scale of values that, however unacademic it may be, is quite constant, a knowledge of good and evil that, however individualistic it may be, is quite unambiguous. The more unacademic this scale of values, and the more individualistic this knowledge, the more deeply do the children experience the encounter. In the former instance the preliminary declaration of what alone was right made for resignation or rebellion; but in the latter, where the pupil gains the realization only after he has ventured far out on the way to his achievement, his heart is drawn to reverence for the form, and educated.

This almost imperceptible, most delicate approach, the raising of a finger, perhaps, or a questioning glance, is the other half of what happens in education.

Modern educational theory, which is characterized by tendencies to freedom, misunderstands the meaning of this other half, just as the old theory, which was characterized by the habit of authority, misunderstood the meaning of the first half. The symbol of the funnel is in course of being exchanged for that of the pump. I am reminded of the two camps in the doctrine of evolution, current in the seventeenth and eighteenth centuries, the animalculists, who believed that the whole germ was present in the spermatozoon, and the ovists who believed it was wholly present in the ovum. The theory of the development of powers in the child recalls, in its most extreme expressions, Swammerdam's "unfolding" of the "pre-formed" organism. But the growth of the spirit is no more an unfolding than that of the body. The dispositions which would be discovered in the soul of a new-born child—if the soul could in fact be analyzed—are nothing but capacities to receive and imagine the world. The world engenders the person in the individual. The world, that is the whole environment, nature and society, "educates" the human being: it draws out his powers, and makes him grasp and penetrate its objections. What we term education, conscious and will, means *a selection by man of the effective world:* it means to give decisive effective power to a selection of the world which is concentrated and manifested in the educator. The relation in education is lifted out of the purposelessly streaming education by all things, and is marked off as purpose. In this way, through the educator, the world for the first time becomes the true subject of its effect.

There was a time, there were times, where there neither was nor needed to be any specific calling of educator or teacher. There was a master, a philosopher or a coppersmith, whose journeymen and apprentices lived with him and learned, by being allowed to share in it, what he had to teach them out of his handwork or brainwork. But they also learned, without either their or his being concerned with it, they learned, without noticing that they did, the mystery of personal life: they received the spirit. Such a thing must still happen to some extent, where spirit and person exist, but it is expelled to the sphere of spirituality, of personality, and has become exceptional, it happens only "on the heights." Education as a purpose is bound to be summoned. We can as little return to the state of affairs that existed before there were schools as to that which existed before, say, technical science. But we can and must enter into the completeness of its growth to reality, into the perfect humanization of its reality. Our way is composed of losses that secretly become gains. Education has lost the paradise of pure instinctiveness and now consciously serves at the plow for the bread of life. It has been transformed; only in this transformation has it become visible.

Yet the master remains the model for the teacher. For if the educator of our day has to act consciously he must nevertheless do it "as though he did not." That raising of the finger, that questioning glance, are his genuine doing. Through him the selection of the effective world reaches the pupil. He fails the recipient when he presents this selection to him with a gesture of interference. It must be concentrated in him; and doing out of concentration has the appearance of rest. Interference divides the soul in his care into an obedient part and a rebellious part. But a hidden influence proceeding from his integrity has an integrating force.

The world, I said, has its influence as nature and as society on the child. He is educated by the elements, by air and light and the life of plants and animals, and he is educated by relationships. The true educator represents both; but he must be to the child as one of the elements.

The release of powers can be only a presupposition of education, nothing more. Put more generally; it is the nature of freedom to provide the place, but not the foundation as well, on which true life is raised. That is true both of inner, "moral" freedom and of outer freedom (which consists in not being hindered or limited). As the higher freedom, the soul's freedom of decision, signifies perhaps our highest moments but not a fraction of our substance, so the lower freedom, the freedom of development, signifies our capacity for growth but by no means our growth itself. This latter freedom is charged with importance as the actuality from which the work of education begins, but as its fundamental task it becomes absurd.

There is a tendency to understand this freedom, which may be termed evolutionary freedom, as at the opposite pole from compulsion, from being under a compulsion. But at the opposite pole from compulsion there stands not freedom but communion. Compulsion is a negative reality; communion is the positive reality; freedom is a possibility, possibility regained. At the opposite pole of being compelled by destiny or nature or men there does not stand being free of destiny or nature or men but to commune and to covenant with them. To do this, it is true that one must first have become independent; but this independence is a footbridge, not a dwelling place. Freedom is the vibrating needle, the fruitful zero. Compulsion in education means disunion, it means humiliation and re-belliousness. Communion in education is just communion, it means being opened up and drawn in. Freedom in education is the possibility of communion; it cannot be dispensed with and it cannot be made use of in itself; without it nothing succeeds, but neither does anything succeed by means of it: it is the run before the jump, the tuning of the violin, the con-firmation of that primal and mighty potentiality which it can-not even begin to actualize.

Freedom—I love its flashing face: it flashes forth from the darkness and dies away, but it has made the heart invulnerable. I am devoted to it, I am always ready to join in the fight for it, for the appearance of the flash, which lasts no longer than the eye is able to endure it, for the vibrating of the needle that was held down too long and was stiff. I give my left hand to the rebel and my right to the heretic: forward! But I do not trust them. They know how to die, but that is not enough. I love freedom, but I do not believe in it. How could one believe in it after looking in its face? It is the flash of a significance comprising all meanings, of a possibility com-prising all potentiality. For it we fight, again and again, from of old, victorious and in vain.

It is easy to understand that in a time when the deterioration of all traditional bonds has made their legitimacy questionable, the tendency to freedom is exalted, the springboard is treated as the goal and a functional good as substantial good. More-over, it is idle sentimentality to lament at great length that freedom is made the subject of experiments. Perhaps it is fitting for this time which has no compass that people should throw out their lives like a plummet to discover our bearings and the course we should set. But truly *their* lives! Such an experiment, when it is carried out, is a neck-breaking venture which cannot be disputed. But when it is talked about and talked around, in intellectual discussions and confessions and in the mutual pros and cons of their life's "problems," it is an abomination of disintegration. Those who stake themselves, as individuals or as a community, may leap and crash out into the swaying void where senses and sense fail, or through it and beyond into some kind of existence. But they must not make freedom into a theorem or a program. To become free of a bond is destiny; one carries that like a cross, not like a cockade. Let us realize the true meaning of being free of a bond: it means that a quite personal responsibility takes the place of one shared with many generations. Life lived in freedom is personal responsibility or it is a pathetic farce.

I have pointed out the power which alone can give a content to empty freedom and a direction to swaying and spinning freedom. I believe in it, I trust those devoted to it.

This fragile life between birth and death can nevertheless be a fulfillment—if it is a dialogue. In our life and experience we are addressed; by thought and speech and action, by producing and by influencing we are able to answer. For the most part we do not listen to the address, or we break into it with chatter. But if the word comes to us and the answer proceeds from us then human life exists, though brokenly, in the world. The kindling of the response in that "spark" of the soul, the blazing up of the response, which occurs time and again, to the unexpectedly approaching speech, we term responsibility. We practice responsibility for that realm of life allotted and entrusted to us for which we are able to respond, that is, for which we have a relation of deeds which may count—in all our inadequacy—as a proper response. The extent to which a man, in the strength of the reality of the spark, can keep a traditional bond, a law, a direction, is the extent to which he is permitted to lean his responsibility on something (more than this is not vouchsafed to us, responsibility is not taken off our shoulders). As we "become free" this leaning on something is more and more denied to us, and our responsibility must become personal and solitary.

From this point of view education and its transformation in the hour of the crumbling of bonds are to be understood.

It is usual to contrast the principle of the "new" education as "Eros" with that of the "old" education as the "will to power."

In fact the one is as little a principle of education as the other. A principle of education, in a sense still to be clarified, can only be a basic relation which is fulfilled in education. But Eros and the will to power are alike passions of the soul for whose real elaboration a place is prepared elsewhere. Education can supply for them only an incidental realm and moreover one which sets a limit to their elaboration; nor can this limit be infringed without the realm itself being destroyed. The one can as little as the other constitute the educational attitude.

The "old" educator, in so far as he was an educator, was not "the man with a will to power," but he was the bearer of assured values which were strong in tradition. If the educator represents the world to the pupil, the "old" educator represented particularly the historical world, the past. He was the ambassador of history to this intruder, the "child"; he carried to him, as the Pope in the legend did to the prince of the Huns, the magic of the spiritual forces of history; he instilled values into the child or he drew the child into the values. The man who reduces this encounter between the cosmos of history and its eternally new chaos, between Zeus and Dionysos, to the formula of the "antagonism between fathers and sons," has never beheld it in his spirit. Zeus the Father does not stand for a generation but for a world, for the olympic, the formed world; the world of history faces a particular generation, which is the world of nature renewed again and again, always without history.

This situation of the old type of education is, however, easily used, or misused, by the individual's will to power, for this will is inflated by the authority of history. The will to power becomes convulsive and passes into fury, when the authority begins to decay, that is, when the magical validity of tradition disappears. Then the moment comes near when the teacher no longer faces the pupil as an ambassador but only as an individual, as a static atom to the whirling atom. Then no matter how much he imagines he is acting from the fullness of the objective spirit, in the reality of his life he is thrown back on himself, cast on his own resources, and hence filled with longing. Eros appears. And Eros finds employment in the new situation of education as the will to power did in the old situation. But Eros is not a bearer or the ground or the principle any more than the will to power was. He only claims to be that, in order not to be recognized as longing, as the stranger given refuge. And many believe it.

Nietzsche did not succeed in glorifying the will to power as much as Plato glorified Eros. But in our concern for the creature in this great time of concern, for both alike we have not to consider the myths of the philosophers but the actuality of present life. In entire opposition to any glorification we have to see that Eros—that is, not "love," but Eros the male and magnificent—whatever else may belong to him, necessarily includes this one thing, that he desires to enjoy men; and education, the peculiar essence bearing this name which is composed of no others, excludes precisely this desire. However mightily an educator is possessed and inspired by Eros, if he obeys him in the course of his educating them he stifles the growth of his blessings. It must be one or the other: either he takes on himself the tragedy of the person, and offers an unblemished daily sacrifice, or the fire enters his work and consumes it.

Eros is choice, choice made from an inclination. This is precisely what education is not. The man who is loving in Eros chooses the beloved, the modern educator finds his pupil there before him. From this unerotic situation the *greatness* of the modern educator is to be seen—and most clearly when he is a teacher. He enters the schoolroom for the first time, he sees them crouching at the desks, indiscriminately flung together, the misshapen and the well-proportioned, animal faces, empty faces, and noble faces in indiscriminate confusion, like the presence of the created universe; the glance of the educator accepts and receives them all. He is assuredly no descendant of the Greek gods, who kidnapped those they loved. But he seems to me to be a representative of the true God. For if God "forms the light and creates darkness," man is able to love both—to love light in itself, and darkness toward the light.

If this educator should ever believe that for the sake of education he has to practice selection and arrangement, then he will be guided by another criterion than that of inclination, however legitimate this may be in its own sphere; he will be guided by the recognition of values which is in his glance as an educator. But even then his selection remains suspended, under constant correction by the special humility of the educator for whom the life and particular being of all his pupils is the decisive factor to which his "hierarchic" recognition is subordinated. For in the manifold variety of the children the variety of creation is placed before him.

In education, then, there is a lofty asceticism: an asceticism which rejoices in the world, for the sake of the responsibility for a realm of life which is entrusted to us for our influence but not our interference—either by the will to power or by Eros. The spirit's service of life can be truly carried out only in the system of a reliable counterpoint—regulated by the laws of the different forms of relation—of giving and withholding oneself, intimacy and distance, which of course must not be controlled by reflection but must arise from the living tact of the natural and spiritual man. Every form of relation in which the spirit's service of life is realized has its special objectivity, its structure of proportions and limits which in no way resists the fervor of personal comprehension and penetration, though it does resist any confusion with the person's own spheres. If this structure and its resistance are not respected then a dilettantism will prevail which claims to be aristocratic, though in reality it is unsteady and feverish: to provide it with the most sacred names and attitudes will not help it past its inevitable consequence of disintegration. Consider, for example, the relation of doctor and patient. It is essential that this should be a real human relation experienced with the spirit by the one who is addressed; but as soon as the helper is touched by the desire—in however subtle a form—to dominate or to enjoy his patient, or to treat the latter's wish to be dominated or enjoyed by him other than as a wrong condition needing to be cured, the danger of a falsification arises, beside which all quackery appears peripheral.

The objectively ascetic character of the sphere of education must not, however, be misunderstood as being so separated from the instinct to power and from Eros that no bridge can be flung from them to it. I have already pointed out how very significant Eros can be to the educator without corroding his work. What matters here is the threshold and the transformation which takes place on it. It is not the church alone which has a testing threshold on which a man is transformed or becomes a lie. But in order to be able to carry out this ever renewed transition from sphere to sphere he must have carried it out once in a decisive fashion and taken up in himself the essence of education. How does this happen? There is an elemental experience which shatters at least the assurance of the erotic as well as the cratetic man, but sometimes does more, forcing its way at white heat into the heart of the instinct and remolding it. A reversal of the single instinct takes place, which does not eliminate it but reverses its system of direction. Such a reversal can be effected by the elemental experience with which the real process of education begins and on which it is based. I call it experiencing the other side.

A man belabors another, who remains quite still. Then let us assume that the striker suddenly receives in his soul the blow which he strikes: the same blow; that he receives it as the other who remains still. For the space of a moment he experiences the situation from the other side. Reality imposes itself on him. What will he do? Either he will overwhelm the voice of the soul, or his impulse will be reversed.

A man caresses a woman, who lets herself be caressed. Then let us assume that he feels the contact from two sides—with the palm of his hand still, and also with the woman's skin. The twofold nature of the gesture, as one that takes place between two persons, thrills through the depth of enjoyment in his heart and stirs it. If he does not deafen his heart he will have—not to renounce the enjoyment but—to love.

I do not in the least mean that the man who has had such an experience would from then on have this two-sided sensation in every such meeting—that would perhaps destroy his instinct. But the one extreme experience makes the other person present to him for all time. A transfusion has taken place after which a mere elaboration of subjectivity is never again possible or tolerable to him.

Only an inclusive power is able to take the lead; only an inclusive Eros is love. Inclusiveness is the complete realization of the submissive person, the desired person, the "partner," not by the fancy but by the actuality of the being.

It would be wrong to identify what is meant here with the familiar but not very significant term "empathy." Empathy means, if anything, to glide with one's own feeling into the dynamic structure of an object, a pillar or a crystal or the branch of a tree, or even of an animal or a man, and as it were to trace it from within, understanding the formation and motoriality of the object with the perceptions of one's own muscles; it means to "transpose" oneself over there and in there. Thus it means the exclusion of one's own concreteness, the extinguishing of the actual situation of life, the absorption in pure aestheticism of the reality in which one participates. Inclusion is the opposite of this. It is the extension of one's own concreteness, the fulfillment of the actual situation of life, the complete presence of the reality in which one participates. Its elements are, first, a relation, of no matter what kind, between two persons, second, an event experienced by them in common, in which at least one of them actively participates, and, third, the fact that this one person, without forfeiting anything of the felt reality of his activity, at the same time lives through the common event from the standpoint of the other.

A relation between persons that is characterized in more or less degree by the element of inclusion may be termed a dialogical relation.

A dialogical relation will show itself also in genuine conversation, but it is not composed of this. Not only is the shared silence of two such persons a dialogue, but also their dialogical life continues, even when they are separated in space, as the continual potential presence of the one to the other, as an unexpressed intercourse. On the other hand, all conversation derives its genuineness only from the consciousness of the element of inclusion—even if this appears only abstractly as an "acknowledgement" of the actual being of the partner in the conversation; but this acknowledgement can be real and effective only when it springs from an experience of inclusion, of the other side.

The reversal of the will to power and of Eros means that relations characterized by these are made dialogical. For that very reason it means that the instinct enters into communion with the fellowman and into responsibility for him as an allotted and entrusted realm of life.

The element of inclusion, with whose recognition this clarification begins, is the same as that which constitutes the relation in education.

The relation in education is one of pure dialogue.

I have referred to the child, lying with half-closed eyes waiting for his mother to speak to him. But many children do not need to wait, for they know that they are unceasingly addressed in a dialogue which never breaks off. In face of the lonely night which threatens to invade, they lie preserved and guarded, invulnerable, clad in the silver mail of trust.

Trust, trust in the world, because this human being exists—that is the most inward achievement of the relation in education. Because this human being exists, meaninglessness, however hard pressed you are by it, cannot be the real truth. Because this human being exists, in the darkness the light lies hidden, in fear salvation, and in the callousness of one's fellowmen the great Love.

Because this human being exists: therefore he must be really there, really facing the child, not merely there in spirit. He may not let himself be represented by a phantom: the death of the phantom would be a catastrophe for the child's pristine soul. He need possess none of the perfections which the child may dream he possesses; but he must be really there. In order to be and to remain truly present to the child he must have gathered the child's presence into his own store as one of the bearers of his communion with the world, one of the focuses of his responsibilities for the world. Of course he cannot be continually concerned with the child, either in thought or in deed, nor ought he to be. But if he has really gathered the child into his life then that subterranean dialogic, that steady potential presence of the one to the other is established and endures. Then there is reality *between* them, there is mutuality.

But this mutality—that is what constitutes the peculiar nature of the relation in education—cannot be one of inclusion, although the true relation of the educator to the pupil is based on inclusion. No other relation draws its inner life like this one from the element of inclusion, but no other is in that regard like this, completely directed to one-sidedness, so that if it loses one-sidedness it loses essence.

We may distinguish three chief forms of the dialogical relation.

The first rests on an abstract but mutual experience of inclusion.

The clearest example of this is a disputation between two men, thoroughly different in nature and outlook and calling, where in an instant—as by the action of a messenger as anonymous as he is invisible—it happens that each is aware of the other's full legitimacy, wearing the insignia of necessity and of meaning. What an illumination! The truth, the strength of conviction, the "standpoint," or rather the circle of movement, of each of them, is in no way reduced by this. There is no "relativizing," but we may say that, in the sign of the limit, the essence of mortal recognition, fraught with primal destiny, is manifested to us. To recognize means for us creatures the fulfillment by each of us, in truth and responsibility, of his own relation to the Present Being, through our receiving all that is manifested of it and incorporating it into our own being, with all our force, faithfully, and open to the world and the spirit. In this way living truth arises and endures. We have become aware that it is with the other as with ourselves, and that what rules over us both is not a truth of recognition but the truth-of-existence and the existence-of-truth of the Present Being. In this way we have become able *to acknowledge*.

I have called this form abstract, not as though its basic experience lacked immediacy, but because it is related to man only as a spiritual person and is bound to leave out the full

reality of his being and life. The other two forms proceed
from the inclusion of this full reality.

Of these the first, the relation of education, is based on a
concrete but one-sided experience of inclusion.

If education means to let a selection of the world affect a
person through the medium of another person, then the one
through whom this takes place, rather, who makes it take place
through himself, is caught in a strange paradox. What is otherwise found only as grace, inlaid in the folds of life—the influencing of the lives of others with one's own life—becomes here
a function and a law. But since the educator has to such an
extent replaced the master, the danger has arisen that the new
phenomenon, the will to educate, may degenerate into arbi-
trariness, and that the educator may carry out his selection
and his influence from himself and his idea of the pupil, not
from the pupil's own reality. One only needs to read, say, the
accounts of Pestalozzi's teaching method to see how easily,
even with the noblest teachers, arbitrary self-will is mixed up
with will. This is almost always due to an interruption or a
temporary flagging of the act of inclusion, which is not
merely regulative for the realm of education, as for other
realms, but is actually constitutive; so that the realm of education acquires its true and proper force from the constant
return of this act and the constantly renewed connection with
it. The man whose calling it is to influence the being of persons
that can be determined, must experience this action of his
(however much it may have assumed the form of non-action)
ever anew from the other side. Without the action of his spirit
being in any way weakened he must at the same time be over
there, on the surface of that other spirit which is being acted
upon—and not of some conceptual, contrived spirit, but all
the time the wholly concrete spirit of this individual and unique
being who is living and confronting him, and who stands with
him in the common situation of "educating" and "being
educated" (which is indeed one situation, only the other is at
the other end of it). It is not enough for him to imagine the
child's individuality, nor to experience him directly as a
spiritual person and then to acknowledge him. Only when he
catches himself "from over there," and feels how it affects
one, how it affects this other human being, does he recognize
the real limit, baptize his self-will in Reality and make it true
will, and renew his paradoxical legitimacy. He is of all men
the one for whom inclusion may and should change from an
alarming and edifying event into an atmosphere.

But however intense the mutuality of giving and taking with which he is bound to his pupil, inclusion cannot be mutual in this case. He experiences the pupil's being educated, but the pupil cannot experience the educating of the educator. The educator stands at both ends of the common situation, the pupil only at one end. In the moment when the pupil is able to throw himself across and experience from over there, the educative relation would be burst asunder, or change into friendship.

We call friendship the third form of the dialogical relation, which is based on a concrete and mutual experience of inclusion. It is the true inclusion of one another by human souls.

The educator who practices the experience of the other side and stands firm in it, experiences two things together, first that he is limited by otherness, and second that he receives grace by being bound to the other. He feels from "over there" the acceptance and the rejection of what is approaching (that is, approaching from himself, the educator)—of course often only in a fugitive mood or an uncertain feeling; but this discloses the real need and absence of need in the soul. In the same way the foods a child likes and dislikes is a fact which does not, indeed, procure for the experienced person but certainly helps him to gain an insight into what substances the child's body needs. In learning from time to time what this human being needs and does not need at the moment, the educator is led to an ever deeper recognition of what the human being needs in order to grow. But he is also led to the recognition of what he, the "educator," is able and what he is unable to give of what is needed—and what he can give now, and what not yet. So the responsibility for this realm of life allotted and entrusted to him, the constant responsibility for this living soul, points him to that which seems impossible and yet is somehow granted to us—to self-education. But self-education, here as everywhere, cannot take place through one's being concerned with oneself but only through one's being concerned, knowing what it means, with the world. The forces of the world which the child needs for the building up of his substance must be chosen by the educator from the world and drawn into himself.

The education of men by men means the selection of the effective world by a person and in him. The educator gathers in the constructive forces of the world. He distinguishes, rejects, and confirms in himself, in his self which is filled with the world. The constructive forces are eternally the same: they are the world bound up in community, turned to God. The educator educates himself to be their vehicle.

Then is this the "principle" of education, its normal and fixed maxim?

No; it is only the *principium* of its reality, the beginning of its reality—wherever it begins.

There is not and never has been a norm and fixed maxim of education. What is called so was always only the norm of a culture, of a society, a church, an epoch, to which education too, like all stirring and action of the spirit, was submissive, and which education translated into its language. In a formed age there is in truth no autonomy of education, but only in an age which is losing form. Only in it, in the disintegration of traditional bonds, in the spinning whirl of freedom, does personal responsibility arise which in the end can no longer lean with its burden of decision on any church or society or culture, but is lonely in face of Present Being.

In an age which is losing form the highly-praised "personalities," who know how to serve its fictitious forms and in their name to dominate the age, count in the truth of what is happening no more than those who lament the genuine forms of the past and are diligent to restore them. The ones who count are those persons who—though they may be of little renown—respond to and are responsible for the continuation of the living spirit, each in the active stillness of his sphere of work.

The question which is always being brought forward—"To where, to what, must we educate?"—misunderstands the situation. Only times which know a figure of general validity—the Christian, the gentleman, the citizen—know an answer to that question, not necessarily in words, but by pointing with the finger to the figure which rises clear in the air, out-topping all. The forming of this figure in all individuals, out of all materials, is the formation of a "culture." But when all figures are shattered, when no figure is able anymore to dominate and shape the present human material, what is there left to form?

Nothing but the image of God.

That is the indefinable, only factual, direction of the responsible modern educator. This cannot be a theoretical answer to the question "To what?," but only, if at all, an answer carried out in deeds; an answer carried out by non-doing.

The educator is set now in the midst of the need which he experiences in inclusion, but only a bit deeper in it. He is set in the midst of the service, only a bit higher up, which he invokes without words; he is set in the *imitatio Dei absconditi sed non ignoti*.

When all "directions" fail there arises in the darkness over the abyss the one true direction of man, toward the creative Spirit, toward the Spirit of God brooding on the face of the waters, toward Him of whom we know not whence He comes and whither He goes.

That is man's true autonomy which no longer betrays, but responds.

Man, the creature, who forms and transforms the creation, cannot create. But he, each man, can expose himself and others to the creative Spirit. And he can call upon the Creator to save and perfect His image.

Bibliography

The bibliography is not intended to include every reference and footnote cited in individual selections. A reduced rather than inclusive bibliography was attempted: one which would provide a framework for the present volume.

Abraham, Karl. *Clinical Papers and Essays on Psychoanalysis*. London: Hogarth Press, 1955, paper numbers 1, 6, 7, 11, 19.

Adorno, Theodor W., Else Frenkel-Brunswik, D. J. Levinson, and R. N. Sanford. *The Authoritarian Personality*. New York: Harper and Bros., 1950.

Aichhorn, August. *Wayward Youth*. New York: Viking, 1925.

Ames, Louise B. and J. Learned, "Imaginary Companions and Related Phenomena." *Journal of Genetic Psychology*, 1963, 69, 147–167.

Anthony, Sylvia. *The Child's Discovery of Death*. London: Routledge and Kegan Paul, 1940.

Bartlett, F. C. *Remembering: A Study in Experimental and Social Psychology*. Cambridge: Cambridge University Press, 1932.

Bender, Lauretta. *Aggression, Hostility and Anxiety in Childhood*. Springfield, Illinois: Thomas, 1953.

——, and J. Frosch. "Children's Reactions to the War." *American Journal of Orthopsychiatry*, 1942, 12, 571–586.

——, and R. Lourie. "The Effect of Comic Books on the Ideology of Children." *American Journal of Orthopsychiatry*, July 1941, 540–549.

——, "Homosexual Trends in Children." *American Journal of Orthopsychiatry*, 1941, 730–742.

Benedict, Ruth. "Child Rearing in Certain European Countries." *American Journal of Orthopsychiatry*, 1948, XIX, No. 2, 342–350.

Bettelheim, Bruno. *The Empty Fortress*. New York: The Free Press, 1967.

——, *Love Is Not Enough*. Glencoe, Illinois: The Free Press, 1952.

——, *Truants from Life*. Glencoe, Illinois: The Free Press, 1955.

Blatz, William E., K. D. Allin and D. A. Millichamp. *A Study of Laughter in the Nursery School Child*. Toronto: University of Toronto Press, 1936.

Blos, Peter. *On Adolescence*. Glencoe, Illinois: The Free Press, 1962.

Bornstein, Berta. "Phobia in a Two-and-a-half-year-old Child." *Psychoanalytic Quarterly*, IV, 1934.

Bowlby, John. "Grief and Mourning in Infancy and Early Childhood." *Psychoanalytic Study of the Child*, Vol. 15, 1960.

——, "Separation Anxiety." *International Journal of Psychoanalysis*, 41, 1960.

Briffault, Robert. *The Mothers*. New York: Macmillan, 1927.

Brill, Abraham A. "The Only or Favorite Child in Adult Life." *New York State Journal of Medicine*, 1912.

Bruch, Hilda. "Obesity in Childhood and Personality Development." *American Journal of Orthopsychiatry*, XI, 1941.

Bühler, Charlotte. *The First Year of Life*. New York: John Day, 1930.

Bühler, Karl. *The Mental Development of the Child*. New York: Harcourt, Brace, 1930.

Burlingham, Dorothy. "Child Analysis and the Mother." *Psychoanalytic Quarterly*, IV, 1935.

Burrow, Trigant. *The Structure of Insanity*. London: Routledge & Kegan Paul, 1930.

Caplan, Gerald (ed.). *Emotional Problems of Early Childhood*. New York: Basic Books, 1955.

Carmichael, L. *Manual of Child Psychology* (Second ed.). New York: John Wiley, 1954.

Chamberlain, A. F. *The Child: A Study in the Evolution of Man*. London: Walter Scott, 1901.

Claparede, Edouard. *Psychology of the Child*. New York: Longmans, Green & Co., 1911.

Clark, Kenneth. *Prejudice and Your Child*. Boston: Beacon Press, 1963.

Coles, Robert. *Children of Crisis: A Study of Courage and Fear*. Boston: Atlantic-Little, Brown, 1967.

Cook, H. Caldwell. *The Play Way*. New York: Frederick A. Stokes Co., 1917.

Daedalus. *Creativity and Learning*. Cambridge: American Academy of Arts and Sciences, Summer 1965.

Dalcroze, Emile J. *Rhythm, Music and Education*. London, 1921.

Darwin, Charles. "A Biographical Sketch of an Infant," *Mind*, II, 1877, 286–294.

Davis, Allison. *Children of Bondage*. American Council on Education, 1940.

Davis, Clara. "Results of the Self-Selection of Diets by Young Children." *Canadian Medical Association Journal*, 1939, 41:257–261.

Deutsch, Helen. "A Two-Year-Old's First Love Comes to Grief." *Dynamic Psychopathology of Childhood*, ed. Lucie Jessner and Eleanor Pavenstedt. New York: Grune & Stratton, 1959.

Dewey, John. *Experience and Education*. New York: Macmillan, 1954.

Dewey, John. *Human Nature and Conduct.* New York: Holt & Co., 1930.

——, *The School and Society.* Chicago: University of Chicago Press, 1915.

——, *Schools of Tomorrow.* New York: E. P. Dutton & Co., 1915.

Dollard, John L. *Caste and Class in a Southern Town.* New Haven: Yale University Press, 1937.

——, and Allison Davis. *Children of Bondage.* Washington, D.C.: American Council on Education, 1940.

——, et al. *Frustration and Aggression.* New Haven: Yale University Press, 1939.

Durkheim, Emile. *Moral Education.* New York: The Free Press, 1961.

Erikson, Erik H. *Childhood and Society.* New York: W. W. Norton & Co., 1950.

——, "Configurations in Play." *Psychoanalytic Quarterly,* 1937, VI, No. 2, 2 139–214.

——, "Identity and the Life Cycle," *Psychological Issues,* 1959, Vol. I, No. 1.

——, *Insight and Responsibility.* New York: W. W. Norton & Co., 1964.

——, "The Problem of Ego Identity." *Journal of American Psychoanalytic Association,* IV, 56–121.

——, "Studies in the Interpretation of Play." *Genetic Psychological Monographs,* 1940, 22, 557–671.

——, *Youth: Change and Challenge.* New York: Basic Books, 1963.

——, "Youth: Fidelity and Diversity." *Daedalus,* 91:5–27.

Escalona, Sibylle. "Early Phases of Personality Development." Child Development Publications, 1953.

Feifel, Herman (ed.). *The Meaning of Death.* New York: McGraw-Hill, 1959.

Fenichel, Otto. "The Means of Education." *Psychoanalytic Study of the Child,* I. New York: International Universities Press, 1945–1946.

——, *The Psychoanalytic Theory of Neurosis.* New York: Norton, 1945.

Ferenczi, Sandor. "Stages in the Development of the Sense of Reality." *Contributions to Psychoanalysis.* Boston: Richard Badger, 1916.

——, "The Unwelcome Child and the Death Instinct." *International Journal of Psychoanalysis,* 1929, 10:125–129.

Frenkel-Brunswik, Else. "Patterns of Social and Cognitive Outlook in Children and Parents." *American Journal of Orthopsychiatry,* 1951, 21, 543–558.

——, "A Study of Prejudice in Children." *Human Relations,* 1948, I, No. 3.

Freud, Anna. *The Ego and the Mechanisms of Defense*. London: Hogarth Press, 1937.

——, *Normality and Pathology in Childhood: Assessments of Development*. New York: International Universities Press, 1965.

Freud, Sigmund. "Analysis of a Phobia in a Five-year-old Boy." *Collected Papers*, Vol. III. New York: Basic Books, 1959.

——, "A Child is Being Beaten." *Collected Papers*, Vol. III.

——, "A Childhood Recollection," from the *Dichtung und Wahrheit*, Vol. II.

——, "The Infantile Genital Organization of the Libido." Vol. II.

——, "Infantile Mental Life: Two Lies Told by Children." Vol. II.

——, "The Passing of the Oedipus Complex." Vol. II.

——, "The Sexual Enlightenment of Children." Vol. II.

——, "On the Sexual Theories of Children." Vol. II.

——, "Three Contributions to the Sexual Theory" (Translated by A. A. Brill). Nervous and Mental Disease Monograph Series, No. 7, 1910.

Friedenberg, Edgar Z. *The Vanishing Adolescent*. Boston: Beacon Press, 1959.

——, *The Dignity of Youth and Other Atavisms*. Boston: Beacon Press, 1965.

Froebel, Friedrich. *Chief Writings in Education*, translated by S. S. F. Fletcher and J. Welton. London, 1908.

Fromm, Erich. *The Forgotten Language: An Introduction to the Understanding of Dreams, Fairy Tales and Myths*. New York: Rinehart & Winston, 1951.

Gesell, Arnold. *The Embryology of Behavior*. New York: Harper, 1945.

——, *Infancy and Human Growth*. New York: Macmillan, 1928.

——, "Jealousy." *American Journal of Psychology*, 1906, 17.

——, and Frances Ilg. *Infant and Child in the Culture of Today*. New York: Harper, 1943.

——, et al. *The Child from Five to Ten*. New York: Harper, 1946.

Goodman, Paul. *Growing Up Absurd*. New York: Random House, 1960.

Hall, Stanley. *Aspects of Child Life and Education*. New York: Appleton, 1921.

——, "The Development of Religious Experience in Children." *American Journal of Sociology*, 5, 112–122.

Harms, Ernest (ed.). "Schizophrenia in Childhood." *The Nervous Child*, I. New York: The Philosophical Library, 1941.

——, "Psychosomatic Aspects of Childhood." *The Nervous Child*, V.

Hartley, Ruth, L. K. Frank and R. Goldenson. *Understanding Children's Play*. New York: Columbia University Press, 1952.

Hartmann, Heinz. *The Ego and the Problem of Adaptation*. New York: Vintage, 1964.

Havighurst, Robert J. "Development of the Ideal Self in Childhood and Adolescence." *Journal of Educational Research,* 40, 241–257.

Horney, Karen. *The Neurotic Personality of Our Time.* New York: Norton, 1937.

——, *Neurosis and Human Growth.* New York: Norton, 1950.

Huizinga, Johan. *Homo Ludens: A Study of the Play Element in Culture.* London: 1950.

Infant Care, 1945 & 1951. Children's Bureau, Washington, D.C.

Isaacs, Susan. *Childhood and After.* New York: International Universities Press: 1949.

——, *Intellectual Growth in Young Children.* New York: Harcourt, Brace, 1931.

——, *The Social Development in Young Children.* New York: Harcourt, Brace, 1933.

——, *The Nursery Years.* New York: Vanguard Press, 1936.

Jersild, Arthur Thomas, Catherine L. Jersild and Frances V. Markey. *Children's Fears, Dreams, Wishes, Daydreams, Likes, Dislikes, Pleasant and Unpleasant Memories.* Child Development Monographs, No. 12, 1935. New York: Teachers College, Columbia University.

Jersild, Arthur Thomas and Francis B. Holmes. *Children's Fears.* Child Development Monographs, No. 20, 1935. New York: Teachers College, Columbia University.

Jung, Carl G. *Collected Works.* New York: Pantheon Books, 1953–1964.

Kardiner, Abram. *The Individual and His Society.* New York: Columbia University Press, 1939, 1955.

Keniston, Kenneth. *The Uncommitted: Alienated Youth in American Society.* New York: Harcourt, Brace & World, 1965.

Kimmins, Charles William. *Children's Dreams: An Unexplored Land.* London: G. Allen & Unwin, 1937.

Kirkpatrick, Edwin A. *Imagination and its Place in Education.* Boston: 1920.

Klein, Melanie. *The Psychoanalysis of Children.* London: Hogarth Press, 1950.

——, and J. Rivière. *Love, Hate and Reparation.* London: Hogarth Press, 1937.

——, *Narrative of a Child Analysis.* London: Hogarth Press, 1929.

——, "Personification in the Play of Children." *International Journal of Psychoanalysis,* 1929, Vol. X.

Koffka, Kurt. *The Growth of the Mind: An Introduction to Child Psychology.* New York: Harcourt, Brace, 1928.

Kohler, Wolfgang. *Gestalt Psychology.* New York: Liveright Publishing Company, 1946.

Leighton, Dorothea and Claude Kluckhohn. *Children of the People.* Cambridge: Harvard University Press, 1947.

Levy, David M. *Maternal Overprotection*. New York: Columbia University Press, 1943.

——, *Studies in Sibling Rivalry*. New York: The American Orthopsychiatric Association, 1937.

Lewin, Kurt. *A Dynamic Theory of Personality*. New York: McGraw-Hill, 1935.

Lindner, Robert M. *Rebel Without a Cause*. New York: Grune & Stratton, 1944.

Locke, John. *Some Thoughts Concerning Education* (Fourth ed.). London: A. and J. Churchill, 1699.

Lowenfeld, Margaret. *Play in Childhood*. London: Gollancz, 1935.

Malinowski, Bronislaw. *Sex and Repression in Savage Society*. New York: Harcourt, Brace, 1927.

Markey, Frances V. *Imaginative Behavior of Pre-School Children*. New York: Columbia University Press, 1935.

Markey, J. F. *The Symbolic Process and its Integration in Children*. London: Kegan Paul, Trench, Trubner & Co., 1928.

Mead, Margaret. *And Keep Your Powder Dry*. New York: William Morrow, 1942.

——, *Coming of Age in Samoa*. New York: William Morrow & Co., 1928.

——, *Continuities in Cultural Evolution*. New Haven: Yale University Press, 1964.

——, *Growth and Culture*. New York: Putnam, 1951.

——, *The School in American Culture*. Cambridge: Harvard University Press, 1951.

——, and Martha Wolfenstein. *Childhood in Contemporary Cultures*. Chicago: University of Chicago Press, 1955.

Miller, Nathan. *The Child in Primitive Society*. New York: Brentano, 1928.

Mitchell, Marjorie Edith. *The Child's Attitude to Death*. New York: Schocken Books, 1967.

Moellenhoff, Fritz. "Ideas of Children about Death." *Bulletin of the Menninger Clinic*, III, 1939.

Montessori, Maria. *Spontaneous Activity in Education*. New York: Schocken Books, 1964.

——, *The Montessori Elementary Material*. Cambridge: Bentley, 1964.

——, *The Secret of Childhood*. New York: Longmans, Green & Co., 1936.

Mott, Francis. *Biosynthesis*. Philadelphia: David McKay, 1948.

——, *Universal Design of Birth*. Philadelphia: David McKay, 1948.

Murchison, C. (ed.). *Handbook of Child Psychology*. Worcester, Mass.: Clark University, 1931.

Murphy, Gardner. *Personality*. New York: Harpers, 1947.

Murphy, Lois B. *Social Behavior and Child Personality*. New York: Columbia University Press, 1937.

Murphy, Lois B. *The Widening World of Childhood: Paths Toward Mastery.* New York: Basic Books, 1962.

Nagy, Maria H. "The Child's View of Death." *Journal of Genetic Psychology,* 73:2–27, 1948.

Neill, Alexander S. *The Free Child.* London: Jenkins, 1953.

——, *The Problem Family.* New York: Hermitage Press, 1949.

——, *Summerhill.* New York: Hart Publishing Co., 1960.

Ogden, Robert Morris. *Psychology and Education.* New York: Harcourt, Brace, 1926.

Osada, A. Compiler of *Children of the A Bomb.* New York: Peter Owen, 1963.

Peller, Lili. "Daydreams and Children's Favorite Books." *Psychological Review,* #14, 1959. International Universities Press.

Pestalozzi, Johann. *The Education of Man.* New York: Philosophical Library, 1951.

——, *How Gertrude Teaches Her Children.* London: Allen, 1915.

Piaget, Jean. *The Child's Conception of Geometry.* New York: Basic Books, 1960.

——, *The Child's Conception of Number.* London: Routledge and Kegan Paul, 1952.

——, *The Child's Conception of Physical Causality.* New York: Harcourt, Brace, 1930.

——, *The Child's Conception of the World.* New York: Harcourt, Brace, 1924.

——, *The Construction of Reality in the Child.* New York: Basic Books, 1954.

——, *Judgment & Reasoning in the Child.* New York: Harcourt, Brace, 1928.

——, *The Language and Thought of the Child.* New York: Harcourt, Brace, 1952.

——, *Play, Dreams and Imitation in Childhood.* New York: W. W. Norton & Co., 1951.

——, *The Psychology of Intelligence.* New York: Harcourt, Brace, 1950.

——, *The Origins of Intelligence in Children.* New York: International Universities Press, 1952.

——, *The Child's Concept of Space.* London: Routledge and Kegan Paul, 1956.

Plato. *The Laws,* Vol. IV, *The Dialogues of Plato.* Oxford: The Clarendon Press, 1871.

——, *The Republic,* Vol. II, *The Dialogues of Plato.* Oxford: The Clarendon Press, 1871.

Preyer, William. *The Mind of the Child.* New York: Appleton, 1919.

Rank, Otto. *Modern Education.* New York: Alfred A. Knopf, 1932.

Read, Herbert. *Education for Peace.* New York: Scribner's, 1949.

Redl, Fritz and David Wineman. *Children Who Hate*. Glencoe, Illinois: The Free Press, 1952.

Reich, Wilhelm. "Character Formation and the Phobias of Childhood." *International Journal of Psychology*, XII, 1931.

Riesman, David. *The Lonely Crowd*. New Haven: Yale University Press, 1964.

Ribble, M. *The Rights of Infants*. New York: Columbia University Press, 1943.

Rickman, John (ed.). *On the Bringing Up of Children*. London: Routledge and Kegan Paul, 1936.

Rivière, Joan. "Symposium on Child Analysis." *International Journal of Psychoanalysis*, XVII, 1936.

Rugg, Harold. *Culture and Education in America*. New York: Harcourt, Brace, 1931.

Russell, Bertrand. *Education and the Good Life*. New York: Liveright Publishing Co., 1926.

——, *Education and the Modern World*. New York: W. W. Norton & Co., 1932.

——, *On Education, Especially in Early Childhood*. London: 1926.

Schachtel, Ernest G. "On Alienated Concepts of Identity." *American Journal of Psychoanalysis*, 1961, 21:120–127.

Schilder, Paul and David Wechsler. "The Attitudes of Children Toward Death." *Journal of Genetic Psychology*, 1934, 45: 406–51.

Sears, Robert R. "Doll Play Aggression in Normal Young Children." *Psychological Monographs*, Vol. 65, No. 6.

——, Eleanor E. Macoby and Harry Levin (ed.). *Patterns in Child Rearing*. Evanston, Illinois: Row, Peterson, 1957.

Shinn, Millicent W. *The Biography of a Baby*. Boston: Houghton Mifflin, 1900.

——, *Notes on the Development of a Child*, Vol. I (1898); Vol. II (1900).

Shirley, Mary M. *The First Two Years: A Study of Twenty-five Babies*. Minneapolis: University of Minnesota Press, 1931.

Silverberg, William. *Childhood Experience and Personal Destiny*. New York: Springer Publishers, 1952.

Spitz, Rene. "Anxiety in Infancy." *International Journal of Psychoanalysis*, XXXI, 1950, 138–143.

Spitz, Rene in collaboration with Cobliner, W. Godfrey. *The First Year of Life: A Psychoanalytic Study of Normal and Deviant Development of Object Relations*. New York: International Universities Press, 1965.

Stern, William. *Psychology of Early Childhood up to the Sixth Year of Age*. London: 1924.

Sullivan, Harry S. *The Conceptions of Modern Psychiatry*. Washington, D.C.: William Alanson White Psychiatric Foundation, 1942.

Sully, James. *Studies of Childhood.* New York: D. Appleton & Co., 1903.

Thrasher, Frederic M. *The Gang.* Chicago: University of Chicago Press, 1936.

Torrance, E. P. *Education and the Creative Potential.* Minneapolis: University of Minnesota Press, 1963.

Washburn, Ruth W. "A Study of Smiling and Laughing of Infants in the First Year of Life." Genetic Psychology Monographs, 6, 397–539.

Watson, J. B. *Psychological Care of Infant and Child.* New York: Norton, 1928.

Whitehead, Alfred N. *The Aims of Education and Other Essays.* New York: Macmillan, 1929.

Wickes, Frances G. *The Inner World of Childhood.* New York: Appleton, 1929.

Witty, Paul (ed.). *The Gifted Child.* Boston: Heath, 1951.

Wolfenstein, Martha. "Some Variants in Moral Training." *Psychoanalytic Study of the Child,* 1950, V, 310–78.

——, "Trends in Infant Care." *American Journal of Orthopsychiatry,* 1953, XXIII, No. 1, 120–30.

Ziegfeld, Edwin (ed.). *Educational Art: A Symposium.* Paris (UNESCO), 1953.